Financial intermediation is currently a subject of active research on both sides of the Atlantic. The integration of European financial markets raises questions concerning the risks to the banking system of increased competition, the appropriate regulation of banks and other financial intermediaries, and the emphasis that should be placed on Anglo-American as against Continental European forms of financial markets. The choice of the most appropriate financial system to promote economic growth is also central to Eastern Europe's transformation.

In this volume, derived from a joint CEPR conference with the Fundación Banco Bilbao Vizcaya (BBV) on 'Financial Intermediation in the Construction of Europe', held in San Sebastián on 27/28 March 1992, leading academics from Europe and North America review 'state-of-the-art' theories of banking and financial intermediation and discuss their policy implications. Individual chapters focus on bank lending to companies, relationship banking, competition in banking, stock markets and banks, banking and corporate control, financial intermediation in Eastern Europe, monetary policy and the banking system, financial intermediation and growth, and bank regulation.

Capital markets and financial intermediation

Executive Committee

Chairman
Anthony Loehnis

Vice-Chairmen
Guillermo de la Dehesa
Adam Ridley

Giorgio Basevi	Otmar Issing
Honor Chapman	Mervyn King
Sheila Drew Smith	Peter Middleton
Jacob A. Frenkel	Mario Sarcinelli
Sarah Hogg	Alasdair Smith

Officers

Director
Richard Portes

Deputy Director
Stephen Yeo

Director of Finance and Research Administration
Wendy Thompson

20 October 1992

Capital markets and financial intermediation

Edited by
COLIN MAYER
and
XAVIER VIVES

CAMBRIDGE
UNIVERSITY PRESS

Published by the Press Syndicate of the University of Cambridge
The Pitt Building, Trumpington Street, Cambridge CB2 1RP
40 West 20th Street, New York, NY 10011-4211, USA
10 Stamford Road, Oakleigh, Melbourne 3166, Australia

First published 1993

Printed in Great Britain at the University Press, Cambridge

A catalogue record for this book is available from the British Library

Library of Congress cataloguing in publication data

Capital markets and financial intermediation / edited by
Colin Mayer and Xavier Vives.
    p.   cm.
Includes bibliographical references and index.
ISBN 0 521 44397 0
1. Intermediation (Finance) – Congresses.
2. Capital market – Congresses.
I. Mayer, C. P. (Colin P.)   II. Vives, Xavier.
HG3891.5.C37 1993
332'.0414 – dc20   92-46587   CIP

ISBN 0 521 44397 0   hardback

CE

Contents

List of figures   *page* xiii
List of tables   xv
Preface   xvii
List of conference participants   xviii

1 Introduction   1
   Colin Mayer and *Xavier Vives*
   1 Theoretical issues   2
   2 Policy issues   7
   3 Conclusions   10

**2 Efficient governance structure: implications for banking
   regulation**   12
   Mathias Dewatripont and *Jean Tirole*
   1 Introduction   12
   2 What do banks do?   14
   3 Efficient governance structure of firms   17
   4 Interpreting the firm as a bank   26
   5 Banking regulation   28
   6 Private remedies   31
   7 Concluding remarks   33
   Discussion
   Richard Kihlstrom   36
   Ailsa Röell   42

3 Bank loan maturity and priority when borrowers can refinance   46
   Douglas Diamond
   1 Introduction   46

2   The model   48
3   Borrowers' desired f_1-contingent contracts   50
4   Assignment of control when f_1 is not verifiable and there
    are no competing future lenders   53
5   Competing future lenders, refinancing and liquidation
    decisions   55
6   Multiple initial lenders and debt priority   58
7   Bank (private) lenders and public bondholders   61
8   Lender competition and dilution   64
9   Conclusion   65
    Discussion
    Patrick Bolton   68
    Martin Hellwig   70

4   **Stock markets and resource allocation**   81
    Franklin Allen
    1   Introduction   81
    2   Traditional analyses   90
    3   The checking role of the stock market   92
    4   Banks versus stock markets   101
    5   The stock market and government ownership   103
    6   Concluding remarks   104
    Discussion
    Sudipto Bhattacharya   108
    Anjan V. Thakor   114

5   **Informational capacity and financial collapse**   117
    Douglas Gale
    1   Introduction   117
    2   The model   121
    3   Equilibrium   124
    4   Equilibrium with positive lending   127
    5   Stability of financial collapse   130
    6   The impossibility of profitable deviations   133
    7   Discussion   134
    Appendix A: Definition of equilibrium   137
    Appendix B: Proofs of Propositions 2–5   139
    Discussion
    Franklin Allen   148
    Oren Sussman   151

6 Financial intermediation and economic development   156
Robert G. King and *Ross Levine*
    1   Introduction   156
    2   Theoretical perspective   158
    3   Financial development and economic activity   166
    4   Financial intermediation and economic growth   172
    5   Implications for the reconstruction of Europe   182
    6   Summary and conclusions   187
         Discussion
         Mark Gertler   190
         Nouriel Roubini   193

**7 Creditor passivity and bankruptcy: implications for economic
    reform**   197
Janet Mitchell
    1   Introduction   197
    2   The history of Hungarian bankruptcy   199
    3   The design of bankruptcy laws and decisions to liquidate   204
    4   Creditor passivity: an implementation problem   207
    5   Towards a link between financial institutions and
         bankruptcy   218
         Discussion
         David Newbery   225
         Philippe Aghion   227

**8 Enterprise debt and economic transformation: financial
    restructuring in Central and Eastern Europe**   230
David Begg and *Richard Portes*
    1   Introduction   230
    2   Identifying the problem   231
    3   Implications of credit market failures   237
    4   Tackling the problem   239
    5   Reforming credit relations in Central and Eastern Europe   245
    6   Monetary policy after credit reform   252
         Discussion
         Rafael Repullo   255
         Ramon Caminal   259

**9 Bank regulation, reputation and rents: theory and policy
    implications**   262
Arnoud W. Boot and *Stuart Greenbaum*
    1   Introduction   262

2   The formal analysis   263
3   The changing environment of banking: the US experience
    and its implications for Western Europe   271
    Appendix   277
    Discussion
    Pierre-André Chiappori   286
    Gary Gorton   289

**10   Relationship banking, deposit insurance and bank portfolio
       choice**   292
David Besanko and *Anjan V. Thakor*
1   Introduction   292
2   The model   295
3   The analysis   299
4   Policy implications   314
5   Conclusion   317
    Discussion
    Richard Gilbert   319
    Carmen Matutes   322

11   Competition and bank performance: a theoretical perspective   328
Michael Riordan
1   Introduction   328
2   A simple model of lending   331
3   Comparative statics of more competition   336
4   Welfare results   337
5   Other issues   339
6   Concluding remarks   341
    Discussion
    David Pyle   344
    Anthony Santomero   345

    Index   349

Figures

2.1   The timing of events   *page* 20
2.2   23
2.3a Debt control   25
2.3b Equity control   25
2B.1 Optimal net debt as a function of visible performance   44
3B.1 The abstract equilibrium contract   74
3B.2 A debt package with $\rho + r_1 X/L > X$ 74
4.1   Net financing of private physical investment by enterprises
      in France, Germany, Japan, the UK and the US, 1970–85   84
4.2   Percentage of total business funds raised through securities
      and bank loans, 1965–89   85
4.3   The relationship between value and actions   91
5A.1 The relationship between the expected profitability of good
      and bad firms and economic outlook with debt contracts   149
5B.1 Bank's profit as a function of beliefs about a typical
      applicant, μ_1 152
5B.2 Borrower's profit as a function of the probability of being
      screened   153
6.1   The traditional view   160
6.2   Accumulation and economic development in the physical
      capital (Solow) model   161
6.3   The new view   163
6.4   Accumulation and development in the comprehensive
      model   164
6.5   Financial size (LLY) and real per capita income, 1970   168
6.6   Financial size (LLY) and real per capita income, 1985   170
6.7   Average financial size and growth, 1960–89   173
6.8   Initial financial size and subsequent per capita growth   175
6.9   Partial association between LLY and contemporaneous per
      capita growth   178

10.1   Evolution of borrower types   297
10.2   Bank's cash flow per dollar of deposits as a function of
       portfolio choice λ 305
10.3   Bank's survival probability as a function of portfolio choice
       λ 306
10.4   Bank's first-period expected profit as a function of portfolio
       choice λ 307
10.5   Bank's second-period expected profit as a function of
       portfolio choice λ 309

Tables

page

4.1 London Stock Exchange: securities quoted (paid-up capital), 1853–1913   82

4.2 All stocks listed on the New York Stock Exchange as of the close of business 31 December 1949   83

4.3 Number of firms covered by financial analysts by country   88

6.1 Financial development and real per capita GDP in 1970   167

6.2 Financial development and real per capita GDP in 1985   169

6.3 Financial development and contemporaneous real per capita GDP growth, 1960–89   172

6.4 Initial financial development and subsequent per capita GDP growth, 1970–89   174

6.5 Sources of growth: links to contemporaneous financial size   177

6.6 Sources of growth: links to contemporaneous importance of banks   180

6.7 Sources of growth: links to contemporaneous credit allocated to private sector   181

6.8 Sources of growth: links to previous financial size   183

6.9 Sources of growth: links to previous importance of banks   184

6.10 Sources of growth: links to previous credit allocated to private sector   185

7.1 Explanations and remedies for creditor passivity   208

8.1 Credit to enterprises and households, CSFR, 1989–91 (Kcs bn)   232

8.2 Money supply, interest rates and prices in the CSFR, 1989–91   232

8.3 Domestic credit, interest rates and prices in Hungary, 1989–91   233

8.4 UK bank lending and inter-enterprise credit, industrial and commercial companies, 1980–90 (£bn)   235

8.5   Real interest rates in Chile, 1975–83 (% per annum)   237
8.6   Interest rates and bank margins in Poland, 1990–1 (% per
       annum)   238
8.7   Bank loans to private manufacturing firms (survey of 125
       such firms in each country)   239
8.8   Recapitalization of banks and cancellation of SOE debt   249
10.1   Financial states of the world for the bank at the end of the
       first period   303
11.1   European banking structure, 1988   329

Preface

On 27–28 March 1992, the Fundación Banco Bilbao Vizcaya (BBV) and the Centre for Economic Policy Research organized an international conference on financial intermediation in San Sebastián in Spain. The conference brought together leading academics and policy-makers from Europe and the United States working in the field of financial intermediation. This book contains all the papers presented at the conference together with discussants' comments.

The conference was generously supported by the Fundación BBV. We are particularly grateful to José Angel Sánchez Asiaín, President of the Fundación BBV, Emilio Ybarra, President of the BBV, Luis Angel Lerena, Director of the Centro de Estudios Bancarios of the Fundación BBV, and María Luisa Oyarzábal, General Secretary of the Fundación BBV, for their support. We are also grateful to Stephen Yeo at CEPR and to Antonio Roldán at Fundación BBV for having devoted considerable effort to ensuring the success of the conference, to Miguel Angel García Cestona as a Rapporteur, to Jennifer Jones and Núria Guinjoan for assistance in organizing the conference, to David Guthrie and Kate Millward for overseeing the preparation of this volume, and to Liz Paton for her patient work in copyediting the volume.

Colin Mayer and Xavier Vives
October 1992

Conference participants

José Luis Alzola *Banco de España*
José Antonio Ardanza *Gobierno Vasco*
Juan Ayuso *Banco de España*
Francisco J. Azaola *BBV*
Ricardo Bajo *BBV*
Pablo Bajo Martínez *Ministerio de Hacienda*
Luis Bastida *BBV*
Paulina Beato *Banesto*
David Begg *Birkbeck College, London, and CEPR*
Juan Bengoechea *Fundación BBV*
Sudipto Bhattacharya *University of Delhi*
Patrick Bolton *Université Libre de Bruxelles and CEPR*
Arnoud Boot *Northwestern University*
Ramón Caminal *Universidad Autónoma de Barcelona*
José Maria Campos *Banco de España*
José-Manuel Chamorro *Universidad País Vasco*
Pierre-André Chiappori *DELTA, Paris, and CEPR*
Angel Corcóstegui *BBV*
Juan Crucelegui *Gobierno Vasco*
Douglas Diamond *University of Chicago*
Juan Domingo Elejada *Basque Television (ETB)*
José Manuel Espinosa *Basque Television (ETB)*
Juan Ferrari *YA*
Xabier Galarraga *Universidad País Vasco*
Eli Galdos *Disputación de Guipúzcoa*
Inmaculada Gallastegui *Universidad País Vasco*
Carmen Gallastegui *Universidad País Vasco*
Javier Gallego *Deia*
Miguel Angel García Cestona *Universidad Autónoma de Barcelona and Stanford University*

Alberto García Garmendia *COPE*
Mark Gertler *New York University*
Richard Gilbert *University of California at Berkeley*
Juan José Goiriena *Universidad País Vasco*
Antonio Gómez Bezares *Universidad de Deusto*
Gary Gorton *University of Pennsylvania*
Stuart Greenbaum *Northwestern University*
Martin Hellwig *Universität Basel and CEPR*
José Antonio Iñurrigarro *BBV*
Bill Javetski *Business Week*
Richard Kihlstrom *University of Pennsylvania*
Robert King *Rochester University*
Xabier Lapitz *SER, San Sebastián*
José Luis Larrea *Gobierno Vasco*
Luis Angel Lerena *Fundación BBV*
Alfredo Martín *Ministerio de Economía*
Miguel Alfonso Martínez-Echevarría *Universidad de Navarra*
Carmen Matutes *Universidad Autónoma de Barcelona and CEPR*
Colin Mayer *City University Business School, London, and CEPR*
Víctor Menéndez *Fundación BBV*
Rafael de Miguel *SER, San Sebastián*
Janet Mitchell *Cornell University*
Víctor Múgica *Gobierno Vasco*
David Newbery *Department of Applied Economics, Cambridge, and CEPR*
Manfred Nolte *Bilbao Bizkaia Kutxa*
María Luisa Oyarzábal *BBV*
Henri Pagès *Banque de France*
José Pérez *Banco de España*
Jesús Pizarro *BBV*
Richard Portes *CEPR and Birkbeck College, London*
David Pyle *University of California at Berkeley*
Francisco Querejazu *Fundación BBV*
Javier Quesada *Instituto Valenciano de Investigaciones Economicas, Valencia*
María José Rapado *Edit Media*
Rafael Repullo *Banco de España and CEPR*
Fernando Restoy *Banco de España*
Michael Riordan *University of California at Berkeley*
José Manuel Rodríguez Carrasco *Fundación Fies*
Ailsa Röell *LSE and CEPR*
Nouriel Roubini *Yale University and CEPR*
Gonzalo Rubio *Universidad País Vasco*

Mariano Rubio *Banco de España*
José Angel Sánchez Asiaín *Fundación BBV*
Garbiñe San Miguel *Basque Television (ETB)*
Anthony Santomero *University of Pennsylvania*
Anjan Thakor *Indiana University*
Jean Tirole *Université des Sciences Sociales, Toulouse, and CEPR*
José Antonio Torróntegui *Senador*
Aitor Ubarretxena *Deia*
Pedro L. Uriarte *BBV*
Eduardo Vilela *Universidad de Navarra*
Xavier Vives *IAE, Universidad Autónoma de Barcelona and CEPR*
Emilio Ybarra *BBV*

1   Introduction

COLIN MAYER and XAVIER VIVES

Under the influence of the Anglo-American systems, corporate finance over the past three decades has been dominated by consideration of the operation of securities markets. Recently attention has begun to switch to the role of financial intermediaries. This has occurred at the same time as financial innovation has led some observers to suggest that there is little future for financial intermediation in financing large corporate activities.

The integration of financial markets in Europe and the possible emergence of a single European currency have raised questions about the regulation of financial markets. Does increased competition endanger the stability of banking systems and should the regulation of banks change in the future? The requirement on banks to perform a central function in restructuring enterprises in Eastern Europe has made reform of banking systems of crucial importance.

A study of financial intermediation is therefore timely from the perspective of both academic analysis and policy relevance. The Fundación Banco Bilbao Vizcaya and the Centre for Economic Policy Research organized an international conference on financial intermediation in San Sebastián in Spain on 27 and 28 March 1992. This brought together academics and policy makers from Europe and North America to discuss the latest advances in the study of financial intermediation.

This introduction begins by discussing four issues in the theory of banks: the rationale for the existence of financial intermediaries, competition in banking, bank regulation and the real effects of banks. It then turns to three policy issues: securitization and the future of banks, increased competition in Europe and the US, and banking in Eastern Europe.

1   Theoretical Issues

1.1   The rationale for banks

A central question that any study of financial intermediation has to address is why do banks exist? This question has a long intellectual pedigree, to which Edgeworth amongst others contributed. Recent literature on banks has emphasized their role in providing **liquidity**, transforming illiquid assets into liquid liabilities (Diamond and Dybvig, 1983), and acting as **delegated monitors** of investors (Diamond, 1984), as well as their traditional functions of providing **payments** and **portfolio** services.

The two functions of liquidity provision and delegated monitoring cannot be considered in isolation. If the illiquidity of banks' assets is taken as exogenous, then von Thadden (1991) has shown that banks cannot provide intertemporal insurance to consumers and bank contracts that offer depositors liquidity may not be sustainable. Instead, bank holdings of illiquid assets should be regarded as a joint product of the asymmetric information problems that afflict the financing of such investments and the comparative advantage of banks in this area. Banks should therefore be viewed as competing with other institutions and securities markets in the market for different classes of loans and deposits.

The view that information collection and processing lie at the heart of the operation of banks is reflected in the contributions to this volume. For example, Arnoud Boot and Stuart Greenbaum consider a model in which banks monitor projects to preserve their reputations. Strong reputations allow banks to raise finance in deposit markets. Besanko and Thakor argue that 'relationship' banking allows banks to acquire proprietary information that is of benefit to both borrower and bank. The screening of investment projects by banks in the presence of adverse selection is also central to the models of Michael Riordan and Douglas Gale.

The precise nature of that information, however, is a source of some controversy. The paper by Franklin Allen suggests that banks have a comparative advantage in monitoring well-established technologies that involve the implementation of standard techniques (for example, agriculture or most manufacturing processes). There the comparative advantage of banks in screening and monitoring at lower costs than individual investors is most in evidence. Where technologies are not known, however, in for example innovative firms, investors can legitimately hold different views about best production techniques. Banks then constrain the diverse views that securities markets allow investors to express. Allen therefore predicts that banks will be associated with the financing of well-established technologies and that securities markets will finance new technologies.

The papers by Mathias Dewatripont and Jean Tirole and by Douglas Diamond emphasize a different aspect of the operation of banks. They draw on the recent literature on financial structure and corporate control. This literature points to the need to have debt in a company's liabilities to effect transfers of control from shareholders to holders of debt during periods of poor financial performance. This is as applicable to banks as it is to any other company. Dewatripont and Tirole therefore argue that the structure of banks' liabilities is a product of an optimal governance structure allowing transfers of control from shareholders to depositors to occur in the event of poor financial performance.

As Douglas Diamond notes, however, in a multi-period context there is a tension between credibly committing to liquidate in the event of default and refinancing to avoid excessive liquidations. Short-term debt allows borrowers who expect their credit rating to improve to benefit from more favourable terms of lending; it also allows lenders to exercise more rapid control over borrowers who are in default. On the other hand, some of the gains to refinancing are private control rights of the borrower. Lenders do not take account of these in their liquidation decisions and short-term debt can therefore lead to excessive liquidation. Long-term debt protects borrowers from this risk.

Diamond then argues that short-term creditors should be banks since they are required to organize restructurings in the event of default. They are clearly in a better position to do this than dispersed bond-holders. Lenders who do not possess information or management expertise hold long-term debt in the form of bonds. These predictions appear to be consistent with observed financing practice in Europe and the US.

1.2   Competition in banking

Competition in banking has been regarded with suspicion. Until recently, legally sanctioned cartels have been more the rule than the exception. Interest rates have been regulated. Competition has been blamed for excessive risk taking, inducing moral hazard problems and undermining financial stability. Matutes and Vives (1992) show that coordination problems in deposit-taking involving multiple equilibria and fragility can arise independently of competition. Excessively high deposit rates involving too high a rate of bank failures are, however, a typical characteristic of unregulated environments.

Besanko and Thakor, and Riordan discuss the possibility of excessive competition in loans as well as deposits. Riordan draws on theories of common value auctions to conclude that an increase in competition may have two adverse consequences. First, with greater competition market statistics used to screen loans may become less informative about the quality of projects, with the result that more bad projects are financed. Second, banks will appreciate that they are afflicted by the 'winner's curse', namely they must have overbid for any loan contract that they secure. This will encourage undue conservatism on the part of banks.

Besanko and Thakor consider a model of 'relationship banking' where there are repeated bilateral transactions between banks and borrowers. Banks with a relationship with customers have informational advantages over other banks. Relationship banking provides banks with rents that encourage them to avoid risk taking. Increased competition reduces these rents and thereby encourages risk taking and failure. This leads to a reduction in the welfare of borrowers. The implication is that a balance has to be struck between the benefits of lower prices that competition creates and the increased risk taking that decreased charter value of banks entails.

The appropriate degree of competition in banking has become of particular relevance in the new deregulated environment under which banks now operate.

1.3   Regulation

There have been at least two primary objectives of bank regulation. The first is to protect the financial system. The second is to provide investor protection.

Banks are subject to a market failure, which gives rise to the risk of runs. Runs can be provoked by panics – rumour, sudden loss of confidence – encouraging depositors to withdraw their funds. This results in the premature liquidation of assets and the collapse of what would otherwise be sound banks (Diamond and Dybvig, 1983). Runs can also occur in response to unfavourable information about the quality of bank investments reaching depositors. Bank runs are costly in terms of real resources because the production process is interrupted and assets are liquidated prematurely. In particular, runs may spread in a contagious fashion through an economy, thereby creating a systemic failure.

Intermediaries in money and capital markets, for example dealers and market makers, provide essential liquidity services which need to be supported by bank credit lines and a guaranteed settlements system. Unexpected settlement demands due to the failure of a large intermediary may trigger a systemic crisis. This will give rise to premature liquidations and welfare costs.

A separate justification for regulation comes from the need to offer investor protection. Small depositors do not have the ability or incentive to undertake adequate monitoring of banks. They free-ride on the monitoring of others and, as a consequence, there is excessive abuse and fraud.

Boot and Greenbaum argue that regulation must be designed to encourage appropriate monitoring by financial intermediaries. They suggest that (i) capital requirements may reduce monitoring by bank managers because of dilution of ownership, (ii) rents and reputations are substitute ways of encouraging monitoring, and (iii) incentives based on reputation are destroyed by risk-insensitive deposit insurance. By raising risk, increased competition and deregulation increase the cost of deposit insurance and encourage the use of direct restrictions rather than deposit insurance.

In the past, tightly regulated banks and less competitive environments encouraged prudent behaviour on the part of banks. The erosion of rents through deregulation and competition has made reputations all the more important. Flat-rate deposit insurance does not, however, give advantages to banks with better reputations. Boot and Greenbaum suggest that this favours the imposition of direct restrictions on the investments that can be made with insured deposits. They therefore propose the implementation of 'narrow bank' schemes by which banks that have insured deposits can invest only in riskless assets.

As noted above, Dewatripont and Tirole view the liability structure of banks as being determined by optimal governance considerations. This involves transfers in control when performance falls below some critical level. This discourages banks from pursuing 'go-for-broke' strategies by which they gamble on small probabilities of likely outcomes at the expense of depositors.

A problem with the transfer of control from shareholders to depositors is that depositors are small and dispersed. It is therefore costly for them to exercise control rights. Instead, a monitoring agency is required to represent their interests. Optimal regulation by this agency involves *ex ante* requirements, such as capital requirements and limits on lending, and *ex post* interventions to rescue failing banks.

The structure described by Dewatripont and Tirole is useful for investigating alternative institutional arrangements to represent the interests of depositors, for example, public versus private monitors, rating agencies versus insurance agencies. Dewatripont and Tirole also discuss the need for separate agencies to undertake monitoring and intervention in the event of failure. This may be required to avoid investors drawing bad inferences about the performance of the regulator from observations on failing banks. This may have important implications for the design of bank regulation, not least in relation to the European Monetary System.[1]

1.4   Real effects of banks

Traditionally, one of the main functions attributed to banks has been as a link in the monetary transmission mechanism. Increases in high-powered money allow banks to raise their lending according to multiplier ratios, which in turn raises aggregate spending. In this story, banks are passive instruments for converting high-powered into broader monetary aggregates. They play no independent role in affecting real activity. Financial systems are products of the real requirements of an economy, not determinants of its performance. The division of financial activity between intermediated and disintermediated sources is of no direct significance.

Economic theory has recently suggested that financial intermediation may be of significance in two ways. The first is through the conjunction of financial intermediation and new growth theory. In this volume, King and Levine view the link as originating from the nexus between entrepreneurship, intangible capital investment and financial intermediation. Much productivity-enhancing investment involves intangible capital goods. These are difficult to evaluate by third parties, and financial intermediaries arise endogenously as part of a market mechanism for screening entrepreneurs and financing intangibles. Countries with superior financial systems are better at evaluating innovations and entrepreneurs and thus at allocating assets more efficiently. This translates into increased productivity and growth through physical capital accumulation, and investments in intangible and human capital.

The second link is through the disturbances created by financial collapse. Bernanke (1983) has pointed to the disruptive effects of bank failures during the 1930s. Consistent with the description of banks having informational advantages over dispersed investors, bank failures have real welfare consequences associated with the destruction of valuable informational assets.

Douglas Gale in this volume describes a model in which the informational screening function of banks can have real consequences. In Gale's model, banks have access to a costly screening technology. Their ability to screen borrowers is limited and it is costly for borrowers to apply for loans. Gale demonstrates that multiple equilibria can result. Some equilibria involve lending by banks; others give rise to 'financial collapse' with little lending. This arises from the fact that if all banks but one decide not to lend then the remaining bank will attract a high proportion of bad borrowers. When a good borrower applies it is always in the interests of a bad borrower to apply because, given the nature of the debt contract, bad borrowers expect higher returns by investing in high variance projects. The ability of the bank to screen is limited so that it has to reject a high proportion of its applicants. Good applicants are discouraged from applying because it is costly for them to apply and there is a low probability of their receiving a loan. Essentially, the low-lending equilibrium that Gale describes arises from a coordination problem. If all banks lent then there would be no screening constraint and good applicants would expect to receive loans. If banks do not lend, then it is not in the interest of any bank to lend because it attracts low-quality borrowers. This may explain instances of 'credit crunches' and raises the possibility that universal banking systems in which banks can make equity as well as debt investments may be less prone to this type of crisis.

2   Policy Issues

2.1   Do banks have a future?

It is frequently suggested that securities markets are destined to displace banks as sources of finance for large corporations. The reasoning behind this is that for many large corporations technological developments, deregulation and losses sustained by banks have combined to reduce the costs of direct financing below those of intermediated finance.

The growth of the Eurobond market is cited as an example of how securities markets have come to displace banks as sources of finance. Since the beginning of the 1970s, Eurobond finance has expanded eight times in real terms. Many large corporations regularly tap Eurobond markets for finance that previously was obtained from banks. It is uncertain what role banks can play in funding companies whose credit ratings are often superior to those of their banks.

While it is clear that securities markets have played an increasing role in the funding of large companies, there are a number of points that should be borne in mind. First, only a small segment of the corporate sector in most countries has access to bond markets. The information requirement of investors makes banks relevant to the financing of all but the largest firms. In the UK, for example, fewer than 200 companies have tapped the Eurobond market since its inception at the end of the 1960s.

Second, even for large companies, banks continue to play a significant role. Davis and Mayer (1992) have documented how large companies rely on banks to fund large projects. The maximum size of finance that is available from syndicated banks is well in excess of that from Eurobonds. Again this may reflect the information requirement on large-scale investments or the greater control that banks can exert in relation to that of bond markets.

Third, Eurobonds do not provide the relationships with investors that Besanko and Thakor argue are an important aspect of bank finance. This is probably particularly relevant to the involvement of investors in restructuring failing companies. Banks appear to play a significant role in restructuring and recapitalizing firms that encounter periods of financial distress. According to the control models (see, for example, Dewatripont and Tirole in this volume), 'hard' external control will be expected to be exerted by investors during periods of poor financial performance. Dewatripont and Tirole argue that debt finance is well suited to perform the function of transferring control from shareholders, who impose soft constraints on managers, to providers of debt finance, who impose tough constraints, during periods of poor financial performance. A large number of highly dispersed investors in bond markets may well not be as well placed as concentrated bank lenders to exert the necessary control during periods of poor financial performance.

The traditional functions of banking in offering liquidity and maturity transformation have also come under question from the proponents of narrow banking (such as Boot and Greenbaum). They argue that, by restricting bank investments to liquid securities (for example Treasury bills), the cost of deposit insurance can be minimized. The narrow bank proposal leaves open two sets of questions: (i) are there enough 'safe' securities to provide the counterpart of transaction deposits and is it appropriate to link public debt to transaction requirements in this way, and (ii), in the absence of banks, who will perform the role of funding illiquid projects and will the risk of runs just be transferred to other institutions?

2.2   Increased competition in Europe and the US

One of the main goals of integration in the European Community has been to encourage greater competition in banking. Domestic banks have been protected from competition by stringent regulatory requirements and the special place that they have been afforded in the operation of the monetary system. According to the home country doctrine, a bank that is registered in any European country is eligible to open branches in any other and to offer services to citizens of any member country. It is thought that integration will increase competition in Europe by removing sources of restrictive practices (Vives, 1991). Intensified competition will reduce margins between borrowing and lending rates, operating costs and profit margins. Proposals to lift restrictions on interstate branching and universal banking in the US would have similar effects.

While increases in competition have desirable results in reducing profit margins, the papers in this volume warn against assertions that competition in banking is necessarily beneficial. Competition may cause valuable relationships between borrower and lender to be extinguished (Besanko and Thakor). It may exacerbate the 'winner's curse' problem that afflicts financial markets (Riordan). It may reduce the profitability of banks and exacerbate the risks of financial failure discouraging reputation building in the presence of flat-rate deposit insurance (Boot and Greenbaum).

Of these, the risk to the financial system is probably the most immediate cause of concern both for European integration and for US restructuring of the banking industry. In Europe, banking systems are being integrated faster than bank regulation is being coordinated. As a consequence, cross-border externalities in bank failure are being revealed. One example of this was the failure of BCCI: the collapse of a Luxembourg-registered bank had consequences for depositors in a large number of countries around the world.

2.3   Banking in Eastern Europe

One area in which control of and by banks is particularly crucial is Eastern Europe. Enterprise sectors in most East European countries are bankrupt. As Janet Mitchell describes in this volume, bankruptcy laws have been introduced to facilitate the imposition of bankruptcy proceedings. Few creditors, however, have availed themselves of this facility. Mitchell argues that there are three reasons for this. First, the expected value of creditors' claims net of bankruptcy costs may be less than zero. In that case, provided that revenues exceed variable costs, there may be no motive for enforcing bankruptcy procedures. Second, creditors may be concerned about the signal transmitted to the market by the revelation that they have a high proportion of non-performing loans. Banks may be worried that this may cause their own creditors to re-evaluate the soundness of their lending to banks. Third, creditors may believe that they can be assured of continuing financial assistance from the government, in which case it is not in their or their customers' interests to initiate bankruptcy procedures. It may therefore be difficult to encourage banks to initiate bankruptcy proceedings even in the presence of a well-functioning bankruptcy law.

David Begg and Richard Portes furthermore argue that recapitalization of banks may be a prerequisite for the successful restructuring of the enterprise sector by banks. They argue that recapitalization is necessary to prevent an inherited stock problem from distorting the efficient allocation of credit through the banking system. In addition to finance, East European banks clearly need to develop the expertise to be able to undertake the necessary evaluations and management of banks. Joint ventures with foreign banks may assist with this.

Notwithstanding Allen's assertion in this volume that stock markets may play a central role in the development of new technologies in developed countries, most East European countries are concerned with the development of quite well-established production processes. It is therefore clear that banks will perform a central function in the development of East European economies. The role for stock markets will be very limited for several years to come and, even then, the experience of Western economies is that the role of stock markets may be limited to quite specific functions, most notably in high-technology sectors.

3   Conclusions

This book records the current state of knowledge about the operation of banks. The first thing that strikes the reader is the gaps in our understanding. Even the rationale for the existence of banks is only imperfectly understood. Despite the limitations, there have been remarkable strides in our understanding over the past decade. We now have a much better appreciation of what contributes to the all-embracing notion of economies of scale, which was traditionally propounded as the rationale for banks. In particular, economies of scale appear to be associated with information gathering in the form of screening and monitoring of firms in the presence of diversification possibilities.

One practical implication of this rationale for banks is that their existence is unlikely to be undermined by financial innovation. Certainly, technological improvements and deregulation may pull back the boundaries of bank activity but there is no question that banks will continue to perform a central function in evaluating and monitoring medium-sized and smaller customers. Bankers can take heart from the inherent limitations of market processes.

The recent control literature also points to another reason for the continuing existence of banks and that is to restructure firms. Debt contracts are better suited than equity contracts to perform this function, and concentrated lending through banks is better than dispersed lending through bond markets. This role for banks in restructuring enterprises is most in evidence in Eastern Europe. East Germany, with its well-developed banking system, has been able to take better advantage of this than other East European countries. Once restructured and recapitalized, however, banks will play a central role in enterprise reform throughout Eastern Europe.

The second main lesson to be learnt from recent developments in financial intermediation is more salutary. Competition in banking is not like competition in sausage production. There are risks and distortions associated with bank competition that make the welfare effects of increased competition uncertain. It is quite conceivable that competition in banking needs to be moderated more than that in other markets.

That leads to the final theme, which is the importance of the regulation of banks. The papers in this volume illustrate the diversity of views on the question of how much and what form of bank regulation is required. This is an area in which existing theoretical models are not sufficiently robust to deliver clear conclusions. Assertions that deposit insurance is necessary or that narrow banking is beneficial are more statements of faith than well-established propositions. That is little consolation for policy makers who are required to make decisions. The value of this type of volume, however, is as much to sound notes of caution as it is to proclaim advances in our state of understanding.

NOTE

1 For a discussion of the merits of establishing separate agencies to license and close banks in the context of the Single European Currency see CEPR (1991).

REFERENCES

Bernanke, B. (1983) 'Non-monetary effects of the financial crisis in the propagation of the Great Depression', *American Economic Review* 73, 257–63.

Centre for Economic Policy Research (1991) 'The making of monetary union', a Report on Monitoring European Integration.

Davis, P. and C. Mayer (1992) 'Corporate finance in the euromarkets and the economics of intermediation', Centre for Economic Policy Research working paper.

Diamond, D. and P. Dybvig (1983) 'Bank runs, deposit insurance and liquidity', *Journal of Political Economy* 91, 401–19.

Diamond, D. (1984) 'Financial intermediation and delegated monitoring', *Review of Economic Studies* 51, 393–414.

Matutes, C. and X. Vives (1992) 'Competition for deposits, risk of failure and regulation in banking', Working Paper 18, ESF Network in Financial Markets.

Vives, X. (1991) 'Banking competition and European integration', in A. Giovannini and C. Mayer (eds.), *European Financial Integration*, Cambridge: Cambridge University Press, 9–31.

Von Thadden, E. (1991) 'The term-structure of investment and the limits to the banks' insurance function', WWZ Discussion Paper No. 9107.

2 Efficient governance structure: implications for banking regulation

MATHIAS DEWATRIPONT and JEAN
TIROLE

1 Introduction

The analysis of banking regulation must start with a careful analysis of the characteristics of banking and of why regulation is needed in that industry. A growing number of economists challenge the traditional view that banking differs from other somewhat competitive industries and needs to be regulated. Meanwhile, practitioners have lost some of their earlier enthusiasm for deregulation. The S&L crisis in the US and the difficulties encountered by a number of other financial institutions have led to stricter regulatory requirements. Furthermore, the 1991 Federal Deposit Insurance Corporation Improvement Act (FDICIA) by and large has removed the regulators' discretionary powers. Europe is also pondering the future of its prudential regulation. The Basle 1988 agreement on the uniformization of capital adequacy requirements has paved the way for a European Monetary Union. In both cases, there is much concern that the requirements do not take sufficient account of bank diversification or of the real riskiness of loans. It is suggested that regulators should use softer information about the quality of loans than the institutional nature of the borrowers. By depriving the requirements of their mechanical aspect, these suggestions raise the issue of who would regulate. Should this close monitoring be performed by a central bank or by private investors (main creditor, multiple creditors, rating agencies)? And should deposit insurance be privately contracted for or should it be publicly provided conditional on the bank having a high credit rating or else some government requirements being met?

This paper studies moral hazard both at the bank level and at the level of its monitors. It sets aside macroeconomic aspects of banking, which we hope to address in future work.

Section 2 discusses the *notion of a bank*. The several characteristics of banking suggested in the literature all relate to the nature of its activities.

12

They do not seem fully convincing however, because they have counter-parts in the non-financial sector. We therefore argue that it is useful to look at a bank as an ordinary firm, and to focus on the optimal control structure of the bank and on the role of its equity holders and depositors. But what is then the distinctiveness of banking? And why might one consider regulation? We argue that an important feature of banks is that their debt is mostly held by a group of dispersed and uninformed small depositors. This fact seriously limits the intensity of monitoring and outside involvement in management. True, our focus on the nature of monitoring raises the question of why banks in our definition tend to be banks, or more generally depository institutions, in the usual parlance. That is, why doesn't the productive sector collect the small depositors' money to a larger extent?[1] At this stage of our research we have little else to offer than a few potential explanations such as historical accident and regulation.

Section 3 develops a model of the *optimal control of firms*. Viewing a bank as a firm enables us to build on our work (Dewatripont and Tirole, 1992) on the optimal financial structure of a firm. There, it was argued that (i) firm's outsiders must be given incentive schemes in the form of securities to intervene appropriately in the firm; (ii) the securities' residual rights of control should therefore be correlated with their return streams; (iii) the firm's managers should be rewarded by low interference by outsiders when performing well, and be punished by substantial outside involvement when having low profits or failing to repay short-term debt; and therefore (iv), under some conditions, control should be given to equity owners when the firm does well and to debt-holders in harsher times. This in turn generates (partial) manager–shareholder congruence.

Section 4 applies these ideas to banks, which indeed themselves have shareholders and creditors. By predicting the coexistence of debt and equity, the model is suited to the consideration of regulatory instruments such as capital adequacy requirements. It also offers a clearer view of bank management by not following the literature in exogenously equating managerial and equity interests.

The model applied to banks predicts that when some verifiable bank performance measure (capital-to-loans ratio, reserves, riskiness of loans, etc.) falls below some threshold, the control of the bank should shift away from its shareholders to its creditors. For instance, this enables the creditors to prevent the bank from 'gambling for resurrection' by limiting borrowing, requiring the choice of safer loans, reducing the discrepancy between the term structures of loans and deposits, or liquidating the bank. More generally, we show that, in the absence of adjustments in borrowing, loans or recapitalization, the mere resolution of uncertainty gives rise to wrong incentives for the bank's claim-holders (as well as for its management). Claim-holders of a shaky bank have more incentives to be passive than claim-holders of a healthy one. Recapitalization in turbulent times and increased borrowing in quiet times can be used to counter these perverse incentives.

The theoretical model assumes that each category of a bank's claim-holders (e.g. shareholders and debt-holders) acts in its own collective interest, which is determined by its contingent revenue stream. It thus ignores the possibility that holders of a security may not perfectly coordinate their monitoring and involvement in the bank. Yet most bank creditors – small depositors – have neither the incentive nor the information or competence to monitor and exert their residual rights of control over the bank. To remedy this, a large private or public monitor representing the interests of the creditors must exert these rights of control on their behalf. Sections 5 and 6 therefore investigate the implementation of the optimal monitoring and control of banks. They analyse the costs and benefits of several institutions and the extent to which they can approximate the optimal control structure: (i) discretionary regulation, (ii) use of rating agencies, (iii) private deposit insurance, (iv) large private monitor holding subordinated or non-subordinated debt.

Finally, section 7 contains concluding remarks.

2   What do banks do?

The traditional discussion of the particularities of banking points to the following activities:[2]

Reduction in the transaction costs associated with direct finance. Financial intermediaries transform the primary securities issued by firms into the indirect financial securities desired by final investors. Firms could issue the demand deposits that are demanded by consumers facing consumption timing risk, but it might be costly for most consumers to lend directly to a diversified array of firms (Gurley and Shaw, 1960).

Transformation. Financial intermediaries transform the mostly short-term liabilities preferred by consumers into the long-term loans desired by firms. This transformation function implies that early withdrawal by consumers who do not face a liquidity need (a bank run) jeopardizes the bank that has lent long (Diamond and Dybvig, 1983).

Delegated monitoring. Scale economies in monitoring imply that it is best performed by a single monitor. A financial intermediary monitors the borrowers on behalf of the final investors (Diamond, 1984).

Provision of the payment mechanism. Banks facilitate payments among consumers. A well-functioning banking system implies that the beneficiary of a cheque does not need to worry about whether or not the issuer has sufficient funds (the banking system is responsible for punishing abuses) and whether or not the issuer's bank is going to fail.

Proponents of regulation have argued that it might be vindicated by the transformation function. Banks may be subject to banking panics, which force them to stop profitable investments.[3] There are several instruments that can prevent 'bank run equilibria'. Private or government deposit insurance[4] suppresses the depositors' incentive to run. Banks may borrow reserves from the Federal Reserve or borrow from other banks. Suspension of convertibility is another method, although there is a debate about who should decide the suspension. Banks themselves face a conflict of interest. Rey and Stiglitz (1991) argue that large debt-holders, when observing poor bank choices, can punish the firm by withdrawing their funds. Bank management clearly would prefer to suspend convertibility in such circumstances. In any case, bank runs are nowadays infrequent and do not seem per se to be a crucial issue, although they should be kept in mind when considering the full array of organizations of the banking industry.

Proponents of regulation have also emphasized the following *externalities* exerted by a bank as a further justification for regulation:

Spillovers of bank failures. The borrowers of a failing bank may have difficulty in finding substitute loans from other banks; if this is the case, valuable investments will need to be stopped or cancelled and the productive sector will suffer. While the bank's failure per se does not inflict an individual stigma on each borrower, it may convey bad information about the bank's management ability to select borrowers and thus inflict a collective stigma on the borrowers. Even good borrowers, so goes the argument, have trouble finding new financing. That precious relationship capital is lost in the failure is one of the arguments used to justify bank bail-outs through recapitalization or merger.

Another worry about bank failures is that, in an interdependent banking system, a bank's failure can propagate and generate other failures. This concern played an important role for instance in the 1984 Continental Illinois debacle where some large debt-holders would have been jeopardized by a failure.

Competition for limited resources. Banks compete for their inputs as well as on their product markets. They bid for a limited volume of money and credit controlled by the central bank. This is sometimes presumed to lead to 'cannibalism', failures and financial shocks (Kaufman, 1991), because banks in trouble try to 'get back on their feet' by attracting more funds, thereby making life more difficult for their competitors.

Externalities in the payment system. A bank's claim-holders who use their asset as a means of payment may have a suboptimal incentive to acquire information about the bank's soundness and to act upon it. For, if the bank goes bankrupt, the claim-holder's loss (if not insured) is shared by those who have cheques drawn on the bank.

Are these activities necessarily to be performed by the financial sector? Do they and the associated externalities justify government intervention?

Transaction costs. The transaction cost theory of banking is subject to the objection that non-financial firms could themselves offer the financial securities desired by final investors such as demand deposits. As Hellwig (1991a) argues, at least sufficiently large non-financial firms should not be concerned by the risk of withdrawal.

Transformation. Transformation does not quite distinguish the financial and non-financial sectors for the reason that financial intermediaries act on behalf of non-financial firms. Again, a non-financial firm could finance long-term investments by borrowing short from final investors instead of using a financial intermediary.

Delegated monitoring. Diamond's view of financial intermediaries as monitors of borrowers is well taken. There is no doubt that final investors are both unable and unwilling to monitor non-financial firms directly. We should note, however, that, when it comes to discussing regulation, this monitoring activity on behalf of outside investors is not specific to banking. Non-financial firms every day screen projects that claim-holders would be unable or unwilling to assess. Furthermore, the Diamond argument that a bank with a well-diversified portfolio can issue riskless, fixed-interest debt claims could equally be applied to a well-diversified non-financial firm.

Payment system. There is no technological obstacle to non-financial firms allowing their debt-holders to write cheques, or more generally make payments, on their claims. It should be noted, though, that some form of oversight is necessary for economic agents to accept payments.

Spillovers. That bank failures may have spillover effects on the rest of the economy is correct, but is not specific to the banking industry. A manufacturer that fails or reduces its production hurts its suppliers and customers.

Competition for inputs. Again, there is no specificity to banking here. Non-financial intermediaries such as wholesalers and retailers, and many producers, compete for intermediate goods, raw materials and labour.

Of course, we do not deny that these features, although not *qualitatively* different, may be *quantitatively* more important for banks than for non-financial firms. We feel, however, that it is worth investigating how far one can go in treating banks as regular firms, and depositors as regular debt-holders. We start with a model of optimal debt and equity control of a firm. In section 3, we derive the optimality of relative shareholder passivity, and we show that standard debt or deposit contracts have the desired incentive properties to discipline managers following bad performance. In section 4, we reinterpret these results for the case where the firm is a bank.

Focusing on the issue of governance structure leads us naturally to emphasize one neglected, although certainly *quantitatively* important, feature of banks, namely the dispersed nature of the debt-holders or depositors. Small depositors typically have no time or expertise to perform the monitoring and control that the optimal governance structure of sections 3 and 4 requires. And even if they did, they would be tempted to free ride on each other's monitoring and exercise of control.[5] We thus depart from Diamond's (1984) banking theory in not assuming that asset diversification solves the problem of monitoring and controlling the intermediary. The widespread problems of the 1929–33 banking crisis in the absence of deposit insurance, and the equally widespread current S&L problems in its presence, lend support to our view of a lack of appropriate depositor control. In sections 5 and 6 we thus investigate the idea of depositors' representatives and we analyse their incentives to discipline banks.

In this paper, we neglect a number of banking particularities. At the microeconomic level, liquidity transformation creates no specific problem per se in our model, and we ignore the role of banks in the payment mechanism. We feel, however, that these are not the essence of the current banking regulatory debate. Indeed, coordination failures leading to bank runs are reasonably easily solved through suspension of convertibility, last resort lending or deposit insurance. And the payment function could be performed by very liquid money market mutual funds. Perhaps more importantly, the paper neglects the macroeconomic issues raised by the banking sector, like spillovers from bank failures or 'cannibalism' in the fight for financial resources. These issues are left for future research.

3   Efficient governance structure of firms

We present here a simplified version of the model in Dewatripont and Tirole (1992). This model considers the provision of incentives for the manager of a firm in a world of incomplete contracts (as in Grossman and

Hart, 1986, and Aghion and Bolton, 1992). Contractual incompleteness means that it is optimal to discipline managers not only through financial incentive schemes based upon verifiable signals but also through granting residual rights of control to outsiders. The idea is that poor performance should induce outsiders in control to take actions that managers dislike, while good performance should lead to actions favourable to managers. Assuming that such actions are non-contractible implies that outsiders in control should be given, through the return streams attached to their claims, appropriate incentives to discipline managers.

3.1   The model

The model has two periods, $t = 1, 2$.

3.1.1 Managerial moral hazard

In period 1, the firm's manager chooses an unobservable effort level $e \in \{\underline{e}, \bar{e}\}$ with $\underline{e} < \bar{e}$. The high effort level is efficient, but costs the manager K in utility terms, while the low effort level costs 0. The low and high effort levels can be interpreted as the choice of a bad or good project. K must then be thought of as the private benefit derived by the manager from choosing the bad project.

At the end of period 1, two signals are commonly observable. Signal v is 'verifiable', 'contractible', 'objective' or 'hard information'. That is, outside claim-holders and the manager can *ex ante* contract on v. Signal u is 'non-verifiable', 'non-contractible', 'subjective' or 'soft information'. It cannot be specified *ex ante* in a contract.

Both signals reflect the performance of the firm as of date 1. Both will be assumed to be correlated with the effort choice of the manager. Signal v contains the verifiable elements of date 1 performance, for example short-term profits and, possibly, the stock price of the company if it is publicly traded. Even in the case of a public corporation, these measures of performances will typically not reveal all information available at that time, which is why we also assume the existence of a publicly observable but non-verifiable component u of performance at date 1.[6]

For simplicity, we will assume that v and u are independently distributed on $[0, 1]$ conditionally on e. Their densities are given by $\bar{f}(v)$ and $\bar{g}(u)$ if $e = \bar{e}$ and $f(v)$ and $\underline{g}(u)$ if $e = \underline{e}$. We assume that higher effort generates better signals.

3.1.2 Monotone likelihood ratio property

$\bar{f}/f$ and $\bar{g}/g$ are increasing functions.

The firm's long-term profit is realized in period 2. It depends on which action or policy A is chosen at the end of period 1 (see below). The density and cumulative distribution given action A and signals v and u are denoted $h_A(\pi|v,u)$ and $H_A(\pi|v,u)$. Their support is $[0,\infty)$, say.

3.1.3 Interference in management

After the effort is chosen and the first-period signals are realized, the outsider(s) who is granted control chooses some non-contractible action A. The firm's capital structure specifies the *control structure*, that is, which claim-holder has the right to choose A for each realization of the contractible signal v. The capital structure also determines the profit-contingent revenue stream of each claim-holder. For each v is, of course, of particular interest to the revenue stream of the claim-holder who has been granted residual rights of control.

For simplicity, we concentrate on two possible actions, 'intervening' or 'stopping' (S), and 'acquiescing' or 'continuing' (C), so $A \in \{S, C\}$. Action S can be interpreted as liquidating or selling a share of the firm's assets, forcing the manager to cancel new projects, firing the manager and so forth.

This interpretation naturally suggests the following assumption, which will play a role in the characterization of the optimal financial structure in terms of debt and equity:

Simple decrease in risk: action S is safer than action C in that it has leaner lower and upper tails. That is, for each (v, u), there exists $\hat{\pi}(v, u)$ such that

$$H_S(\pi|v,u) < H_C(\pi|v,u) \quad \text{for } 0 < \pi < \hat{\pi}(v,u)$$

and

$$H_S(\pi|v,u) > H_C(\pi|v,u) \quad \text{for } \hat{\pi}(v,u) < \pi$$

3.1.4 Timing

The timing of the model is summarized in Figure 2.1. At stage (i), securities are issued. They involve financial return streams (contingent on v and π), as well as residual rights of control (contingent on v) for stage (v) concerning the choice of action.

Events taking place at stages (ii), (iii) and (vi) are self-explanatory. Note that the choice of action at stage (v) is, in the absence of renegotiation, determined by the income stream established by the firm at stage (i) for the controlling party. Because this choice may be inefficient, parties may have an incentive to renegotiate, which we allow at stage (iv) once v and u have been realized. In fact, we assume that renegotiation completely eliminates *ex post* inefficiencies, as renegotiation takes place under

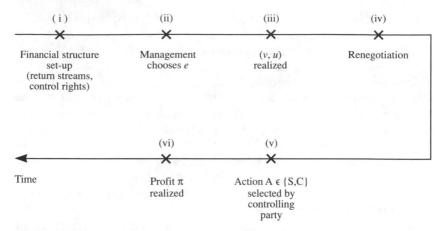

Figure 2.1   The timing of events

symmetric information. Our qualitative results carry over if renegotiation is infeasible.[7] We choose to develop the case of renegotiation for two reasons. First, the exposition is notationally simpler because of the absence of *ex post* inefficiency terms. Second, in the absence of renegotiation (or under imperfect renegotiation), the securities' income streams play a dual role: disciplining managers and inducing optimal actions by outsiders. We will discuss monitoring by outsiders later, but want to focus on managerial incentives for the moment.

3.1.5 Preferences

Our theory is based on the (tautological) idea that managers do not like outside interference in their management. In our model, interference will correspond to action S. In reality, there are several reasons why managers dislike their projects being interrupted or altered; for instance:[8] (1) they are likely to receive high monetary rewards (bonuses, stock options) if the project they started is pursued because continuation yields a fatter upper tail for the distribution of profits; (2) they enjoy private benefits as long as the project continues. We here focus on the private benefit reason.

The manager is assumed for simplicity not to respond to monetary incentives[9] and thus receives a constant wage 0. The manager receives no private benefit if the project is stopped. If the project is pursued, the manager receives private benefit $B > 0$. This private benefit is non-appropriable by the claim-holders because they do not have enough information to capture it. But the manager can also release the relevant information and let the claim-holders raise π by B in case of continuation (for notational simplicity; more generally, the cost savings could differ from B). For instance, an empire builder may point out that the firm could raise its profit by dispensing with some activity that gives the manager private benefits. The idea here is to allow for the possibility of concession by the manager to claim-holders even when the manager receives no monetary reward. That is, in states of nature in which the controlling outsider prefers to stop the project in the absence of renegotiation, the manager will be willing to give up the private benefit associated with continuation.[10] Similarly, we assume *transferable utility* when stopping is *ex post* efficient, but the controlling outsider prefers continuation in the absence of renegotiation. Voluntary renegotiation can be achieved by giving the manager *another position* which yields the manager B as private benefits too,[11] and costs the claim-holders B to create. Alternatively, our theory would apply if renegotiation were excluded, which would occur, for instance, if the private benefits cannot be appropriated with the help of the manager.

We also assume that, although renegotiation is voluntary (i.e. requires the manager's approval in particular), the manager has no bargaining power in the renegotiation process, so that their utility is not affected by it (what is crucial for our analysis is more generally that either renegotiation is imperfect or the manager must make at least some concession to prevent the controlling party from going against the manager's will).

3.2 Managerial incentive scheme

Since we assume efficient renegotiation, maximizing the total value of outside claims is equivalent to minimizing the agency cost (AC) in the absence of renegotiation, that is, to choosing the probability of action C prior to renegotiation. If the manager's outside opportunity is zero, the individual rationality constraint is not binding, and only the incentive constraint has to be taken care of.

This subsection determines the optimal managerial incentive scheme (which is fully defined by the optimal financial structure if the manager does not respond to monetary incentives), that is, the optimal probability $x(v, u)$ of choosing action C in the absence of renegotiation for each (v, u). In subsection 3.3, we turn to the implementation of the function x through specific financial structures. Thus, while this subsection considers the managerial incentive scheme, subsection 3.3 focuses on outsiders' incentive schemes. Our two-step approach is vindicated by the fact that the optimal function x derived in this subsection will be implementable by some financial structure.

Minimizing agency costs is equivalent to programme (I):

$$\operatorname*{Min}_{\{x(.,.)\}} AC = B \int \bar{f}(v)\bar{g}(u)x(v,u)\,dv\,du$$

subject to

$$AC \ge B \int \underline{f}(v)\underline{g}(u)x(v,u)\,dv\,du + K.$$

Letting μ denote the multiplier of the constraint, the Lagrangian is

$$B[(\mu - 1)\bar{f}(v)\bar{g}(u) - \mu\underline{f}(v)\underline{g}(u)]x(v,u).$$

Because the Lagrangian is linear in x, it is not optimal to set x strictly between 0 and 1. The monotone likelihood ratio property implies that action C should be chosen with probability 1 if:

$$\frac{\bar{f}(v)\bar{g}(u)}{\underline{f}(v)\underline{g}(u)} \ge \frac{\mu}{\mu - 1}. \tag{1}$$

Otherwise, action S should be chosen with probability 1. Indeed, since high v's and u's are good news about effort, the agency cost is minimized by rewarding the manager only for good realizations of these signals. Condition (1) in fact defines a target level of u, $u^*(v)$, which has to be met for action S not to be taken. And $u^*(v)$ is decreasing in v: a high v is good news about effort, which means that the target in terms of u need not be as severe as for lower v's.

3.3   Outsiders' incentive schemes

We now show how the optimal managerial incentives can be provided by a financial structure consisting of debt and equity. Let $\tilde{u}(v)$ be such that continuation and stopping are socially optimal:

$$\Delta(v, \tilde{u}(v)) = \int_0^\infty \pi\{h_C[\pi \,|\, v, \tilde{u}(v)] - h_S[\pi \,|\, v, \tilde{u}(v)]\}\,d\pi + B$$

$$= \int_0^\infty \{H_S[\pi \,|\, v, \tilde{u}(v)] - H_C[\pi \,|\, v, \tilde{u}(v)]\}\,d\pi + B$$

$$= 0$$

We thus assume for simplicity that $\tilde{u}(v)$ is interior for all v. We also assume that a higher soft signal is good news for action C:

$$\frac{\partial}{\partial u}(H_S - H_C) > 0. \tag{2}$$

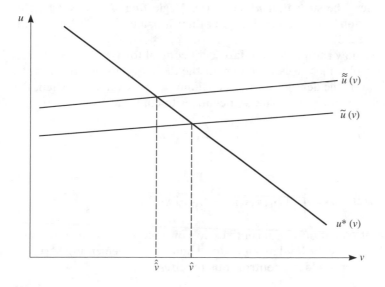

Figure 2.2

We further assume that $\partial/\partial v(H_S - H_C) \leq 0$. For example, if v is simply the firm's first-period profit, one has $\partial/\partial v(H_S - H_C) = 0$. (More generally, one could allow $(H_S - H_C)$ to grow with v as long as it does not grow too fast.) Then $\tilde{u}(v)$ is weakly increasing. Let $\hat{v}$ be such that $u^*(\hat{v}) = \tilde{u}(\hat{v})$ (see Figure 2.2).

Minimizing agency costs thus requires threatening the manager with *excessive intervention* $(u^*(v) > \tilde{u}(v))$ for low realizations of v (that is, $v < \hat{v}$) and *excessive passivity* $(u^*(v) < \tilde{u}(v))$ for high realizations of v (that is, $v > \hat{v}$). Note that the threat facing the manager is *ex post* efficient with probability zero (namely, only for $v = \hat{v}$).

How can these *ex post* inefficient threats[12] be made credible? Given that action S has been assumed to be *safer* than action C, *excessive intervention* can be obtained if the payoff of the outsider in control is *concave* in π. Similarly, *excessive passivity* can be obtained through a payoff *convex* in π for the outsider in control.

Note, however, that outside investors will neglect managerial private benefits B in their choice of action (prior to renegotiation). Define $(\tilde{u}, v)$ such that continuation and stopping are equivalent from the point of view of *monetary benefits*.

$$\Delta_m[v, \tilde{u}(v)] = \int_0^\infty \{H_S[\pi \mid v, \tilde{u}(v)] - H_C[\pi \mid v, \tilde{u}(v)]\}\, d\pi = 0.$$

Similarly, let $\hat{\hat{v}}$ be such that $u^*(\hat{\hat{v}}) = \tilde{\tilde{u}}(\hat{\hat{v}})$. Neglecting B means a bias in favour of action S, so that $\tilde{\tilde{u}}(v)$ is higher than $\tilde{u}(v)$, and thus $\hat{\hat{v}}$ is lower than $\hat{v}$ (see Figure 2.2).[13]

In fact, we now show that standard debt control for $v < \hat{\hat{v}}$ and standard equity control for $v > \hat{\hat{v}}$ can implement the desired managerial incentive scheme. Call $\hat{D}$ the debt level to be repaid in period 2 out of π. Then, the debt-holders' and equity holders' incentives to continue are respectively:

$$\Delta_D(\hat{D}, v, u) = \int_0^{\hat{D}} [H_S(\pi \mid v, u) - H_C(\pi \mid v, u)] d\pi$$

and

$$\Delta_E(\hat{D}, v, u) = \int_{\hat{D}}^{\infty} [H_S(\pi \mid v, u) - H_C(\pi \mid v, u)] d\pi.$$

Because of condition (2), incentives to continue increase in u for any given v, for both debt-holders and equity holders. Implementing $u^*(v)$ for a given v by debt-holders' control thus requires:

$$\Delta_D(\hat{D}, v, u^*(v)) = 0. \tag{3}$$

This can be done through an appropriate choice of $\hat{D} = \hat{D}(v)$ provided $\Delta_m(v, u^*(v)) > 0$, that is, provided $u^*(v) > \tilde{u}(v)$, or, equivalently, $v < \hat{v}$. Indeed, debt-holders always have a bias in favour of action S, which is safer than action C. More precisely, Figure 2.3(a) shows that, whenever $\Delta_D(\hat{D}, v, u) = 0$, then $\Delta_m(v, u) > 0$.[14]

Consequently, we can rely on debt-holders only to implement $u^*(v) > \tilde{u}(v)$. In such cases, for each v, $\hat{D}$ is chosen as in Figure 2.3(a).

Similarly, implementing $u^*(v)$ for a given v by equity holders' control requires

$$\Delta_E(\hat{D}, v, u^*(v)) = 0. \tag{4}$$

Ignoring private benefits, equity holders have a bias in favour of the riskier action C (see Figure 2.3(b)), so that equity control implements $u^*(v)$ only for such v's for which $u^*(v) < \tilde{u}(v)$ or $v > \hat{v}$. Figure 2.3(b) shows how $\hat{D}$ is chosen in such cases.

We can thus summarize our findings as follows:

> *Debt-holders always have socially excessive incentives to interfere while equity holders are typically too passive.*

Yet is is optimal to give contingent control to one of these two asset-holders in order to discipline managers:

Turbulent times ($v < \hat{v}$). The optimal managerial incentive scheme specifies

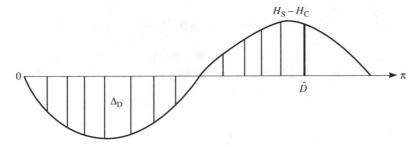

(a) Debt control

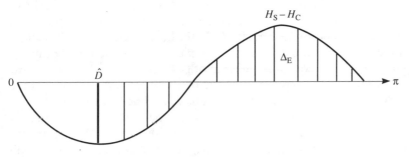

(b) Equity control

Figure 2.3 (a) Debt control (b) Equity control

more interference than is socially optimal ($u^*(v) > \tilde{u}(v)$). Hence it can be implemented only by giving control to *debt* for $v < \hat{\hat{v}} < \hat{v}$. Equity is instead required for $\hat{\hat{v}} < v < \hat{v}$, that is, when times are 'not too bad'.

Quiet times ($v > \hat{v}$). The optimal incentive scheme can be implemented only by giving control to *equity* in this case.

This is all very natural: managers are rewarded in good times by letting relatively passive shareholders retain control. Bad times require tough interference by debt-holders. The transfer of control from equity holders to debt-holders can be triggered by the inability of the firm to reimburse *short-term debt* out of period 1 profits. If v is interpreted strictly as period 1 profit, short-term debt can be set at the level $\hat{\hat{v}}$, and this will automatically induce the desired contingent control rule.

To implement $u^*(\cdot)$, note finally that the level of (long-term) debt $\hat{D}$ should be contingent on the verifiable signal. It can be shown that both in turbulent and in quiet times the firm's allowed level of debt is an increasing function of v. This is because more debt softens the controlling outsiders and thus can be used to reward the manager. Let us for example derive this property for equity control. The cut-off soft signal $u = u^*(v)$ satisfies:

$$\int_{\hat{D}(v)}^{\infty} [H_S(\pi \,|\, v, u^*(v)) - H_C(\pi \,|\, v, u^*(v))] \mathrm{d}\pi = 0.$$

Given that u^* is decreasing, the integrand is decreasing in v. Furthermore $\{H_S[\hat{D}(v)\,|\,v,u^*(v)] - H_C[\hat{D}(v)\,|\,v,u^*(v)]\}$ negative (see Figure 2.3(b)) implies that $\hat{D}$ must increase with v.

4   Interpreting the firm as a bank

What lessons can we draw from this analysis? In this section, we reinter-pret the firm as a bank. Long-term debt D is then the level of deposits of the bank. At the start (stage (i)), the bank's liability is thus composed of D, the level of deposits, and equity E. In the benchmark, either depositors do not withdraw their deposits until the end, or any amount withdrawn is compensated by an equivalent accrual of new deposits; we later will allow for a change in the deposit level. So, with a zero rate of interest, D is the debt owed at stage (iv). The value of equity is defined as a residual.

The verifiable signal v can include first-period bank profit, capital-to-loans ratio, categories of loans, current default rates on loans, and so forth. For notational simplicity, we will ignore first-period profits and will think of v as an objective measure of the riskiness of outstanding loans and of the bank's fragility. Thus, v corresponds to the *mechanistic grades* defined by, say, the 1991 FDICIA rules.[15]

In contrast, the non-verifiable signal u stands for other dimensions of the riskiness of loans and their correlation. A rating agency's or a govern-ment's rating of bank soundness thus is based on both v and u.

On the asset side of the bank, loans to businesses will result in total final profits $v + \pi$, where π concerns those loans for which uncertainty is not yet fully resolved at stage (iii), while v concerns loans where all uncertainty is resolved at that stage.[16]

The features of the optimal control structure of banks in our model are as follows:

(1)   Following good performance (high v), control rests with (passive) equity holders.

(2)   Increased bank fragility (average v) should be followed by more interventionist, but still accommodating, equity holder behaviour.

(3)   Finally, bad performance (low v) should trigger depositor control, with excessively interventionist behaviour.

We now investigate the consequences of the fact that bank deposits are typically held by *small depositors*.

As an aside, we should note that, if those small depositors are risk averse, it makes sense to insure their deposits (as they are not insured against bank failure, that is against the possibility that $v + \pi < D$). The insurance can be private or governmental at this stage. The traditional argument against deposit insurance is that insured small depositors have no incentives to monitor the banks. It seems doubtful, however, that small depositors would monitor banks even in the absence of deposit insurance. At best they would watch ratings supplied by private rating agencies or by the FDIC. A bank with a poor rating would then see its flow of uninsured deposits drained. Yet the same outcome can be achieved more simply (and without asking depositors to grasp the meaning of ratings) by imposing a limit on the deposits a bank can take for a given rating. We will thus work under the assumption that small depositors are fully insured. Their insurer (private insurer or FDIC), which bears the risk of bank failure, is then the debt-holder of the model.

In our model, small depositors need to be represented for two reasons. First, we saw that the level of deposits should be tailored to the bank's performance. While equity holders and managers prefer larger levels of deposits D, the bank should be allowed to take more deposits the higher its verifiable performance. Someone must therefore check that deposits match performance. Second, depositors ought to exercise their control rights when the bank's performance is poor. This exercise realistically can be performed only by a representative because of informational and free-riding problems.

Coming back to the necessary adjustment of the level of deposits to the bank's performance, we should point out that the mere evolution of the bank's balance sheet gives rise to incentives that are opposite to those derived in section 3. Namely, the more fragile the bank, the more incentives its claim-holders have to take risk, while an optimal governance structure would call for more conservative policies.

The perverse incentives problem

In a first step, let us assume away changes in assets and liabilities other than those associated with the resolution of v. In section 3.3, we saw that the claim-holders' (equity holders' or debt-holders') incentive to continue at stage (v) increases with the (net) debt level. Here the net debt level is $D - v$. Therefore a lower-grade v induces more passivity from claim-holders.[17] But we saw that an optimal financial structure would punish the bank's management by a high level of interference in turbulent times! Thus, keeping assets and liabilities unchanged, the mere accrual of information about existing loans gives the bank's financial structure the wrong incentives.

For instance, equity holders have an incentive to *gamble for resurrection*, that is, to choose action C when action S is far superior when the firm is ridden with debt, that is, when $D - v$ is large. The bank then suffers from a form of debt overhang. Our analysis is here similar to that of Kane (1989), who calls such banks (or thrifts in his particular study) *zombie firms*. Kane argues that managers and stockholders of decapitalized firms benefit from going for broke by attracting additional funds at above-market interest rates and placing the funds thus raised into high-risk, high-yield assets such as junk bonds or speculative real estate and construction ventures (p. 48).

The manager, of course, has even more incentives to conceal difficulties and to try to escape interference by outsiders, possibly by running Ponzi schemes, or even by manipulating hard information, i.e. the level of v. While this is true in general for the control of firms, it seems that it is particularly relevant in the case of banks, which can raise insured deposits even in bad times, in the absence of depositor control.

5   Banking regulation

The above sections have demonstrated the limitation of laissez-faire in the banking sector: one cannot rely solely on equity holders to discipline management. They are by essence biased in favour of managers, and can thus be relied upon only in good times (and even so the level of deposits should not be under their control). Debt-holders have to take an active role in disciplining management in turbulent times. Small depositors, however, the typical debt-holders of banks, cannot be relied upon to perform this task. In the absence of a threat of debt-holder control, equity holders face perverse incentives, siding with management in a strategy of gambling for resurrection.

These problems suggest a role for a public agency like FDIC that would: (1) regulate banks *ex ante*, forcing adjustments in the liability structure to counter the perverse incentive problem; (2) intervene *ex post*, thereby acting on behalf of small depositors in turbulent times.

5.1   Ex ante *regulation: capital requirements and deposit expansion*

Our analysis suggests that *capital requirements* and *limits to the growth of deposits*, policies that are often part of the regulatory environment of the banking sector, are appropriate to counter the perverse incentive problem described above. To eliminate this problem, the bank can be constrained to issue equity when the net debt $D - v$ is high. The new equity E', if invested in a safe asset, has the effect of reducing net debt to $D - v - E'$. Note that a decrease in v must be compensated by a higher issue of new equity so that turbulent times are associated with more interference. Conversely, when net debt is low, the bank should be allowed to take on more deposits and distribute the proceeds to shareholders. Note that the bank's management is always eager to have more deposits, as this induces more passivity. It thus suffices to fix *ex ante* a ceiling on deposits that increases with v.

Ceteris paribus (that is, keeping risky assets unaltered), a recapitalization makes claim-holders tougher, while an increase in the level of deposits makes them more passive. Therefore recapitalization should take place in turbulent times, and deposit expansion should be allowed in quiet times.

5.2   Ex post *regulation: incentives to intervene, sell or liquidate*

Our analysis is also consistent with the observed practice that allows the agency, when mechanistic grades fall below some threshold ($\hat{v}$ in our model), to take control of the bank and *directly interfere* in management if it finds it desirable. Often such interference takes the form of forcing the bank to act safely. But the agency can also manage the bank, as occurs when it gets ownership through capital injections.[18] Last, the government may look for another bank to purchase the bank in distress.

One striking implication of our analysis for regulation is that, in its intervention policy, the agency *should not maximize* ex post *social welfare*. Rather it should stand for the interests of depositors, were those not being insured; or, equivalently, the interests of taxpayers when depositors are insured. Let us see what would happen under a benevolent government that internalizes not only the taxpayers', but also the bank's and equity holders' interests. The agency would remain passive if and only if

$$\Delta_E + \Delta_D + B > 0.$$

Note that whenever Δ_D is positive, so is Δ_E *a fortiori*, and therefore the benevolent agency would not interfere when the debt-holder of section 3 would not. But the agency would also remain passive for some values of the signals for which debt-holders would interfere. We thus conclude that *the agency's internalization of bank or equity-holder welfare induces excessive passivity from the point of view of* ex ante *optimality*.

This suggests that regulatory agencies like FDIC be given missions that, in the spirit of the finance ministers, are monetary in nature. Such agencies could thus be instructed to stand for taxpayers (assuming they insure deposits), and not attempt to maximize *ex post* social welfare. The independence of the agency here might be a facilitating factor. One would expect politicians to be subject to pressures to internalize the bank's and its equity holders' welfare.

This pressure to internalize the welfare of other parties than taxpayers is particularly strong when the bank is 'too big to fail', that is, when its failure is deemed to exert substantial externalities on the local or national economy. The pressure is similarly quite strong in the presence of macro-economic shocks (lowering v for all banks, say). The correlation of shocks implies that the bank's failure coincides with other bank failures and thus with a high social shadow value of credit and employment. On the other hand, our analysis assumes that the decision making concerning the bank exerts no externality on the rest of the economy. The internalization by the regulator of such externalities on the rest of the economy is desirable, but our general point that the bank's and its equity holders' welfare should be ignored carries over.

Finally, note that the excessive passivity problem is further aggravated when the regulator is captured by the industry and thus favours the bank's and its equity holders' interests over those of taxpayers.

5.3   Regulatory and political cover-ups: monitoring and intervention

We just saw that regulation does not yield the optimal governance of banks if regulators define their tasks too broadly. Another limit to regulatory efficiency is the intrinsic tension between the two tasks allocated to the regulatory agency: monitoring and intervention. What drives bureaucrats and politicians alike is not monetary incentives but their career concerns or reputations. Bureaucrats seek promotions and attractive jobs in the private sector, and politicians seek re-election. And, independently of career concerns, none of them enjoys looking dumb. Yet, when they are asked to intervene when a bank is in trouble, they are de facto asked to confess that they may not have properly monitored the bank and prevented distress. This gives an incentive for bureaucrats and politicians to cover up and remain passive. Depending on their job horizon (date of promotion or hiring for the bureaucrat, and date of re-election for the politician), this cover-up is tantamount to (regulatory) gambling for resurrection if the horizon is long, and to passing the buck to the next administration if the horizon is short.

This conflict between monitoring and intervention suggests that it might be desirable to divide tasks. The monitoring role could be given to a private or governmental rating agency. The intervention role might remain with the FDIC, say. FDIC bureaucrats would then not be concerned with the bad inferences drawn from their intervention.

This division of labour would not be without cost. It may be hard for a rating agency to assess a bank's risk when the specificities of bank failure are later determined by the regulator's policy. Clear criteria such as the amount of taxpayer money spent therefore ought to be defined. More importantly, the division of labour creates a problem of 'moral hazard in teams'. A bank may fail either because the rating agency failed to give sufficient warning of possible trouble or because the regulator took inappropriate steps to control the bank. None of the two would want to take responsibility for the bank's failure.

6   Private remedies

Many private solutions, or more precisely remedies with a limited use of regulation, have been proposed. We examine them informally in the light of our framework. Remember that, for an optimal governance structure, the bank should be exposed to more external interference in turbulent times; this can be accomplished, for instance, by forcing the bank to recapitalize or suspending the distribution of dividends, and insisting that new loans be safe. An optimal governance structure also requires a shift of control to depositors in very difficult times, which raises the issue that depositors do not have the information or the incentive to perform this control.

Private ratings
A substitute for depositors' monitoring is the use of well-publicized ratings by agencies such as Moody's. While rating agencies have no financial stake in the bank, they have a reputation to sustain. For example, they might be commissioned by the government to monitor banks and might lose their contract if they committed too many type I and type II errors (unnecessary warning of distress, and ignorance of real distress). It is argued that bank mismanagement would be deterred by the use of ratings because a poor grade would induce depositors to select or switch to other banks.

Ratings per se are not a satisfactory solution however: a poor rating (following a poor combination of v and u) forces the bank to raise interest rates in order to retain its depositors. This impoverishes the bank and makes its claim-holders even more prone to let the managers gamble for resurrection than in the absence of ratings. Furthermore, spontaneous recapitalization is not desired by shareholders because it amounts to a gift to debt-holders.

Private deposit insurance
Private insurance resembles the use of ratings. Both raise the bank's cost of deposits in the event of bad signals. And both create a private monitor that substitutes for small depositors. One difference between the two is that the insurer has direct monetary incentives while the rating agency

tries to preserve its reputational capital. The arguments for and against private deposit insurance are similar to those for and against ratings. On the one hand, private insurance that designs risk-based insurance premia for banks acts as a deterrent to *ex ante* bank misbehaviour. On the other hand, an increase in deposit insurance aggravates the bank's difficulties in turbulent times without eliminating the perverse incentive problem for equity holders. Note also that private insurance raises the issue of what to do with failing insurance companies (where the failure can be triggered by correlated, macroeconomic shocks at the insured banks' level, say).

Large debt-holder

Several proposals have suggested that banks should be forced to have at least one large debt-holder besides small depositors. A large debt-holder has the same financial incentives as a deposit insurer. The difference between the two possibly lies with the exercise of residual rights of control. When the bank is in distress, the insurer contents itself with raising the insurance premium. The large debt-holder can interfere with management (choose action A in our model). A large debt-holder thus partly solves the intervention and monitoring problems, while an insurer or a rating agency supplies only the monitoring activity. To have full incentives to monitor and intervene on behalf of debt-holders, the large debt-holder could also be required to insure deposits as well.

There are a couple of potential problems with the use of a large debt-holder. First, a large debt-holder that does not insure small depositors and exercises the control rights associated with debt has an incentive to collude with management and equity to rip off the small depositors (or the insurer).[19] If the coalition internalizes the interests of everyone but small depositors, it will in fact be excessively passive in turbulent times, instead of excessively tough.

Incentives to collude with management and equity are lower if the large debt-holder's claim is junior to that of small depositors. In bad times, however, incentives to intervene are lower for a junior creditor than for a senior one: in the extreme case where equity has become worthless, the junior creditor is the residual claimant and is thus excessively soft, not excessively tough.

The second potential problem with the use of large debt-holders is that they must indeed be large to have an incentive to monitor the bank. This raises the general equilibrium question of whether there is enough large equity and debt capital in the economy to invest in banks. Or, turning things around, the small depositors must invest their money somewhere, and, wherever they invest it (a 'bank' in the definition of section 2), the monitoring and intervention issues will arise.[20]

7   Concluding remarks

In this paper, we started investigating the issue of banking regulation from the point of view of the optimal governance structure of firms. We built on previous work developing a theory of debt and equity and emphasized the optimality of shareholder passivity and of debt-holder interventionism. In this view, shareholders act as 'good times' principal while debt-holders act as 'bad times' principal. Each principal should moreover be tougher with management when performance deteriorates.

The distinctiveness of banks emphasized in this paper is the nature of the debt-holders, who are small dispersed depositors, typically unable meaningfully to exert residual rights of control. This would justify the existence of an agency like FDIC representing depositors and acting like a 'bad times' principal. That is, the agency should be given incentives to intervene in management more than *ex post* efficiency would require.

In the absence of regulation, banks face perverse incentives. Instead of being induced to be tougher when performance deteriorates, i.e. when bank solvency worsens, equity holders are tempted to 'gamble for resurrection', especially if the threat of depositor involvement is not credible. This would justify measures like capital adequacy requirements to counter such perverse incentives and ensure that equity holders take a more active stance in the case of deteriorating performance.

The paper has also suggested directions for research, by emphasizing issues like the political economy of banking regulation or the potential for private remedies to complement the regulation of banks. Another worthwhile avenue concerns the risk structure of bank assets and the optimal regulation of bank activities. We hope to pursue these issues in the above framework in the future.

NOTES

We thank Martin Hellwig, Richard Kihlstrom, Colin Mayer, Ailsa Röell and Xavier Vives for comments.

  1 During 1985–8, US households held 46.1 per cent of their financial assets (which represented about two-thirds of their total assets) in indirect securities. Non US Government debt securities amounted to only 7.1 per cent of their financial holdings (Kopcke and Rosengren, 1989).

  It should also be noted that much of the public debt of corporations is issued by firms with well-established reputations and low probability of bankruptcy (see Diamond, 1991, for a theory rationalizing this fact). In 1989, 52 per cent of outstanding corporate bonds had a credit rating of 'A' or better, a low figure by historical standards (the 1982 and 1972 figures being 72 and 73 per cent; Kaufman, 1991).

  2 Hellwig (1991a) contains an excellent discussion of some of these activities.

3 When banks that perform the delegated monitoring role emphasized by Diamond compete, the presence of returns to scale in monitoring due to diversification leads to multiplicity of equilibria and fragility of the banking system (self-fulfilling pessimism by depositors). This provides another rationale for regulation (for more on this, see Yanelle, 1989, 1991, and Matutes and Vives, 1991).

4 Possibly indexed to reflect the evolution of interest rates, as advocated by Hellwig (1991b).

5 Calomiris and Gorton (1991) point out that allowing runs gives depositors incentives to monitor as only the first to run get their money back. Monitoring by small depositors, however, may be quite costly owing to increasing returns in this activity. Also, run mechanisms do not solve the interference problem.

6 See Dewatripont and Tirole (1992) for a more extensive discussion of this point. Some implications of our theory can be obtained in the absence of a non-verifiable signal.

7 It suffices to add to the maximand in programme (I) below the expected *ex post* inefficiency associated with socially suboptimal decision making by outsiders.

8 They may also enjoy a better reputation in the labour market if their decisions are not reversed.

9 In Dewatripont and Tirole (1992), we show that our main results generalize to the case where managers care about monetary incentives; this moreover allows us to explain why managerial compensation depends on the value of equity rather than the total value of the firm.

10 The manager would be strictly willing to do so in exchange for keeping at least a small fraction of B.

11 We thank Ailsa Röell for pointing out the need to make such an assumption.

12 By assumption, renegotiation will ensure they are not carried out. However, they need to be credible *prior* to renegotiation in order to have an impact on the manager's payoff.

13 We thank Ailsa Röell for correcting the previous version of the paper by pointing out the need to define both $\Delta(.,.)$ and $\Delta_m(.,.)$.

14 That $\hat{D}$ can be found such that $\Delta_D(\hat{D}, v, u^*(v)) = 0$ results from the following facts: for $\hat{D}$ small, Δ_D is negative (again refer to Figure 2.3(a)), and $\Delta_D(\infty,.,.) = \Delta_m(.,.)$. Thus for $u^*(v) > \tilde{u}(v)$, there exists an appropriate $\hat{D}$ by continuity.

15 The FDICIA creates five grades for banks: well-capitalized, adequately capitalized, undercapitalized, significantly undercapitalized and critically undercapitalized.

16 As earlier, v and π are random variables whose distribution is determined by effort e. High and low efforts generate distributions $\bar{f}$ and $\bar{g}$ and f and g for v and u. And π has density $h_\Lambda(\pi|v,u)$. Note that π no longer denotes total profits, but still stands for profits that are risky at stage (iii).

17 Note that claim-holders are equally, and not more, passive if v is a first-period profit immediately distributed as a dividend to shareholders.

18 For instance, in the Continental Illinois case, the FDIC provided $1 billion of additional capital and bought from the bank $4.5 billion of shaky loans at face value, and received 80 per cent of the equity.

19 Collusion is a relevant issue for debt-holders and management of non-financial firms too. It is more acute, however, if there exists one large debt-holder facing many small ones.

20 This does not explain why small depositors do not invest in equity rather than debt. Insurance may be one reason. Another reason is that it is costly for firms to be held mainly by liquidity traders (on this, see Holmström and Tirole, 1992).

REFERENCES

Aghion, P. and P. Bolton (1992) 'An "incomplete contract" approach to bankruptcy and the financial structure of the firm', *Review of Economic Studies* **59**, forthcoming.

Calomiris, C.W. and G. Gorton (1991) 'The origins of banking panics', in G. Hubbard (ed.), *Financial Markets and Financial Crises*, Chicago: University of Chicago Press.

Dewatripont, M. and J. Tirole (1992) 'A theory of debt and equity: diversity of securities and manager–shareholder congruence', mimeo, Université Libre, Brussels, and IDEI, Toulouse.

Diamond, D. (1984) 'Financial intermediation and delegated monitoring', *Review of Economic Studies* **51**, 393–414.

Diamond, D. (1991) 'Monitoring and reputation: the choice between bank loans and directly placed debt', *Journal of Political Economy* **99**, 689–721.

Diamond, D. and P. Dybvig (1983) 'Bank runs, deposit insurance and liquidity', *Journal of Political Economy* **91**, 401–19.

Grossman, S. and O. Hart (1986) 'The costs and benefits of ownership: a theory of lateral and vertical integration', *Journal of Political Economy* **94**, 691–719.

Gurley, J. and E. Shaw (1960) *Money in a Theory of Finance*, Washington, DC: Brookings Institution.

Hellwig, M. (1991a) 'Banking, financial intermediation and corporate finance', in A. Giovannini and C. Mayer (eds.), *European Financial Integration*, Cambridge: Cambridge University Press.

Hellwig, M. (1991b) 'The regulation of banking: a theoretical appraisal', paper presented at the Bank of France Symposium.

Holmström, B. and J. Tirole (1992) 'Market liquidity and performance monitoring', mimeo.

Kane, E. (1989) *The S&L Insurance Mess: How Did this Happen?*, Washington: Urban Institute Press.

Kaufman, H. (1991) 'How Treasury's reform could hurt free enterprise', speech given at the Financial Association's 21st Annual Banking Symposium, New York City, 27 March.

Kopcke, R. and E. Rosengren (1989) 'Regulation of debt and equity', in R. Kopcke and E. Rosengren (eds.), *Are the Distinctions between Debt and Equity Disappearing?* Conference Series No. 33, Boston: Federal Reserve Bank of Boston.

Matutes, C. and X. Vives (1991) 'Competition for deposits, risk of failure, and regulation in banking', mimeo, Universitat Autònoma de Barcelona.

Rey, P. and J. Stiglitz (1991) 'Short-term contracts as a monitoring device', mimeo, INSEE and Stanford University.

Yanelle, M.O. (1989) 'The strategic analysis of intermediation', *European Economic Review* **33**, 294–304.

Yanelle, M.O. (1991) 'On endogenous intermediation', mimeo, Delta, Paris.

Discussion

RICHARD KIHLSTROM

In an earlier paper, Dewatripont and Tirole (1992), the authors have developed a model to explain why it is efficient for creditors to take control of a firm when it experiences difficulties and why shareholders should retain control of the firm in good times. In this model there is a verifiable signal of the firm's financial position and creditors take control of the firm when this signal indicates that profits will be low. When the verifiable signal indicates high profits, the firm is left under the control of shareholders. The model uses the well-known facts that the creditors' welfare is a concave function of the firm's profit and the shareholders' welfare is a convex function of the firm's profit. The part in control of the firm, then, uses a non-verifiable, i.e. non-contractible, signal as the basis for deciding whether or not to allow the firm's manager to remain in control of the firm. When a manager is in control of the firm, the firm's profit distribution is more 'risky' (in the sense of second-order stochastic dominance) than when they are not in control. For this reason, the risk-averse creditors will replace the manager more often than the risk-preferring shareholders. This is the efficient regime when the verifiable and unverifiable signals are both positively correlated with high profits as assumed. In their paper on bank regulation, Dewatripont and Tirole apply this model of debt to a bank. In this application, the bank's creditors are its depositors. It is argued that, because the depositors are each small creditors and are, therefore, unable to act concertedly to assume control when it is efficient to do so, regulators should act on their behalf. It is also argued that regulation which requires the bank to raise more equity capital in bad times and allows the banks to take on more deposits in good times is efficient.

  The Dewatripont–Tirole model of debt is quite creative and is the first that I am aware of to provide an interesting theoretical explanation of the legal arrangement which transfers control of financially troubled firms to creditors. The application to the discussion of banking regulation is also quite insightful and useful. As the authors emphasize, however, their discussion ignores many of the other aspects of the relationship between banks, depositors and borrowers.

  In the Dewatripont and Tirole (1992) model of debt, a moral hazard arises because the firm manager makes an effort decision that is unobserved by creditors and shareholders alike. While this effort decision presumably affects the distribution of profits, it is through its effect on the distribution of the verifiable and unverifiable signals that this unobserved effort level plays an explicit role. While it assumed that a high effort level is efficient, the model does not explicitly discuss the efficiency of the manager's effort level choice nor is it explicit about the effect of the effort level choice on the firm's profits. In this respect the model differs significantly from the earlier work of Grossman and Hart (1982). In the Grossman–Hart model, debt acts as an incentive device that can motivate the manager to choose an efficient level of a variable that affects profit but is unobserved by outside investors. While debt does not explicitly play this role in the Dewatripont–Tirole model, one might conjecture that the Dewatripont–Tirole and Grossman–Hart models could be combined to yield a more complete model of debt. Because the Grossman–Hart model has not received the attention that I believe it deserves, I would like to give a very brief exposition of an example of this model. In the example, the incentives provided by debt do, indeed, motivate the manager to choose an efficient level of the variable that affects profit but is unobserved by outside investors.

In the Grossman–Hart model of capital structure, a firm manager raises capital from outside investors by issuing debt and equity. The manager can invest this capital productively or use it for their own purposes by consuming 'perquisites'. Outside investors are unable to tell whether the capital is being used productively or consumed as perquisites. Thus, the investment level chosen by a manager is unobserved by the capital market. We will assume that they can choose only two investment levels, I_1 and I_2, where

$$I_1 > I_2.$$

Grossman and Hart assume that the mean of the profit distribution, $g(I)$, is an increasing function of investment, I. We will introduce this assumption in the following way. We suppose that the profit of the firm can be either $\bar{\pi}$ or $\underline{\pi}$, where

$$\bar{\pi} > \underline{\pi}.$$

The probability of the higher profit level, $\bar{\pi}$, depends on the amount invested in the firm. If $I = I_i$ then the probability of the $\bar{\pi}$ is μ_i and the probability of $\underline{\pi}$ is, therefore, $[1 - \mu_i]$. We assume that

$$\mu_1 > \mu_2$$

so that

$$g(I_1) \equiv \mu_1 \bar{\pi} + [1 - \mu_1]\underline{\pi} > \mu_2 \bar{\pi} + [1 - \mu_2]\underline{\pi} \equiv g(I_2),$$

and, as Grossman and Hart assume, the mean of the profit distribution, $g(I)$, is, indeed, an increasing function of investment, I.

Since investors are assumed to be risk neutral, and R is one plus the discount rate, the firm would have a market value of

$$V(I_i) \equiv g(I_i)/R$$

if the investors believed that the manager had invested I_i. Although the investors don't observe I, they observe the firm's capital structure and from the capital structure they can infer the manager's incentive to invest. The investors specifically observe the firm's debt level, D, and they know the manager has the incentive to invest $I(D)$ when the firm's debt level is D. The investors, therefore, expect the manager to invest $I(D)$ when they observe debt level D. Thus, when the debt level D is observed, the firm's market value is

$$V[I(D)] \equiv g[I(D)]/R.$$

We now describe the manager's preferences and their implied incentives. A manager's utility, u, is a function $u(W)$ of the value, W, of the perquisites they consume. This function is such that

$$u(0) = 0$$

and

$$u' > 0.$$

If the manager issues debt in the amount D and there is a default then they are assumed to lose control of the firm and receive no perquisites. If no default occurs, the value of the perquisites consumed by the manager is $V - I$ where V is the market value of the firm and I is their investment. Thus, a manager's incentives to invest are determined by the possibility of a default. These incentives depend entirely on whether they issue debt with a face value D in excess of $\underline{\pi}$ but less than $\bar{\pi}$ or issue debt with a face value below $\underline{\pi}$. Of course, they will never issue debt with a face value in excess of $\bar{\pi}$, because, in that case, a default is certain and the manager never has any perquisites.

We assume that the parameters are such that

$$u[V(I_1) - I_1]\mu_1 > \max\{u[V(I_1) - I_2]\mu_2, \quad u[V(I_2) - I_2]\}. \tag{1}$$

Recall that the investors expect the manager to invest $I(D)$ when they observe debt level D. When

$$D > \underline{\pi},$$

there will be a default when profits equal $\underline{\pi}$. Thus, if the manager chooses to invest I_i, their expected utility will be

$$u[V(I(D)) - I_i]\mu_i.$$

When, however,

$$D \leq \underline{\pi},$$

there is no possibility of a default. In this case, if the manager chooses to invest I_i, their expected utility is simply

$$u[V(I(D)) - I_i].$$

When

$$D > \underline{\pi},$$

the market knows that the manager chooses the investment level

$$\hat{I}(D) = \underset{I_i}{\operatorname{argmax}}\ u[V(I(D)) - I_i]\mu_i.$$

When

$$D \leq \underline{\pi},$$

the market knows that the manager chooses the investment level

$$\hat{I}(D) = \underset{I_i}{\operatorname{argmax}}\ u[V(I(D)) - I_i].$$

Since

$$I_1 \geq I_2,$$

$$I_2 = \underset{I_i}{\operatorname{argmax}}\ u[V(I(D)) - I_i]$$

and

$$\hat{I}(D) = I_2$$

when

$$D \leq \underline{\pi}.$$

In any rational expectations equilibrium we must, therefore, suppose that the investors expect the manager to invest

$$I(D) = \hat{I}(D) = I_2$$

when they observe a debt level D equal to or below $\underline{\pi}$. Thus, when the manager chooses to issue debt in an amount D such that

$$D \leq \underline{\pi},$$

their expected utility is

$$U(D) \equiv u[V(I_2) - I_2].$$

Suppose now that the investors expect the manager to invest

$$I(D) = I_1$$

when they observe a debt level D in excess of $\underline{\pi}$. When

$$D > \underline{\pi},$$

the manager will choose the investment level

$$\hat{I}(D) = \underset{I_i}{\operatorname{argmax}}\, u[V(I_1) - I_i]\mu_i.$$

Since it is assumed that

$$u[V(I_1) - I_1]\mu_1 > u[V(I_1) - I_2]\mu_2,$$

we must have

$$I(D) = \hat{I}(D) = I_1 = \underset{I_i}{\operatorname{argmax}}\, u[V(I_1) - I_i]\mu_i$$

when

$$D > \underline{\pi}.$$

Thus, the hypothesis that

$$I(D) = I_1$$

when

$$D > \underline{\pi}$$

is consistent with rational expectations. Note also that, when the manager chooses to issue debt in an amount D such that

$$D > \underline{\pi},$$

their expected utility is

$$U(D) \equiv u[V(I_1) - I_1]\mu_1.$$

The level of debt issued by the manager is

$$\hat{D} = \underset{D}{\operatorname{argmax}}\, U(D) = \begin{cases} u[V(I_1) - I_1]\mu_1, & \text{if } D \geq \underline{\pi}, \\ u[V(I_1) - I_2], & \text{if } D \leq \underline{\pi}. \end{cases}$$

Since it is assumed that

$$u[V(I_1) - I_1]\mu_1 > u[V(I_2) - I_2],$$

the level of debt, $\hat{D}$, issued by the manager will exceed $\underline{\pi}$ and the manager will invest $\hat{I}(\hat{D}) = I_1$.

Note that

$$u[V(I_1) - I_1]\mu_1 > u[V(I_1) - I_2]\mu_2$$

is equivalent to

$$\frac{u[V(I_1) - I_2]}{u[V(I_1) - I_1]} < \mu_1/\mu_2.$$

Note also that

$$u[V(I_1) - I_1]\mu_1 > u[V(I_2) - I_2]$$

is equivalent to

$$\frac{u[V(I_2) - I_2]}{u[V(I_1) - I_1]} < \mu_1 < 1.$$

Since

$$\mu_1 < 1,$$

this inequality implies

$$V(I_2) - I_2 < V(I_1) - I_1.$$

Thus, in the equilibrium described here, there is no underinvestment even though the investors invest more, viz. $V(I_1)$, in the firm than I_1, the amount that is ultimately invested.

Note that if we had

$$u[V(I_1) - I_1]\mu_1 < u[V(I_2) - I_2],$$

which is equivalent to

$$\frac{u[V(I_2) - I_2]}{u[V(I_1) - I_1]} > \mu_1,$$

then the optimal investment level could still have been I_1 so that we would have had

$$1 > \frac{u[V(I_2) - I_2]}{u[V(I_1) - I_1]} > \mu_1.$$

In this case, however,

$$u[V(I_1) - I_1]\mu_1 < u[V(I_2) - I_2]$$

would imply that the level of debt raised in equilibrium would have been less than π and the equilibrium investment level would have been I_2. Thus, in this case there would be underinvestment.

REFERENCES

Dewatripont, M. and J. Tirole (1992) 'A theory of debt and equity: diversity of securities and manager–shareholder congruence', mimeo, Université Libre de Bruxelles and IDEI, Toulouse.
Grossman, S. and O. Hart (1982) 'Corporate financial structure and managerial incentives', in J. McCall (ed.), *The Economics of Information and Uncertainty*, Chicago: University of Chicago Press, pp. 107–37.

AILSA RÖELL

The paper proposes an ingenious scheme for providing performance-based managerial incentives in a setting where not all aspects of a bank's performance are 'hard' enough information to make payments contingent upon. The idea is that publicly verifiable performance indicators can be made to trigger both changes in control of the bank among claim-holders and adjustments in its debt–equity mix. The changes in financial structure can be designed in such a way that *ex post* bargaining among equity holders, depositors/creditors and the manager implements the appropriate fully state-contingent reward scheme for the manager.

The model presented in the paper is a special, simplified case of a more general model presented in a companion paper (Dewatripont and Tirole, 1992). In the simple case, the manager is assumed not to attach utility to money; instead, they derive a 'private benefit' from being in charge when the bank 'continues' its risky activities rather than 'stopping' (adopting a safer policy). The simplified model requires somewhat strained assumptions concerning the transferability of the manager's 'private' benefit (though it is private, they can agree to give it up if they choose to; similarly, it can be given to them even if the bank does not 'continue'). In this respect the more general model is superior.

The assumptions about the bargaining power of the various parties are rather special. It is assumed that the controlling class of claim-holders has absolute power to determine whether the firm 'stops' or 'continues'; yet, the manager has the power to veto any restructuring of claims in renegotiation that might lead the controlling claim-holders to prefer a different course of action. In effect, the manager has no control over the bank's operating decisions but veto power over any financial restructuring. This is a strong assumption as it means, for example, that the bank's equity holders cannot purchase its debt on the open market (as they might wish to do in the south-eastern quadrant of Figure 2.2), which would induce them to 'stop' without rewarding the management. Indeed it means that debt-holders cannot even unilaterally renounce a small part of their claims, even though this would be to their advantage along the lower reaches of that quadrant (because the equity holders would become more conservative and voluntarily choose to 'stop' rather than 'continue'). In principle it is possible to give such extreme powers to managers, but this is rarely observed in practice. Research into the robustness of the model to changes in assumptions regarding bargaining power seems worthwhile.

While the model of the paper is relevant to firms in general, it seems particularly applicable to banks. This is because the model requires either a provision in the corporate charter or action by an outside monitoring agency to ensure that the debt–equity mix of the firm adjusts in the light of its visible performance, v. In practice, in an ordinary firm such decisions are taken *ex post* by managers and other stake-holders; it seems unrealistic to suppose that such complex schemes would be written into the corporate charter at the time the firm is first set up. Banks, however, are subject to monitoring by government agencies. These explicitly prescribe adjustments to their capital structure in the light of their performance. Thus the model serves as a model of optimal regulatory intervention into banks' capital structure.

The authors prefer to take a somewhat different view, stressing the bank regulator's role as a representative of the fragmented depositors in the *ex post* bargaining process. They regard the debt–equity mix, and its changes in response to verifiable performance indicators, as written into the corporate charter.

Leaving aside the question of how the debt–equity mix is imposed, one question that is not fully addressed in the paper is the comparative statics of the relationship between visible performance, v, and the net debt level, $\hat{D}$. The model calls for the firm to exploit debt-holders' bias towards safe projects when visible performance is bad, and equity holders' bias towards risky projects when visible performance is good. What does this imply for the optimal level of net debt, $\hat{D}$, as a function of visible performance, v?

Surprisingly, the optimal level of $\hat{D}(v)$ corresponding to any particular level of visible performance, v, is neither unique nor monotonic. It is also discontinuous in v at $\hat{v}$, the level of performance that triggers a change in control. To see this, take for simplicity the special case where $H_S - H_C$

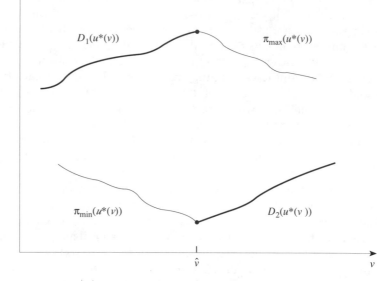

Figure 2B.1   Optimal net debt as a function of visible performance

does not depend directly on the visible signal, v. Consider first the optimal debt–equity mix at $\hat{v}$. Here, optimal managerial compensation requires the socially efficient decision to be the status quo for renegotiation. Then $\hat{D}$ must either equal $\pi_{\min}(u^*(\hat{v}))$ or $\pi_{\max}(u^*(\hat{v}))$ (where $\pi_{\min}(u)$ and $\pi_{\max}(u)$ will denote the lower and upper endpoints of the interval of long-run profits π where $H_S(\pi|u) \neq H_C(\pi|u)$ in Figure 2.3 of the paper). Thus at $\hat{v}$, the firm must be to all intents and purposes either 100 per cent debt-financed or 0 per cent debt-financed (or rather, to be precise, $\hat{D}$ must be so low that debt is riskless even if the firm 'continues'). For other values of v there are two optimal values of $\hat{D}(v)$. Since $H_S - H_C$ is increasing in u, $\pi_{\min}(u)$ and $\pi_{\max}(u)$ are increasing in u, while the interior cut-offs D_1 and D_2 defined by

$$\int_0^{D_1} H_S - H_C = 0 \quad \text{and.} \quad \int_{D_2}^{\infty} H_S - H_C = 0$$

are both decreasing in u. Since $u^*(v)$ is decreasing, it follows that $D_1(u^*(v))$ and $D_2(u^*(v))$ are increasing in Figure 2B.1.

The authors focus their discussion of regulation on the $D_1(u^*(v))$ arm of the picture, where depositors/debt-holders are in control and a deterioration of visible performance, v, requires regulators to lower deposits $\hat{D}$. They do not make explicit that, as v increases towards $\hat{v}$, the optimal level of deposits rises to 100 per cent of the firm's financing, after which it drops suddenly to (effectively) 0 per cent, to rise again slowly as v increases along the $D_2(u^*(v))$ arm of the picture. At $\hat{v}$, where control switches to the equity holders and risky debt must be reduced abruptly from 100 per cent down to zero, the equity holders are in effect required to operate a 'narrow bank' that does not in any way put its depositors'/creditors' money at risk. This scheme seems too sensitive to parameter changes to be taken as a literal policy prescription for banking regulators or designers of corporate charters.

Like the authors I have ignored the $\pi_{\min}$ and $\pi_{\max}$ branches of the picture, though it is not clear why these are less deserving of attention. The model seeks to manipulate the level of risk aversion of those in control by varying the level of debt; there are always two solutions because, as debt increases, the convexity (concavity) of the equity holders' (creditors') objective function over the relevant range first increases, then decreases. Thus the desired level of risk aversion can generally be obtained in two different ways.

In summary, the paper makes a valuable contribution in bringing the issue of managerial incentives and control into the debate about banking regulation. As my comments indicate, I am somewhat hesitant about the specificities of the model. But the issues raised are important enough to merit further research along these lines.

REFERENCES

Dewatripont, M. and J. Tirole (1992) 'A theory of debt and equity: diversity of securities and manager–shareholder congruence', mimeo, Université Libre de Bruxelles and IDEI, Toulouse.

3 Bank loan maturity and priority when borrowers can refinance

DOUGLAS W. DIAMOND

1 Introduction

This paper provides a theory of how highly levered borrowers with private information about their credit prospects choose the seniority and maturity of their debt. The main result is that when different lenders own the short-term and long-term debt issues, short-term debt will be senior to long-term debt. This result follows from the difficulty of restructuring and renegotiating bonds that are held by the public. I develop the implications of choosing an optimal debt structure for the decisions of banks to make concessions on their loans. Recent empirical evidence on debt concessions by banks is discussed in light of the results.

The debt maturity and priority choice trades off protection of the borrower's control rents against increasing the sensitivity of the borrower's financing costs to new information. Short-term debt provides information sensitivity; this is desired because it benefits a borrower who expects his credit rating to improve. If the borrower cannot repay the debt in full, however, the lender has the right to remove the borrower from control (I term this a liquidation), and shorter-term debt makes this possibility happen sooner. Liquidation has beneficial effects, and ought not be eliminated. Lenders may, however, be too prone to liquidate. Some related papers on the effects of debt structure on control arc Aghion and Bolton (1992), Harris and Raviv (1990), Hart and Moore (1989, 1990), Jensen (1989), and Jensen and Meckling (1976). Flannery (1986) examines the effect of debt maturity on information sensitivity.

Lenders might liquidate too often because part of the future returns of the project can be assigned only to the borrower, and not to lenders. The part of the value that must go to the borrower is termed a control rent: it accrues to management (if it keeps control) but cannot be assigned to lenders. Lenders neglect control rents when they choose to liquidate. Lenders can then inefficiently choose to liquidate a solvent but illiquid

46

borrower, when one includes the control rents in the solvency value. There are many motivations for the existence of non-assignable control rents. Moral hazard or future bargaining power of the borrower are two sufficient motivations.[1]

My previous work on the structure of debt contracts (Diamond, 1991a, 1992a) shows how the existence of multiple future lenders can be used to provide some impact of new information on a borrower's cost of finance while allowing the borrower to retain control more often than any single lender would permit. The ability to go to the market and refinance maturing debt from competing lenders serves to limit the control that outside lenders have over borrowers. If the contracts are properly structured, the outside lenders will retain control when they need it most. This implies that one can fine-tune the amount of control that lenders possess, using the added freedom of having two types of lender: current and future.

This paper describes the implications of these models for the restructuring actions taken by various types of lenders when the borrower cannot meet its contracted obligations. The model has implications for the maturity structure of debt when a single lender owns all of the debt. When differing lenders own the various debt maturities, and there is some possibility that the lenders cannot renegotiate their contracts, there are implications for debt priority as well. I do not explain why there are various owners of the different maturities. I appeal to the ideas in Diamond (1992b), where only a subset of lenders, those I call banks, have both the timely information required to make liquidation decisions and the specific expertise to implement them. The control right over these liquidation decisions, which is ownership of the short-term debt, ought to be assigned to these lenders. The lenders who do not have the information or expertise to make liquidation decisions should own the publicly traded bonds. Free-rider problems and government regulation limit the public's ability to renegotiate their bonds, but do not eliminate this ability. Under the assumption that there is a positive probability, but not a certainty, of renegotiating public bonds, I obtain a strong prediction on priority. Bank loans, which are short term, should be senior to long-term public bonds.

This paper also illustrates how the ability to refinance from competing future lenders improves the set of contracts available to the borrower. The improvement occurs even if the market for initial financing is competitive. I contrast the contracts available with competing future lenders with those available when the initial lender is the only source of refinancing.

Section 2 outlines the basics of the model. Section 3 describes the information-contingent payments and liquidation decisions that borrowers would choose if they could write explicitly information-contingent contracts. Section 4 shows how close one can come to the desired policy by contracting with a single lender who faces no competition when the borrower attempts to refinance maturing debt. Section 5 demonstrates how the ability to write contracts that are implicitly contingent on future information is increased when the initial lender faces competition in providing refinancing. Section 6 introduces multiple initial lenders to the model with competing refinancing lenders, and develops the potential effects of debt priority. Section 7 studies the implications of using bank loans together with publicly traded bonds if there is uncertain negotiation of public bonds. This delivers a strong prediction on the priority of these two lenders' debt. In section 8, I interpret some models where the initial lender has an information monopoly, which leads to imperfect competition, in terms of the contrast between the models in sections 4 and 5. Section 9 concludes the paper, and relates it to recent empirical evidence.

2   The model

There are three dates, 0, 1 and 2. Long-term debt is issued on date 0 and matures on date 2, with no coupon payment on date 1 (the results do not depend on the zero coupon assumption). Short-term debt is single period. Either or both types of debt can be used. To keep units simple, assume that riskless interest rates are zero. Borrowers and lenders are risk neutral and consume on date 2. Lenders will then lend at an expected rate of return of zero.[2] The model abstracts from unexpected changes in riskless interest rates. One interpretation of this is that the borrower hedges these changes using interest rate futures, options or swaps. Because borrowers have no private information about future riskless interest rates, they could hedge these risks without revealing any information about themselves.

There are many potential lenders who all observe the same information. With all lenders observing the same information, borrowers face a competitive loan market on each date: lenders will lend if they get a competitive (zero) expected rate of return. I examine the case where the date-0 short-term and long-term lenders are different parties, and the case where a single lender owns both maturities. The borrower can borrow from a competitive loan market when refinancing at date 1; the new lender can be a different party from any of the date-0 lenders.

To illustrate the effects of facing a competitive loan market in the future, section 4 contrasts the case where the initial date-0 lender is the only available lender at date 1. The contracts available with this *ex post* monopoly are not as desirable for borrowers. In particular, the contract with *ex post* monopoly does not allow borrowers as much benefit if favourable information arrives about them in the future.

There is no outside equity: all equity is owned by the borrower (or, more generally, by those in control). To focus on the refinancing risk of short-term debt, and its effect on the borrower's ability to retain control, assume that projects produce cash flows only on date 2. All short-term debt issued on date 0 must then be refinanced at date 1. New public information arrives to lenders on date 1, but the data cannot be used to condition contingent contracts because the information is not verifiable and is not observed by any court of law. Covenants in the long-term debt cannot depend on this information. The information observed at date 1 is about the continued creditworthiness of the borrower, and this is implicitly information about a borrower's type.

There are two types of borrower, who differ in their type of investment project. No one but a borrower knows the type of their project. Borrowers have no capital of their own. Denote the amount of initial capital required for each project by $I > 0$ (projects are indivisible). *Each project yields a date-2 cash flow of* $X > I$ *when successful, returns 0 otherwise, and each project also produces a non-assignable control rent of* C *if the management has control at date 2.*[3] All projects can be liquidated at date 1 for a liquidation value of $L < I$. Liquidation value is the maximum value in alternative use that can be obtained without the management of the borrower (see Diamond, 1991a, section IV). A successful project yields a higher return when not liquidated at date 1, because $L < I < X$. The two types of project differ only in the probability that the return X is received. The two types of borrower are described as follows.

Type G   The project returns a cash flow of $X > I$ for sure at date 2. This is a positive net present value project.

Type B   The project returns a cash flow of X, with probability π, and returns zero with probability $1 - \pi$. The project has a negative net present value: $\pi X < I$.

Both types of project also deliver a control rent of C to the borrower if they have control on date 2, but this cannot be assigned to lenders. The value of control, C, is large enough that there will never be liquidation when lenders do not have the control right to force liquidation, because borrowers would turn down any deal that lenders would offer.[4] If lenders learn that a borrower has a sufficiently high probability of being of type B, it is in lenders' collective interest to liquidate: I assume that $L > \pi X$.

The prior of all lenders on date 0 is that the borrower is of type G with probability f. A borrower's date-0 credit rating is summarized by f. The lower is f, the higher is the promised interest rate, owing to the higher default rate of type Bs. As of date 0, the probability of repayment of a loan maturing on date 2 made to a borrower with credit rating f is: $q(f) = \pi + f(1 - \pi)$.

On date 1, all lenders will observe new information about the type of each borrower. The new information, with realization f_1, is the conditional probability that a borrower is of type G. To keep this discussion simple, I assume that f_1 takes on only three possible values: 0, f^d and 1, where $f^d \in (0,1)$. Only type Bs receive an f_1 of 0, only type Gs receive an f_1 of 1, and both types can receive the value f^d. I refer to f^d as the downgrade credit rating, but do not assume that $f^d < f$. From Bayes' law, if the unconditional probability of a realization f_1^i is P^j, then the probability that a type G receives the realization is $g^j = P^j f_1^i / f$.

3   Borrowers' desired f_1-contingent contracts

I assume that contracts that are contingent on the date-1 information, f_1, are not available. It is useful, however, to examine the contract the borrower would choose if the contingent contracts were available. This allows a comparison of how close to the optimum are some alternative contracts. The contract preferred by type G borrowers is chosen by *all* borrowers. Borrowers offer contracts to lenders, and offering a contract that only type Bs would prefer would reveal that a borrower was of type B, and then no loan would be made. Control rents are sufficiently large that it is impossible to separate the borrower types. Diamond (1991a) discusses the reasonable borrower beliefs that support this outcome.

Given a date-1 credit rating, f_1, with probability f_1 a borrower is of type G. Type Gs want to make liquidation decisions and required payments contingent on f_1. They want to maximize their expected payoff in cash plus control rents, subject to giving lenders a sufficient return to induce them to lend. Let $Z(f_1) \le X$ be the date-2 promised payment that the borrower makes when there is not liquidation, given f_1. This payment is made when the borrower's project returns X (no payment is made if the project returns 0). This gives the lender an expected return of $q(f_1) Z(f_1)$, where $q(f_1) = f_1 + (1 - f_1)\pi$ is the probability that a borrower with date-1 information f_1 makes the promised payment. A type G borrower's payoff is $X - Z(f_1) + C$ when there is not liquidation given f_1, because type Gs make the payment with certainty. Let $z(f_1)$ be the date-1 payment to the lender where there is liquidation given f_1. When there is liquidation given f_1, the control rent C is destroyed, and the payoff of a borrower is $L - z(f_1)$. Let $\mathcal{L}(f_1)$ be the probability of liquidation given a value of f_1. A type G chooses f_1-contingent payments and liquidation rules that solve:

$$\max_{Z(f_1) \le X,\, z(f_1) \le L,\, \mathcal{L}(f_1) \in [0,1]} \frac{1}{f} \sum_{j \in J} P^j f_1^i \{\mathcal{L}(f_1^i)[L - z(f_1^i)]$$
$$+ [1 - \mathcal{L}(f_1^i)][X - Z(f_1^i) + C]\}$$

Subject to $\sum_{j \in J} P^i\{\mathcal{L}(f^i_1)z(f^i_1) + [1 - \mathcal{L}(f^i_1)][q(f^i_1)Z(f^i_1)]\} \geq I.$

There are three possible date-1 realizations of the information f_1: $0, f^d, 1$. This is the set, J. When $f_1 = 0$, the cash payments $Z(0)$ and $z(0)$ and the control rent C do not directly enter the objective function, because only type Bs can receive a credit rating $f_1 = 0$ (recall that a type G receives information f^i_1 with probability $g^i = P^i f^i_1/f$). The liquidation decisions and payments given $f_1 = 0$ are relevant to type Gs only through their effect on the budget constraint that lenders receive an expected return of at least I. As a result, the decision that results in the maximum payment given $f_1 = 0$ is desired by type Gs. This decision is liquidation (because $L > \pi X$), and, with liquidation, the payment ought to be $z(0) = L$, to loosen the budget constraint as much as possible. Similarly for a fixed liquidation decision given $f_1 = f^d$, type Gs prefer that payments be at their maximum to allow the payment given $f_1 = 1$ to be reduced. Type Gs prefer high payments for lower values of f_1 and lower payments for higher values of f_1 because they are more likely than type Bs to receive a high f_1. If there is to be liquidation given $f_1 = f^d$ then $z(f^d) = L$, and if not then $Z(f^d) = X$ is preferred.

If lenders are to get an expected return of I, then

$$I = P^z L + \mathcal{L}(f^d)P^d L + [1 - \mathcal{L}(f^d)]P^d q(f^d)X + P^u Z(1),$$

or

$$Z(1) = (1/P^u)\{I - P^z L - P^d\{\mathcal{L}(f^d)L + [1 - \mathcal{L}(f^d)]q(f^d)X\}.$$

A type G's payoff is then:

$$(P^d f^d/f)([1 - \mathcal{L}(f^d)]C) + (P^u/f)\{X + C - Z(1)\}.$$

Liquidation given $f_1 = f^d$ reduces $Z(1)$ by $(P^d/P^u)(L - q(f^d)X)$, which a type G pays with probability P^u/f, at the cost, C, in lost control rents, which a type G borrower loses with probability $(P^d f^d/f)$. Liquidation is then preferred when C is less than $(L - q(f^d)X)/f^d$. This means that a type G desires liquidation given $f_1 = f^d$ if the expected lost control rents given $f_1 = f^d$ of the type G are less than the increased return that liquidation provides to lenders, that is if $f^d_1 C \leq L - q(f^d_1)X$. For sufficiently large control rents, C, type G borrowers will want to avoid liquidation when $f_1 = f^d$, but they will still desire liquidation when $f_1 = 0$. In this case the *ex ante* desired liquidation policy is $\mathcal{L}(0) = 1$, $\mathcal{L}(f^d) = \mathcal{L}(1) = 0$. I assume that C is large enough so that this is the desired liquidation policy.

3.1 An example

To illustrate the contingent policy desired by borrowers, and because no proofs are provided in this paper, the following example is presented. The example will be used throughout the paper, to make points more precise. As of date 0, the lenders believe the borrower is of type G with probability $f = .7$. The value of a successful project is $X = 1.3$. A type B borrower's project is successful with probability $\pi = .5$. Projects require initial capital of $I = 1$. Liquidation at date 1 yields $L = 0.9$. The non-assignable value of keeping control until date 2 is $C = 0.4$.

The three possible values of f_1 are 0, .25 and 1, and the unconditional probabilities of these realizations are, respectively, $P^z = .15$, $P^d = .2$, and $P^u = .65$. The implied conditional probabilities of debt repayment, $q(f_1)$, are 0, .625 and 1, respectively. The probabilities that a type G borrower receives each realization of f_1 are, respectively, 0, .07143 and .92857. Recall that the probability that a type G receives the realization is the unconditional probability multiplied by f_1/f. Consequently, type G borrowers want a larger payment to lenders when f_1 is smaller. For a fixed liquidation decision, a type G borrower prefers the payment given $f_1 = 0$ to be as high as possible, and that there be liquidation. Liquidation provides lenders with return $L = 0.9$, as compared with a maximum without liquidation of $\pi X = 0.65$. No type Gs receive $f_1 = 0$, implying that control rents lost when $f_1 - 0$ are not relevant to a type G. This implies $\mathcal{L}(0) = 1$ and $z(0) = L$ is preferred by type Gs. There will not be liquidation given $f_1 = 1$, because the cash flow from the borrower's project is more valuable than the liquidation proceeds, $X > L$, and liquidation is in no one's interest.

For a given liquidation decision, type Gs want the maximum payment, given $f_1 = f^d = .25$, to produce a lower payment when $f_1 = 1$: type G borrowers prefer $Z(f^d) = X$ and $z(f^d) = L$. I showed that liquidation given $f_1 = f^d$ is not desired when C exceeds $(L - q(f^d)X)/f^d$. Using the parameters from the example, one obtains $C = 0.35$ as the maximum C such that liquidation is preferred given $f_1 = f^d$. For all $C > 0.35$, type G borrowers prefer $\mathcal{L}(f^d) = 0$: no liquidation given $f_1 = f^d$. For $C < 0.35$, type G borrowers prefer $\mathcal{L}(f^d) = 1$: certain liquidation given $f_1 = f^d$. The example assumes $C = 0.4$, implying that the desired liquidation policy is $\mathcal{L}(0) = 1$, and $\mathcal{L}(f^d) = \mathcal{L}(1) = 0$: liquidate only when $f_1 = 0$. The f_1-contingent payments desired are $z(0) = L = 0.9$, $Z(f^d) = X = 1.3$, and $Z(1) = (1/P^u)\{I - P^z L - P^d q(f^d)X\} = 1.081125$.

I will show that this can be implemented with a properly chosen set of debt contracts, with the possibility of refinancing from a competing lender at date 1. In general, however, debt contracts cannot duplicate all contracts available with f_1-contingent contracts. To show the importance of refinancing from a competing lender, the next section analyses the case where the date-0 lender is the only available lender at date 1. With a single lender, the desired payment policy cannot be implemented.

4   Assignment of control when f_1 is not verifiable and there are no competing future lenders

Suppose that the assignment of liquidation rights and promised payments cannot depend directly on f_1. Lenders are willing to lend given an expected return of I, but the lender will face no competition on date 1. The borrower and the lender can assign the unconditional right to liquidate to one party or the other. In addition, they can specify a date-1 payment to the lender, z, if liquidation is chosen, and a date-2 payment to the lender, Z, if there is not liquidation (this is paid only if the borrower's project returns X). Both the borrower and the lender will know f_1 on date 1.

The *ex post* desire of all borrowers is to avoid liquidation. If borrowers have the right to choose whether to liquidate, there will never be liquidation. The maximum increase in value from liquidation over date-2 expected value is $L - \pi X$. Because $C > L - \pi X$, borrowers cannot be compensated for their lost control rent and still make lenders better off. When borrowers have control at date 1, the liquidation policy is $\mathscr{L}(0) = \mathscr{L}(f^d) = \mathscr{L}(1) = 0$: never liquidation.

Renegotiation of contracts at date 1 works as follows. The lender can propose an alternative contract, specifying date-1 payments given liquidation and date-2 payments if there is not liquidation. The borrower either accepts the new contract or rejects it. If it is rejected, the original contract remains in force. Then, the lender chooses between liquidation or allowing the borrower to continue, if the lender has that right.

If the lender has the right to choose whether to liquidate, the lender will liquidate given the original contract if $z > q(f_1)Z$, absent renegotiation. If the lender would not liquidate given the original contract, then the borrower will reject any new contract that has a higher value of date-2 payment, Z. But the lender has no interest in proposing a contract with a lower value of Z. The only situation, therefore, where renegotiation will occur is if the lender would liquidate given the original contract, but can be given enough of the date-2 cash flow to induce them not to liquidate. This requires $z > q(f_1)Z$ (for liquidation given the original contract), and $z \le q(f_1)X$ (for there to be a way for the borrower to induce the lender not to liquidate).[5] A necessary condition for renegotiation is $Z < X$ (there is future cash to assign to the lender) and $L < q(f_1)X$ (liquidation does not increase the value of cash flow).

Any contract that implements the *ex ante* desired liquidation policy of $\mathscr{L}(0) = 1$, $\mathscr{L}(f^d) = \mathscr{L}(1) = 0$ has the payment to the lender given liquidation, z, satisfy $z \in [\pi X, q(f^d)X]$. If $z < \pi X$, the lender would not liquidate given $f_1 = 0$. If $z > q(f^d)X$, the lender would liquidate given $f_1 = f^d$. With $z \in [\pi X, q(f^d)X]$, there will be liquidation without renegotiation given

$f_1 = 0$, because the borrower's total date-2 cash flow is worth only $q(0)X < q(f^d)X$. When $f_1 = f^d$, liquidation will be avoided, but renegotiation will be required if $Z < X$. Without renegotiation, liquidation will yield the lender $q(f^d)X$, implying that the borrower will accept a contract with z less than or equal to its original value and with $Z = X$. This will induce the lender not to liquidate, and there is no other contract that makes both borrower and lender weakly better off than the original contract.

When $f_1 = 1$, the lender will not liquidate given the original contract so long as $Z > z = q(f^d)X$. If this condition is true, the contract will not be renegotiated. If, instead, $Z < z$, the contract would need to be renegotiated, and the lender would propose $Z = X$, which the borrower would accept. It is then in the borrower's interest to set $Z > z$, to keep the payment contingent on $f_1 = 1$ below X.

The borrower wants the payments given $f_1 = 0$ and $f_1 = f^d$ to be as large as possible (to reduce the payment given $f_1 = 1$). This implies that $z = q(f^d)X$ is the choice. This provides lenders with the expected return of $(P^z + P^d)q(f^d)X + P^uZ$, which must be at least equal to I if the project is financed. The desired liquidation policy is then implementable with a single lender when the contract cannot depend on f_1 if and only if $Z = \{I - (P^z + P^d)q(f^d)X\}/P^u < X$. Even if the liquidation policy is implementable, no contract with a single lender can achieve the contingent payment policy desired by type G borrowers. Type G borrowers also desire information sensitivity: higher repayments from those who get low future credit ratings. This implies that $z(0) = L$ is desired, and that $Z(1)$ ought to be as small as possible.

The assumption of *ex ante* private information of borrowers is critical in only one way. It implies that larger cash payments from borrowers with low f_1 are desired. Without private information, only the liquidation decision is relevant. For a given f_1-contingent decision, borrowers are indifferent between all cash payments $z(f_1)$ and $Z(f_1)$ with a given expected value. Without private information, the single-lender contract is a desirable one for the borrower. If, however, the desired liquidation policy is not implementable with a single lender (because $\{I - (P^z + P^d)q(f^d)X\}/P^u) > X$), then the ability to contract with competing future lenders has value even with no private information.

With access to additional lenders in the future, the borrower can raise funds to make date-1 payments. The lender can then be given the unconditional right to liquidate whenever the date-1 payments are not made. This can be achieved without requiring an explicit or verifiable announcement by any new lender on date 1. I do not need to write a contract that is contingent on date-1 announcements by any new lender. The dependence on the information of new lenders is only through the resources that they will lend the borrower to make date-1 payments.

4.1   The example

With a single lender, the best way to implement the desired liquidation policy $\mathcal{L}(0) = 1$, and $\mathcal{L}(f^d) = \mathcal{L}(1) = 0$, is to set $Z = \{I - (P^z + P^d) q(f^d)X\}/P^u) = 1.10096$, and $z = q(f^d)X = 0.8125$. This gives a type G borrower an expected payoff of $(P^d f^d/f)(C) + (P^u/f)(X + C - Z) = 0.58482$. The contract assigns a just sufficient portion of the liquidation proceeds to the borrower to deter the lender from liquidation. This claim assigned to the lender results in the desired liquidation policy, but reduces information sensitivity relative to the desired f_1-contingent policy: $z(1) = 0.8125$, but $z(0) = L = 0.9$ is desired. As a result, the payment given $f_1 = 1$, $Z(1)$, is 1.10096, rather than the 1.081125 desired by the type G borrower.

5   Competing future lenders, refinancing and liquidation decisions

The ability of the borrower to raise money from competing lenders at date 1 allows the borrower to implement the desired liquidation policy and make the cost of capital depend on the date-1 information in the way desired. In particular, the ability to refinance allows the payment to the lender when liquidation occurs to be larger than is possible in the single-lender case. In the single-lender case, to deter liquidation given $f_1 = f^d$, the maximum payment from liquidation the lender can receive is $z = q(f_1)X < L$. In this section, I examine claims where $z = L$, and there is no payment to the borrower when there is liquidation.

The right to continue when a new lender will advance the funds fully to repay the maturing debt is given to the borrower. The competitive behaviour of the new lender despite the *ex post* harm done to the existing lender (who prefers liquidation) is the limit of an implicit game of coalition formation. If the borrower were to offer just above a normal return to the date-1 lender, the new lender would get a small profit. To deter every lender from making the small profit, the existing lender would need to pay this small amount, $\epsilon > 0$, to each potential lender. There are many potential lenders ($N \to \infty$), and the existing lender cannot bribe them all (at cost ϵN) to prevent each from making a profitable loan. I go to the limit where $\epsilon \to 0$.

To implement the desired f_1-contingent policy requires a mix of debt maturities. With a single initial lender this is equivalent to a mix of coupon payments on each date of a single security. All long-term debt would then imply no required date-1 payment (this is zero-coupon long-term debt). All short-term debt would imply that all of the capital is raised with debt that must be repaid on date 1: no debt with date-2 coupons would be sold on date 0. Before examining the proper maturity mix, these two extremes are examined.

5.1   All long-term debt

With all long-term debt, no date-1 debt payment is required and the lender has no right to liquidate. All long-term debt implies that date-1 information does not influence any rate-setting or liquidation decisions. Based on date-0 information, a borrower repays long-term debt with probability $q(f) = f(1 - \pi) + \pi$, and pays zero otherwise. To raise initial capital of I requires long-term debt with face value $I/q(f)$ if this does not exceed X, which is the most any borrower can repay (if it exceeds X, the borrower cannot borrow long term because the lender would receive a sub-normal return). This implies no liquidation when $f_1 = 0$. With all long-term debt, $\mathcal{L}(f_1) = 0$ for all f_1, and $Z(f_1) = I/q(f)$ for all f_1.

5.2   All short-term debt

When there is some short-term debt, the lender will have the right to liquidate at date 1 if not repaid in full. The borrower can issue new debt at date 1, priced in the competitive loan market, to raise funds to repay the maturing short-term debt. The new date-1 information will determine both the amount that the market offers for this new debt, and the liquidation decision that the existing lender makes if the borrower does not repay in full.

Suppose that *all* the debt issued on date 0 is short term. On date 1, all lenders and the borrower then know f_1, the updated credit rating. The borrower can issue new short-term debt with face value r_2, but r_2 cannot exceed X (the most that can be repaid). The new date-1 lenders will pay $q(f_1)r_2$ for such a debt issue. If fully repaid, the old lender has no other rights. The old lender knows f_1, and can choose to accept less than the amount owed, r_1, or can choose liquidation. The old lender offers to accept less than r_1 only if the borrower cannot raise r_1 in the market, or only if $q(f_1)X < r_1$. If the borrower cannot raise r_1, the old lender liquidates if the most that can be raised, $q(f_1)X$, is less than the proceeds of liquidation, L. If liquidation yields less, and $L < q(f_1)X$, the old lender settles for $q(f_1)X$, or equivalently extends maturity to date 2 in exchange for an increase in face value to X. In summary, when the new date-1 lenders will lend the borrower enough to repay the old lender, there is not liquidation. When less than r_1 can be raised, the old lender compares the present value of future cash flows with the value of liquidation. The future control rents, C, are not considered by old lenders because they will not be paid to them, but instead to the borrower. If $r_1 > q(f^d)X$ and $L > q(f^d)X$, there will be liquidation when $f_1 = f^d$.

When r_1 exceeds $q(f^d)X$, the lender will have the right to liquidate given $f_1 = f^d$, because the debt will not be able to be refinanced. If the desired liquidation policy is $\mathscr{L}(f^d) = 0$, then the borrower will desire a debt structure that is not exclusively short-term debt.

5.3 Multiple maturities with a single initial lender

In this case, there is a single lender at date 0, and a competitive loan market at date 1. Choosing multiple maturities of initial debt describes the promised time series of cash flows promised to the single lender. Let the promised date-1 payment be r_1 and the promised date-2 payment be p. If there is liquidation on date 1 the payment of the long-term debt is accelerated to date 1. The lender will have the right to liquidate whenever the borrower cannot raise r_1 on date 1. Because the lender owns all of the initial debt, if the initial lender owns total debt $r_1 + p$ in excess of $q(f_1)X$, and liquidation is worth more than $q(f_1)X$, the lender will choose to liquidate.

The debt contracts are as follows. The long-term debt has face value p, and prohibits any future debt senior to it.[6] This implies that, when refinancing at date 1, the most that the borrower can promise to new lenders is $X - p$. The new lender will lend $q(f_1)r_2$ if offered a date-2 claim of r_2. This implies that the borrower can raise up to $q(f_1)(X - p)$, conditional on f_1. By refinancing, the borrower can possibly avoid a liquidation that is in the lender's interest, although the project delivers no date-1 cash. If the firm is liquidated at date 1, the long-term debt is accelerated to date 1, giving the lender a claim of $r_1 + p$ (priority of these claims is not relevant because one lender owns both issues).

5.4 The example

To implement the desired liquidation policy, with all liquidation proceeds to the lender, requires that the borrower be able to refinance when $f_1 = f^d = .25$: this implies that $r_1 \leq q(f_1)(X - p)$. The borrower must not be able to refinance when $f_1 = 0$, because liquidation is desired then. This requires that $r_1 > \pi(X - p)$. If there is liquidation at date 1, the lender will receive the smaller of $r_1 + p$ and L. When the debt is refinanced, the lender will receive r_1, plus they will retain their long-term claim, which will then be worth $q(f_1)p$. A debt structure that leads to the desired liquidation policy will then raise:

$$P^z \min\{r_1 + p, L\} + P^d(r_1 + q(f^d)p) + P^u(r_1 + p).$$

In the example, setting $r_1 = 0.36585$ and $\rho = 0.715375$ raises exactly $I = 1$. To show that it implements the desired liquidation policy, note that

$$q(f^{\mathrm{d}})(X - \rho) = .625(1.3 - 0.715375) = 0.36585 = r_1.$$

The short-term debt can be refinanced given $f_1 = f^{\mathrm{d}}$ but not given $f_1 = 0$. This leads to the desired liquidation policy, and provides information sensitivity: $z(0) = L$, $Z(f^{\mathrm{d}}) = X$, and $Z(1) = 1.081125$. This leads to a type G payoff of $(P^{\mathrm{d}}f^{\mathrm{d}}/f)C + (P^{\mathrm{u}}/f)(X + C - r_1 - \rho) = 0.603571$.

When there is a single initial lender, but additional competing future lenders, the ability to refinance and fully repay the maturing debt limits the liquidation rights of the lender. This describes the way in which debt maturity influences the state-contingent control rights. Because a single lender owns all initial debt claims, the priority of these claims will be relevant only through its limit on the amount that new debt issues can raise on date 1. When there are multiple initial lenders, then the priority of their claims might be relevant, depending on the ability of the initial lenders to renegotiate their claims in the future. The next section describes the liquidation decisions with two initial lenders, one owning the long-term debt, the other the short-term debt.

6   Multiple initial lenders and debt priority

I assume that different lenders own the two maturities of the borrower's debt. This is exogenously imposed, and I do not analyse why this would be desirable. In section 7, I examine the effects if one lender, a bank, is better able to exercise the control right to liquidate. In this section, there is no such difference between the two lenders.

The effect of there being two date-0 lenders depends on whether they can reach a renegotiated agreement among themselves on date 1, in circumstances where the short-term lender has the right to liquidate. When the two lenders can negotiate, they will maximize the total value of their claims, and will make the same liquidation decision as a single lender. If they cannot renegotiate, then the priority of their claims might influence the liquidation decision made when the date-1 maturing debt cannot be fully repaid. The lender who owns the short-term debt will have the right to liquidate, and will then make the decision in their own interest.

The short-term lender will have the right to liquidate whenever the short-term debt cannot be fully refinanced, or $r_1 > q(f_1)(X - \rho)$. If renegotiation occurs, lenders prefer to liquidate only if it is in their collective interest, implying $L > q(f_1)X$. If they cannot renegotiate and the maturing debt cannot be refinanced, the short-term lender receives at most $q(f_1)(X - \rho) < r_1$ without liquidation. With liquidation, the short-term lender receives $\min\{L, r_1\}$ if senior, and $\min\{L - \rho, r_1\}$ if junior. Lemma 1 describes the liquidation policy implied by this situation.

Lemma 1: The incentives and rights to liquidate of a short-term lender at date 1, given the face value of short-term debt, r_1, and of long-term debt, ρ, are as follows. The probability of repayment given date 1 information is $q(f_1) = f_1(1 - \pi) + \pi \equiv q_1$.

Conditions for liquidation at date 1	Right (debt not repaid)	Incentive with no negotiation	Incentive with negotiation
All short-term	$q_1 < r_1/X$	$q_1 < L/X$	$q_1 < L/X$
All long-term	No	(not relevant)	
Short senior, with ρ of junior long-term	$q_1 < \dfrac{r_1}{X - \rho}$	$q_1 < \dfrac{L}{X - \rho}$	$q_1 < L/X$
Short junior, with ρ of senior long-term	$q_1 < \dfrac{r_1}{X - \rho}$	$q_1 < \dfrac{L - \rho}{X - \rho}$	$q_1 < L/X$

Without negotiation a junior short lender has less incentive to liquidate than the senior short or all-short lender. With negotiation, the incentive to liquidate is independent of initial debt priority.

When the initial lenders can renegotiate, the priority of their claims does not influence their liquidation decision. As in the case of the single initial lender, the debt priority is irrelevant. If initial lenders cannot renegotiate, priority can influence liquidation decisions when maturing short-term debt cannot be fully repaid by refinancing. The problem with giving the unconditional right to liquidate to lenders is the potential for lost control rents. As a result, it can be useful to choose a structure where the short-term lender would not liquidate given the right, although liquidation is in the collective interest of the two lenders. From lemma 1, this occurs only when the short-term debt is junior to the long-term debt. If renegotiation is impossible, this implies that another way to implement the desired liquidation policy is to make short-term debt junior to long-term debt. This can force the short-term lender to make a unilateral concession, to avoid a liquidation that is not in their interest.

The debt structure with junior short-term debt can implement the same policy as that with senior short-term debt that can be fully repaid given $f_1 = f^d$. To make subordination implement the liquidation policy $\mathcal{L}(0) = 1$, and $\mathcal{L}(f^d) = \mathcal{L}(1) - 0$, requires the following. $\mathcal{L}(0) = 1$ requires $\pi < (L - \rho)/(X - \rho)$, or $\rho < (L - \pi X)/(1 - \pi)$. $\mathcal{L}(f^d) = 0$ requires $q(f^d) \geq (L - \rho)/(X - \rho)$, or $\rho \geq [L - q(f^d)X]/[1 - q(f^d)]$, and this also implies that $\mathcal{L}(1) = 0$. These conditions do not put an upper bound on the amount of short-term debt, r_1, because, if the short-term lender makes a concession, the maturing short-term debt does not need to be fully refinanced to avoid liquidation. The next section illustrates this in the example. Section 7 then shows that making short-term debt junior is generally a bad idea when there is a possibility (but not a certainty) of renegotiation.

6.1   The example

The implemention of the desired liquidation policy with full renegotiation is the same as the single-lender case already described: priority is irrelevant. With renegotiation impossible, one can exploit the asymmetric incentives induced by subordination. The asymmetry can induce a short-term lender to make a concession to avoid liquidation even when liquidation is in the collective interest of existing lenders. To implement $\mathcal{L}(f^d) = 0$ (deter liquidation given $f_1 = f^d$) requires that $p \geq [L - q(f^d)X]/[1 - q(f^d)]$, or, in the example, $p \geq 0.2333$. If $p = 0.2333$, then liquidation yields the short-term lender $L - p = 0.6667$, while refinancing with new debt with face value of $X - p = 1.1667$, which is received with probability $q(f^d) = .625$: $q(f^d)(X - p) = 0.6667$. This will deter liquidation given f^d, even if the maturing short-term debt cannot be fully refinanced.

To implement $\mathcal{L}(0) = 1$ (liquidation given $f_1 = 0$), requires $p < (L - \pi X)/(1 - \pi) = 0.5$, and that the maturing debt cannot be refinanced given $f_1 = 0$. The maturing short-term debt cannot be fully refinanced given $f_1 = 0$ if $r_1 > \pi(X - p) = .5(1.3 - p) = 0.65 - p/2$. Any $p \in [0.2333, 0.5)$, and $r_1 > 0.65 - p/2$ will implement the desired liquidation policy. If, in addition, $r_1 + p = Z(1) = 1.081125$, it will also implement the desired f_1-contingent payment policy. For example, let $r_1 = 0.847825$ and $p = 0.2333$. When $f_1 = 0$, there is liquidation and the long-term lender gets p while the short-term lender gets $L - p$, implying that $z(0) = L = 0.9$. When $f_1 = f^d = .25$, the short-term lender does not liquidate, but accepts a claim with date-2 face value $X - p$, implying that date-2 debt given $f_1 = f^d$ is X. When $f_1 = 1$, the short-term debt with face value r_1 is refinanced in full, with new debt having face value $r_1 = 0.847825$, implying total date-2 debt is $r_1 + p = 1.081125$. These are the payments desired when f_1 can condition contracts. If renegotiation is impossible, then relying on subordination to induce short-term bank lenders to make concessions is an alternative method of implementing the liquidation policy desired. Even public debt can sometimes be renegotiated, however. The next section shows that making short-term debt junior is undesirable when there is a possibility, but not a certainty, of renegotiation.

7   Bank (private) lenders and public bondholders

Suppose there are two kinds of lenders, which I call banks and the public respectively. I use the term bank loosely to mean private institutional lenders in general. The public is not able to implement liquidation decisions. This is motivated in Diamond (1992b) by the liquidation decision requiring some specific expertise, or by the public not always observing the information f_1 as quickly as other lenders. Those lenders who can implement liquidation decisions are banks. A bank is delegated the task of monitoring the information about liquidation, as in Diamond (1984, 1991b). In addition, I examine the implications of the public being less able to renegotiate and restructure debt. There are many banks, and they provide perfect competition for each other. The information about the borrower is observed by many competing banks. If each date-0 bank lender has some information monopoly, they will face imperfect competition. This is discussed in section 8.

Only the bank lenders have the specific expertise to implement a liquidation. They will then be the short-term lenders. Long-term lenders need do nothing on date 1, unless renegotiation is required. When no renegotiation is required, this implies that public lenders can own the long-term debt without distorting date-1 decisions. This could be beneficial by allowing some of the borrower's capital to be raised from the public. The public might require a lower rate of return, for example. I do not explain why the borrower contracts with the public, but simply examine the implications for priority of issuing public bonds.

I follow Diamond (1992b), and assume that the original debt contracts can possibly be renegotiated in the future when new information arrives. Bulow and Shoven (1978) examine bank renegotiation with a borrower when the public can never renegotiate. I assume that there is an exogenous probability $R \in (0,1)$ that the contracts can be renegotiated and restructured. With probability $1 - R$ the contract will not be renegotiated even if it is in everyone's interest to renegotiate. This imperfect renegotiation is motivated by the difficulty of restructuring public debt issues, owing to free-rider problems and information asymmetries where public bondholders do not have rapid access to the information observed by bank lenders. In addition, the US Federal Trust Indenture Act requires unanimous consent for public bondholders to make principal interest or maturity concessions outside the bankruptcy court (see Smith and Warner, 1979; Roe, 1987; Gertner and Scharfstein, 1991). Such concessions from publicly traded bonds require an exchange offer, the success of which is uncertain. One source of uncertainty is the distribution of ownership of the bond when the exchange offer is made.

Lemma 1 describes the incentives of the short-term lender to liquidate with, and without, renegotiation. When the maturing short-term debt is fully repaid, there is not liquidation. The liquidation rule is as follows when the maturing short-term debt cannot be fully repaid. If liquidation is in the short-term lender's interest both with and without renegotiation, there is certain liquidation. If liquidation is not in the short-term lender's interest either with or without renegotiation, then there is certainly not liquidation. If liquidation is not in the short-term lender's interest without renegotiation, but is with renegotiation, then the probability of liquidation is R. If liquidation is in the short-term lender's interest without renegotiation, but not with renegotiation, then the probability of liquidation is $1 - R$.

The uncertain ability to renegotiate with the public makes the liquidation policy random whenever a contract requiring renegotiation is used. Borrowers want to choose contracts that have f_1-contingent liquidation probabilities that are either 0 or 1. This rules out many debt contracts.

Contracts where the liquidation decision is different with and without renegotiation are potentially dominated. There are two circumstances where the renegotiated and non-renegotiated liquidation decisions differ. When short-term debt is senior, it has a unilateral incentive to liquidate even when liquidation is worth less than the expected cash flow from continuation. When short-term debt is junior, and there is sufficient long-term debt, the short-term lender has a unilateral incentive not to liquidate when liquidation produces more cash than continuation. If a debt contract is to lead to f_1-contingent liquidation probabilities that are either 0 or 1, the maturing short-term debt must be fully refinanced for all possible realizations of f_1 where renegotiation would otherwise be required.

To implement the liquidation and pricing rule desired by type Gs then requires the following. Because it is in the collective interest of lenders to liquidate when $f_1 = f^d$, ruling out liquidation requires that maturing short-term debt be fully refinanced when $f_1 = f^d$ (requiring $r_1 \leq q(f_1)(X - \rho)$). Making liquidation certain when $f_1 = 0$ requires two conditions: that the maturing short-term debt not be fully refinanced when $f_1 = 0$, and that the short-term lender have the incentive to liquidate without renegotiation. The former requires $r_1 > \pi(X - \rho)$ and the condition for the latter depends on the priority of the debt. If the short-term debt is senior, it is satisfied automatically. If the short-term debt is junior, the incentive to liquidate without requiring renegotiation is present only if the face value of long-term debt satisfies $\rho \leq (L - \pi X)/(X - \pi X)$.

The implications of structuring the contract to avoid the undesirable effects of uncertain renegotiation are as follows. The short-term debt must be fully refinanced whenever the borrower wishes to avoid a liquidation that is in the collective interest of lenders. This imposes an upper bound on the amount of short-term debt no matter what is its priority. In addition, if the short-term debt is junior, there is a separate upper bound on the amount of long-term debt. If this bound is exceeded, the short-term lender will not liquidate, even when it is desirable to do so (when $f_1 = 0$), thus excessively entrenching the borrower. These two conditions impose an upper bound on total debt, long-term plus short-term, that can be less than X (the amount of cash that a borrower can pay on date 2). When short-term debt is senior, there is no upper bound on the total amount of debt, other than that it not exceed X.

With junior short-term debt, it can be impossible for the borrower to raise sufficient capital to finance their project and simultaneously implement the desired liquidation policy. This is the case in the example.

7.1   The example

The upper bound on long-term debt p, such that the short-term lender will liquidate without renegotiation given $f_1 = 0$, is

$$p \leq \frac{L - \pi X}{X - \pi X} = 0.5.$$

The upper bound on r_1 such that maturing short-term debt is refinanced in full is

$$r_1 \leq q(f^d)(X - p) = .625(X - p).$$

This implies that $r_1 + .625p < 0.8125$.

The total date-2 payment to lenders when $f_1 = 1$ will be $r_1 + p$. The maturing short-term debt will be refinanced with new debt with face value r_1, because, given $f_1 = 1$, it will be repaid for certain. For lenders to get an expected return of $I = 1$ with the liquidation policy $\mathcal{L}(0) = \mathcal{L}(f^d) = 0$ and $\mathcal{L}(1) = 1$ requires that the payment contingent on $f_1 = 1$ be at least $Z(1) = 1.081125$. The lender's expected return is then $p^z L + p^d q^d X + p^u Z(1) = I$. Requiring both $r_1 + .625p < 0.8125$ and $r_1 + p > 1.081125$, implies $p > 0.76428$. This contradicts $p < 0.5$. The f_1-contingent liquidation policy cannot be implemented by junior short-term debt. The example in section 5.4 shows that it can be implemented with senior short-term debt. The senior debt is fully refinanced given $f_1 = f^d$ (implying no renegotiation). Given $f_1 = 0$, the short-term debt is not fully refinanced, and the senior short-term lender has the individual incentive to liquidate given $f_1 = 0$.

8   Lender competition and dilution

Competition between lenders implies that the borrower is able to refinance on terms that give no rents to the new lenders. If there is imperfect competition between lenders, they will capture some of the rents. For example, if it costs the borrower a fixed cost, ϕ, to verify the original (date-0) lender's information to another lender on date 1, then the original lender can capture some of ϕ, because the borrower would need to pay ϕ to attract a competitive bid from the second lender. Alternatively, if two lenders observe information that is imperfectly correlated, then competitive bidding will allow them to capture some rents, because each is afraid to bid aggressively owing to the fear of outbidding the other due to the imperfectly correlated error in their information (see Milgrom and Weber, 1982, for a model of bidding in this information setup). This imperfectly correlated (common value) bidding model has each lender bidding a date-1 interest rate a bit above the competitive level given f_1. As such, if there are several bidders, it is a minor change from the perfectly competitive setup I use.

A severe limit on competition occurs if only the original lender observes the date-1 information. The only competition in date-1 bidding against the lender then comes from uninformed bidders, who realize that they face a severe adverse selection/winner's curse problem. With no information, competitors must put in a bid that is not f_1 contingent, and will win only when the original lender gets sufficiently bad news. This is the setup in Englebrecht-Wiggans, Milgrom and Weber (1983) and Rajan (1990). Because the initial lender faces no competition for those borrowers who get good news (high f_1), those borrowers get little benefit from the chance to refinance. Information monopoly would be a major change in the model, and it would suggest that private lenders make large *ex post* profits from their loan customers who do well, and there would be substantial competition for the *ex ante* right to exploit the customers later.

This model is based on the belief that the monopoly-in-information problem is not severe. Rajan (1990) examines a model with information monopoly leading to imperfect competition.[7] He concludes that bank debt is junior to the public, to control the information monopoly. Rajan's conclusion is opposite to the prediction of this model. One can see a point close to his in the single date-1 lender model of section 4. The monopolist lender successfully bargains to obtain most of the date-2 cash flow from the borrower, whenever they have a credible threat to liquidate. In section 4, the liquidation incentive of the single lender is limited by giving the borrower a senior claim that assigns to them some liquidation proceeds.

Rajan assumes that existing lenders cannot renegotiate, and then limits the bargaining power by making long-term debt senior to the short-term debt that has liquidation rights. In contrast, my approach relies on competition in the refinancing market to limit the lender's bargaining power.

9   Conclusion

The analysis suggests that the structure of debt contracts and the actions that lenders take when the borrower is in financial distress depend on the type of lender providing the funds. If the borrower combines bank loans with public debt, the model predicts that the bank loan will be shorter term and senior to the public debt. If the borrower gets into financial distress, the bank will not make concessions. Instead, the bank will use its power to force a restructuring, such as asset sales or liquidation.

If all of the debt is bank debt, possibly owned by different banks, then the priority prediction is not clear. Banks, especially those that are part of a syndicate for a given loan participation, can renegotiate rather easily. Because bank loans often have strict covenants that allow even long-term lenders to exercise control, banks may always have the 'right to liquidate'. The model then predicts that, if all of the debt is bank debt, then at times the banks will make concessions, extending maturity or forgiving interest or principal.

Two recent empirical studies present results consistent with this model. Asquith, Gertner and Scharfstein (1991) study restructuring decisions of firms that have large amounts of public debt. They study firms that issued long-term, junior junk bonds and later experienced financial distress. The theory predicts that, in this case, banks would not make concessions. They conclude:

> Outside of bankruptcy proceedings, banks almost never (there is one exception) forgive principal on their loans and they rarely provide new financing. [Banks] often waive covenants and defer principal and interest payments, but they also often force accelerated payments and increase their collateral.
>
> (Asquith, Gertner and Scharfstein, 1991, p. 1).

Gilson, John and Lang (1990) examine a sample of firms in financial distress and examine the characteristics of firms that successfully renegotiate their debt outside of bankruptcy court. Their sample includes firms with and without public debt. They find that a firm with a higher fraction of its debt as bank debt is more likely to renegotiate, with the banks making concessions. This is consistent with the theory discussed in this paper. The bank will make concessions if the amount of bank debt is high enough, and if concessions are in the mutual interest of lenders $(r_1 > q(f^d)(X - \rho)$ and $L < q(f^d)X)$. They also find that a firm is less likely to reach a negotiated settlement if there are more distinct issues of debt, a proxy for the cost of renegotiation.

A study of the universe of Euromarket syndicated publicly traded bonds and bank loans by Davis and Mayer (1992) documents that bank loans are of shorter maturity than bonds, even for firms that use both forms of finance. They also find that larger firms and firms that raise less capital have longer-maturity bank loans and are more likely to issue publicly traded bonds. If one assumes that the smaller firms are marginal firms that cannot raise sufficient funds if they choose a structure that limits the banks' control right to liquidate when it is in the collective interest of the lenders, this is consistent with the theory in this paper.

NOTES

I am grateful to Patrick Bolton, Michael Dotsey, Robert Gertner, Martin Hellwig, Colin Mayer and Robert Vishny for helpful comments and for financial support from Dimensional Fund Advisors and the Center for Research in Securities Prices.

1 The most obvious motivation for control rents is moral hazard. If outsiders receive 100 per cent of future cash flows, then management will not act properly if its interests conflict with those of outsiders. The future cash flows that must be pledged to management to provide incentives cannot be assigned to outside investors (see Diamond, 1991a). Similarly, if the manager cannot commit to stay with the firm in the future, there is a state-contingent floor on the manager's compensation (see Hart and Moore, 1991).

2 To be concrete in a simple way, assume that lenders use a constant returns-to-scale investment technology that returns 1 per unit invested per period.

3 There is, implicitly, also a control rent associated with having control from date 0 to 1, but all borrowers who can borrow at date 0 get this. It is therefore a 'sunk benefit', and is not explicitly introduced.

4 The lowest possible value of expected cash flow is πX, and liquidation yields L. Assume that $C > L - \pi X$; then borrowers can never be bribed to give up control voluntarily. Without this assumption, borrowers might negotiate a deal to liquidate at date 1 independent of the debt structure.

5 Even if a payment conditional on liquidation could not be specified, the same result can be attained by giving the borrower a senior claim on all cash payments of $L - z$. The lender can then get at most z if liquidation is chosen against the wishes of the borrower.

6 This is without loss of generality given my assumption of the three possible realizations of f_1. In Diamond (1992a), there is a continuum of possible realizations of f_1. Approaching the desired f_1-contingent payments can then require that new refinanced debt be senior to existing long-term debt. Other qualitative implications of the model are preserved in the three-realization case used here.

7 Another model of information monopoly in bank lending is Sharpe (1990).

REFERENCES

Aghion, P. and P. Bolton (1992) 'An incomplete contracts approach to financial contracting', *Review of Economic Studies* **59**, 473–94.

Asquith, P., R. Gertner and D. Scharfstein (1991) 'Anatomy of financial distress: an examination of junk bond issuers', working paper, University of Chicago, October.

Bulow, J. and J. Shoven (1978) 'The bankruptcy decision', *Bell Journal of Economics* **9**, 437–56.

Davis, E.P. and C.P. Mayer (1992) 'Corporate finance in the Euromarkets and the economics of intermediation', CEPR working paper.

Diamond, D.W. (1984) 'Financial intermediation and delegated monitoring', *Review of Economic Studies* **51**, 393–414.

(1991a) 'Debt maturity structure and liquidity risk', *Quarterly Journal of Economics* **106** (August), 709–37.

(1991b) 'Monitoring and reputation: the choice between bank loans and directly placed debt', *Journal of Political Economy* **99** (August), 689–721.

(1992a) 'Seniority and maturity of debt contracts', *Journal of Financial Economics*, forthcoming.

(1992b) 'Seniority and maturity structure of bank loans and publicly traded debt', working paper, University of Chicago, revised March 1992.

Englebrecht-Wiggans, R., P. Milgrom and R. Weber (1983) 'Competitive bidding and proprietary information', *Journal of Mathematical Economics* **11**, 161–9.

Flannery, M.J. (1986) 'Asymmetric information and risky debt maturity choice', *Journal of Finance* **41**, 19–38.

Gertner, R. and D. Scharfstein (1991) 'A theory of workouts and the effects of reorganization law', *Journal of Finance* **46** (September), 1189–222.

Gilson, S.C., K. John and L. Lang (1990) 'Troubled debt restructurings: an empirical study of private reorganization of firms in default', *Journal of Financial Economics* **27** (October), 315–54.

Harris, M. and A. Raviv (1990) 'Capital structure and the informational role of debt', *Journal of Finance* **45**, 321–50.

Hart, O. and J. Moore (1989) 'Default and renegotiation: a dynamic model of debt', LSE discussion paper 57, June.

(1990) 'A theory of corporate financial structure based on the priority of claims', MIT working paper, July.

(1991) 'A theory of debt based on the inalienability of human capital', NBER working paper 3906, November.

Jensen, M. (1989) 'The eclipse of the public corporation', *Harvard Business Review*, September.

Jensen, M. and W. Meckling (1976) 'Theory of the firm: managerial behavior, agency costs and ownership structure', *Journal of Financial Economics* **3**, 305–60.

Milgrom, P. and R. Weber (1982) 'A theory of auctions and competitive bidding', *Econometrica* **50**, 1089–122.

Rajan, R. (1990) 'Insiders and outsiders: the choice between relationship and arms-length debt', MIT working paper, October; forthcoming in *Journal of Finance*.

Roe, M. (1987) 'The voting prohibition in bond workouts', *The Yale Law Journal* **97**, 232–79.

Sharpe, S. (1990) 'Asymmetric information, bank lending and implicit contracts: a stylized model of customer relationships', *Journal of Finance* **45** (September).
Smith, Clifford W. and Jerrold B. Warner (1979) 'On financial contracting: an analysis of bond covenants', *Journal of Financial Economics* **7** (June), 111–61.

Discussion

PATRICK BOLTON

This paper contributes to a recent literature concerned with optimal debt structure. Until very recently corporate finance theorists have mostly been concerned with agency theories or control theories of the optimal choice of debt/equity ratio. These theories do not differentiate between different forms of debt. Typically, only one form of debt instrument is considered. In practice, however, firms' liabilities are composed of many different forms of debt held by different lenders. The larger firms (e.g. Fortune 500 firms) have liabilities in the form of bank debt, trade credit, bonds (which may be callable, convertible and what not). Given this observed diversity of debt instruments and given the importance of debt financing (over 80 per cent of firms' external funding in the US in the last decade was in the form of debt), the recent literature concerned with optimal debt structure fills an important gap in the theory of corporate finance.

The specific aspect of debt structure which Diamond is concerned with here and in previous research is how the firm's liabilities can be designed so as to use future information about the firm's creditworthiness efficiently. His approach to this problem is similar to that taken in the recent literature on vertical restraints (see Tirole, 1988): he begins by characterizing the optimal principal/agent contract with full commitment and then asks how this contract can be replicated with a combination of standard debt contracts of differing maturities and a given priority rule.

In the model considered here, the optimal full-commitment contract specifies liquidation of all the assets in place when $f_1 = 0$ and continuation with all assets in place when $f_1 = f^d$ and $f_1 = 1$. In addition, the contract with full commitment specifies that the lender gets all the proceeds from liquidation, that the borrower makes a maximum repayment when $f_1 = f^d$ and that a smaller repayment is made when $f_1 = 1$. This outcome cannot be implemented with a long-term standard debt contract. Indeed, with such a contract there is no liquidation when $f_1 = 0$. Similarly, it cannot be implemented with only a short-term contract, since there would be excessive liquidation with such a contract (there may be liquidation when $f_1 = f^d$; excessive liquidation can be avoided only if the lender gives up some of the proceeds from liquidation).

The optimal full-commitment solution can be implemented if the firm holds both short-term and long-term debt. More precisely, when the firm can obtain refinancing from competing future lenders then there exists a combination of short-term and long-term debt which implements the full-commitment solution.

When a single lender holds both debt instruments the issue of priority between the two instruments does not arise. When different lenders hold the short-term debt and long-term debt then priority is relevant. Diamond shows that, if short-term debt-holders are unable to renegotiate their claims (e.g. because they are dispersed bond-holders), then short-term debt should be junior. If, however, there is a possibility (but not a certainty) of renegotiation, then short-term debt should be senior. These are the main conclusions in Diamond's analysis.

The result about the seniority of short-term debt is the most intriguing in my opinion. It is not obvious *a priori* why short-term debt needs to be senior to long-term debt. After all, short-term debt is repaid earlier and this is already a form of priority. When then should short-term debt get further protection? The answer is that senior short-term lenders are more likely to liquidate when it is desirable to do so (when $f_1 = 0$). If short-term debt was junior there might be excessive continuation, since in the event of liquidation most of the proceeds might go to long-term lenders.

This is an important general insight. My only criticism of Diamond's paper is that it fails to convey the full generality of this idea. Other versions of this idea have been proposed independently and simultaneously by Dewatripont and Tirole (1992) and Berglof and Von Thadden (1992). The general principle has been put very clearly by Dewatripont and Tirole: when decisions such as liquidation or continuation must be taken in the future, the person(s) in control must be given adequate incentives to take the right decision. This means that the borrower must have the right incentives when they are in control, but also that the outside investor(s) must be given the right incentives when they are in control. Giving the right incentives to outside investors may require that they should be senior, short-term debt-holders. As Berglof and Von Thadden explain, when senior short-term debt-holders are in control (following a default) the firm's bargaining position in reorganization is weak, so that the firm's incentives to default strategically are diminished.

By reducing the risk of strategic default in this way, more outside funding can be obtained *ex ante*.

Perhaps one other criticism of Diamond's paper is that it does not explain why the firm should have multiple creditors and why these creditors should hold different types of instrument. If one wants to address these questions one is led to an analysis of multilateral bargaining as in Bolton and Scharfstein (1992) or Berglof and Von Thadden (1992). These papers show how multiple creditor arrangements can dominate single creditor arrangements through their effects on *ex post* renegotiation outcomes. Diamond argues that only those outside investors who have the expertise to make efficient liquidation/continuation decisions would hold short-term debt. This is an interesting idea which is worth exploring further. However, it can provide an explanation only for why short-term debt is concentrated in banks; it cannot explain why banks do not hold long-term debt.

REFERENCES

Berglof, E. and E.L. Von Thadden (1992) 'Long term and short term debt: a theory of contracting with multiple creditors', mimeo, ECARE, Brussels.
Bolton, P. and D. Scharfstein (1992) 'A theory of debt structure', mimeo, MIT.
Dewatripont, M. and J. Tirole (1992) 'A theory of debt and equity: diversity of securities and manager–shareholder congruence', mimeo, Université Libre, Brussels, and IDEI, Toulouse.
Tirole, J. (1988) *The Theory of Industrial Organisation*, MIT Press.

MARTIN HELLWIG

Diamond's paper makes an interesting contribution to a research programme that has dominated the analysis of financial institutions since its first formulation by Jensen and Meckling (1976). According to this research programme, institutional arrangements in financial markets should be interpreted and explained as solutions to incentive and information problems in situations involving moral hazard (hidden actions) and/or adverse selection (hidden characteristics).

Diamond wants to explain the well-known phenomenon that debt finance of a firm typically involves a multiplicity of instruments with different maturities, different priority rights and different financiers. In particular he wants to explain the role of short-term bank loans in the financing of long-term investments.

Diamond proposes to explain this phenomenon as an equilibrium response to a particular information problem which arises because certain payoff-relevant characteristics of the potential borrowers, which they are well aware of, are hidden from the potential lenders. Different potential borrowers have different probabilities of being 'successful', i.e. with return distributions of *all* borrowers concentrated at the two points 0 and $X > 0$, the probability of the positive return realization X is relatively higher for 'good' types of borrowers than for the 'bad' types. Indeed the different success probabilities are taken to be such that a potential borrower whose type is known to be 'bad' will not get a loan at all because their expected return does not cover the opportunity costs of the loan. This assumption rules out the possibility of screening borrowers through some self-selection mechanism involving different types choosing different loan contracts; to get a loan contract at all, the 'bad' types must be pooled with the good types. By standard arguments, an 'equilibrium' contractual arrangement in a loan market with Bertrand competition among potential lenders will then be one that maximizes the 'good' types' expected payoffs subject to the participation constraint that lenders break even on the pool of 'good' and 'bad' types together.

What is a 'contract'? As usual, this depends on the precise specification of the information that is available at different dates. Diamond makes the key assumption that, at some date between the initial investment and the final realization of returns, lenders receive additional information about the borrowers' types. When this information has been received, there is still time to shut the prospect down if this is deemed preferable. More generally, anything that happens after the information is received can be made to depend on it. This concerns not only the decision to liquidate or to continue the project, but also the division of the final return, 0 or X in the case of continuation, L in the case of liquidation, between the borrower and the lender.

In abstract terms, a contract can thus be seen as a system of rules linking the liquidation/continuation decision and the division of final returns to the realizations of the intervening information variable. The choice of a contract involves the following considerations:

(a) Borrowers who know that their type is 'good' assign a relatively higher probability to favourable realizations of the information variable than the lender, who doesn't know the borrower's type. Thus, from the *ex ante* point of view, Pareto efficiency requires a division of returns such that the lender gets everything if the realization of the information variable is sufficiently unfavourable and the borrower gets everything if the realization of the information variable is sufficiently favourable.

(b)   The lender wants the project to be liquidated if the realization of the information variable is sufficiently unfavourable. Given the information, the borrower never wants the project to be liquidated because this would involve a loss of control rents. However, from the *ex ante* point of view, borrowers who know their type to be 'good' are willing to agree to a contract involving liquidation if the realization of the information variable is sufficiently unfavourable; since they consider the probability of such unfavourable information to be small, this doesn't cost them much, and the lender is more than willing to compensate them by giving them a larger share of returns when the realization of the information variable is favourable.

Under the assumption that the information variable has three possible realizations, Diamond characterizes the equilibrium contract. He shows that the abstract equilibrium contract can be implemented by a single lender providing initial finance through a mixture of short-term and long-term debt. Here short-term debt is a claim that comes due after the information variable has been realized but before the project has been completed; long-term debt comes due after the project has been completed and the returns on it have been realized.

Diamond also shows that the equilibrium contract cannot generally be implemented if initial finance is provided *only* through long-term or *only* through short-term debt. If initial finance is provided only through long-term debt, there is no mechanism to implement the desired liquidation of the project when the realization of the information variable is unfavourable. In contrast, if initial finance is provided *only* through short-term debt, there may be excessive liquidation.

The key idea is that short-term debt allows for a contingent assignment of control over the liquidation/continuation decision: if the realization of the intervening information variable is favourable, a borrower can service the debt by refinancing themselves in the open market. In this case they retain control and opt for continuation. In contrast, if the information is unfavourable, the borrower cannot raise the funds needed to service the short-term debt and must default; control passes to the lender, who opts for liquidation if the information is really bad. The precise incidence of the change of control depends on the level of short-term debt; under pure short-term finance, this level may be so high as to entail liquidation in cases when the abstract equilibrium contract requires continuation; under pure long-term finance, it is too low to provide for any liquidation at all.

At first sight, this analysis looks like a variant of the observation of Aghion and Bolton (1992) that (i) it may be desirable to have a state-contingent assignment of control and (ii) financial packaging may be used to implement such a state-contingent assignment of control (see also Hart and Moore, 1989). It should be noted though that Diamond has a rather neat answer to a question that bugs practically all the literature on financial contracting and control, namely, why are control assignments and return patterns correlated the way they are. To explain, e.g., why it is desirable to have a debt contract involve a transfer of control to lenders if and only if current obligations cannot be met, Aghion and Bolton have to introduce an additional *ad hoc* assumption that current returns and future prospects are correlated so that an inability to meet current obligations is a signal of bad prospects for the future. In Diamond's analysis the correlation between current debt service capacity and future prospects arises naturally, without any additional assumption, because, with the possibility of refinancing in the open market, current debt service capacity is directly determined by the market's evaluation of future prospects. To be sure, the argument makes heavy use of the assumption that the refinancing of short-term debt is not hampered by any further information asymmetries. Even so, I find the link between debt service capacity and control assignments more convincing than in most other recent work.

This being said, I have some doubt about the robustness of Diamond's analysis. Some conclusions depend crucially on the assumption that there are only three possible realizations of the information variable (and that the realizations are arranged the way they are). If there is a continuum of realizations, the equilibrium contract that is derived from the given information and incentive problem can no longer be implemented by a suitable combination of short-term and long-term debt.

To see the difficulty, compare Figures 3B.1 and 3B.2. In both figures, the information variable is parametrized by f_1, the posterior probability that the borrower's type is good; the prior distribution of f_1 is assumed to be continuous. Figure 3B.1 exhibits the typical shape of the abstract *equilibrium contract*, namely, there are two critical values f_1^* and $f_1^0 > f_1^*$ such that

(i)   the equilibrium contract involves liquidation if $f_1 < f_1^*$, continuation if $f_1 \geq f_1^*$, and
(ii) the financier gets the entire return if $f_1 \leq f_1^0$, the borrower gets the entire return if $f_1 > f_1^0$ (for details see the appendix).

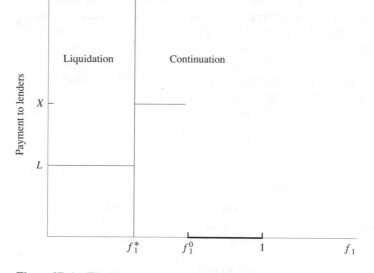

Figure 3B.1   The abstract equilibrium contract

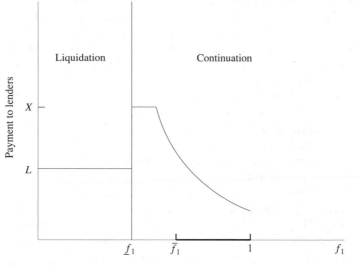

Figure 3B.2   A debt package with $\rho + r_1 \, X/L > X$

In contrast, Figure 3B.2 exhibits the typical shape of a contract involving a packaged short-term and long-term debt finance by the initial financier. Here there are critical values $\underline{f}_1$ and $\bar{f}_1 \geq \underline{f}_1$ such that

(i)   the debt finance package involves liquidation if $\underline{f}_1 < f_1$, continuation if $f_1 \geq \underline{f}_1$, and

(ii)   the financier gets the entire return if $f_1 \leq \bar{f}_1$; in the case of success they get $p + r_1/q(f_1)$ and the borrower gets $X - p - r_1/q(f_1)$, if $f_1 > \bar{f}_1$. Here p is the nominal obligation on long-term debt, r_1 is the nominal obligation on short-term debt, and $q(f_1)$ is the probability of success given f_1.

Upon comparing Figures 3B.1 and 3B.2, one finds:

(a*)   A debt finance package can never be used to implement a contract that prescribes that for some realizations of the information variable *all* the returns go to the borrower.[1]

(b*)   If $\bar{f}_1 > f_1$, as in Figure 3B.2, then f_1 is strictly greater than $f\dagger$, so the debt finance package involves excessive liquidation. This is because f_1 satisfies the equation $L - q(\underline{f}_1)X = 0$, requiring that the lender be indifferent between liquidation and continuation, without regard to control rents. In contrast, $f\dagger$ satisfies $L - q(f\dagger)X > 0$, being based on a trade-off between the marginal loss of money, $L - qX$, of the lender from not liquidating and the marginal loss of expected control rent, Cf_1/f, of the borrower from liquidating.

The problem of excessive liquidation is eliminated if the level r_1 of short-term debt is reduced sufficiently so that the critical ratio $r_1/(X - p)$ falls below L/X, and hence f_1 falls below the solution to $L - q(f_1)X = 0$. Because of the lender's participation constraint, however, the reduction in r_1 entails an increase in the level p of long-term debt. Thereby the borrower's payment to the lender becomes less sensitive to f_1, and the inability of debt finance to mimic the discontinuous return pattern in Figure 3B.1 is exacerbated.[2]

The problem of excessive liquidation can be eliminated *without* a change in the mix of short-term and long-term debt if there is a possibility of dilution of long-term debt, i.e. if the short-term debt can be refinanced by issuing new claims that have priority over long-term debt. As shown in Diamond (1992), the original piece on which the paper under discussion draws, if $Y \in (X - p, X)$ is the amount of priority refinancing that is permitted, then the borrower can service the short-term debt, and the project is continued, whenever $q(f_1)Y > r_1$. If $r_1/Y < L/X$, this means that the liquidation region is smaller than in Figure 3B.2 where $q(f_1) = L/X$. With a suitable choice of the dilution right Y, one can thus take account of the loss of control rents through liquidation regardless of what continuation of short-term debt r_1 and long-term debt p is chosen. The problem of excess liquidation, problem (b*) above, can thus be handled within the context of short-term and long-term debt contracts with refinancing of short-term debt in the open market.

The same cannot be said of problem (a*), the discrepancy between return patterns on the abstract equilibrium contract and on combinations of short-term and long-term debt. As shown by Diamond (1992), the consideration that the 'good' type of borrower wants to obtain returns conditional on favourable information in exchange for returns conditional on unfavourable information makes it desirable to set dilution rights at the maximum, $Y = X$, so that, for a given ratio r_1/Y, r_1 is at a maximum and the borrower's effective payment in the event of success, $\min[X, \rho + r_1/q(f_1)]$, is most sensitive to changes in the assessed success probability $q(f_1)$. Even then, however, the package of short-term and long-term debt fails to implement the abstract equilibrium contract in Figure 3B.1.

At this point, Diamond argues that the equilibrium contract in Figure 3B.1 may be unavailable because the posterior probability f_1 of the borrower's type being 'good' is not verifiable. I am not entirely convinced by the argument. There is a one-to-one relation between f_1 and $q(f_1)$, the posterior probability of success from the perspective of the financiers. The success probability $q(f_1)$ in turn is equal to the market price of a long-term bond or indeed of the newly issued claims that serve to refinance the short-term debt. I find it hard to believe that this market price should be observable and not verifiable. If, however, $q(f_1)$ is verifiable, one can write contracts on it, and indeed the equilibrium contract of Figure 3B.1 is feasible.

The dilemma that we are facing here is one that affects most work in the Jensen–Meckling tradition, beginning with the paper by Jensen and Meckling itself (Jensen and Meckling, 1976). On the one hand, the consideration of information and incentive problems enhances our understanding of the trade-offs between *given* financial instruments, debt and equity in Jensen and Meckling (1976), between short-term and long-term debt in Diamond's papers. On the other hand, the abstract analysis of information and incentive problems does not allow us to derive the use of these financial instruments from first principles. Optimal contracts or equilibrium contracts that are derived from first principles typically involve discontinuities (as well as other strange features) that make it impossible to implement these contracts by standard financial instruments. We may consider such discontinuities to be pathological, ruled out by other considerations, but then we ought to make these considerations explicit and show why they lead to the use of the instruments that we observe.

Appendix

In this appendix, I give the general solution to the abstract contracting problem underlying Diamond's analysis. I assume that Diamond's f_1, i.e. the conditional probability of type G given the intervening signal, can be treated as the realization of a random variable $\tilde{f}_1$ with cumulative distribution function $P(\cdot)$ and expected value $f = (\int f_1 dP(f_1))$. As indicated by Diamond, Bayes' law implies that, for an agent who knows that they are of type G, the conditional distribution of $\tilde{f}_1$ is given by the function $P_G(\cdot)$, where, for any f_1,

$$P_G(f_1) = \int_0^{f_1} x\, dP(x)/f.$$

The problem of finding the best contract for type G subject to the participation constraint for the lender can thus be written as:

$$\text{Max } \frac{1}{f} \int_0^1 f_1\{\lambda(f_1)[L - z(f_1)] + [1 - \lambda(f_1)][X - Z(f_1) + C]\}dP(f_1)$$

subject to

$$\int_0^1 \{\lambda(f_1)z(f_1) + [1 - \lambda(f_1)]q(f_1)Z(f_1)\}dP(f_1) \geq I,$$

and, for all f_1, $z(f_1) \in [0, L]$, $Z(f_1) \in [0, X]$, and $\lambda(f_1) \in [0, 1]$. To ensure that the problem is well defined, I assume that

$$\int_0^1 \max[L, q(f_1)X]dP(f_1) > I,$$

so that the constraint set is non-empty.

The analysis is somewhat less than straightforward because the problem is not convex. Let μ be the Kuhn–Tucker multiplier of the creditor's participation constraint. Then an optimal contract satisfies: for any f_1,

$$\lambda(f_1)z(f_1) = \begin{cases} 0 & , \text{ if } f_1 > \mu f, \\ \lambda(f_1)L, & \text{ if } f_1 < \mu f; \end{cases} \tag{1}$$

$$[1 - \lambda(f_1)]Z(f_1) = \begin{cases} 0 & , \text{ if } f_1 > \mu f q(f_1), \\ [1 - \lambda(f_1)]X, & \text{ if } f_1 < \mu f q(f_1); \end{cases} \tag{2}$$

$$\lambda(f_1) = \begin{cases} 0, & \text{ if } Cf_1 + X \max[f_1, \mu f q(f_1)] > L \max[f_1, \mu f], \\ 1, & \text{ if } Cf_1 + X \max[f_1, \mu f q(f_1)] < L \max[f_1, \mu f]. \end{cases} \tag{3}$$

From (1) one immediately finds that there exists some $f_1^1 \in [0, 1]$ such that

$$\lambda(f_1)Z(f_1) = \begin{cases} 0 & , \text{ if } f_1 > f_1^1, \\ \lambda(f_1)L, & \text{ if } f_1 < f_1^1. \end{cases} \tag{1*}$$

From (1) and (3), one also finds that there exists some $f_1^* \in [0, f_1^1)$ such that

$$\lambda(f_1) = \begin{cases} 0, & \text{ if } f_1 > f_1^*, \\ 1, & \text{ if } f_1 < f_1^*. \end{cases} \tag{3*}$$

To prove this, observe first that $f_1 \geq f_1^1$ implies $f_1 \geq \mu f$, hence $f_1 \geq \mu f q(f_1)$), and $C f_1 + X \max[f_1, \mu f q(f_1)] - L \max[f_1, \mu f] = (C + X - L) f_1 > 0$, so (3) implies $\lambda(f_1) = 0$. Next, in the interval $(0, f_1^1)$, one has

$$C f_1 + X \max[f_1, \mu f q(f_1)] - L \max[f_1, \mu f]$$
$$= C f_1 + X \max[f_1, \mu f q(f_1)] - L \mu f,$$

and there is at most one point f_1^* at which $C f_1 + X \max[f_1, \mu f q(f_1)] = L \mu f$. This proves (3*).

As for (2), we must distinguish whether

$$\mu f (1 - \pi) < 1 \quad (\text{Case A})$$

or

$$\mu f (1 - \pi) \geq 1 \quad (\text{Case B})$$

In case A, the difference $f_1 - \mu f q(f_1) = f_1 - \mu f[\pi + (1 - \pi) f_1]$ is increasing in f_1, so (2) implies that for some $f_1^0 \in [0, 1]$,

$$[1 - \lambda(f_1)] Z(f_1) = \begin{cases} 0 & , \quad \text{if} \quad f_1 > f_1^0, \\ [1 - \lambda(f_1)] X, & \text{if} \quad f_1 < f_1^0. \end{cases} \quad (2^*A)$$

The critical value f_1^0 in (2*A) must be larger than the critical f_1^* in (3*) since $f_1^0 \leq f_1^*$ would imply an expected return $LP(f_1^*)$ for the creditor, contrary to the participation constraint.

In case B, the difference $f_1 - \mu f q(f_1) = f_1[1 - \mu f (1 - \pi)] - \mu f \pi$ is negative for all $f_1 \in [0, 1]$, so (2) implies

$$[1 - \lambda(f_1)] Z(f_1) = [1 - \lambda(f_1)] X \quad (2^*B)$$

for all f_1.

The critical values f_1^0, f_1^1, f_1^* in (1*A), (2*A) and (3*) are related to the multiplier μ by the conditions

$$f_1^1 = \mu f \tag{4}$$

$$f_1^0 = \max\left(1, \frac{\mu \pi f}{1 - \mu f (1 - \pi)}\right) \tag{5}$$

$$f_1^* = \max\left(0, \frac{\mu f (L - \pi X)}{C + \mu f (1 - \pi X)}\right) \tag{6}$$

In computing (6), one must rely on the information that $f_1^* < f_1^0$ and $f_1^* < f_1^1$, so that in the neighbourhood of f_1^*, $\max[f_1, \mu f q] = \mu f q$ and $\max[f_1, \mu f] = \mu f$.

An optimal contract can thus be characterized by the conditions

$$\lambda(f_1) = 1 \quad \text{and} \quad z(f_1) = L, \quad \text{if} \quad f_1 < f_1^*, \tag{7}$$

$$\lambda(f_1) = 0 \quad \text{and} \quad Z(f_1) = X, \quad \text{if} \quad \mu f(1 - \pi) < 1 \quad \text{and} \quad f_1 \in (f_1^*, f_1^0) \quad (8)$$

$$\lambda(f_1) = 0 \quad \text{and} \quad Z(f_1) = 0, \quad \text{if} \quad \mu f(1 - \pi) < 1 \quad \text{and} \quad f_1 \in (f_1^0, 1) \quad (9)$$

$$\lambda(f_1) = 0 \quad \text{and} \quad Z(f_1) = X, \quad \text{if} \quad \mu f(1 - \pi) \geq 1 \quad \text{and} \quad f_1 \in (f_1^*, 1). \quad (10)$$

The behaviour of λ, z and Z at the critical points f_1^* and f_1^0 is arbitrary if these points have zero mass under the measure μ. If f_1^* has positive mass, one has $Z(f_1) = X$, and $\lambda(f_1) \in [0, 1]$ will be determined by the creditor's participation constraint. If f_1^* has positive mass and $f_1^0 = 1$, one again has $Z(f_1) = X$.

If the critical points f_1^*, f_1^1 have zero mass, e.g. if the distribution P is nonatomic, the creditor's expected returns are given as

$$\int_0^{f_1^*} L \, dP + \int_{f_1^*}^{\bar{f_1}} X q(f_1) \, dP, \quad (11)$$

where

$$\bar{f_1} = \begin{cases} f_1^0, & \text{if} \quad \mu f(1 - \pi) < 1, \\ 1 & \text{if} \quad \mu f(1 - \pi) \geq 1. \end{cases} \quad (12)$$

Upon substituting (11) into the participation constraint and using (5) and (6), one obtains a condition for μ, which is easily seen to have a single solution. This solution in turn determines the optimal contract.

An explicit solution for μ cannot be given as it depends on P, which has been left unspecified. It is, however, possible to give a simple classification as to when $\bar{f_1} < 1$ and when $\bar{f_1} = 1$. Let

$$f_1^{**} = \frac{L - \pi X}{C + (1 - \pi) X}. \quad (13)$$

If

$$LP(f_1^{**}) + \int^1 q(f_1) X \, dP > I, f_1^{**}$$

then μ must be less than $1/f$ and hence $\bar{f_1} = f_1^0 < 1$ (and $f_1^* < f_1^{**}$). In contrast, if

$$LP(f_1^{**}) + \int_{f_1^{**}}^1 q(f_1) X \, dP \leq I,$$

then μ must not be less than $1/f$, and hence $\bar{f} = 1$ and $f^* \geq f^{**}$ (with equality *only* if there is equality in the premise). Hence the constellation drawn in Figure 3B.1 is an optimal contract if and only if

$$L > \pi X$$

and

$$LP(f_1^{**}) + \int_{f_1^{**}}^1 q(f_1)X\mathrm{d}P > I.$$

NOTES

1 This observation is independent of the number of states, so it applies to Diamond's three-state case as well as to the continuum. There it does not matter, however, because, with a mass point at $f_1 = 1$ Diamond's equilibrium contract involves a positive payment to the lender even when $f_1 = 1$.
2 Note that Hart and Moore (1989) discuss the choice between short-term and long-term debt in terms of a trade-off between increased information sensitivity and increased excessive liquidation as more short-term debt is used.

REFERENCES

Aghion, P. and P. Bolton (1992) 'An incomplete contracts approach to financial contracting', *Review of Economic Studies* **59**, 473–94.
Diamond, D. (1992) 'Seniority and maturity structure of bank loans and publicly traded debt', mimeo, University of Chicago.
Hart, O. and J. Moore (1989) 'Default and renegotiation: a dynamic model of debt', LSE Discussion Paper 57, June.
Jensen, M. and W. Meckling, (1976) 'Theory of the firm: managerial behavior, agency costs and capital structure', *Journal of Financial Economics* **3**, 305–60.

4 Stock markets and resource allocation

FRANKLIN ALLEN

1 Introduction

As West European countries integrate their economies and East European countries move away from communism, both are reassessing their economic and financial institutions. One of the most important choices they face concerns the emphasis they should place on stock markets (including equity, bond and other markets) as opposed to banks for providing finance to their industries.

Although both stock markets and banks have existed in most advanced countries for many years, the relative importance of the two has varied. Stock-market-based financial systems have been associated with the nineteenth-century UK, which was the first country to go through the Industrial Revolution, and the twentieth-century US, which was the first country to go through the post-Industrial Revolution. Bank-based financial systems have been associated with France, Germany and Japan.

In the second half of the nineteenth century the stock market played an important role in the financing of industry in the UK. According to Michie (1987), roughly one-quarter of capital formation was raised through the London Stock Exchange in 1853; by 1913 this had grown to one-third.[1] Table 4.1 gives a detailed breakdown of the distribution of securities by industry between 1853 and 1913. It can be seen that railways were the most important category apart from government debt. Urban services, financial services and commercial and industrial firms were all significant and constituted most of the remainder. Agriculture was a very minor component and consisted entirely of overseas investments.

In the first half of the twentieth century, the role of the London Stock Exchange in raising funds for industry declined and it was in the US that stock markets came to have the greatest relative importance. Table 4.2 shows the stocks listed on the New York Stock Exchange at the end of

Table 4.1. *London Stock Exchange: securities quoted (paid-up capital),*
1853–1913 (as a percentage of overall and individual totals)

Category	1853	1863	1873	1883	1893	1903	1913
Government							
Domestic	92.5	84.0	63.8	48.4	46.6	43.8	38.8
Foreign	7.5	16.0	36.2	51.6	53.4	56.2	61.2
Total	76.0	67.0	59.3	52.0	39.5	36.0	34.8
Railways							
Domestic	86.1	55.4	51.4	44.6	35.3	35.8	29.4
Foreign	13.9	44.6	48.6	55.4	64.7	64.2	70.6
Total	18.5	27.7	32.1	40.6	49.4	44.2	43.4
Urban services							
Total	2.0	1.7	1.4	2.8	2.9	2.9	4.6
Financial services							
Total	1.1	1.6	5.4	2.8	4.1	6.3	6.4
Commercial and industrial							
Total	1.8	1.7	1.4	1.2	3.5	9.9	9.6
Mining							
Domestic	—	19.6	16.9	2.9	0.9	—	—
Foreign	—	80.4	83.1	97.1	99.1	100.0	100.0
Total	0.6	0.3	0.3	0.6	0.7	0.6	1.0
Agriculture							
Total (all foreign)	—	—	0.1	—	—	0.1	0.3
Total (£million)	1,215.2	1,601.4	2,269.1	3,634.3	4,899.2	6,978.3	9,550.3
Domestic	97.1	76.7	62.6	50.1	46.3	50.7	46.8
Foreign	8.5	23.3	37.4	49.9	53.7	49.3	53.2

Source: Michie (1987), Table 2.4, p. 54.

1949. It can be seen that manufacturing industries dominated and that
agriculture was again unimportant.

Mayer (1988) has examined the importance of various sources of funds
for financing investment in a number of major industrialized countries in
more recent years. His comparison between France, Germany, Japan, the
UK and the US, using data from the period 1970–85, is shown in Figure
4.1. The most important source of funds was retained earnings; stock
markets were relatively unimportant. The exception is the US, where
significant amounts were raised in the bond markets.

Table 4.2. *All stocks listed on the New York Stock Exchange as of the close of business 31 December 1949*

Group	No. of issuers	Market value US$ '000
Aircraft	24	733,622
Amusement	22	990,202
Automotive	69	5,597,060
Building trade	29	1,150,761
Chemical	78	10,661,300
Electrical equipment	20	2,105,845
Farm machinery	8	956,488
Financial	32	1,667,982
Food products & beverages	70	4,646,688
Leather & its products	12	339,010
Machinery & metals	103	2,612,936
Mining	40	1,958,759
Office equipment	10	883,151
Paper & publishing	35	1,198,242
Petroleum & natural gas	45	10,046,827
Railroad & R.R. equipment	86	4,391,592
Real estate	11	240,588
Retail trade	73	4,729,705
Rubber	10	621,731
Shipbuilding & operating	11	167,453
Steel & iron	41	3,086,983
Textile	44	1,302,786
Tobacco	15	1,710,630
Utilities	94	11,696,454
Miscellaneous	17	623,017
US companies operating abroad	25	980,200

Source: Neill (1950), p. 323.

A more direct comparison of the relative importance of banks and stock markets is given in Figure 4.2, which is from Frankel and Montgomery (1991). It can be seen that the US is dramatically different from the other countries in terms of the proportion of funds raised with securities, a category which includes both stocks and bonds. Apart from 1985–9, when companies were borrowing to repurchase shares, securities have been much more important in the US.

Why do these stark differences in the role of banks and stock markets between the US and other countries arise? In order to answer this question, it is necessary to start by contrasting banks and stock markets. As suggested by Hellwig (1990), the main distinction is between the

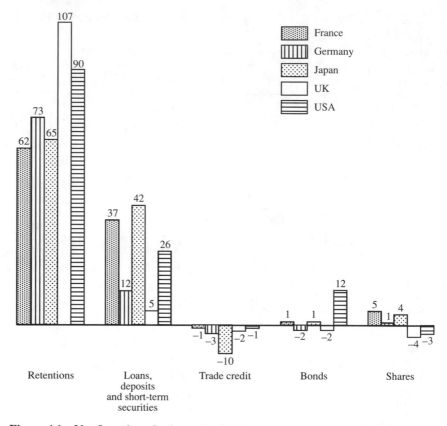

Figure 4.1   Net financing of private physical investment by enterprises in France, Germany, Japan, the UK and the US, 1970–85

Source: Mayer (1988), Figure 2, p. 1174.

structure of the financial institutions rather than the financial instruments they issue. There are countries where banks lend using debt and equity and countries where bonds and shares are traded in stock markets. The important difference between the two institutions is that banks individually negotiate contracts with borrowers and it is rare for a borrower to deal with more than a few banks; in stock markets there are a large number of anonymous lenders who take the contract form specified by the borrower or an intermediary as given. In the US this difference between stock markets and banks is particularly evident. The stock markets have many participants and are very competitive. In other countries, the difference is not as clearcut. In Germany, for example, the stock market is not as competitive and firms can seek financing from several different

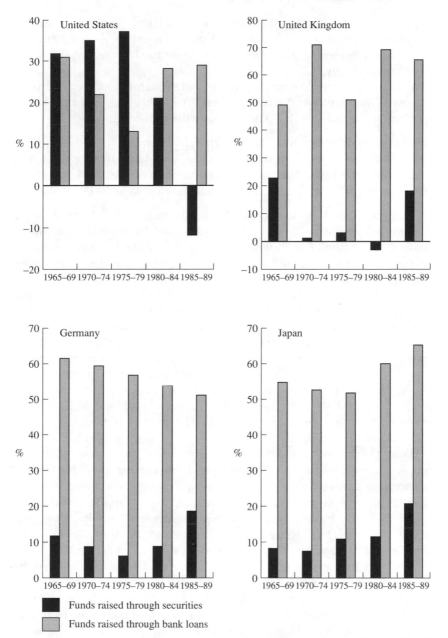

Figure 4.2   **Percentage of total business funds raised through securities and bank loans, 1965–89**

Source: Frankel and Montgomery (1991), Figure 6, p. 267.

banks. However, as the globalization of financial markets continues, the number of participants in most major stock markets is growing and the markets are becoming more competitive while bank loans are still negotiated individually.

What are some of the advantages and disadvantages that have been suggested for banks and stock markets? It has been argued that banks perform a number of roles. These include the following:

Banks act as delegated monitors of firms (Diamond, 1984).
In contrast to stock markets, they allow long-term relationships and commitments (Mayer, 1988; Shleifer and Summers, 1988; Berkovitch and Greenbaum, 1990; and Boot, Thakor and Udell, 1987, 1991).

Diamond's (1984) notion is that the management of a firm needs to be 'monitored' to ensure they act in the interest of the investors providing finance to the firm. This monitoring needs to be done by only one party; duplication does not result in improved monitoring. If finance is provided through a stock market, diverse ownership means that security-holders may waste resources by costly repetition of monitoring. They cannot combine to hire somebody to monitor because of a free-rider problem; each would want others to bear the costs of monitoring the monitor. Diamond suggests that a bank lending to corporations allows the advantages of a single monitor to be captured and solves the problem of monitoring the monitor. By holding a large portfolio of loans to different firms, the bank can guarantee to its depositors that it is undertaking the monitoring and thus overcomes the free-rider problem; if it did not monitor it would be unable to make the promised payment to the depositors.

Mayer (1988) and Shleifer and Summers (1988) have pointed to the importance of long-term relationships. They suggest that, because of incomplete contracting possibilities, it is desirable for firms to make long-term implicit contracts with their workers, suppliers and other groups they do business with. These long-term relationships allow significant *ex ante* gains to be made. For example, workers and suppliers may be willing to acquire firm-specific capital, whereas without an implicit contract they would not be willing to do so. *Ex post*, a firm may be required to make payments to fulfil its implicit contracts, which it is not legally obligated to. For a firm that is listed on a stock exchange, there is an incentive for somebody to take it over and cease making the payments required under the implicit contract. Recognizing this possibility, workers and others will be wary of entering into implicit contracts and *ex ante* gains will be lost. In contrast, one of the advantages of bank-oriented financial structures is that this problem is not so serious. Banks will encourage long-term relationships in order to be able to share in the *ex ante* gains; *ex post* they will want to keep the implicit contracts from a desire to maintain their long-term reputation. Their position and incentives are very different from those of stock market raiders. Similarly, Berkovitch and Greenbaum (1990) and Boot, Thakor and Udell (1987, 1991) have stressed the importance of banks' ability to make credible long-term commitments.

Bank loans have many other desirable characteristics that arise from the fact that they are provided on an individual basis. For example, bank loans can be renegotiated more easily than securities sold in stock markets (Wilson, 1991). There are also better incentives for various types of information about borrowers to be gathered than with stock markets (Sharpe, 1990). A comprehensive survey of these and other recent theories of banking is provided in Bhattacharya and Thakor (1992).

A number of advantages of stock markets have been stressed in the literature. These include the following:

Stock markets allow efficient risk sharing (e.g. P. Diamond, 1967).
They provide incentives to gather information, which becomes reflected in stock prices. These prices provide signals for the efficient allocation of investment (Grossman, 1976, 1978; Grossman and Stiglitz, 1980; and Diamond and Verrecchia, 1981).
Information in stock market prices allows effective managerial incentive schemes (Diamond and Verrecchia, 1982; Holmstrom and Tirole, 1990).

Diamond (1967) and others have suggested that one of the important advantages of stock markets is that they allow efficient risk sharing between investors. However, the absence of agriculture from stock markets is somewhat surprising if risk sharing is one of their major roles. Although futures markets exist to spread some of the risk in agriculture, the residual uncertainty is still considerable and is larger than in many industries that figure prominently on the stock market. Also, in comparing the US with other countries there does not appear to be any evidence that risk is shared better in the US. In France, Germany and Japan the portfolios held by banks and other financial institutions appear to spread risk across the population as effectively as happens in the US.

The number of firms that analysts gather information about differs significantly in different countries. Table 4.3 shows the number of firms covered by financial analysts by country. It can be seen that in France and Germany, in particular, very little information is gathered and stock prices are unlikely to reflect much information. At the other extreme, many firms in the US are covered by analysts so stock prices are likely to incorporate more information. Grossman (1976, 1978), Grossman and

Table 4.3. *Number of firms covered by financial analysts by country*

Country	No. of firms covered
France	303
Germany	210
Japan	1,152
UK	1,183
US	> 4,600

Source: Nelson's Directory of Investment Research 1992.

Stiglitz (1980) and Diamond and Verrecchia (1981) have suggested models where investors have diverse information and stock prices aggregate this information. This allows stock prices to provide efficient signals for the allocation of resources. Diamond and Verrecchia (1982) and Holmstrom and Tirole (1990) have extended this idea to suggest that the information in stock prices allows effective managerial incentive schemes to be provided. Similarly to risk sharing, however, it does not appear that the US has had a significant advantage over other countries in terms of the efficiency of investment allocation or the provision of managerial incentives. In this view, an advantage of bank-oriented systems is the absence of wasteful expenditures involved when analysts gather information.

It would appear that stock-market-based systems have few advantages and a number of disadvantages when compared with bank-based systems. This suggests that bank-based systems are superior. The purpose of this paper is to claim that the standard arguments presented above do not capture all the benefits of stock markets and that, depending on the circumstances, stock markets can play an important role. It is suggested in section 2 that, from the classical economists onwards, the typical starting point of analysis has been that the production technology is well known and the essential resource allocation problems considered have been static in nature. With competitive industries like agriculture, repetition ensures that a consensus will soon be reached and this assumption is appropriate. In industrial economies, with oligopolistic or monopolistic industries, however, the actions that managers of large corporations should take are far from clear. The problems they face are extraordinarily complex and there will be a divergence of opinions on what a firm should do. Although there may be some sharing of information, the complexity of the problems involved means that a consensus on how firms should be run will not be reached; it is simply too time consuming and costly to transfer all the relevant information. In this type of situation the crucial issue in allocating resources is one of checking whether the strategies the management undertake are sensible ones. The great advantage of a stock market is that it provides incentives for large numbers of investors to check what the firm is doing. These arguments are developed more fully in section 3.

Given this checking role for the stock market, what is the role of banks? The crucial difference between this framework and those of Diamond (1984) and Mayer (1988) is that repetition of the decision-making process is valuable. The weakness of banks is that they allow checking to occur only relatively few times; if there is one bank lending, checking occurs just once. It is argued in section 4 that banks are institutions which will be advantageous when there is a consensus on the actions that management should take and the problem is to ensure that they actually take them, as in Diamond (1984). This suggests that, in industries where the optimal actions of management are widely agreed upon, banking will predominate; thus banking will be important in competitive industries such as agriculture. In industries where there is wide disagreement on optimal policies, however, stock markets will be important; these include industries dominated by large corporations and those with high technology.

The idea that the stock market provides a checking role also has implications for government ownership. The extreme case of government ownership was in the former communist countries. One of the defects of centrally planned systems is that there are no checks in the sense of decisions being replicated. Thus managers might have information about the effects of various actions that are far from the truth but this may not become apparent for a considerable time. In a number of non-communist countries there has also been substantial government ownership of firms, particularly those that have natural monopolies. The only checks on these firms are those provided by politicians, which again rarely involve replication of decisions. In contrast a quotation on the stock market means that analysts have a constant incentive to consider how the firm is being run and what alternative strategies there are. These arguments suggest that private ownership of firms may be preferable to government ownership even when firms have natural monopolies. They are considered more fully in section 5. Section 6 contains concluding remarks.

The approach taken in this paper is related to that in Sah and Stiglitz (1985, 1986). They consider the optimal structure of firms given that people make mistakes in screening projects. In contrast, the issue addressed here is the optimal structure of financial institutions given that people have different views on how firms should be run. Both approaches, however, are concerned with the allocation of resources when the traditional assumption that production functions are known to all is dispensed with.

2   Traditional analyses

Starting with the classical economists, the traditional view of the firm in economics has been that it combines a vector of inputs, such as various types of capital and labour, to produce a vector of outputs. The role of the owners or managers of the firm is to choose the vector of inputs to maximize profits given the technological relationship between inputs and outputs.

This approach to modelling the firm, which assumes that its production function is well known, was appropriate for economies prior to the Industrial Revolution. The industries in these economies had a number of features that made the assumption of a known technology reasonable:

(a)   the industries were competitive, with many producers;
(b)   production cycles were relatively short;
(c)   technology was constant.

The classic example of an industry with these characteristics was agriculture. There were many farmers, production occurred in a matter of months and was repeated every year and technology changed only slowly. In this type of situation, assuming that the production function was well known was appropriate. Many producers and the short production cycle meant that a wide range of actions would be tried and their consequences discovered. Movement between farms and direct observation ensured that this knowledge became widely spread and there was wide agreement throughout the industry on the technology. Similar arguments will apply in other competitive industries.

At this point it is helpful to develop these ideas more formally. Suppose a firm is run by a manager who may or may not be the owner. For large corporations 'the manager' should be thought of as the management team that runs the firm. The manager can choose various courses of action a for the firm. These courses of action are multidimensional and may include a wide range of things. Examples would include how much to invest in equipment, research and development, what personnel policies to pursue, and so on. Manager i's opinions of the effectiveness of the various possible actions will be determined by his or her information set η_i. This is again multidimensional. It includes the information that the manager has about the particular firm that is being managed, his or her education, any relevant political views and so forth. The manager's perception of the value of the firm depends on this information set and the course of action

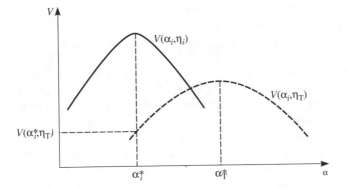

Figure 4.3   The relationship between value and actions

undertaken. The value of the firm as perceived by manager i given a course of action a is

$$V_i = V(a, \eta_i). \tag{1}$$

The true information set is denoted η_T. Each individual manager's view of the information set is initially a function of η_T and a vector of random disturbances ϵ_i:

$$\eta_i = \eta_T + \epsilon_i \tag{2}$$

where $E\epsilon_i = 0$ and the ϵ_i are independent.

The relationship between firm value and the manager's information and actions is represented in Figure 4.3 for the special case where a has one dimension. It is important to stress that in practice a will have many dimensions. The optimal course of action as perceived by manager i is a_i^* whereas the optimal course of action is in fact a_T^*. The value of the firm as perceived by the manager is $V(a_i^*, \eta_i)$ but the true value is $V(a_i^*, \eta_T)$.

An important issue is how managers acquire the information that determines their opinions. This is a long, complex process. Part of it occurs during their education, part of it is the information they acquire to make actual decisions about the running of the firm. The amount of information involved is so large that it can be directly transferred only at great cost.

For firms in competitive industries where the production cycle is brief, it will soon be the case that the effect of actions will be empirically established. Empirical information will come to dominate and there will be a consensus on the relationship between actions and value:

$$V(a_i, \eta_i) = V(a_i, \eta_T) \quad \text{for all } i. \tag{3}$$

The convergence of information sets will come about in a variety of ways, including through the educational system, trial and error, the movement of personnel between firms and the direct observation of competing firms.

In this view, one of the advantages of competitive industries with many firms is that the information that is the basis of management decisions is widely agreed upon and has been verified numerous times. Thus, in competitive industries with the features listed above, it is natural to assume that the production technology is known to everybody.

This was essentially the view of the production process taken by the classical economists and it provided very useful insights into the role of the price system in allocating resources efficiently. In this type of economy there is little role for a stock market and indeed the classical economists rarely mentioned its existence. For example, even though Ricardo had made a fortune on the stock market before turning to economics, he ascribed it no special place in his economic theories.[2]

The static theory of resource allocation culminated with the Arrow–Debreu model and the fundamental theorems of welfare economics. Provided markets are complete, an efficient allocation of resources can be attained. An important component of markets being complete is that the appropriate financial markets are available to consumers. Equity and bond markets may perform this role but there is no need that they do so; any other types of financial security that complete the market can perform this function. Apart from this possible role in sharing risk, the stock market is also not important in the Arrow–Debreu theory.

3   The checking role of the stock market

In modern economies, a number of factors mean the assumption that the relationship between actions and outcomes is widely agreed upon is problematic in many industries. These include the following:

(a)   increasing returns to scale result in there only being a few firms in an industry;
(b)   there is often a long time between the adoption of policies and the time that their success or failure is realized;
(c)   technological change is important and rapid.

An example of an industry that displays these characteristics in varying degrees is biotechnology.

These factors contrast sharply with those underlying industries before the Industrial Revolution listed above. In some industries, instead of there being many firms there are now only a few; instead of production cycles being short, they can be up to several decades in length; instead of technological change being unimportant, it often changes rapidly.

All this suggests that in many cases there will be very little consensus about the effects of managerial actions. Even after expending considerable effort gathering information, the complexity of running modern corporations means that there will not be a uniform view of the best actions to undertake. It is important to stress that it is not just a difference in the data that are collected that is important here. Even if people collected the same information about the industry, they might interpret it differently because of differences in education, personal experiences and background. The range of relevant information is so large that in practice it cannot be shared between people. The length of time taken to complete projects and the fact that the technology changes mean that few actual data points will be gathered. In the absence of a large sample of data points on the effect of various policies it is likely that differences in views of the production function will persist. This divergence of opinions is an important feature of many industries.

How do these differences in opinion relate to standard Bayesian decision theory? In an important contribution, Aumann (1976) showed that if two people have the same priors for a given event and their posteriors are common knowledge then they cannot agree to disagree. Geanokoplos and Polemarchakis (1982) demonstrated that if the two agents receive different information then, by communicating their posteriors back and forth, they will converge to a common posterior. McKelvey and Page (1986) extended these results to n individuals and showed that public announcement of posteriors was not necessary for convergence; public announcement of other aggregate statistics can have the same effect. The crucial point here is that, if the information that each person observes is sufficiently complex, the number of iterations required to obtain convergence will be large. The process of making public announcements and updating priors is not costless and takes time. In addition, the underlying technology is continually changing. In practice, therefore, agents will update only a limited amount and will agree to disagree.

The fact that each manager's information set is the true one plus a disturbance (as in (2)) and these disturbances are independent means that the more values of η_i that are obtained the better is the aggregate information set. This is why competitive industries do well in this framework; there are multiple 'draws' and in the long run a consensus as to the true production function is reached. In oligopolistic and monopolistic industries this will not be the case; there will be only a limited number of views and each will have a certain amount of idiosyncratic noise.

In this type of situation the resource allocation problem becomes one of trying to ensure that the information sets that managers of firms make decisions on are as close to the true one as possible. One way to do this is to increase the number of firms so that the industry becomes more competitive in the sense that there are more draws of η_i. However, if there are significant returns to scale this will not be a very good way of obtaining checking. Another way to achieve checking is to set up a stock market. In a stock market with many investors there is an incentive for many people to estimate η_i.

In a series of papers Grossman (1976, 1978) has argued that, if some agents are better informed than others about the value of a financial asset, then the price of that asset aggregates the information possessed by all the traders. In terms of the literature on agreeing to disagree, McKelvey and Page (1976) showed that, provided markets are complete, public revelation of the asset price is sufficient for there to be consensus on the asset return distribution.

Grossman and Stiglitz (1980) pointed out that if acquiring information is costly there is a paradox in the complete market framework. If the price reflects all investors' information there is no incentive to expend resources to gather information and nobody will do so. However, if nobody collects information there is an incentive to expend resources and profitably trade on it. Grossman and Stiglitz's solution to this paradox is to argue that there may be a number of variables which are unobservable to participants so that markets are incomplete and this limits the ability of the uninformed to deduce the information of the informed from the price. In this case those that gather costly information can recover the costs of doing so. Uninformed investors deduce some information from price but they do not end up with the same posteriors as the informed. In general, the more variables that are unobservable, the less information that can be deduced from price and the greater the difference in posteriors between the informed and uninformed.

When there are many different dimensions of information that are relevant for determining optimal actions, as there are here, a stock price will transfer very little of it. The stock price may be a relatively accurate signal of $V(a_i^*, \eta_T)$ where a_i^* is the current set of actions proposed by management. Given the large dimension of η_i that is postulated here, however, and the lack of knowledge about the structure of the economy, the stock price may reveal a very limited amount about η_T itself. For example, the stock price of General Motors may be a reasonable estimate of the value of General Motors given current management policies. At the same time the stock price may reveal relatively little about others' views of optimal strategies for General Motors.

If there are many small investors it will typically not be worthwhile for each individual investor to undertake the necessary research. However, even in this case the existence of an information market as considered in Admati and Pfleiderer (1986, 1990) and Allen (1990) may mean that a number of groups will go through the process of estimating η_i. In the US, many financial analysts are employed and the information they create is sold to investors in a number of ways. Hence there is a wide range of circumstances where the stock price comes to reflect $V(a_i^*, \eta_T)$.[3]

In summary, it has been argued that:

(a)   the stock price tends to reflect the true value of the firm given current management policies $V(a_i^*, \eta_T)$;
(b)   the stock price does not provide much information about the optimal policies a firm should pursue, a_T^*.

The first result means that the stock price can help allocate resources efficiently. The second result underlines the importance of other means of transferring the information about policies for running the firm. We consider these in turn.

3.1   Stock prices and resource allocation

Stock prices affect resource allocation in a number of ways. A firm first raises money in the stock market through an initial public offering (IPO). The offering will fail if the market ascribes a value to the firm that is less than the start-up cost. Hence in this case there is a direct allocational effect of checking by investors.

There has been a large literature in recent years on IPOs. Ibbotson (1976) and others have documented the fact that IPOs are underpriced: their stock price on average rises about 15 per cent during the first day of trading.[4] For some time this was regarded as a puzzle. However, Rock (1986) presented a model in which underpricing comes about because some investors collect information and value the firm. This means that uninformed investors face an adverse selection problem. The informed investors will identify which stocks are worth more than the issue price and will order a large amount. As a result the uninformed will be rationed when buying the stock is profitable. In contrast, when a stock has an issue price above its value the informed will not demand any and the uninformed will receive their full allocation. It follows from this that, in order for the uninformed to be willing to participate, there must be underpricing on average.

An alternative explanation of the IPO underpricing phenomenon is based on the assumption that the owners of firms are better informed about its value than are investors in the market. Allen and Faulhaber

(1989), Grinblatt and Hwang (1989) and Welch (1989) have suggested that in this case underpricing can act as a signal. Good firms signal they are good by underpricing their IPOs and this subsequently enables them to raise capital on better terms than they would if they did not signal.

The important distinction between these two types of model is whether it is the firm itself that has the best information about its value or whether it is the market that has the best information. Michaely and Shaw (1992) consider data from firms with IPOs in the period 1984–8 to test between these two hypotheses. Their results do not support the signalling hypothesis but instead suggest that the market has superior information about the value of the firm. Jegadeesh, Weinstein and Welch (1991) investigate a similar issue using IPOs between 1980 and 1986; their results also suggest that the market has better information about the value of the firm.

At first sight it appears unlikely that the market could have better information than the managers of a firm undergoing an IPO. However, the important point here is that, even though the firm may be better informed about its prospects than any single investor, in the aggregate the market may be better informed than the firm. Initial public offerings thus provide an example where checking by investors ensures that resources are allocated to viable firms. If the firms' managers have information that is sufficiently different from the truth, the stock market mechanism ensures that they will not be allocated resources. What is important here is that there is multiple checking by investors. In aggregate their information ensures an efficient allocation of resources. When there is a large degree of underpricing, investors will have a strong incentive to become informed. Hence, the information that is collected initially will tend to be relatively good.

Once a firm has gone public, its equity trades on the stock market. As long as it is publicly quoted, investors have an incentive to value it. This involves continually evaluating η_i and deducing $V(a_i^*, \eta_i)$. The stock price again reflects the average valuation of investors. In this case, however, the allocational effect is not the same as in initial public offerings. As Mayer's (1988) findings indicate, even companies in the US resort relatively infrequently to the capital market to raise money and instead prefer to rely on internal finance.

There are a number of points here. The first is that, as long as a firm is making reasonable earnings, it will not have to rely on raising funds in the market. In terms of the analysis of this paper, provided managers' information is sufficiently close to the truth, η_T, they will be able to generate earnings and need not be extensively checked by the market. Should η_i be very different from η_T, then the firm will not be successful; its earnings will not be sufficient to finance its needs and it will have to resort to the outside markets. In this case its stock market valuation is important in the same way as in an IPO; only firms that investors on average think have a value greater than their costs will receive funds. Again the checking function of the stock market ensures an efficient allocation of resources.

An important determinant of the effectiveness of the stock market as a check on firms' activities is the financial policies they pursue. Firms that use a significant amount of debt and pay out a large portion of their earnings will have continually to raise finance and the average valuation of investors reflected in the stock price will be an important determinant of the level of resources allocated to the firm. This is clearly related to Jensen's (1986) free cash flow theory. Here, however, resources are wasted because managers have bad information whereas in Jensen's theory managers pursue their own ends.

Why is it that investors do not always insist on keeping firms on a short rein so that the firms continually have to return to the market? So far no distinction has been made about the ease with which the managers and investors can acquire values of η_i. In many cases once a firm is in operation the manager may be able to acquire information that is more accurate than that available to outside investors and it may be optimal to give the manager a relatively long rein. Thus for firms such as IBM and Kodak, where research and development are important components of the firm's long-term viability and investors have very limited access to the results of the firm's R&D programme, this is likely to be the case. Investors may be prepared to give the managers a lot of freedom, which corresponds to firms adopting fairly conservative debt and dividend policies. For other firms where the technology is relatively well known, such as utilities, it may be optimal to restrict the actions of managers and force them to return to the capital market relatively frequently. In this case high debt and payout ratios are optimal. This type of theory of corporate financial policies may provide some insights into why taxes appear to have such little influence on corporate financial policies.

It has been argued that the stock market helps allocate resources efficiently because it provides incentives for investors to gather information and check that what the managers of firms do is sensible. The process of going through this exercise multiple times ensures that stock prices reflect values accurately. The effect on the allocation of resources in the case of IPOs is immediate. For stocks that are traded in the secondary market, the effect may be important even though the firms raise funds in the markets relatively infrequently. In this view the primary purpose of corporate financial policy is to determine the extent to which firms can rely exclusively on their perception of η_i. There remains the issue of how information is directly transferred; this is considered next.

3.2   *The direct transfer of information and the market for corporate control*

It was argued above that in competitive industries a consensus on η_T is reached over time through a transfer of information by various mechanisms. In non-competitive industries subject to technological change, the stock market ensures that only managers who have information that is sufficiently close to the consensus of the market will be allocated resources. Given the complexity of the information set η_T, the stock price allows relatively little of it to be deduced. Clearly, an important part of allocating resources efficiently in this type of situation will be to ensure that some type of information transfer takes place. No doubt a certain amount of transfer will occur directly. Analysts will discuss what they think of various actions a firm could take and the likely effectiveness of these. Some of these views will reach management and may affect their view of η_i.

Firms may also be willing to engage voluntarily in direct exchanges of information. Examples of this type of direct exchange are trade associations, cartels and research joint ventures. The literature on exchange of information through trade associations includes Novshek and Sonnenschein (1982), Clarke (1983), Vives (1984) and Gal-Or (1985). In the model of Novshek and Sonnenschein (1982), firms that have access to the same amount of private information are indifferent between revealing their information and not revealing it. In the papers of Clarke (1983) and Gal-Or (1985), sharing information is not optimal in equilibrium. Vives (1984), however, showed that, if goods are substitutes and there is Bertrand competition, or if goods are complements and there is Cournot competition, sharing information is optimal.

There is also a literature on the formation of cartels and the exchange of information, which includes Roberts (1985), Cramton and Palfrey (1990) and Kihlstrom and Vives (1989). Roberts (1985) considered a duopoly where costs could be high or low but were not publicly observable. He showed that, if firms are sufficiently similar, then information about costs will not be shared and collusion cannot be achieved unless there are sidepayments. Cramton and Palfrey (1990) generalize Roberts' analysis by considering a model with a continuum of firms and a finite number of types. They show that as the number of firms becomes large then, even if there are sidepayments, the exchange of information and the formation of a cartel will not occur. Kihlstrom and Vives (1989) consider a similar model to Cramton and Palfrey but with a continuum of firms and a finite number of types. In this case the adverse selection problem is less severe, information is exchanged and the monopoly outcome is enforceable.

Research joint ventures are another important way information is exchanged. Katz (1986) showed that firms have an incentive to share the costs and knowledge created by research projects. Bhattacharya, Glazer and Sappington (1990) analyse the optimal level of knowledge sharing and show how this can be implemented.

In addition to these methods for direct voluntary exchange of information there is another important mechanism for the direct transfer of information, namely the market for corporate control. Manne (1965) has argued that an important element of market economies is the ability of different management teams to compete for the control of assets. There are essentially three mechanisms for transferring control:

(i)   proxy fights;
(ii) direct purchase of shares;
(iii) mergers.

These three mechanisms can be interpreted in terms of the framework suggested above. Suppose there is a raider R whose information set η_R is such that the optimal set of actions $a_R{}^*$ is different from that pursued by the current management $a_i{}^*$ and

$$V(a_R{}^*, \eta_R) > MV, \tag{4}$$

where MV is the market value of the firm. How can the raider take advantage of this apparent opportunity?

One possibility is a proxy fight. In this case, in order to persuade the shareholders to vote with the raider so that the optimal policies $a_R{}^*$ can be implemented, it is necessary to transfer η_R to them and convince them it is better than their own information set. Unless the current management of the firm is adopting policies that are clearly suboptimal, this will be difficult. As argued above, transferring an information set can be exceedingly complex. Even if there is agreement about the data gathered, differences in education may mean interpretations of the data differ, which will make it necessary to share information about educational processes to obtain consensus. If there are a large number of shareholders it is likely that it will be impractical in most cases to engage successfully in a proxy fight. This is consistent with the evidence that proxy fights are in fact relatively rare.

A second possibility is a tender offer. Here there is no need to persuade the shareholders directly; a large enough offer will induce them to sell. In determining the amount that must be paid, it is the information set of the median holder η_M conditional on the offer that is important. The size of the offer the raider R will need to make will depend on

$$\text{Max}\{V(a_i{}^*,\eta_M),\ V(a_R{}^*,\eta_M)\}. \tag{5}$$

Shareholders will update their beliefs in response to the raider's offer. As before, however, given significant differences in information arising from differences in education and background, they may not update very much on the basis of this single piece of information. In this case the holdout problem identified by Grossman and Hart (1980) does not necessarily arise. Suppose $V(a_i{}^*,\eta_M) > V(a_R{}^*,\eta_M)$, so the median shareholder thinks the value of the firm will go down when the raider gets control. They will require only their reservation value $V(a_i{}^*,\eta_M)$ in order to be willing to sell. There will be a holdout problem only if $V(a_R{}^*,\eta_M) \geq V(a_i{}^*,\eta_M)$ so the median holder has similar views to the raider. In this case the raider will need to pay the full price unless there are possibilities for dilution as in Grossman and Hart (1980). Takeovers will therefore be most profitable from the perspective of the raider if the raider's views are different from those of the shareholders. It is therefore desirable that there be as little transfer of information as possible before the takeover occurs.

The third type of mechanism for transferring control is a merger. If the merger occurs after a tender offer then it is the tender offer that is the mechanism for transferring control. Hence the case of interest is where the merger is agreed to by both firms and there is no tender offer. In the framework here, one of the advantages of mergers can be the sharing of information about the effects of management actions. When η is very complex, a merger may be the most effective way of sharing information and obtaining a superior information set on average.

3.3   Discussion

This section has suggested that one of the main roles of the stock market is to provide a way of checking that firms are well run when there are divergences of opinion on how firms should be run. Where a firm is publicly quoted there is a built-in incentive for investors to assess what the management is doing. Thus firms where the managers obtain a 'bad draw' are likely to be identified. The stock price comes to reflect the views of a wide range of different investors and hence is likely to be representative of the true value of the firm.

Even when the firm is not continually raising capital in the market but is financing its investments through retained earnings, a stock market quotation is still important. It ensures continuous checking. Firms where the managers get a long way out of line with the consensus in the market will eventually be forced to relinquish control either because they cannot raise the necessary capital or because of a takeover attempt.

One important implication of the analysis above is that stock market quotation may be preferred to individual or family ownership. Although the incentive effects of private ownership are preferable to stock market ownership, the checking function associated with listing may allow a better allocation of resources overall.

4   Banks versus stock markets

In Diamond's (1984) theory of banks as delegated monitors, information about the management of the firm needs to be collected to ensure that they do not take suboptimal actions. If the equity of the firm is owned by many shareholders, none of them has the correct incentives to monitor the firm. They could combine to hire somebody to do this but that person would effectively be another manager. The essential problem is who monitors the monitor. Diamond points out that, if a bank undertakes to monitor a number of firms, it can diversify the unique risk associated with each. By promising a certain return to its depositors, it can guarantee that it is undertaking the cost of monitoring the firms; if it did not, it would be unable to pay the promised return. This theory relies on the assumption that there is a consensus on the way the firm should be run and the probability distribution of returns on loans. If there was disagreement on the expected return on loans, depositors would not be able to evaluate properly whether or not the bank had done the required monitoring.

When there is no consensus on the way in which firms should be run, as in the previous section, banks may not be as effective in allocating financial resources as stock markets. When banks evaluate loans to companies, they will produce an estimate of η in order to value the firm. They thus provide a check on the manager's estimate. The problem is that there is only one check. In situations where there are diverse views on η this does not permit much of a consensus to be reached.

Implicit in this argument is the notion that the bank cannot simply hire more people and produce an information set that is equivalent to the stock market. In order to negotiate a loan individually with a borrower it would be necessary to aggregate the information. Ultimately there would be a loan officer in charge of the negotiation and his or her biases will affect the weights given and determine η_i. The subjective nature and complexity of the information that forms the basis of the negotiation cannot be aggregated simply. Of course, the bank could exactly replicate a stock market but, if there are any fixed costs, setting up an actual market would dominate this strategy.

A criticism of Diamond's theory made by Hellwig (1990) is that it predicts that firms will transact with only one bank, but in practice this is not usually the case. If there are differences in information sets, an increase in the number of banks the firm deals with may be advantageous for all. The problems associated with coordinating negotiations that are likely to occur as the number of banks increases, however, mean that it will usually be worth only a few banks lending.

In summary, the essential difference between Diamond's theory and that suggested here is that multiple opinions are valuable. Banks do not give repeated evaluations in the same way that stock markets do and may be an inefficient way of allocating resources when there are large differences in views on production functions.

The two theories can thus be combined to explain why in some circumstances banks will be the optimal way of allocating resources and in others stock markets will be. Banks will be a good way to provide financing in traditional industries such as agriculture where the technology is well known and there is a wide consensus on how things should be done. Here the bank can monitor firms effectively and take advantage of the scale economies in monitoring. In industries where there is little consensus on how the firms should be managed, an allocation of resources through a stock market is desirable. The theory predicts that stock market quotations will be observed among large corporations and in industries where there is continuous technological advance. Countries that will have a significant stock market will be those with a significant amount of technological innovation in the sense of developing entirely new industries and those with industries with a significant amount of concentration.

It was the UK that first underwent the Industrial Revolution in the nineteenth century with the development of the railways and other new industries, which were to a large extent financed through the London Stock Exchange. Similarly, in the US the New York Stock Exchange played a critical role in the development of the major twentieth-century industries such as the automobile, aircraft, electronics and computer industries. Among current emerging industries such as biotechnology, stock markets are again major sources of finance.

In nineteenth-century Germany, in contrast, industrial development took place when the technologies were not as new and untried as in the UK. Similarly, in the twentieth century Japan's most important achievements have mainly been in existing industries rather than in entirely new ones. In both these cases, the factors that favour stock market finance are less prevalent and those that favour bank finance are more prevalent than in the US and the UK.

5   The stock market and government ownership

During the early part of the twentieth century there was an important debate among economists about whether or not planned socialist economies where the means of production were owned by the state could allocate resources efficiently. Lange and Lerner argued that there was no reason why such an economy could not achieve the same allocation of resources as a capitalist economy. This debate took as its starting point the traditional classical model discussed in section 2 above, where it was essentially assumed that there is a consensus on production functions. Thus, for example, Lange (1938/1971, p. 34) argued: 'The administrators of a Socialist economy will have exactly the same knowledge, or lack of knowledge, of the production functions as the Capitalist entrepreneurs have.'

The defence of capitalism conducted by Robbins and von Hayek among others took the traditional framework of analysis as given. They argued that the practical difficulty of calculating the necessary prices would be the main problem with socialist systems. For example, Robbins (1934) argued that:

> On paper we can conceive this problem to be solved by a series of mathematical calculations ... But in practice this solution is quite unworkable. It would necessitate the drawing up of millions of equations on the basis of millions of statistical data based on many more millions of individual computations. By the time the equations were solved, the information on which they were based would have become obsolete and they would need to be calculated anew. The suggestion that a practical solution of the problem of planning is possible on the basis of the Paretian equations simply indicates that those who put it forward have not grasped what these equations mean.
>
> (Quoted by Lange, 1938/1971, p. 36)

These arguments by and large followed the classical tradition of ignoring the stock market, and it was assigned no special role in the debate. There was very little discussion of the basic assumptions of the static model. The question of private versus state ownership is not really very important in this framework. Since the technology is known, managers employed by the state can run firms as efficiently as managers employed by stockholders. Although most countries did not go as far as the Soviet bloc in terms of central planning, state ownership became a central plank of many socialist parties. After the Second World War many of these parties attained power and large sectors of industry were nationalized. For example, in the UK the railways and the coal and steel industries were acquired by post-war Labour governments. Many third world countries such as India were also heavily influenced by Lange and Lerner's ideas and large sectors of industry came under state control.

The theory presented in sections 3 and 4 suggests that public ownership will be inefficient because there is only one group that tries to estimate the relationship between firms' actions and outcomes. There is no checking by replication except that undertaken by the ministries in charge of the industries and politicians. There is no automatic incentive for doing this, in the way that there is in a stock market economy. If managers have inaccurate information, their misperceptions can persist almost indefinitely. State-owned industries thus provide a stark contrast to those where the firms are listed on stock exchanges.

In many countries natural monopolies are directly owned by the state. Traditional theory has very little to say in terms of the efficacy of this compared with having a company that is owned by shareholders and regulated by the government. The theory of section 3 suggests that there is an important difference. With government ownership there is again no checking, but with private ownership stock market investors will constantly evaluate what the management of the firm is doing. It is interesting to note in this regard that many of the early listings on exchanges were monopolies. For example, in the UK the first joint stock companies were trading monopolies such as the East India Company and other monopolies such as those providing water supplies. More recently in the US, regulated utilities comprise a large proportion of listed stocks. Of course, it is important to stress here that the desirability of ownership of natural monopolies will depend on the effectiveness of the government regulation; the disadvantages of this may offset the advantages associated with stock market listings.

6   Concluding remarks

Divergence of opinions about how firms should be run is an important feature of many industries. Standard theories do not incorporate this factor in a satisfactory way. This paper has argued that stock markets can play an important role in industrialized economies when there is disagreement about production functions. Stock markets work relatively well when there is little consensus on how a firm should be run since they provide checks that the manager's view of the production function is a sensible one. They therefore work best in industries which are not very competitive or where there is a long period before the results of actions become apparent or where technology is constantly changing. The theory is thus consistent with the observation that the stock market was important in the UK during the nineteenth century when it was the first country to go through the Industrial Revolution. It is also consistent with the fact that the US has relied heavily on stock markets in the twentieth century when it was the first country to go through the post-Industrial Revolution. In contrast, it has been argued that banks are desirable institutions for allocating resources in situations where there is a consensus on the technology and the main problem is monitoring firms.

These conclusions have a number of implications for the development of financial institutions in Europe. For the advanced economies of Western Europe the implication is that active stock markets are important if developing new industries where there is no consensus on technology are desired. Banks are clearly also very important, however, and will remain so in the foreseeable future. The countries of Eastern Europe, on the other hand, face a different problem. They will be building basic industries where the technology is well known for some time to come. This indicates that they should concentrate on developing bank-based financial systems. Stock markets should be given relatively little emphasis for a number of years.

In most countries, stock markets and banks are only one way in which funds for industry are raised. Self-financed owner-managed firms and informal networks are also crucial. It is important that in Western Europe these methods of finance be maintained and that in Eastern Europe these channels be actively encouraged and developed.

This paper has focused on the provision of funds for industry. Another important role of stock markets is the provision of funds for governments. To the extent that this role is important, stock markets oriented to public finance should be developed.

NOTES

I am grateful to my discussants Sudipto Bhattacharya, Jean-Charles Rochet and Anjan Thakor, the editors Colin Mayer and Xavier Vives, participants at the conference, Marc Debroeck, Richard Stehle and other members of the Finance Lunch Group at Wharton, Douglas Gale, Michel Habib, Stephen Morris and particularly Gary Gorton (who presented the paper at the conference) for helpful comments and suggestions. Financial support from the NSF is gratefully acknowledged.

1 See Michie (1987), p. 110.
2 See Soule (1935), pp. 5–6.
3 In Allen (1990), analysts are provided with the correct incentives to reveal their information truthfully. This may not always be possible in practice. In such cases analysts may be compared with their peers. As a result they may tend to 'herd' together and there will be an insufficient diversity of views relative to the truth. It is an empirical issue as to which is the correct description of information gathering in stock markets.
4 See Smith (1986) for a summary of the empirical evidence on underpricing.

REFERENCES

Admati, A. and P. Pfleiderer (1986) 'A monopolistic market for information', *Journal of Economic Theory* **39**, 400–38.

(1990) 'Direct and indirect sale of information', *Econometrica* **58**, 901–28.

Allen, F. (1990) 'The market for information and the origin of financial intermediation', *Journal of Financial Intermediation* **1**, 3–30.

Allen, F. and G. Faulhaber (1989) 'Signaling by underpricing in the IPO market', *Journal of Financial Economics* **23**, 303–23.

Aumann, R. (1976) 'Agreeing to disagree', *The Annals of Statistics* **4**, 1236–9.

Berkovitch, E. and S. Greenbaum (1990) 'The loan commitment as an optimal financing contract', *Journal of Financial and Quantitative Analysis* **26**, 83–95.

Bhattacharya, S. and A. Thakor (1992) 'Contemporary banking theory', Discussion Paper No. 504, Graduate School of Business, Indiana University.

Bhattacharya, S., J. Glazer and D. Sappington (1990) 'Sharing productive knowledge in internally financed R & D contests', *Journal of Industrial Economics* **39**, 187–208.

Boot, A., A. Thakor and G. Udell (1987) 'Competition, risk neutrality and loan commitments', *Journal of Banking and Finance* **11**, 449–71.

(1991) 'Off-balance sheet liabilities, deposit insurance and capital regulation', *Journal of Banking and Finance* **15**, 825–46.

Clarke, R. (1983) 'Collusion and incentives for information sharing', *Bell Journal of Economics* **14**, 383–94.

Cramton, P. and T. Palfrey (1990) 'Cartel enforcement with uncertainty about costs', *International Economic Review* **31**, 17–47.

Diamond, D. (1984) 'Financial intermediation and delegated monitoring', *Review of Economic Studies* **51**, 393–414.

Diamond, D. and R. Verrecchia (1981) 'Information aggregation in a noisy rational expectations model', *Journal of Financial Economics* **9**, 221–35.

(1982) 'Optimal managerial contracts and equilibrium security prices', *Journal of Finance* **37**, 275–87.

Diamond, P. (1967) 'The role of a stock market in a general equilibrium model with technological uncertainty', *American Economic Review* **57**, 759–66.

Frankel, A. and J. Montgomery (1991) 'Financial structure: an international perspective', *Brookings Papers on Economic Activity*, 257–310.

Gal-Or, E. (1985) 'Information sharing in oligopoly', *Econometrica* **53**, 329–43.

Geanokoplos, J. and H. Polemarchakis (1982) 'We can't disagree forever', *Journal of Economic Theory* **28**, 192–200.

Grinblatt, M. and C. Hwang (1989) 'Signalling and the pricing of unseasoned new issues', *Journal of Finance* **44**, 393–420.

Grossman, S. (1976) 'On the efficiency of competitive stock markets where traders have diverse information', *Journal of Finance* **31**, 573–85.

(1978) 'Further results on the informational efficiency of competitive stock markets', *Journal of Economic Theory* **18**, 81–101.

Grossman, S. and O. Hart (1980) 'Takeover bids, the free-rider problem, and the theory of the corporation', *Bell Journal of Economics* **11**, 42–64.

Grossman, S. and J. Stiglitz (1980) 'On the impossibility of informationally efficient markets', *American Economic Review* **70**, 393–408.

Hellwig, M. (1990) 'Banking, financial intermediation and corporate finance', in

A. Giovannini and C. Mayer (eds.), *European Financial Integration*, Cambridge: Cambridge University Press.

Holmstrom, B. and J. Tirole (1990) 'Corporate control and the monitoring role of the stock market', Working Paper Series D, No. 48, Yale School of Organization and Management.

Ibbotson, R. (1976) 'Price performance of common stock new issues', *Journal of Financial Economics* **2**, 235–72.

Jegadeesh, N., M. Weinstein and I. Welch (1991) 'An empirical investigation of IPO underpricing and subsequent equity offerings', Working Paper, UCLA.

Jensen, M. (1986) 'Agency costs of free cash flow, corporate finance, and takeovers', *American Economic Review* **76**, 323–9.

Katz, M. (1986) 'An analysis of cooperative research and development', *Rand Journal of Economics* **17**, 527–43.

Kihlstrom, R. and X. Vives (1989) 'Collusion by asymmetrically informed firms', Working Paper, University of Pennsylvania, forthcoming in *Journal of Economics and Management Strategy*.

Lange, O. (1938) 'On the economic theory of socialism'; in H. Townsend (ed.), *Price Theory*, London: Penguin, 1971, pp. 32–56.

McKelvey, R. and T. Page (1986) 'Common knowledge, consensus, and aggregate information', *Econometrica* **54**, 109–27.

Manne, H. (1965) 'Mergers and the market for corporate control', *Journal of Political Economy* **73**, 110–20.

Mayer, C. (1988) 'New issues in corporate finance', *European Economic Review* **32**, 1167–88.

Michaely, R. and W. Shaw (1992) 'Asymmetric information, adverse selection, and the pricing of initial public offerings', Working Paper, Cornell University.

Michie, R. (1987) *The London and New York Stock Exchanges 1850–1914*, London: Allen & Unwin.

Neill, H. (1950) *Inside Story of the New York Stock Exchange*, New York: B.C. Forbes and Sons.

Nelson's Directory of Investment Research 1992, New York: Nelson Publications.

Novshek, W. and H. Sonnenschein (1982) 'Fulfilled expectations Cournot duopoly with information acquisition and release', *Bell Journal of Economics* **13**, 214–18.

Robbins, L. (1934) *The Great Depression*, London: Macmillan.

Roberts, K. (1985) 'Cartel behavior and adverse selection', *Journal of Industrial Economics* **33**, 33–45.

Rock, K. (1986) 'Why new issues are underpriced', *Journal of Financial Economics* **15**, 187–212.

Sah, R. and J. Stiglitz (1985) 'Human fallibility and economic organization', *American Economic Review* **75**, 292–7.

 (1986) 'The architecture of economic systems: hierarchies and polyarchies', *American Economic Review* **76**, 716–27.

Sharpe, S. (1990) 'Asymmetric information, bank lending, and implicit contracts: a stylized model of customer relationships', *Journal of Finance* **45**, 1069–88.

Shleifer, A. and L. Summers (1988) 'Breach of trust in hostile takeovers', in A. Auerbach (ed.), *Mergers and Acquisitions*, NBER, University of Chicago Press.

Smith, C. (1986) 'Investment banking and the capital acquisition process', *Journal of Financial Economics* **15**, 3–29.

Soule, G. (1935) 'The stock exchange in economic theory', *The Security Markets*, 3–18, New York: Twentieth Century Fund.

Vives, X. (1984) 'Duopoly information equilibrium: Cournot and Bertrand', *Journal of Economic Theory* **34**, 71–94.

Welch, I. (1989) 'Seasoned offerings, imitation costs and the underpricing of initial public offerings', *Journal of Finance* **44**, 421–49.

Wilson, P. (1991) 'Public ownership, delegated project selection and corporate financial policy', Working Paper, Indiana University.

Discussion

SUDIPTO BHATTACHARYA

The literature on applications of information economics to the problems of financial contracting and markets has almost come of age. Beginning with the seminal paper of Green (1973) on Rational Expectations equilibria with *a priori* heterogeneous information, and Rothschild and Stiglitz (1976) on adverse selection in insurance markets, this literature has progressed to provide us with analyses of phenomena such as: endogenous collection of information and its reflection in stock market prices (Grossman and Stiglitz, 1980), signalling with financial policy and disclosure choices (Bhattacharya, 1979; Bhattacharya and Ritter, 1983) by firms, the role of financial intermediation in efficient gathering and utilization of information about investment prospects (Leland and Pyle, 1977; Diamond, 1984), and the function of financial structure in dealing with various agency problems. As a result of these exciting developments, there exists the possibility today of building new approaches to the theories of alternative or complementary institutional structures and (comparative) economic systems in intertemporal settings, in order to examine the roles that these institutional mechanisms may play in attaining allocational efficiency and (perhaps) distributional objectives.

The essence of Franklin Allen's discursive and suggestive paper, as well as that of several other recent papers – such as those of Sharpe (1990), von Thadden (1990), and Dewatripont and Maskin (1990) – is to look at scenarios that go beyond environments in which direct, unduplicated, prudential monitoring of investment projects/firms by efficiently diversified intermediaries (Diamond, 1984) is sufficient to obtain (first-best) allocational efficiency. Papers such as Sharpe (1990) or von Thadden

(1990) focus on learning over time by lending banks about borrowers in ongoing business relationships, either about interim *ex post* cash flows (Sharpe) or about *ex post* trade-offs between long-term versus short-term investment strategies (von Thadden). In both these models, the informational advantage attained by incumbent bank lenders gives rise to the possibility of opportunistic interim rate-raising on their part, which may thwart the (inappropriate extent of) adoption of the more efficient (long-term) investment strategy by borrowers.

Partial remedies to this problem include:

(1)   reputational rents for banks which they stand to lose if such opportunistic behaviour is detected; or
(2)   multiple lending/monitoring banks for each borrower, in order to eliminate the lender's interim informational monopoly, to maintain competitive financing terms.

The second solution is an answer to Hellwig's (1990) observation that most borrowers in the 'Franco-German–Japanese' intermediated financing systems have multiple bank creditors, in contrast to the conclusion of the simple prudential monitoring story of Diamond (1984). The first solution, on the other hand, needs further explicit analysis, in the light of the problems of attaining the analogues of single-market (Walrasian or reputational) equilibrium outcomes with strategic (Bertrand) competition among competing intermediaries in interlinked markets for projects/firms and deposits in finitely elastic supply; see Bhattacharya (1982) and Yanelle (1989). These analyses also suggest that governmental policies, such as restrictions on deposit interest rates, could be relevant in shoring up the efficient institutional mechanisms for investment allocation.

In Allen's paper, the desirability of multiple information gatherers/monitors for investment projects/firms is ascribed to a different set of factors. Allen argues that, in many sectors of modern industrial economies, (a) the number of firms is small owing to increasing returns, (b) production functions are evolving owing to technological change, and (c) agreement on these across firms is absent owing to the lack of sufficient numbers of (statistically stable) replicated observations on actions and their consequences. In such situations, he argues, outside investors/researchers may well have information that firms do not have, and the *aggregation* of such information through prices, as with a stock market, may be extremely important, at least in pointing out to managers the aggregated 'consensus' on the valuation consequences of their existing operating policies.

In less coherently developed corollary observations, Allen appears to suggest that the likely persistence of informational asymmetries or disagreements among investors, in the type of environments he focuses on, may allow easier functioning of takeover bids by investors' coalitions aiming at better (value-enhancing) operating policies, because 'free-rider problems' of the Grossman and Hart (1980) variety among small shareholders may not matter. He does not, however, deal satisfactorily with the revision of their beliefs about the valuational consequences/possibilities of alternative policies that small shareholders may undergo when faced with a higher bid price than current stock market prices. Nor does he examine simple alternatives such as two-part bids (for controlling against other shares) by takeover bidders. On the other hand, he suggests an advantage for intermediated financing mechanisms in these environments by noting that short-run, opportunistic behaviour by controlling shareholders towards other coalitions that have incurred firm-specific investments (such as workers) may be less likely with reputations built up by such financial institutions, in contrast to corporate raiders. Given that most corporate takeover bids are largely financed by intermediaries/ banks, however, and are not by and large made by 'unknowns', this point remains somewhat obscure and unpersuasive.

More pertinently, Allen's attempt to translate from observations about the (greater) desirability of multiple external information monitors in some economic environments to answers to questions about the relative performances of different institutional mechanisms for financing in different economic environments is not particularly successful, on either theoretical or empirical grounds. He is rather vague on why information aggregation about borrowers within a lending bank needs necessarily to boil down to opinions/biases of a single loan officer. Nor does he convince us that realistic multi-bank lending coalitions in modern industrial economies in effect generate any lesser degree of economic information pertinent to technology and demand than would the efficient scale of functioning by multiple stock market analysts. Thus, although Allen is careful to note that, in the type of environment he outlines, the relatively static, conventional Rational Expectations equilibrium notion probably needs modification to incorporate equilibria with multiple, and competing, information sellers who are *not* negligible in their (derived) impact on market prices, he does not achieve a successful comparison between such institutional mechanisms and a financing system with multiple (informed) intermediaries for each borrower, each of which efficiently diversifies idiosyncratic risk across many borrowers (see also Bhattacharya and Pfeiderer, 1985).

On the empirical side, Allen's anecdotal evidence and suggestive advice are contradictory in many respects. For example, if information aggregation is unimportant in relatively static, established industries, such as agriculture, then why are commodity futures markets so prevalent in modern capitalist economies (to aggregate diverse information about demand, presumably)? Similarly, if it is the case that Germany and Japan adopted predominantly intermediary- (rather than market-) oriented financing systems because they achieved large-scale industrialization at a later stage of the evolution of technology, then why is it that, within the USA, utilities with more established technologies adopt financial policies that necessitate far more frequent returns to (and scrutiny in) publicly traded stock (and bond) markets, compared with firms like IBM where fast-changing computer technology and the role of R&D are of far greater importance, as Allen himself notes?

A lesson of Allen's paper is that one must be careful in making the transition from 'micro-micro' models within alternative institutional paradigms to theories of the functioning of alternative institutional set-ups in the financing of investments. A case in point is the recent paper of Dewatripont and Maskin (1990), who build on an analysis of the type of von Thadden (1990) to suggest the following contrast between 'Franco-German–Japanese' (dominantly intermediary-oriented with continuing relationships) and 'Anglo-Saxon' (dominantly financed by sequences of decentralized investors) modes of financing. They observe that, in the intermediated institutional set-up, learning in ongoing relationships may mitigate any bias toward short-term investment strategies to signal good prospects to the uninformed, decentralized investors of the market-based set-up. On the other hand, intermediated systems with informational advantage for extant lenders may lead to failing long-term investment strategies being continued for too long, in the hope of recouping unpaid debt from past periods. The whole analysis of Dewatripont and Maskin ignores the possibility, emphasized in Allen's paper, that analysts and/or information sellers in stock markets may be just as important as are intermediaries in gathering, aggregating and disseminating information about firms to decentralized stock market investors.

All of this brings us to the topic of suggestions for additional research on this important topic of the alternative/complementary roles of different financing arrangements, some aspects of which necessarily belong to the realm of somewhat speculative conjecture. In making these suggestions, we need to recognize that a sound theory of comparative financial economic systems must, as Allen emphasizes, incorporate technologically dynamic environments with increasing returns and oligopolistic product market structure, and it should at least allow us to examine the relative advantages of three dominant modes of 'Anglo-Saxon', 'Franco-German–Japanese' and 'market socialist' patterns of organizing investment and its financing from primary sources of savings.

A major issue in technologically dynamic environments in which R&D

and new knowledge are important is that of knowledge *spillover*, namely that information that is revealed (for pricing) to financing sources may also reach firms that are competitors in R & D/product market 'contests', and hence the private value of such information to its generator may be diminished. On the other hand, there may be social gains from such spillover in speeding up overall innovative activity in the economy, and, with repetition of innovations, such social gains may come to be reflected in privately chosen institutional mechanisms for (the dominant component of) external financing, above and beyond the empirically very important element of retained earnings. In two papers (Bhattacharya and Ritter, 1983, and Bhattacharya, Glazer and Sappington, 1992), my co-authors and I have examined financial market and efficient contractual arrangement resolutions in such 'proprietary information' environments, under contrasting assumptions about the feasibility of writing licensing contracts for disclosed knowledge or 'intellectual property'. An extension of this line of work to examine private versus social benefits under stock market versus diversified intermediary modes of financing, with the latter perhaps resulting in less spillover to competing firms, could prove to be very helpful in answering some of the questions that Allen's paper suggests, and in distinguishing the comparative advantages of 'Anglo-Saxon' versus 'Franco-German–Japanese' modes of financing. Bhattacharya (1992) takes a step in this direction.

Second, understanding stock market versus other modes of financing is likely to require a major improvement in our understanding of equilibrium theory, in decentralized markets and in small-numbers bargaining environments. With items of technological information (rather than scalar and easily aggregatable information about, say, demand shocks) being predominant, and these being complex enough to be understood *a priori* by a small number of analysts in any sector, the aggregation of such information into market prices (which are partially revealing of it) is likely to require a major reworking of Rational Expectations equilibrium theory. Similarly, with the alternative of a small-number-of-lenders intermediated mode of financing, our understanding of the problems of coordination and delays in bargaining over the terms of financing in common-value environments, when each lender (and borrower) may have different and complementary technological information, needs to be significantly enhanced.

Third, to augment our understanding of key differences between 'Franco-German–Japanese' versus 'market socialist' modes of investment financing, we need perhaps to extend extant theories of information processing in decision-making hierarchies versus polyarchies (Sah and Stiglitz, 1985) to related models of the efficiencies of information aggregation in these contrasting organizational set-ups, with different degrees of ease of communication (and incentives for doing so) among originators and processors of information in 'organizations' that involve competitive versus bureaucratic interactions among their constituent members.

NOTE

This discussion was written while I was a visiting scholar at the Institut d'Anàlisi Econòmica, Universitat Autónoma de Barcelona, under the Sabbatical Programme of the Spanish Ministry of Education. I am grateful to the Ministry and the Institute, and to CEPR and Fundacion BBV, which organized the San Sebastian conference, for financial support and gracious hospitality.

ADDITIONAL REFERENCES

Bhattacharya, S. (1979) 'Imperfect information, dividend policy, and the "bird in the hand" fallacy', *Bell Journal of Economic Studies*, Spring.

(1982) 'Aspects of monetary and banking theory and moral hazard', *Journal of Finance* (Papers and Proceedings), May.

(1992) 'Financial intermediation with proprietary information', Paper presented at the European Summer Symposium on Economic Theory, Gerzensee, Switzerland, July.

Bhattacharya, S., J. Glazer and D. Sappington (1992) 'Licensing and the sharing of knowledge in research joint ventures', *Journal of Economic Theory*, February.

Bhattacharya, S. and P. Pfeiderer (1985) 'Delegated portfolio management', *Journal of Economic Theory*, June.

Bhattacharya, S. and B. Ritter (1983) 'Innovation and communication: signaling with partial disclosure', *Review of Economic Studies*, April.

Dewatripont, M. and E. Maskin (1990) 'Credit and efficiency in centralized and decentralized economies', Harvard University working paper.

Green, J. (1973) 'Information, efficiency and equilibrium', Harvard University working paper.

Leland, H. and D. Pyle (1977) 'Informational asymmetries, financial structure and financial intermediation', *Journal of Finance* (Papers and Proceedings), May.

Rothschild, M. and J.E. Stiglitz (1976) 'Equilibrium in competitive insurance markets', *Quarterly Journal of Economics*, November.

Von Thadden, E.-L. (1990) 'Bank finance and long-term investment', University of Basel working paper.

Yanelle, M.-O. (1989) 'The strategic analysis of intermediation', *European Economic Review* 33 294–304.

ANJAN V. THAKOR

This paper by Franklin Allen is an essay on *comparative financial systems*. The question posed cuts to the very heart of how capital should be allocated in the economy: should the emphasis be on the stock market or on banks and other depository intermediaries? In light of the impending transition of so many former Communist bloc countries in Eastern Europe to market-based economic systems, this question is timely and important. It is also important for developed capitalist economies like the US, as I will argue later.

The answer to the question posed in this paper is novel. The stock market is viewed as a mechanism for aggregating many diverse opinions and hence providing information about optimal decision rules in corporations that is superior to that attainable through bank borrowing; the bank provides a 'single check' as opposed to the 'multiple checks' of the stock market. It follows from this that the stock market will be the preferred institution for capital allocation when optimal decision rules are hard to formulate; for instance, when information decays rapidly and new information arrives almost constantly. Examples are firms in highly competitive industries with constantly changing market conditions, or firms in industries where technology evolves at a fast pace.

While this idea is provocative and new, the question itself has been posed previously in a variety of different contexts. This is recognized in the paper and there is a good discussion of where the paper fits in the overall literature. The main message emerging from previous research on the choice between bank loans and capital market financing appears to be as follows. Bank financing is likely to be preferred when asset substitution moral hazard is great and borrowers do not have sufficient credit reputation, so that bank monitoring is valuable (Diamond, 1989, and Rajan, 1991), when long-term financing commitments that banks can make are effective in attenuating underinvestment (Berkovitch and Greenbaum, 1990) and other forms of moral hazard (Boot, Thakor and Udell, 1991), and when contract renegotiation is likely so that the flexibility offered by bank financing is of value (Berlin and Mester, 1992). On the other hand, capital market financing is preferred when *intrafirm* incentive problems are severe for the borrowing firm (Wilson, 1991), and when banks are likely to develop monopoly power that could distort allocations (Rajan, 1991, and Sharpe, 1990).

Allen provides a perspective that seems consistent with all but one of these theories. Since renegotiation is likely to be important when significant new information arrival is possible after the contract has been signed, Berlin and Mester (1992) suggest that bank financing is likely to be preferred when the informational environment is volatile. This appears to be in contrast with the conclusion of the present paper.

It is useful to note, however, that these two papers focus on two distinct aspects of the choice of financing source. It may well be that, in informationally volatile settings, the choice of financing source depends critically on the *tension* between the value of renegotiation flexibility with a bank loan and the value of the information aggregation provided by the stock market.

Another issue pertinent to the choice is corporate governance. The paper views control contests in the stock market as valuable information-generating devices. Of course, the financing source also impinges quite directly on corporate governance. If banks are allowed to hold stock in the companies they provide financing to, then we can expect potentially significant bank representation on the boards of directors of non-financial corporations. This, in turn, could improve corporate governance in these companies. It has been pointed out that many of today's abuses in large corporations are attributable to a failure of the corporate governance process, and that this failure can be traced in part to the passive nature of institutional investors' ownership behaviour. Thus, there is reason to believe that the stock market may not be highly efficient in inducing corporate managers to behave in their shareholders' best interests. A bank, sitting on the borrower's board as a shareholder, may be able to provide monitoring that would be of value to *all* shareholders.

When this observation is combined with the insight in Allen's paper, we see a role for the *simultaneous* existence of bank financing and capital market financing. Shareholders would like their managers to access the capital market to obtain valuable information signals that can guide their decisions. And they would like them to obtain capital from banks so that, once the information necessary for good decisions has been acquired, managers will indeed make good decisions.

I very much enjoyed reading Allen's paper. It provides interesting new insights and tantalizes the reader with the promise of a plethora of additional insights that could result from formally tackling some of the issues taken up in the paper. In particular, an interesting question in the context of the US banking system is the extent to which deregulation should reduce the current emphasis on banks in the capital allocation process. Since the information environment in the US has admittedly become more volatile, Allen's paper seems to suggest that the diminishing role of banks – as manifested in both the growth in commercial paper issues and the upsurge in securitization – may well be part of the natural process of evolution to a superior capital allocation system.

REFERENCES

Berkovitch, E. and I. Greenbaum (1990) 'The loan commitment as an optimal financing contract', *Journal of Financial and Quantitative Analysis* **26** (March) 83–95.

Berlin, M. and L. Mester (1992) 'Debt covenants and renegotiation', forthcoming in *Journal of Financial Intermediation*.

Boot, A.W.A., V. Thakor and G.F. Udell (1991) 'Credible commitments, contract enforcement problems and banks: intermediation as credibility assurance', *Journal of Banking and Finance* **15** (June), 605–32.

Diamond, D.W. (1989) 'Monitoring and reputation: the choice between bank loans and directly placed debt', mimeo, University of Chicago.

Rajan, R. (1991) 'Insiders and outsiders: the choice between relationship and armslength debt', CRSP working paper, University of Chicago.

Sharpe, S.A. (1990) 'Asymmetric information, bank lending, and implicit contracts: a stylized model of customer relationships', *Journal of Finance* **45** (September), 1069–87.

Wilson, P. (1991) 'Public ownership, delegated project selection and corporate financial policy', Working Paper, Indiana University.

5 Informational capacity and financial collapse

DOUGLAS GALE

1 Introduction

The starting point for the work reported in this paper is the observation that banks are information-gathering and information-processing institutions. When a bank makes a loan, it investigates the borrowing firm's assets and business plan. It later acquires information in the course of handling the firm's accounts and conducting routine banking transactions. It observes the firm's repayment history. All of this information is proprietary and may be excluded from the public domain. When a bank fails, this information may be lost. Records may be destroyed or falsified and they may be hard to interpret when key personnel leave. One important consequence of bank failures may be the loss of information: borrowers with good credit histories may be forced to seek new sources of finance without the benefit of the information that has been accumulated over the years.

Even without a bank failure, there may be separations that lead to a similar type of information loss. When a bank decides to recall a loan, it may withdraw credit from good risks, forcing them to find new sources of credit on the open market. One reason for this apparently inefficient behaviour is an example of risk shifting. If the bank is in difficulties, it has an incentive to hold on to risky assets (loans) and liquidate safe assets, because it benefits from high returns and the depositors (or the deposit insurance system) bear the losses from low returns. Alternatively, the bank may decide not to recall a loan from a bad risk because it does not want to signal the fact that it has made bad loans, which it will certainly do if it forces the debtors into bankruptcy. So it has an incentive to call in the loan of a solvent firm. Another reason for calling in a loan from a good firm is simply that the bank cannot get cash from a firm that has none. If the object of the exercise is to get cash, the bank must go to solvent firms. For all these reasons, then, a bank may have incentives to recall loans from a firm that has made its repayments on time and has good prospects. Here again, we have a case where good credit risks may be forced to look for new sources of credit without the benefit of the information accumulated by the previous bank.

The US banking industry has recently experienced a large number of bank failures. In addition, loss of bank capital and pressure from regulators have led other banks to reduce lending in certain areas. As a result, there may be substantial numbers of good borrowers seeking credit who face a 'lemons' problem in trying to obtain credit. Some of the firms seeking credit may be good credit risks and know it, but others will be bad risks, who have been turned down for good reasons. In order to distinguish these different risks, banks have to engage in information gathering and processing. Of course, if the banking system has unlimited information-processing capacity, the loss of information may cause only a 'wealth effect'. But if, as seems more reasonable, there is some limit to the banking sector's capacity to gather and process information, any sudden increase in the number of firms seeking credit may strain the system's ability to deal with the informational demands on it.

In this paper, I want to explore the possibility that congestion of the information system may lead to market failure. The informational capacity constraint leads to rationing in the first instance, but the uncoordinated responses of the banks may amplify the impact of the initial shock, with the result that bank lending may collapse completely. The recent difficulty some potential borrowers have had obtaining credit in some regions of the US has led to speculation about the existence of a 'credit crunch' (see Green and Oh, 1991a).[1] Although the existence and nature of a 'credit crunch' are subject to much debate, it seems worth asking whether informational issues have anything to contribute to the understanding of these phenomena.

I begin with a standard model of a credit market.[2] There is a large number of entrepreneurs, each of whom is endowed with a risky project. There is a large (but finite) number of banks, each of whom has unlimited access to funds at the riskless rate of interest. Entrepreneurs and banks are risk neutral and maximize the expected value of their final wealth, measured in terms of money. Since the entrepreneurs have no resources of their own, they have to borrow from banks in order to finance their projects. Borrowing takes the form of standard debt contracts. The imperfection in this market takes the form of adverse selection. Some of the entrepreneurs have good projects and some have bad projects. Entrepreneurs know their types, but the banks do not.

Three essential features are added to this standard model. The first is the assumption that banks gather costly information. Formally, it is assumed that each bank has access to a costly screening technology that allows the bank to distinguish good projects from bad projects. This assumption is intended to capture the role of banks as information-gathering and information-processing institutions. In the standard model, by contrast, the banks infer an entrepreneur's type by observing their choice from the set of available loan contracts.

The second essential feature is that the banks' capacity to screen borrowers is limited. More precisely, it is assumed that each bank can screen a maximum of K borrowers per period.[3] Capacity constraints on banks arise quite naturally both on the deposit side and on the lending side, but it is the lending side that is relevant here. If we think of the bank as an information-gathering and information-processing institution, it is clear there is a limit to the amount of information that can be processed by a finite number of people in a finite amount of time. But we can also think of the capacity constraint as a way of capturing the possibility that mistakes are made when the volume of lending is high.

The third essential feature is the assumption that it is costly for borrowers to apply for loans.[4] More precisely, each borrower has a fixed cost of applying to any lender. These costs need not be large, but it turns out that they have a significant effect on the behaviour of the market.

Once the model is defined, it is used to investigate the possibility of coordination failure. We can show that there are multiple equilibria, some of which involve positive levels of lending and some of which involve the complete cessation of lending or 'financial collapse'.[5] Suppose that the screening technology is not perfect, so that, even if all applicants are screened, there is some possibility that a borrower with a bad project can slip through. Then, if all banks but one decide not to lend to borrowers in this market, it may not be optimal for the remaining bank to lend. The problem is that the entrepreneurs with bad projects have a greater incentive to apply than the entrepreneurs with good projects (because the former have higher variance and so benefit from the 'risk-shifting' effect). Whenever the good borrowers are (weakly) willing to apply, the bad borrowers are (strictly) willing to apply. To attract any of the good borrowers, it is necessary to attract all of the bad borrowers. In that case, the number of applicants is large, the capacity constraint is binding, and the screening probability is low. But if the probability of acceptance is too low, the good risks will not find it worthwhile to apply. Then it will not be profitable for the bank to screen or make loans either.

For the same parameter values, however, there can exist an equilibrium with positive lending. If all banks simultaneously decide to lend, there is enough informational capacity to absorb applications from the bad risks and, at the same time, offer the good risks a sufficiently high probability of screening and acceptance to encourage them to apply. And, if the pool of applicants contains enough good risks, it will be profitable for the banks to screen and offer loans to the successful applicants.

Mankiw (1986) has pointed out that a standard 'lemons' problem can lead to financial collapse. There is also a substantial literature on credit rationing arising from adverse selection (e.g. Stiglitz and Weiss, 1981) and moral hazard (Bester and Hellwig, 1987). The emphasis on multiple equilibria and coordination distinguishes the results in this paper from the work of Mankiw (1986) and Stiglitz and Weiss (1981). The role of induced changes in the pool of applicants suggests that similar results might not obtain if the market imperfection arose from moral hazard rather than adverse selection.

This possibility of coordination failure illustrates the potential importance of industrial organization. The crucial factor here is the size of an individual bank. When a single bank controls a large fraction of the industry's capacity, we can tell an equilibrium story in which the bank successfully deviates from the zero-lending equilibrium. Even if it decides to lend in a market where no one else is lending, a sufficiently large capacity may allow it to avoid the congestion problem, thus destabilizing the 'equilibrium'. In this sense, oligopolistic markets are less fragile than competitive ones.

The importance of these ideas becomes clear when we contrast the structure of the US banking system, with its thousands of banks, with the banking systems of Canada, Europe and Japan, which are dominated by a handful of commercial banks. Similarly, the contrasting experiences of Canada and the US in the 1930s, when the US suffered massive bank failures, suggest the relevance of industrial organization as a factor in bank stability.

The analysis of credit rationing and financial collapse is a first step toward understanding how the banking system responds to external shocks. Bernanke (1983) has argued that the failure of large numbers of banks in the 1930s increased the costs of intermediation and had a significant impact on real activity.[6] The ideas developed here may help to explain the ramifications of historical episodes like the Great Depression and earlier banking panics.

The rest of the paper is organized as follows. Section 2 presents the model. Section 3 describes the equilibrium informally and characterizes the equilibrium outcomes. A formal definition of equilibrium is given in Appendix A. In section 4, equilibria with positive lending are characterized and shown to exist. Section 5 shows that there can exist 'stable' equilibria with no lending, and section 6 demonstrates the impossibility of breaking this equilibrium. Formal proofs are contained in Appendix B.

2 The model

Imagine a credit market consisting of M entrepreneurs and N bankers and lasting a single period. Bankers and entrepreneurs are risk neutral and maximize the expected value of their wealth at the end of the period.

Each entrepreneur has a single, indivisible project that he wants to finance with money borrowed from one of the banks. A project requires an input of one unit at the beginning of the period and yields a (possibly random) return at the end. Projects are divided into two types, indexed by $t = 0, 1$. Projects of type 0 are risky: they yield a high return R_0 with probability π and zero otherwise. Projects of type 1 are safe: they yield a return of R_1 with probability one.

Entrepreneurs know their own type, i.e. whether their projects are safe or risky, but their bankers do not. The number of entrepreneurs (projects) of type t is denoted by M_t, for $t = 0, 1$. Also, for future reference, let $m_t \equiv M_t / N$ denote the number of entrepreneurs of type t per banker and let $m \equiv M/N$ denote the number of entrepreneurs per banker.

Applying for a loan is costly. We can think of the cost as representing the time and effort the entrepreneur puts into the application process (preparing a business plan, collecting and verifying data, discussing the proposed financing with a loan officer). The level of effort must be chosen before the entrepreneur knows whether he will obtain financing or not.

Although bankers cannot observe an entrepreneur's type directly, they have access to a screening technology that distinguishes safe projects from risky projects. Screening is costly. The bank pays a fixed cost $B > 0$ per borrower screened. Also, a banker's screening capacity is limited. At most K applicants can be screened by a single banker during the period.

The screening technology is a 'black box' for whatever methods a bank might use to gather information about the quality of an entrepreneur's project. For present purposes, it can be thought of as a 'test' that takes as an input information provided by the applicant and produces as an output either success or failure. The probability of success depends on the amount of effort taken by the applicant as well as his type. There are two possible effort levels, $A_1 > A_0 > 0$. Think of A_0 as the minimum amount of effort required for the applicant to have any chance of success. Taking a greater amount of effort will, in some cases, increase the chance of obtaining finance. Formally,

$$\text{Prob(success} \mid A, t) = \begin{cases} 1 & \text{if } t = 1 \text{ and } A = A_1 \\ \epsilon & \text{if } t = 1 \text{ and } A = A_0 \\ \epsilon & \text{if } t = 0 \text{ and } A = A_0, A_1. \end{cases}$$

If entrepreneurs with a safe project make a lot of effort, they are certain to pass the test. If they make a low level of effort, they may pass the test by accident, but only with a small probability ϵ. Entrepreneurs with risky projects can pass the test only by accident, regardless of the effort they put in. For example, think of A as the cost of documenting the entrepreneur's information about the project. Then a well-documented, safe project will pass the test with probability one; but a poorly documented application will pass the screen only by accident. In what follows, it will be assumed that A_0 is 'small'.

Bankers have access to an unlimited amount of capital at an exogenous cost of ρ per unit.

Banks are assumed to use standard debt contracts. A borrower receives one unit at the beginning of the period, in exchange for which the banker demands a gross repayment r (principal plus interest) at the end of the period. If the project's random return is $\tilde{R}$, the banker's return is $\text{Min}\{\tilde{R}, r\}$ and the borrower's return is $\text{Max}\{\tilde{R} - r, 0\}$.

2.1 Assumptions

To set the stage for the analysis of market failure, several restrictions are imposed on the parameters of the model. In the first place, it is assumed that risky projects are 'bad' projects, in the sense that they have negative net present value, while safe projects are 'good' projects, in the sense that they have positive net present value.

$$\pi R_0 - \rho < 0 < R_1 - \rho. \tag{A.1}$$

If bankers had complete information, risky projects would never be financed and safe projects would always be financed.

The next assumption places a constraint on the population of borrowers. Suppose a banker makes a loan to an entrepreneur selected at random from the population. Since the banker cannot charge more than R_1 without driving the safe entrepreneurs from the market and she will not willingly lend to the risky entrepreneurs, the most she can charge in equilibrium is R_1. The expected return from a loan at this rate is assumed to be less than the opportunity cost of funds.

$$\bar{\mu}_0 \pi R_1 + \bar{\mu}_1 R_1 < \rho, \quad \text{where } \bar{\mu}_t \equiv M_t / M. \tag{A.2}$$

(A.2) implies that for the credit market to function at all, some of the entrepreneurs with risky projects must be screened from the market. This makes the capacity constraint much more important to the smooth functioning of the market.

The third assumption says that entrepreneurs with risky projects earn higher expected profits than those with safe projects. If an entrepreneur with a safe project can borrow at the opportunity cost of funds, his expected profit will be $R_1 - p$. If an entrepreneur with a risky project were offered a loan on the same terms, he would make a profit of $R_0 - p$ if the project were a success and zero otherwise, so his expected profit is $\pi(R_0 - p)$. I assume that

$$\pi(R_0 - p) > R_1 - p. \tag{A.3}$$

Note that, if (A.3) is satisfied, the risky entrepreneur's expected profit will always be higher than the safe entrepreneur's on any loan with the repayment $r > p$. Although the risky projects are bad, in the sense of having negative net present value, an entrepreneur with a risky project is always more eager to borrow because of risk shifting.

2.2   The contracting game

Bankers and entrepreneurs play the following extensive-form game.

Stage 0: Borrowers observe their types (a move by Nature).
Stage 1: Bankers announce the rates at which they are willing to lend.
Stage 2: Borrowers observe the rates offered by the bankers. They choose whether to apply for a loan and, if they do apply, the bank they apply to and their effort level A.
Stage 3: Bankers observe the rates charged by other banks and the number of potential applicants. They decide how many applicants to screen and whether or not to give loans to each category (those screened successfully, those screened unsuccessfully and those not screened).

2.3   Information sets

Since there are no decisions to be made at the first stage, information sets are defined only for Stages 1, 2 and 3.

Stage 1: At the second stage, bankers have no information except for their prior beliefs about the distribution of types (and, of course, the parameters of the game, which are common knowledge).
Stage 2: Let r_i denote the gross repayment chosen by banker i at stage 2 and let $r \equiv (r_1, \ldots, r_N)$. The information set of a typical entrepreneur at the third stage is (r, t), where r is the vector of repayments chosen by the bankers at the previous stage and t is the type of the entrepreneur's project, observed at the first stage.
Stage 3: At the last stage, the bankers have observed the repayment profile r and the distribution of applicants across banks. Let q_i denote the number of entrepreneurs who apply to banker i and let $q \equiv (q_1, \ldots, q_N)$. Then the information set of each entrepreneur is denoted by (r, q).

3 Equilibrium

Before writing down the equilibrium conditions, we can note one fact that will make the characterization of equilibrium a little simpler.

Fact: Without loss of generality, we can assume that entrepreneurs with bad projects choose $A = A_0$ and entrepreneurs with good projects choose $A = A_1$.

The first part of the statement is clear enough, since it is always a dominant strategy for the high-risk entrepreneurs to choose the minimum level of effort. Choosing the higher level of effort increases their costs but will not increase the probability of getting a loan. On the other hand, if entrepreneurs with safe projects do not choose the higher level of effort, the screening technology does not discriminate between the two types of entrepreneur, since both pass the test with the same probability ϵ. In that case, lending is unprofitable by (A.2). But if there is no lending, there will be no applications and the choice of effort is immaterial.[7]

In what follows, I shall consider only symmetric equilibria, that is, equilibria in which two players who find themselves in the 'same' situation will choose the same actions, have the same beliefs and be treated in the same way. In describing a symmetric equilibrium, I focus first on the actions actually chosen by the agents in equilibrium and then consider what might happen if one of them deviates from his or her equilibrium strategy.[8] It is easiest to do this backwards, beginning with the last stage of the game and then working forwards to the start of the game.

3.1 The lending decision at stage 3

Since we are dealing with a symmetric equilibrium, all bankers choose the same repayment r and receive the same number of applicants q. So the information set of a typical banker at stage 3 is an ordered pair (r,q), where r and q are now treated as scalars. Let β_0 denote the fraction of applicants who receive a loan without screening from the typical banker and let β_1 denote the fraction of applicants who are screened.

A banker's beliefs about the typical applicant are represented by her probability assessment $\mu = (\mu_0, \mu_1)$, where μ_t is the probability that a typical applicant is of type t. If the banker chooses an entrepreneur at random from the pool of applicants and offers him a loan without screening, the expected profit on the loan is

$$W_u \equiv \mu_0 \pi r + \mu_1 r - \rho.$$

With probability μ_0 the applicant is of type 0 and the expected return is πr; with probability μ_1 the applicant is of type 1 and the expected return is r, and the opportunity cost of the loan is ρ.

Conversely, if the banker selects an applicant at random and screens him, the expected profit from screening is

$$W_s \equiv \mu_0 \epsilon(\pi r - \rho) + \mu_1(r - \rho) - B.$$

With probability μ_0 the applicant is of type 0, he passes the test with probability ϵ and the expected net return is $\pi r - \rho$; with probability μ_1 the applicant is of type 1 and the expected net return is $r - \rho$, and the cost of screening is B.[9]

The banker chooses $\beta = (\beta_0, \beta_1)$ to maximize her expected profits, subject to the constraint that the sum of β_0 and β_1 cannot exceed unity and that the total number of applicants screened, $\beta_1 q$, cannot exceed the capacity constraint K. Formally, the banker's choice must solve

$$\text{Max}_{\beta} \ \beta_0 W_u + \beta_1 W_s \tag{E.1}$$
$$\text{s.t.} \quad \beta_0 + \beta_1 \leq 1 \quad \text{and} \quad \beta_1 q \leq K.$$

If W_u is negative, there will be no unscreened loans; if W_s is negative, there will be no screening. If either W_u or W_s is positive, at least one of the constraints must be binding. For example, if $W_s > W_u > 0$, then the banker will screen as much as possible and give unscreened loans to the remaining applicants; if $W_u > W_s > 0$ then all applicants will get unscreened loans; and so on.

3.2   The application decision at stage 2

Now consider the entrepreneur's decision whether to apply for a loan at the third stage. We are assuming that each banker charges the same repayment r and chooses the same probabilities β; so the entrepreneur is indifferent about the choice of banker. Since there is a continuum of entrepreneurs, the fraction of entrepreneurs who apply can vary continuously. Let a_t denote the fraction of entrepreneurs of type t who decide to apply for a loan. We can think of a_t as being chosen by a representative entrepreneur of type t, in which case we may want to think of a_t as the probability that a single entrepreneur applies. If the entrepreneur is of type 0, he takes effort A_0, receives a loan with probability $(\beta_0 + \epsilon\beta_1)$ and makes an expected profit of $\pi(R_0 - r)$ on the loan. Then a_0 must satisfy

$$a_0 = \begin{cases} 1 & \text{if} \quad (\beta_0 + \beta_1 \epsilon)\pi(R_0 - r) - A_0 > 0 \\ 0 & \text{if} \quad (\beta_0 + \beta_1 \epsilon)\pi(R_0 - r) - A_0 < 0. \end{cases} \tag{E.2.0}$$

Similarly, a representative entrepreneur of type 1 receives a loan with probability $(\beta_0 + \beta_1)$ if they take effort A_1 and the expected profit from the loan is $R_1 - r$. So they choose the probability a_1 to solve

$$a_1 = \begin{cases} 1 & \text{if} \quad (\beta_0 + \beta_1)(R_1 - r) - A_1 > 0 \\ 0 & \text{if} \quad (\beta_0 + \beta_1)(R_1 - r) - A_1 < 0. \end{cases} \tag{E.2.1}$$

In keeping with our symmetry assumption, an equal number of entrepreneurs of a given type applies to each banker.

3.3   The pricing decision at stage 1

Given the entrepreneurs' strategies, each bank has a well-defined payoff for each profile of repayments. Then banker i chooses a repayment r_i to maximize her payoff, taking as given the choices of all the other players.

3.4   Beliefs

Lastly, it is necessary to specify a banker's beliefs. At stage 1, her beliefs are determined by the prior probability distribution $\bar{\mu}$. At stage 3, her beliefs are conditioned on the information available to her at that moment. In equilibrium, these beliefs must be consistent with the actions of the entrepreneurs. If a fraction a_t of the entrepreneurs of type t apply for a loan and there are m_t entrepreneurs of type t per banker, then the number of entrepreneurs of type t applying to a typical banker is $a_t m_t$. The fraction of applicants who are of type t is $a_t m_t / q$, where $q \equiv (a_0 m_0 + a_1 m_1)$, and the beliefs must satisfy

$$\mu_t = a_t m_t / q, \quad \text{for} \quad t = 0, 1, \tag{E.3}$$

whenever $q > 0$.

3.5   Symmetric outcomes and existence of equilibrium

The outcome of a symmetric equilibrium is described by the vector (r, a, β, μ), where r denotes the common repayment chosen by all of the bankers, $a = (a_0, a_1)$ represents the entrepreneurs' application decisions (a_t is the proportion of type t entrepreneurs who apply for a loan), $\beta = (\beta_0, \beta_1)$ represents the bankers' lending behaviour (β_0 is the proportion of applicants who get a loan without screening and β_1 is the proportion who are screened) and $\mu = (\mu_0, \mu_1)$ represents the common probability assessments of the bankers. An equilibrium outcome describes what happens in equilibrium, but it does not describe a complete equilibrium because it does not say what happens off the equilibrium path, i.e. if one of the players deviates. It turns out that there are many ways of specifying what can happen off the equilibrium path, as we shall soon see.

An equilibrium outcome must obviously satisfy the conditions (E.1)–(E.3). Conversely, if an outcome $(r a, \beta, \mu)$ satisfies these conditions, it can be supported as an equilibrium outcome. To see this, one needs only to specify the off-the-equilibrium-path moves, and this can be done trivially as follows. Suppose that, whenever the bankers observe an information set that is off the equilibrium path, they adopt the worst possible beliefs, that is, they assume that all applicants will have high-risk projects. By assumption it can never be profitable to give loans to entrepreneurs of this type, so the bankers neither screen nor offer loans without screening. Anticipating this, no entrepreneurs will apply for a loan, so the bankers' beliefs will not be contradicted by experience. Similarly, it will never be profitable for any banker to deviate from the equilibrium interest-rate offer, since this would result in an outcome in which they get no applicants and no profits. All the equilibrium conditions are trivially satisfied and we have proved the following proposition.

Proposition 1: An array (r, a, β, μ) is an equilibrium outcome if and only if it satisfies the conditions (E.1)–(E.3).

The details of a formal proof are omitted.

Although the construction of an equilibrium supported by extremely pessimistic beliefs is used to prove Proposition 1, *we do not have to rely on extreme beliefs to support an equilibrium outcome*. In fact, for each outcome (r, a, β, μ) satisfying the conditions (E.1)–(E.3), there will be a continuum of equilibria, with different off-the-equilibrium-path beliefs but supporting the same outcome. Most of these beliefs put positive weight on the possibility of the applicant belonging to the good type.

Proposition 1 allows us to restrict attention, in what follows, to equilibrium outcomes characterized by conditions (E.1)–(E.3). The fact that there is no equilibrium condition for the repayment r alerts us to a serious problem of indeterminacy: there is an equilibrium for every possible value of r (of course, for many there will be no lending).[10]

4 Equilibrium with positive lending

Before discussing the possibility of financial collapse, it will be useful to examine the benchmark case of an equilibrium that supports a positive level of lending. The existence of equilibria with positive lending is important because it establishes the potential viability of the market. The possibility of coordination failure arises because of the existence of *multiple* equilibria, in some of which there is no lending and in some of which there is a positive level of lending.

For the first result, which characterizes the equilibrium, some additional notation is needed. Recall that $\bar{\mu}_1$ is the proportion of good projects in the initial population. For a fixed value of r, the profitability of screening depends on μ_1, the banker's beliefs about the proportion of good types in the pool of applicants. If there are too few good types, it is not worth screening: even if the banker can identify a good type, they will have to screen too many applicants to find one. Let μ_1^* denote the value of μ_1 at which screening just becomes profitable. In the same way, the profit on unscreened loans is increasing in μ_1. Denote the breakeven proportion by μ_1^{**}.

The next result characterizes an equilibrium outcome with positive lending.

Proposition 2: Suppose that A_0 is very small but positive and $\mu_1^* < \bar{\mu}_1 < \mu_1^{**}$. Then an equilibrium outcome with positive lending (r, a, β, μ) has the following properties:

  (i) good types choose A_1 and bad types choose A_0;
  (ii) both types apply with probability 1;
  (iii) beliefs must satisfy $\mu_1 = \bar{\mu}_1$;
  (iv) banks choose $\beta_0 = 0$ and $\beta_1 = \min\{K/q, 1\}$.

A formal proof is contained in Appendix B.

The statement of the proposition requires $\bar{\mu}_1$ to lie between μ_1^* and μ_1^{**}. Suppose that all entrepreneurs apply for a loan. Then a banker's probability assessment that a typical applicant is type 1 will just be $\bar{\mu}_1$, the proportion of good types among the population as a whole. The condition $\bar{\mu}_1 < \mu_1^{**}$ is just a restatement of (A.2): it says that granting an unscreened loan is not profitable. The condition $\bar{\mu}_1 > \mu_1^*$ says the proportion of good types $\bar{\mu}_1$ is high enough for screening to be profitable. This is a necessary condition for positive lending since unscreened lending has been ruled out as unprofitable.

The first property (i) has already been noted: in order to have positive lending, there must be screening and screening will be effective only if the good types make more effort.

Property (ii) follows from the fact that A_0 is small. In order for some lending to take place, it must be worthwhile for good types to apply and make effort A_1. But it is worth doing this only if the probability of getting a loan is substantial, i.e. bounded away from zero. Then if A_0 is small enough, both types will find it strictly profitable to apply.

Property (iii) follows immediately from the consistency condition: if everyone applies, the banker's beliefs must mirror the initial make-up of the population.

Property (iv), which states that no unscreened loans are offered and the maximum number of applicants is screened, follows directly from the hypothesis that unscreened lending is unprofitable ($\bar{\mu}_1 < \mu_1^{**}$) and screening is profitable ($\mu_1^* < \bar{\mu}_1$) when all entrepreneurs apply.

Proposition 3 characterizes an equilibrium with positive lending, but we need to make sure that such an equilibrium exists. The next result does just this.

We have seen that, in an equilibrium with positive lending, there will be no unscreened loans ($\beta_0 = 0$). The willingness of entrepreneurs to apply for a loan will depend, at a given interest rate, on the probability of being screened. Let β_t^* denote the probability of screening that just makes an entrepreneur of type t willing to apply for a loan, when there is no possibility of getting a loan without screening. By assumption (A.3), the bad type is more eager to borrow, other things being equal, so

$$\beta_0^* < \beta_1^*.$$

Let β_1^{**} denote the probability of screening that is required to make the good type make extra effort. When A_0 is small, both types are willing to apply making effort A_0 before the good type is willing to make extra effort. That is,

$$\beta_1^* < \beta_1^{**}.$$

The relative magnitudes of A_0 and A_1 are important in determining the values of β_0^*, β_1^* and β_1^{**}. If A_0 were zero, so there was no cost of applying, both types would be willing to apply when $\beta_0 = \beta_1 = 0$. But for any positive value of A_0, the bad types will apply first. Similarly, the fact that A_0 is small relative to A_1 ensures that, if the probability of being screened is big enough to make the good types willing to make extra effort, it will surely attract all the bad types.

Now it is fairly easy to show that the main requirements for the existence of these equilibrium outcomes are (i) sufficient informational capacity and (ii) a sufficiently good distribution of types. The next proposition makes this precise.

Proposition 3: For some fixed but arbitrary value of $p < r < R_1$, suppose that $\bar{\mu}_1 \leq \mu_1^{**}$ and that $\beta_0^* < \beta_1^* < \beta_1^{**}$. Then an equilibrium outcome of the kind described in Proposition 2 (i.e. with positive lending) exists if and only if

   (i) $\beta_1^{**} \leq K/m$;

   (ii) $\mu_1^* \leq \bar{\mu}_1$.

The proof is in Appendix B.

In order to have an equilibrium with positive lending, the good types must make extra effort and this requires $\beta_1 \geq \beta_1^{**}$. Since everyone applies, the number of applicants q is equal to the number of entrepreneurs per bank m. Then the number of applicants screened must be at least $\beta_1^{**} m$ and the capacity constraint says that $\beta_1^{**} m \leq K$, which is just condition (i). The second condition says that screening is profitable, which is clearly a necessary condition and is here seen to be sufficient as well.

Proposition 4 describes an equilibrium outcome. One shows in the usual way that every outcome of this type in fact defines an equilibrium, by assuming pessimistic beliefs off the equilibrium path.

5 Stability of financial collapse

What the preceding discussion has shown is that, in spite of the severe adverse selection problem, the loan market can be viable. There does exist an equilibrium with positive lending if the market has sufficient information capacity. But this is not the only possibility. In order for positive lending to be viable, the actions of bankers and entrepreneurs have to be coordinated so that they all choose the appropriate equilibrium strategies. There may be another equilibrium, in which each agent rationally pursues his or her interests, given what the other agents are doing, and yet no lending takes place. In fact, we have seen that there is a trivial way to achieve this outcome simply by assuming the bankers have such pessimistic beliefs that they withdraw from the market. If bankers expect only bad entrepreneurs to apply, it will be rational for them to withdraw from the market (i.e. they will neither screen applicants nor make unscreened loans). If bankers refuse to make loans, it is rational for entrepreneurs not to apply and so the bankers' beliefs are not contradicted by the entrepreneurs' equilibrium behaviour. Although these beliefs are not irrational, they are not necessarily very plausible. Is there any reason to believe that only the worst types will apply?

The reason it is easy to support an equilibrium with no lending is that there is nothing to 'tie down' the beliefs of the bankers at information sets that are never reached in equilibrium. Since no one ever applies for a loan, a banker can rationally believe whatever she wants about a hypothetical applicant.[11] One way out of this impasse is to admit the possibility that agents make mistakes, so that, even in an equilibrium in which no one is supposed to apply for a loan, a small number of entrepreneurs do so by accident. What this small 'perturbation' of the model does is to ensure that the bankers' beliefs are determined by the consistency condition. Since there are always some entrepreneurs applying in equilibrium, the probability that one of them is the good type is well defined. The original model of the market is the limiting case in which these mistakes vanish. If the equilibrium in which no lending occurs is the limit of perturbed equilibria as the size of the mistakes vanishes, we have found one way of rationalizing the bankers' beliefs.

The problem is, of course, that the beliefs may depend crucially on how we perturb the model, that is, on the proportions of good and bad types who are assumed to apply by accident. For this reason, a stronger criterion may be required: this is to consider all possible perturbations and require that, as the size of the perturbations or mistakes becomes vanishingly small, the equilibria of the perturbed model converge to the given one. Put another way, if some perturbation of the model necessitated a large change in the equilibrium, we should consider that a failure of robustness or plausibility.[12]

To get some feeling for how this might work, consider the following example. Suppose we are given an equilibrium in which no one applies for a loan because the bankers have very pessimistic beliefs about the (non-existent) applicants. Perturb the model by assuming that a small number of good entrepreneurs (only) apply by accident, even if it is not optimal for them to do so. Then in any equilibrium of the perturbed model, there will always be some applicants, so the bankers' beliefs are determined by the actual proportion of good and bad types among the applicants.

What kind of beliefs can the bankers have in the perturbed equilibrium? If it is not a best response for the optimizing entrepreneurs to apply, then the only entrepreneurs who do apply are the good types who apply by accident. Consistency requires that bankers' beliefs reflect this fact, i.e. they believe that applicants are good types with probability one. Then the best response for the bankers will be to offer unscreened loans to all applicants ($\beta_0 = 1$). But in that case, all the entrepreneurs will want to apply, so a small perturbation has caused a large change in the equilibrium outcome.

On the other hand, suppose the type 0 entrepreneurs are indifferent about applying, though they choose not to apply in the original equilibrium. Then, in response to a perturbation that causes a small number of type 1 entrepreneurs to apply, it will be optimal for a small number of type 0 entrepreneurs to apply. In fact, the number of type 0 entrepreneurs can be chosen so that the bankers' equilibrium beliefs and hence their behaviour remain unchanged. The equilibrium conditions continue to hold, so a small perturbation causes only a small change in the outcome. The outcome should therefore be considered 'robust'.

The perturbation we have considered will cause a large change in the equilibrium unless one of two conditions is satisfied. Either the bankers must be very optimistic, i.e. they believe all applicants belong to type 1, or the type 0 entrepreneurs must be indifferent between applying and not applying. In the latter case, either the beliefs are determined by the consistency condition or they can be rationalized in the following way. Perturb the model by forcing some good types to apply; then an optimal response by the other entrepreneurs will lead to the beliefs in question. The next proposition shows that there does exist an equilibrium outcome with this property.

Proposition 4: There exists a symmetric equilibrium (r^*, f^*, g^*, h^*) with the following properties:

(i) for any $i = 1, \ldots, N$ and any $R_1 < r_i < R_0$, there is no lending in the equilibrium of the continuation game beginning with the bankers' choice of (r^*_{-i}, r_i);

(ii) furthermore, in the same continuation game equilibrium, *either* it is not a weak best response for either type to apply and the banker's beliefs are $\mu_1 = 1$ *or* it is a weak best response for the bad type of entrepreneurs to apply for loans.

The proof, which is given in Appendix B, depends on the assumption that A_0 is small. The proposition holds whenever the conditions of Proposition 3 are satisfied.

Although we have discussed only one possible perturbation of the model, it seems plausible that this perturbation is the critical one. If the equilibrium is not destabilized by forcing some type 1 entrepreneurs to apply, it seems unlikely that a mixture of type 1 and type 0 entrepreneurs will cause any problems. And this is indeed the case. We can show that for *any* small perturbation there is an equilibrium of the perturbed model in which the amount of lending is very small.[13]

The equilibrium described in Proposition 4 was motivated by a story in which entrepreneurs made mistakes. But the beliefs in this equilibrium are intuitively plausible in their own right. On the one hand, if there is no lending when bankers have the most optimistic beliefs, then any other beliefs will support the same outcome so there is really nothing to discuss. On the other hand, if the type 0 entrepreneurs are indifferent and the type 1 entrepreneurs strictly prefer not to apply, there is a sense in which type 0 entrepreneurs are more likely to apply. It seems reasonable for the bankers' beliefs to put positive weight on the possibility of type 0 entrepreneurs applying.[14]

Note that the capacity constraint plays no role in this rationalization of the no-lending outcome, for the simple reason that no entrepreneurs apply and none are screened. (In the next section, the possibility of profitable deviations from a no-lending outcome is considered and there capacity is a crucial part of the argument.) However, the expectation of rationing ($\beta_0 = 0$ and $\beta_1 < 1$) is crucial in determining which type is most likely to apply and hence in justifying the bankers' beliefs and their behaviour.

6   The impossibility of profitable deviations

Proposition 4 can be interpreted as showing that there exists a credible or plausible set of beliefs that support an equilibrium with no lending. But it does not show or even attempt to argue that these are the only or the most plausible beliefs. We might instead have asked the following question: given that banks have chosen to behave in such a way that there is no lending in equilibrium, is there any plausible story according to which a deviation by a single banker would give them a positive profit? To be more precise, suppose that, in the original equilibrium, all the bankers choose the repayment $r^* > R_0$. At this rate, no one will want a loan even if they could get one. Now suppose that one banker deviates by offering a lower rate $r < R_1$. Obviously, this is not a profitable move in the original equilibrium. The question is, can we think of a story in which this deviation by the banker leads to rational responses by the entrepreneurs such that the banker ends up making a profit? If the answer is no, it suggests that no-lending equilibrium is robust in a fairly strong sense. If the answer is yes, we would then have to ask whether this story is more or less plausible than the one we told about the original equilibrium.

Let r^* denote the repayment chosen by $N - 1$ bankers and let r denote the repayment chosen by the remaining banker. Let $\mathbf{r} \equiv (r^*, r)$ and let $\Gamma(\mathbf{r})$ denote the continuation game that describes what happens in stages 2 and 3, once the repayments $\mathbf{r}$ have been chosen. Note that in any equilibrium of $\Gamma(\mathbf{r})$, it is still a dominant strategy for the entrepreneurs not to apply to any of the bankers charging r^*, so the beliefs and responses of these bankers are irrelevant. Then an equilibrium of $\Gamma(\mathbf{r})$ can be described by the array $(a, \beta, \mu, \mathbf{A})$, where a denotes the probabilities with which entrepreneurs apply to the deviant, β and μ denote the deviant's response and beliefs, respectively, and $\mathbf{A}$ denotes the effort choices of the two types.

Proposition 5: Let $(a, \beta, \mu, \mathbf{A})$ denote a fixed but arbitrary equilibrium of the continuation game $\Gamma(\mathbf{r})$, where $r^* > R_0$. For A_0 sufficiently small and N sufficiently large (holding $m_t \equiv M_t/N$ constant, for $t = 0, 1$) the deviant banker makes non-positive profits in $(a, \beta, \mu, \mathbf{A})$.

The proof is given in Appendix B.

If a single banker offers terms at which the good types are willing to apply (and this is a necessary condition for any lending) then all the bad types will want to apply. But then the capacity constraint means that the probability of being screened and obtaining a loan must be very low. In that case, the good types will not want to apply or, at least, will not want to make a high level of effort, so it is not profitable for the banker to screen applicants.

It is crucial to have a large number of small banks for this result. The capacity of the entire banking system is large, at least large enough to support an equilibrium in which all entrepreneurs apply and some of them get loans. But because the capacity of an individual bank is small relative to the whole market, a single bank cannot overcome the congestion problem when other banks have withdrawn from the market. The bank gets 'swamped' by applicants because it does not have enough screening capacity to attract the good applicants. If there were fewer banks and each one had more capacity, this outcome might be avoided. This suggests the importance of industrial organization for the stability of the banking system. While large numbers of banks may encourage competition, they may also encourage financial collapse.

As a corollary of the proposition, we can see that it is *never a weak best response* for the good type to apply in any equilibrium of the continuation game $\Gamma(\mathbf{r})$. This is another reason for assuming that the applicant is a bad type.

7   Discussion

There is a large literature on coordination failure. In a macroeconomic context, Cooper and John (1988) survey a number of models in which strategic complementarities lead to multiple, Pareto-ranked equilibria. The common theme in all of these models is that an increase (decrease) in the activity of one agent encourages an increase (decrease) in the activity of all the others. Games with strategic complementarities have been studied by Vives (1990) and Milgrom and Roberts (1990).

In a banking context, Diamond and Dybvig (1983) model bank runs as a multiple equilibrium phenomenon. In their model, the strategic complementarity arises from the fact that a depositor's incentive to 'run' increases with the number of other depositors who choose to 'run', since the last depositor ends up with nothing.

Matutes and Vives (1991) also study the fragility of the financial sector in terms of multiple equilibria. A bank can be thought of as a network. The safety of the bank depends on the size of the network. Since depositors care about market share, the bank's quality may be unstable: an increase in market share will increase the attractiveness of the bank and this will amplify the initial change.

The model in this paper addresses the stability issue from the supply side rather than the deposit side. The multiplicity of equilibria arises from the fact that the mix of good and bad types applying for loans depends on the probability of getting a loan and hence on the relationship between the total number of applicants and the capacity of the market. A reduction in capacity, caused by the withdrawal of one bank, has an impact on the quality of applicants, which in turn affects the profitability of lending for the other banks and may encourage them to withdraw, thus further reducing capacity.

The model used is extremely simple and it would be absurd to pretend that the results are completely robust. None the less, I think the conclusions have some validity outside the special circumstances described by the model.

One of the most restrictive features of the model is the assumption of standard debt contracts. This rules out the use of several screening devices that might be helpful to the bank. For example, the banker might offer a debt contract under which the repayment r is a random variable rather than a fixed amount. This kind of contract might be less attractive to an entrepreneur with a risky project than to an entrepreneur with a safe project.[15]

Another alternative is to let the banker charge an application fee. By altering the relative application costs for the two types of entrepreneur, the bank could alter their incentives to apply, possibly even discouraging the bad type altogether. For example, if the application fee were returned to anyone who successfully obtained financing, this scheme would punish any borrower with a low probability of success. As with many other possible remedies, there is a moral hazard inherent in this scheme: the bank may manipulate the probability of getting a loan in order to keep the fees, or simply refuse to return them as promised.

Another possibility is to use a different form of financing altogether, for example, equity financing. It is not clear what the implications of using equity here are. Clearly, it would be preferable to endogenize the form of the contract, but, if the object is to get some understanding of how markets for debt work, this seems a reasonable way to begin.

Clearly, there is some loss of generality in restricting the bankers to standard debt contracts. The question is, how much? In the most general case, one could imagine bankers offering entrepreneurs a menu of mechanisms to choose from. Each mechanism would specify a probability of being screened, a probability of receiving a loan conditional on whether the applicant was screened and on what the outcome was if screened, and a repayment that might be random and would be conditional on all the preceding data. If bankers were able to commit to arbitrary mechanisms, they could discourage entrepreneurs with risky projects from applying in the first place. For example, a 'forcing contract', which imposes a large penalty with small probability if the applicant is found to have a risky project, will do the trick. This would effectively eliminate the adverse selection problem. Such complicated mechanisms do not seem to be used in practice, however, and there are several reasons why this sort of solution seems unconvincing.

In the first place, it is necessary for the bank to make a credible commitment to a mechanism before the applicant approaches the bank. How does the bank communicate the terms of the mechanism to the applicant? Announcing a complex series of stochastic decision rules is much more difficult than announcing the interest rate at which loans are available.

Even if the mechanism can be communicated to potential applicants, there remains the problem of verification. A third party, such as the courts, may be unable to observe either the proposal of the mechanism or the way in which the mechanism is implemented. Since the banker will typically have an incentive *ex post* to implement a different mechanism from the one proposed, the lack of verifiability makes it difficult for the banker to make a credible commitment to implement the mechanism.

What I assume in this paper is that the only verifiable elements of the loan contract are the repayment of the loan and whether the loan is made or not. For this reason, it is not possible for a banker to promise credibly to make the screening probability depend on announcements made by the applicant, or to make the probability of issuing a loan conditional on the result of the test, or to make the terms of the loan contract stochastic and conditional on announcements or the outcome of the screening process. On the other hand, the banker can credibly commit to offer loans at a certain interest rate.

The motivation for all these restrictions is, of course, to simplify the analysis in the hope that it will be tractable as well as transparent. Undoubtedly some sort of restriction is necessary in order to introduce a degree of inefficiency into the contracting process, but as long as there is some lack of commitment, arising from problems of verifiability or moral hazard, there will still be a non-trivial adverse selection problem and the possibility of coordination failure should remain.

A different set of issues arises when we consider changes in the structure of the market. For example, if the capacity constraint is important, why not endogenize capacity by allowing banks to choose the level of capacity at an earlier stage? This is an interesting line of research, which should be pursued (by someone). It is not clear that it would lead to a different conclusion. Much would depend on the game form used. The market could be modelled so that a single bank could capture a monopoly of the entire market by first acquiring large capacity (cf. Yanelle, 1989). But one could just as easily choose a model in which this does not occur. Consider a situation in which financial collapse has occurred or is anticipated. If a single banker acquires large capacity, it may be possible for her to reactivate the market. If other bankers can successfully invade the market, however, a not implausible scenario, investment in excess capacity may turn out to be very unprofitable. Anticipating this outcome, no bank will have an incentive to invest in enough capacity to prevent the collapse of the market.

One could also imagine different rules of the game. For example, it is assumed that entrepreneurs can apply only to a single banker. If the costs of applying for a loan are largely the fixed costs of collecting information and preparing a business plan, it might be no more costly to apply several times. What would happen then? The assumption that entrepreneurs can apply only once is obviously a simplification, one that rules out the sort of phenomena arising in Broecker (1990). The analysis would be much more complicated without it. In particular, if entrepreneurs apply sequentially, there is a lemons problem. If they apply simultaneously, banks have to worry about their offers subsequently being rejected by entrepreneurs who have offers from several banks. It is not clear that this game form will lead to more efficient outcomes, but the complications are worth thinking about.

Another alternative would be to allow for signalling as well as screening. In the present model I have deliberately made the adverse selection problem quite intractable simply to force the banks to rely on their screening technology. This makes sense because the analysis focuses on the informational role of banks and the possibility of collapse due to congestion. I think the phenomenon is somewhat more robust than this model, but the work of Bester (1985) alerts us to the fact that these results are unlikely to hold universally.

Appendix A: Definition of equilibrium

A.1   The lending decision at stage 3

Consider the decision of banker i at the information set (r, q) at stage 3. The banker's beliefs conditional on this information set are denoted by μ_i. The expected profit on an unscreened loan is

$$W_u \equiv \mu_{i0} \pi r_i + \mu_{i1} r_i - \rho,$$

and the expected profit from screening is

$$W_s \equiv \mu_{i0} \epsilon (\pi r_i - \rho) + \mu_{i1}(r_i - \rho) - B.$$

A strategy for the banker at stage 3 is a function g_i that maps (r, q) into a lending decision $\beta_i = g_i(r, q)$.

The banker's decision problem is

$$\underset{\beta}{\text{Max}} \ \beta_{i0} W_0 + \beta_{i1} W_1$$

$$\text{s.t.} \quad \beta_{i0} + \beta_{i1} \leq 1 \quad \text{and} \quad \beta_{i1} q_i \leq K. \tag{P.3}$$

A.2   The application decision at stage 2

Now consider the decision of an entrepreneur whether to apply to banker i at the second stage. The representative entrepreneur of type 0 chooses a vector $a \equiv (a_1, \ldots, a_N)$, with the interpretation that a_i is the probability the entrepreneur applies to banker i. Alternatively, a_i is the fraction of entrepreneurs of this type who apply to banker i. The decision problem is

$$\underset{a}{\text{Max}} \sum_{i=1}^{N} a_i \{ (\beta_{i0} + \beta_{i1} \epsilon) \pi (R_0 - r_i) - A_0 \} \tag{P.2.0}$$

$$\text{s.t.} \quad \sum_{i=1}^{N} a_i \leq 1.$$

The a_i's do not necessarily sum to unity, since the entrepreneurs may choose not to apply.

The representative entrepreneur of type 1 makes effort A_1 and chooses a vector $a = (a_1, \ldots, a_N)$ to solve

$$\underset{a}{\text{Max}} \sum_{i=1}^{N} a_i \{ (\beta_{i0} + \beta_{i1})(R_1 - r_i) - A_1 \} \tag{P.2.1}$$

$$\text{s.t.} \quad \sum_{i=1}^{N} a_i \leq 1.$$

A strategy for the representative entrepreneur at stage 2 is a function f that maps the information set (r, t) into an application decision $a = f(r, t)$.

A.3   The pricing decision at stage 1

Given the entrepreneurs' strategies, f, each bank has a well-defined payoff $V_i(r, f)$ for each profile of repayments. Then banker i chooses r_i to solve

$$\underset{r_i}{\text{Max}} \ V_i(r_i, r_{-i}, f(r_i, r_{-i})), \tag{P.1}$$

taking as given the other bankers' choices $r_{-i} \equiv (r_1, \ldots, r_{i-1}, r_{i+1}, \ldots, r_N)$.

A.4   Beliefs

At stage 1, a banker's beliefs are determined by her priors $\bar{\mu}$. At stage 3, $h_i(r,q)$ denotes banker i's probability assessment, at the information set (r,q), that an application comes from an entrepreneur of type 1. These beliefs are *consistent* if, for any information set (r,q),

$$h_i(r,q) = \frac{f_i(r,1)m_1}{\sum_t f_i(r,t)m_t} \quad \text{whenever} \quad \sum_t f_i(r,t)m_t > 0. \tag{C}$$

Definition: An equilibrium consists of a strategy profile $f = (f(t))$ for entrepreneurs, a strategy profile $(r,g) = ((r_i, g_i))$ for bankers, and the probability assessment $h = (h_i)$ for bankers, satisfying the following conditions.

(a)   For every banker $i = 1, \ldots, N$, r_i solves the problem (P.1).
(b)   For each type of entrepreneur $t = 0, 1$ and every profile r, $a_t = f(r,t)$ solves (P.2.t), when $\beta_i = g_i(r,q)$ and $q_i = a_{i0}m_0 + a_{i1}m_1$ for $i = 1, \ldots, N$.
(c)   For every banker $i = 1, \ldots, N$, and every information set (r,q), $\beta_i = g_i(r,q)$ solves the problem (P.3).
(d)   For every information set (r,q), the bankers' beliefs satisfy the consistency condition (C).

An equilibrium (r,f,g,h) is *symmetric* if it satisfies the following requirements. *First*, all bankers charge the same repayment:

$$r_i = r_j, \quad \forall i,j = 1, \ldots, N.$$

Second, entrepreneurs divide themselves equally among bankers charging the same interest rate:

$$f_i(r) = f_j(r), \quad \forall i,j = 1, \ldots, N, \quad \forall r \ni r_i = r_j.$$

Third, bankers who charge the same interest rate and face the same number of applicants make the same lending decisions:

$$g_i(r,q) = g_j(r,q), \quad \forall i,j = 1, \ldots, N, \quad \forall (r,q) \ni (r_i, q_i) = (r_j, q_j).$$

Fourth, bankers who charge the same interest rate and face the same number of applicants have the same beliefs:

$$h_i(r,q) = h_j(r,q), \quad \forall i,j = 1, \ldots, N, \quad \forall (r,q) \ni (r_i, q_i) = (r_j, q_j).$$

Appendix B: Proofs of Propositions 2–5

B.1   Proof of Proposition 2

The profit from screening a typical applicant is

$$(1 - \mu_1)\epsilon(\pi r - p) + \mu_1(r - p) - B.$$

The profit is clearly increasing in μ_1 and will equal zero for some value μ_1^*, say, where

$$\mu_1^* = \frac{B - \epsilon(\pi r - \rho)}{(r - \rho) - \epsilon(\pi r - \rho)}.$$

In exactly the same way, the profit on unscreened loans,

$$(1 - \mu_1)\pi r + \mu_1 r - \rho,$$

is increasing in μ_1 and the breakeven probability μ_1^{**} is

$$\mu_1^{**} = \frac{\rho - \pi r}{r - \pi \rho}.$$

Property (i) in the proposition is simply a restatement of Fact 1. The remaining properties are immediate once it is established that $a_0 = a_1 = 1$.

Clearly some good types must apply or there can be no lending in equilibrium. To encourage good types to take extra effort,

$$\beta_0 + \beta_1 \geq \frac{A_1}{(R_1 - r)} \geq \frac{A_1}{(R_1 - \rho)}.$$

Since $(\beta_0 + \beta_1)$ is bounded away from zero, $(\beta_0 + \beta_1 \epsilon)$ must be bounded away from zero too. Then, for A_0 sufficiently small, it must be strictly optimal for the bad type of entrepreneur to apply, i.e. $a_0 = 1$ (Property ii). It follows immediately that it cannot be profitable to offer unscreened loans, because $\mu_1 \leq \bar{\mu}_1 < \mu_1^{**}$, for any $r \leq R_1$. Consequently, we must have $\beta_0 = 0$ in any equilibrium (Property iv).

We have seen that positive lending implies that some good types apply and make extra effort. Therefore,

$$\beta_1 \geq \beta_1^{**}.$$

(In particular, this implies that $r < R_1$.) But if A_0 is sufficiently small, this implies that $\beta_0^* < \beta_1$, i.e. the good type gets a positive payoff from applying. Then $a_1 = 1$ (Property ii).

Since both types of entrepreneur apply with probability 1, the proportion of good types in the pool of applicants will be $\mu_1 = \bar{\mu}_1$ (Property iii). Since the good types make effort A_1, the bankers will make positive profits on screening if and only if $\mu_1^* < \bar{\mu}_1$. Then the amount of screening is determined by the capacity constraint $\beta_1 q = K$ or by the constraint $\beta_1 = 1$, whichever is binding (Property iv).□

B.2   Proof of Proposition 3

Since the bad type's payoff is $\beta_1 \epsilon \pi (R_0 - r) - A_0$,

$$\beta_0^* = \frac{A_0}{\pi(R_0 - r)\epsilon}.$$

The good type's payoff is $\beta_1 \epsilon (R_1 - r) - A_0$ when there is no chance of getting an unscreened loan, so

$$\beta_1^* = \frac{A_0}{(R_0 - r)\epsilon}.$$

From assumption (A.3), $\beta_0^* < \beta_1^*$.

The payoff when the good type makes extra effort is $\beta_1(R_1 - r) - A_1$. The increase in the good type's payoff resulting from making extra effort is $(1 - \epsilon)\beta_1(R_1 - r)$. So if there is no chance of getting an unscreened loan, the good type will be just willing to make extra effort if

$$\beta_1^{**} = \text{Max}\left\{ \frac{A_1 - A_0}{(R_1 - r)(1 - \epsilon)}, \frac{A_1}{(R_1 - r)} \right\}.$$

If A_0 is sufficiently small, then

$$\beta_1^{**} = \frac{A_1 - A_0}{(R_1 - r)(1 - \epsilon)}$$

and $\beta_1^* < \beta_1^{**}$. So the good type will be willing to make extra effort only if they are already willing to apply minimum effort.

The necessity of the claim is immediate. If $\mu_1^* > \bar{\mu}_1$ then $\beta_1 = 0$, which is inconsistent with positive lending. If $\beta_1 \geq \beta_1^{**}$ (which is necessary for $a_1 = 1$ and $A = A_1$) then $\beta_1^{**} > K/m$ implies that $\beta_1 m = \beta_1 q > K$, which is impossible.

To see that these conditions are sufficient, note that $a_0 = a_1 = 1$ is optimal for entrepreneurs if $\beta_1 \geq \beta_1^{**}$, because we have assumed $\beta_0^* < \beta_1^* < \beta_1^{**}$. Then $\mu_1 = \bar{\mu}_1$ if $a_0 = a_1 = 1$. Next $\beta_0 = 0$ is optimal for banks since $\bar{\mu}_1 < \mu_1^{**}$ by assumption. Finally, it is optimal to put $\beta_1 = K/m$ if $\mu_1^* \leq \bar{\mu}_1$ since $a_0 = a_1 = 1$ implies that $q = m$. By assumption, this value of β_1 is at least as great as β_1^{**}, so the condition needed for the first step is satisfied.$\square$

B.3   Proof of Proposition 4

The equilibrium can be defined in three steps, first along the equilibrium path, then in the distinguished continuation games and then in all other continuation games.

Step 1

Let (r^*, f^*, g^*, h^*) denote the equilibrium to be defined. Choose $r_i^* > R_0$ for $i = 1, \ldots, n$. Choose $f_j^*(r^*, t) = (0, A_0)$ for $j = 1, \ldots, n$ and $t = 0, 1$. In words, for any type of entrepreneur t, the probability of applying to banker j is zero and the effort that would be expended if an application were made is A_0. The entrepreneurs' strategy is optimal, because all the bankers choose such a high repayment that no one would ever want to apply. As a result, the beliefs and responses of the bankers along the equilibrium path are irrelevant, so (g^*, h^*) can be chosen arbitrarily.

Step 2

Now consider the continuation game defined by the bankers' choices (r^*_{-i}, r_i). Define the entrepreneurs' strategies to be

$$f_j^*(r^*_{-i}, r_i, t) = (0, A_0) \quad \text{for} \quad j = 1, \ldots, N \quad \text{and} \quad t = 0, 1.$$

For each banker $j \neq i$, define beliefs and responses as before. Since it is a dominant strategy not to apply to these banks, the specification of g^* and h^* for $j \neq i$ can be arbitrary.

Recall that screening is profitable for banker i if and only if $\mu_1 \geq \mu_1^*$ and unscreened loans are profitable for banker i if and only if $\mu_1 \geq \mu_1^{**}$, where

$$\mu_1^* = \frac{B - \epsilon(\pi r_i - \rho)}{(r_i - \rho) - \epsilon(\pi r_i - \rho)}$$

and

$$\mu_1^{**} = \frac{\rho - \pi r_i}{r_i - \pi r_i}.$$

Consider the following cases:

Case (a). Suppose that $\mu_1^*, \mu_1^{**} > 1$. Then put

$$h_i^*(r^*_{-i}, r_i, q) = 1$$

and

$$g_i^*(r^*_{-i}, r_i, q) = (\beta_0, \beta_1) = (0, 0).$$

Given the assumed values of μ_1^* and μ_1^{**}, it is optimal to set $\beta = 0$. Also, the requirements of the theorem are satisfied: the banker's beliefs are $\mu_1 = 1$ and, since $\beta = 0$, it is not a weak best response for any type to apply.

Case (b). Suppose now that $\mu_1^{**} \leq 1$ and $\mu_1^{**} < \mu_1^*$. Define beliefs by putting

$$h_i^*(r^*_{-i}, r_i, q) = \mu_1^{**}$$

and define the banker's response by putting

$$g_i^*(r^*_{-i}, r_i, q) = (\beta_0, \beta_1),$$

where

$$\beta_0 = \frac{A_0}{\pi(R_0 - r_i)}.$$

and $\beta_1 = 0$. For the given beliefs, the banker's response is obviously optimal. Also, the requirements of the proposition are satisfied since it is a weak best response for the bad type to apply.

Case (c).   Finally, suppose that $\mu_1^* \leq \min\{1, \mu_1^{**}\}$. Then set

$$g_i^*(r_{-i}^*, r_i, q) = (\beta_0, \beta_1),$$

where

$$\beta_1 = \min\left\{1, K/q, \frac{A_0}{\epsilon \pi (R_0 - r_i)}\right\}.$$

If $\mu_1^{**} > 1$ set $\beta_0 = 0$. If $\beta_1 = A_0/\epsilon \pi (R_0 - r_i)$ set

$$h_i^*(r_{-i}^*, r_i, q) = \mu_1^*;$$

if $\beta_1 < A_0/\epsilon \pi (R_0 - r_i)$ set

$$h_i^*(r_{-i}^*, r_i, q) = 1.$$

It is clear from inspection that the banker's response is optimal given their beliefs. Also, the requirements of the proposition are satisfied, since either it is a weak best response for the bad type to apply or the banker's beliefs are $\mu_1 = \mu_1^*$.

If, on the other hand, $\mu_1^{**} \leq 1$, set $\beta_0 = 0$ and $h_i^*(r_{-i}^*, r_i, q) = \mu_1^*$ if $\beta_1 = A_0/\epsilon \pi (R_0 - r_i)$. Otherwise, set $h_i^*(r_{-i}^*, r_i, q) = \mu_1^{**}$ and choose β_0 so that

$$\beta_0 + \epsilon \beta_1 = \frac{A_0}{\pi (R_0 - r_i)}.$$

Again, it is clear from inspection that the requirements of the theorem are satisfied.

It remains to show that the entrepreneurs' strategy f^* is a best response to the bankers' strategy profile g^* defined above. As noted above, the entrepreneurs will never want to apply to bankers $j \neq i$. By construction, it is always a weak best response for the bad types not to apply. Whenever $\beta_1 = 0$, not applying is a weak best response for the good types because it is a weak best response for the bad types. So we need only to consider the case (c). The problem is to show that, for any $p < p_i < R_1$,

$$\beta_0 + \epsilon \beta_1 \leq \frac{A_0}{\pi (R_0 - r_i)}$$

implies that

$$\beta_0 + \epsilon\beta_1 \leq \frac{A_0}{(R_1 - r_i)} \quad \text{and} \quad \beta_0 + \beta_1 \leq \frac{A_1}{(R_1 - r_i)}.$$

The first inequality follows from the preceding one and (A.3). The second follows from the first if A_0 is sufficiently small, as has been assumed. This completes the proof that $(f^*(r^*_{-i}, r_i), g^*(r^*_{-i}, r_i), h^*(r^*_{-i}, r_i))$ is an equilibrium for this continuation game.

Step 3

For continuation games other than those distinguished in the statement of the proposition, one can simply put

$$f_j^*(r, t) = (0, A_0) \quad \text{for} \quad j = 1, \ldots, N \quad \text{and} \quad t = 0, 1;$$

$$h_j^*(r, q) = 0 \quad \text{for} \quad j = 1, \ldots, N \quad \text{and any } q \geq 0;$$

and

$$g_j^*(r, q) = (0, 0) \quad \text{for any} \quad j = i, \ldots, N \quad \text{and} \quad q \geq 0.$$

This is just the trivial equilibrium which obviously satisfies the equilibrium conditions.$\square$

B.4   *Proof of Proposition 5*

If $r \geq R$, it is a dominant strategy for the good types of entrepreneurs not to apply, so it is impossible for the deviant banker to make profits. Similarly, the banker cannot make positive profits if $r \leq p$. Then, without loss of generality, we can assume that $p < r < R_1$.

I claim that for any $\beta = (\beta_0, \beta_1)$, if it is a weak best response for the good type to apply, it must be a strict best response for the bad type to apply. This is clearly the case if both types choose $A = A_0$, since

$$(\beta_0 + \epsilon\beta_1)(R_1 - r) - A_0 \geq 0$$

implies that

$$(\beta_0 + \epsilon\beta_1)\pi(R_0 - r) - A_0 \geq 0,$$

by (A.3). Suppose then that the good type makes extra effort. It is easy to see that, for some A_0 sufficiently small, any β satisfying

$$\beta_0 + \beta_1 \geq \frac{A_1}{(R_1 - r)}$$

must also satisfy

$$\beta_0 + \epsilon\beta_1 > \frac{A_0}{\pi(R_0 - r)}.$$

We conclude that $a_1 > 0$ implies that $a_0 = 1$.

In order to have a positive amount of lending, it is necessary to have some of the good entrepreneurs apply for loans in equilibrium ($a_1 > 0$). As we have seen, this implies that $a_0 = 1$ and hence $q \geq M_0$. M_0 is large because N is large, so the feasibility constraint $\beta_1 q \leq K$ implies that β_1 is very close to zero. We know that $\beta_0 = 0$ whenever $a_0 = 1$, so for N sufficiently large we have $\beta_0 = 0$ and $\beta_1 \approx 0$. This is inconsistent with $a_1 > 0$ and $A = A_1$, so the banker cannot make positive profits.□

NOTES

I am grateful to a variety of seminar participants for helpful comments and particularly to Franklin Allen, Dan Bernhardt, Martin Hellwig, Peter Howitt and David Webb. Xavier Vives made a number of helpful suggestions that have materially improved the exposition. While writing this paper, I was a guest of the Financial Markets Group at LSE. Alison Hole and Ernst Maug of the FMG provided valuable assistance. The financial support of the National Science Foundation under Grant No. SES 9196061 is gratefully acknowledged.

1 The empirical evidence on the existence of a 'credit crunch' seems rather unclear (see Bernanke and Lown, 1991), but this may be partly due to the lack of theoretical agreement on what the 'credit crunch' is and how it should be modelled. Meltzer (1991) has argued against the existence of a 'credit crunch', basing his argument on the absence of excess reserves; but Haubrich (1991) has criticized this use of excess reserves as a measure of bank willingness to lend, arguing that excess reserves may simply be absorbed by the Federal Reserve. Others have argued that the sharp drop in certain kinds of lending has resulted either from lower demand for loans or from banks' recognition of sharply reduced quality in the ventures needing finance, i.e. it does not represent 'rationing'. Green and Oh (1991a) do not dispute the existence of credit rationing, but suggest that it may be optimal to have such rationing. They regard the credit market as an optimal dynamic insurance mechanism (see Green and Oh, 1991b). *Ex post* distortions such as rationing funds to 'good' borrowers provide the incentives necessary for an *ex ante* optimal (second-best) insurance mechanism.
2 The basic model is similar to Stiglitz and Weiss (1981).
3 In models of credit markets, it is typically assumed that competition takes the form of Bertrand competition among a large number of risk-neutral banks with unconstrained capacity (Stiglitz and Weiss, 1981; Diamond, 1984; Hellwig, 1987). It is well known, of course, that Bertrand competition has rather peculiar properties (Winton, 1990; Yanelle, 1989). The addition of capacity constraints is both a step in the direction of realism and an attempt to avoid some of the peculiar properties of competition among banks with unlimited capacity.
4 We can motivate these costs in various ways. They may represent the cost of searching for an appropriate lender or the cost of preparing and documenting a proposal for a bank. The important thing is that the costs are incurred independently of whether the borrower actually gets the loan.
5 There is always the possibility of a trivial equilibrium with 'financial collapse'.

If banks expect all applicants to be bad risks, they will refuse to issue any loans. If borrowers expect to be rejected with probability one, they will not bother to apply, so the banks' beliefs are never contradicted by experience (i.e. beliefs are rational in a weak sense). Such equilibria may not be 'stable', depending as they do on arbitrary off-the-equilibrium-path beliefs.

6 In Bernanke and Gertler (1989), the real impact of financial shocks is explained in terms of balance sheet effects: loss of entrepreneurial capital increases agency costs and reduces aggregate investment. An alternative story would run in terms of loss of informational capacity. (A similar analysis might be carried out under the assumption that bank capital was the binding constraint on lending.) When the number of banks suddenly shrinks, there is reduced informational capacity and, at the same time, an increased demand because large numbers of borrowers have been separated from their lenders. The cost of intermediation goes up because the probability of being rationed goes up. But this congestion leads to a change in the average quality of applicants, since the costs are different for different types of borrowers. This in turn will give banks an increased incentive to screen loans, but that only worsens the congestion. In extreme cases, this downward spiral may lead to financial collapse: the pool becomes so bad that banks are not willing to incur the cost of screening and so are not willing to lend.

7 Note that, in making this argument, we are ignoring the possibility that entrepreneurs choose 'mixed' strategies, i.e. that some of them might choose A_0 while others choose A_1. In what follows, it will always be assumed that entrepreneurs choose a 'pure' strategy in this sense.

8 In other words, first define the strategies and beliefs along the equilibrium path and then show how the definition can be extended to information sets off the equilibrium path.

9 In making this calculation, it is assumed that an applicant is offered a loan only if he successfully passes the screening test. We are ruling out the use of mixed strategies conditional on the outcome of the screening process, which is a slight restriction on the set of equilibria considered but probably not important. We are also ruling out the possibility that the banker gives loans to all the entrepreneurs who are screened or to none of them. Both these options are dominated strategies, however. Since screening is costly, it never pays to screen unless the banker's decision depends on the outcome.

10 Although the issue is not pursued here, it turns out that, for any value of r, the set of equilibrium outcomes is finite. The results presented below all hold for a given value of r.

11 Technically, the problem is that the posterior probability conditional on a zero probability event is not well defined, so the consistency condition does not apply.

12 This rather loose statement omits some important details. First, there may be several equilibria of the perturbed model. We require only that one of them be close to the equilibrium of the original model. Second, since these equilibria have quite different beliefs and strategies off the equilibrium path, they cannot all be close to the same equilibrium. One needs a set-valued solution concept: a set of equilibria of the original model may have this robustness property. All of these equilibria may have the same outcome, however, i.e. they differ only with respect to what happens off the equilibrium path.

What is being described here is akin to the concept of strategic stability proposed by Kohlberg and Mertens (1986). They study finite games and call a set of equilibria strategically stable if it is the minimal set with the property that, for any sufficiently small perturbation of the game, there is an equilibrium of the perturbed game that is close to the given set. This is not a precise definition, but I think it gives the flavour of the original. No attempt is made here to give a precise account of what strategic stability might mean in the present context. An analysis along the lines proposed by Kohlberg and Mertens is quite impossible in the space available.

13 This claim provides the link between stability in the sense of Kohlberg and Mertens and the property described in Proposition 4. Let (r^*_{-i}, r_i) be given and consider the continuation game that follows this choice of repayments. Perturb the model by assuming that a small measure $\epsilon_{it} > 0$ of entrepreneurs of type t apply to banker i, for every $i = 1, \ldots, N$ and $t = 0, 1$. For any $\delta > 0$ and all sufficiently small perturbations of the form $\eta\epsilon$, we can find an equilibrium outcome of the perturbed continuation game that is δ-close to the original outcome.

14 A similar conclusion is suggested by the concept of Universal Divinity (Banks and Sobel, 1988). Roughly, Universal Divinity asserts that if, for any best response by the bankers, it is a strict best response for the type 0 entrepreneurs to apply whenever it is a (weak or strict) best response for type 1 entrepreneurs to apply, then the bankers' beliefs should be concentrated on the type 0 entrepreneurs. In other words, the most pessimistic beliefs are asserted to be plausible.

15 Instead of demanding a fixed repayment r, suppose the banker asks for R_0 with probability p and 0 with probability $1 - p$, where p is chosen so that $(1 - p)R_1 = R_1 - r$. From the point of view of the safe entrepreneur, this contract is equally attractive, but it may be less attractive to the risky entrepreneur, who now pays R_0 with probability πp. If

$$(1 - p)\pi R_0 < \pi(R_0 - r),$$

the risky entrepreneur is worse off under the stochastic repayment scheme.

REFERENCES

Banks, J. and J. Sobel (1988) 'Equilibrium selection in signalling games', *Econometrica* 55, 647–61.

Bernanke, B. (1983) 'Non-monetary effects of the financial crisis in the propagation of the Great Depression', *American Economic Review* 73, 257–63.

Bernanke, B. and M. Gertler (1989) 'Agency costs, net worth and business fluctuations', *American Economic Review* 79, 14–31.

Bernanke, B. and C. Lown (1991) 'The credit crunch', *Brookings Papers on Economic Activity*, 205–47.

Bester, H. (1985) 'Screening versus rationing in credit markets with imperfect information', *American Economic Review* 75, 850–5.

Bester, H. and M. Hellwig (1987) 'Moral hazard and equilibrium credit rationing: an overview of the issues', in G. Bamberg and K. Spremann (eds.), *Agency Theory, Information and Incentives*. Heidelberg: Springer Verlag.

Broecker, T. (1990) 'Credit-worthiness tests and interbank competition', *Econometrica* 58, 429–52.

Cooper, R. and A. John (1988) 'Coordinating coordination failures in Keynesian models', *Quarterly Journal of Economics* **103**, 441–63.

Diamond, D. (1984) 'Financial intermediation and delegated monitoring', *Review of Economic Studies* **51**, 393–414.

Diamond, D. and P. Dybvig (1983) 'Bank runs, deposit insurance and liquidity', *Journal of Political Economy* **91**, 401–19.

Green, E. and S. Oh (1991a) 'Can a "credit crunch" be efficient?' *Quarterly Review*, Federal Reserve Bank of Minneapolis, Autumn, 3–17.

   (1991b) 'Contracts, constraints and consumption', *Review of Economic Studies* **58**, 883–99.

Haubrich, J. (1991) 'Do excess reserves reveal credit crunches?' *Economic Commentary*, Federal Reserve Bank of Cleveland, 15 July, 1–4.

Hellwig, M. (1987) 'Some recent developments in the theory of competition in markets with adverse selection', *European Economic Review Papers and Proceedings* **31**, 319–25.

Kohlberg, E. and J.-F. Mertens (1986) 'On the strategic stability of equilibria', *Econometrica* **54**, 1003–37.

Mankiw, G. (1986) 'The allocation of credit and financial collapse', *Quarterly Journal of Economics* **101**, 455–70.

Matutes, C. and X. Vives (1991) 'Competition for deposits, risks of failure and regulation in banking', Institut d'Analisi Economica, Universitat Autónoma de Barcelona (unpublished).

Meltzer, A. (1991) 'There is no credit crunch', *The Wall Street Journal*, 8 February, A-14.

Milgrom, P. and J. Roberts (1990) 'Rationalizability, learning and equilibrium in games with strategic complementarities', *Econometrica* **58**, 1255–78.

Stiglitz, J. and A. Weiss (1981) 'Credit rationing in markets with imperfect information', *American Economic Review* **71**, 393–410.

Vives, X. (1990) 'Nash equilibrium with strategic complementarities', *Journal of Mathematical Economics* **19**, 305–21.

Winton, A. (1990) 'Three Essays on Information, Contracting and Financial Intermediation', unpublished PhD dissertation, University of Pennsylvania.

Yanelle, M.-O. (1989). 'The strategic analysis of intermediation', *European Economic Review* **33**, 294–301.

Discussion

FRANKLIN ALLEN

During the recent recession there has been a considerable amount of discussion in the US and UK about the existence of a 'credit crunch'. Some small borrowers have claimed that banks were unwilling to lend to them even for projects with good prospects. Bernanke and Lown (1991) and others suggest that this credit crunch was due to banks having a

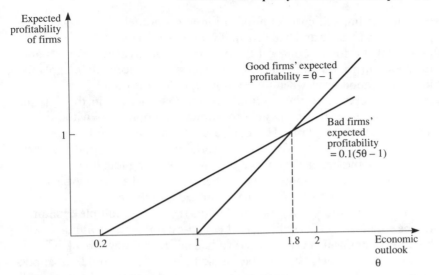

Figure 5A.1   The relationship between the expected profitability of good and bad firms and economic outlook with debt contracts

shortage of equity capital. Gale provides a different theory of credit crunches. This theory can be explained with the help of a simple example. Suppose there are two types of firm, good and bad. Both types of firm can undertake a project with a cost of 1 each period. Firms' profitability depends on the overall economic outlook for that period, which is represented by the variable θ. At the beginning of each period, θ is known. A good firm has a return at the end of the period of θ with probability 1; a bad firm has a return 5θ with probability 0.1 and a return of θ with probability 0.9. Firms do not have the necessary funds to undertake the project but may be able to borrow them from a bank. Firms know their own type but banks cannot observe this. Banks are assumed to lend using a debt contract. For simplicity, the banks' required rate of return is 0. All agents are risk neutral.

If firms were using their own funds, they would undertake projects when $\theta > 1$ if they were good and when $\theta > 2$ if they were bad; firms' decisions would be socially optimal. If, however, firms borrow from banks, this is no longer the case. Figure 5A.1 illustrates the profitability of good and bad firms as θ varies. The use of a debt contract results in the bad firms having an incentive to apply for a loan and undertake a project when $\theta > 0.2$ even though this is socially inefficient. Good firms' incentives are the same as before because their returns are with certainty. For $\theta > 1.8$, good firms are more profitable than bad firms. By setting the sum of the explicit and implicit costs of application appropriately (i.e. between the profitability of good and bad firms), it is possible to ensure that only good firms apply for loans. For $\theta < 1.8$, however, bad firms are more profitable than good firms. Bad firms therefore have a greater incentive to apply for loans than good firms when the economic outlook is poor.

Gale is interested in the operation of the loan market in this type of situation where it is not possible to attract the good firms without also attracting all the bad firms. He considers the case where banks can screen applicants imperfectly. The more effort good firms expend on their application, the better the chance they have of being identified as good; bad firms always have some chance of being identified as good even if they expend minimal effort. Banks have limited processing capacity. As a result of the interaction of these two factors there exist multiple equilibria. In one equilibrium the credit market collapses; no bank is willing to lend because all applicants are expected to be bad. If any single bank were to try to lend, these beliefs would be fulfilled. Good firms would not apply; they would perceive that their chance of being granted a loan is small because of the bank's limited processing capacity and the large number of bad firms applying. Bad firms, on the other hand, would find it worth applying because of the greater (private) profitability of their projects. There also exist other equilibria in which banks do lend. Suppose, for example, all banks do lend, then there is no congestion and good applicants find it worthwhile to apply.

Gale's model provides an interesting alternative interpretation of the recent credit crunch to that provided by Bernanke and Lown (1991). The critical issue is whether it has empirical content. Consider the simple example introduced initially. Suppose that banks were not restricted to using debt contracts and could instead lend and obtain a share a in the revenues of the firm. Setting $a = 1/\theta$ means that the good firms have expected profits of $(1 - a)\theta = \theta - 1$, whereas the bad firms have expected profits of $(1 - a)0.1(5\theta) = 0.5(\theta - 1) < \theta - 1$. In other words, if equity is used the good firms again have a greater incentive to apply for loans than the bad firms for $0 < \theta < 1.8$. This removes the condition required for Gale's theory to be applicable. A lender using an equity contract can simply design the application process so that the sum of the explicit and implicit costs of application, F, are such that $0.5(\theta - 1) < F < \theta - 1$. In this case, only good firms apply and banks cover their outlays with revenues of $a\theta = 1$ per firm.

This observation that the use of equity by lenders can avoid the collapse of the credit market leads to a number of predictions. First, financial collapse will be limited to countries such as the US and UK where banks lend using only debt contracts. In countries such as France and Germany with universal banking systems, banks can make equity loans and financial collapse will not occur. Instead, as the economic outlook deteriorates, there will be a switch away from debt towards equity. Second, even in countries such as the US and UK, financial collapse will predominantly occur in the banking sector; public markets will be less affected because of the availability of equity.

Casual empiricism suggests that the credit crunch was a more important phenomenon in the US and UK than in France and Germany and that it was confined more to the banking sectors in the US and UK than the public credit markets (see, e.g., Brady, 1991). These observations are consistent with Gale's theory of financial collapse. It would be interesting to obtain data on the composition of bank lending in France and Germany between debt and equity as the economic outlook deteriorated. If the data show that there was a move towards equity finance, this would further suggest that Gale's theory captures important features of actual credit markets.

NOTE

I am grateful to Gary Gorton for helpful discussions. Financial support from the NSF is gratefully acknowledged.

REFERENCES

Bernanke, B. and C. Lown (1991) 'The credit crunch', *Brookings Papers on Economic Activity*, 205–47.
Brady, S. (1991) 'Credit crunch? What credit crunch?' *Euromoney*, March, 22–32.

OREN SUSSMAN

The paper is an extension of the Stiglitz–Weiss (1981) model of lending under adverse selection (risky and safe projects, with safe projects having a higher expected rate of return but a lower income when successful). The major addition to this framework is a screening technology available to lenders (banks): at a cost of B a bank can get a (noisy) signal on the type of the borrower. Screening is costly not only to the bank but to the loan

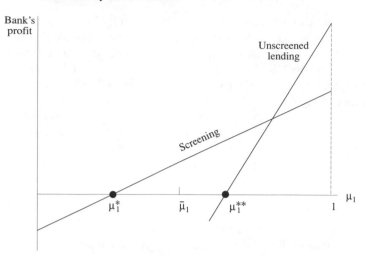

Figure 5B.1   Bank's profit as a function of beliefs about a typical applicant, μ_1

applicant as well because applying for a loan requires some effort A_0. Moreover, a safe borrower can eliminate the noise of their signal by investing a higher level of effort A_1. Another important assumption is that the bank is constrained in its information-processing capacity and cannot screen more than K projects.

This framework is used in order to study the possibility of a financial collapse, i.e. an equilibrium where no lending takes place in spite of the fact that some profitable investment opportunities are available. The novelty relative to other discussions of financial collapse (c.f. Mankiw, 1986) is the analysis of multiple equilibria: for a given set of fundamental parameters equilibria with and without lending exist. The market may collapse due to the breakdown of coordination, and not just as a result of some arbitrary change in the fundamental parameters.

Some assumptions are made about the fundamental parameters, so that, typically, there exist a lending rate, r, such that agents' profits are described by Figures 5B.1 and 5B.2. Figure 5B.1 describes the bank's profit from unscreened lending and from screening (and subsequent lending if the signal is good) as a function of its beliefs about the population of applicants: μ_1 is the probability that an applicant has a safe project, given they had applied for a loan. The profit from screening is calculated under the assumption that applicants with a good project put a high level of effort into the application, otherwise the signal is not informative and screening is not profitable (see discussion and proof of Proposition 2 for more detail). Similarly, Figure 5B.2 describes the profit

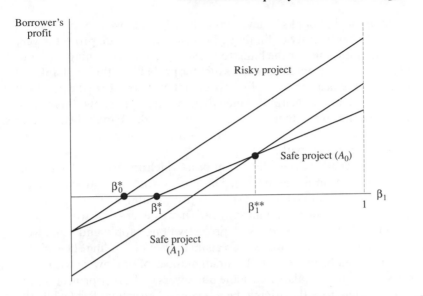

Figure 5B.2   Borrower's profit as a function of the probability of being screened

level of a borrower (who has a risky or a safe project and may choose to invest a high or low level of effort in the application process) as a function of the probability that the bank will screen them β_1 (and provide the loan if the signal is good). It is assumed in Figure 5B.2 that no unscreened lending is available (see discussion and proof of Proposition 3 for more detail).

An equilibrium with positive lending is quite straightforward. Denote by $\bar{\mu}_1$ the share of safe projects in the population (note the distinction between the population of loan applicants and the population of entrepreneurs in general). If bankers' beliefs are $\mu_1 = \bar{\mu}_1$, screening is profitable (if $\mu_1^* < \bar{\mu}_1$ as in Figure 5B.1) while unscreened lending is not. The bank will screen any applicant (provided the capacity constraint is not binding), so $\beta_1 = 1$. At that probability of the bank processing the loan application, it is profitable for borrowers with either safe or risky projects to make the effort of applying for a loan. Moreover, it is profitable for a borrower with a safe project to invest a high level of effort in the application (see Figure 5B.2). Thus, the bank's beliefs are consistent with the realization of the game along the equilibrium path. The information-processing capacity constraint may bind, but for this equilibrium still to exist it should allow the bank to set $\beta_1 > \beta_1^{**}$ so that it is still profitable for the safe borrower to invest a high level of effort in the application (see Propositions 2 and 3 for exact proofs of the above statements).

For the same set of parameters, an equilibrium with no lending also exists. Suppose that banks believe that only risky borrowers apply, so that $\mu_1 = 0$. If the probability of finding a borrower with a safe project is very low, it is unprofitable for the bank to spend money on screening and thus $\beta_1 = 0$. Thus, the entrepreneur knows that the probability that the bank will process their application is very low, so it is not profitable to make the effort involved in a loan application. Since there are no applicants, there is no lending, and no event that is inconsistent with the bank's beliefs ever happens, so that beliefs are consistent with the realization of the game along the equilibrium path.

There are a few other no-lending equilibria (which are discussed in Proposition 4). For example: assume beliefs are $\mu_1 = \mu_1^*$ so that unscreened lending is not profitable and screening is just profitable. Thus, the probability that a bank will process an application can be set arbitrarily at a level of β_0^* so that borrowers with a safe project will not apply and borrowers with a risky project are indifferent, so again there is no lending. The advantage of this equilibrium is that, if a small number of borrowers with good projects apply (by mistake), and some borrowers with risky projects apply also (by indifference), the original beliefs can still be rationalized while the new equilibrium is 'close' to the old one. A concept of 'robustness' can be developed along these lines.

Bankers' behaviour is optimal given their beliefs. What happens, however, if a certain bank deviates unilaterally (maybe because it understands that entrepreneurs don't apply only because they believe that their application will not be processed)? Such a bank, however, will not be able to increase β_1 significantly because the capacity constraint will bind, so that borrowers still will not apply. Note that the economy does not face a capacity constraint in the lending equilibrium because entrepreneurs are spread over a large number of banks so that each has a number of applications it can handle. Thus, capacity constraints are used to argue that 'equilibrium is robust in a fairly strong sense' (see Proposition 5 for a rigorous treatment of this idea).

It is noteworthy, however, that the meaning of the application effort (of the good borrower) is stretched here beyond the original motivation given in section 2. It is said there that a 'well-documented' safe project has a better chance of giving a good signal relative to a 'poorly documented application'. It is assumed in the proof of Proposition 5 that the applicant has to do all this documentation before the bank even decides whether to process the application. Why isn't it possible for the bank to choose (randomly) the borrowers to be processed, let these borrowers document the information and only then evaluate the prospects? This possibility is not discussed in the paper (it is excluded by the definition of the game) but it is an important possibility if the model is applied to actual credit markets.

Another important assumption in the proof of Proposition 5 is that screening capacity cannot be shared by banks. If, for example, the deviating bank rents screening capacity from other banks, or it can pay other banks to do the screening for it, or the screening capacity is owned by a few big credit-rating agencies that specialize in screening only, then Proposition 5 will hold for a smaller subset of the parameter's space (maybe an empty subset in some cases).

This problem is actually just another aspect of a problem which is discussed by the author in the paper: that financial structure is assumed exogenously rather than derived endogenously. Bankers are not allowed to construct and offer incentive schemes that will discourage risky bor-rowers from applying for credit (a few ideas are mentioned in section 7 of the paper), nor are they allowed to reorganize their business or industry in a way which will allow them to use capacity more efficiently.

I would like to conclude this discussion by stressing that this paper deals with a tremendously important issue. For about twenty-five years after World War II financial markets in Europe and the United States looked quite sheltered (by regulation), and the 'real' economy was 'insulated' from potential instability. In the last fifteen years or so things have changed gradually, and it seems the world is heading for a situation in which a financial collapse will mark the downturn of any business cycle. Financial theorists have thus renewed their interest in the somewhat vague idea of 'financial fragility' (and the related concept of a 'credit crunch' which is discussed in the paper).

From that point of view, it seems that the main question which remains unanswered in the paper is what triggers the breakdown of coordination. More important, the breakdown of coordination is not a random event, and is related to the business cycle. The concept of congestion discussed in the paper may be interesting in that respect: maybe credit markets get congested during the boom phase of the business cycle, which triggers the financial collapse. This event starts the bust phase of the business cycle during which some of the congestion is eliminated so that a new boom can start.

I therefore agree with the author that there is much scope for future work in this area.

6 Financial intermediation and economic development

ROBERT G. KING and ROSS LEVINE

1 Introduction

How important are financial markets to the construction of a European economic system which fosters growth, development and international trade? The traditional view is that financial markets are simply the 'handmaiden of industry', but recent economic research suggests otherwise. In this new view, financial markets play a central role in determining a country's patterns of trade and growth.

The emerging new view of the links between financial markets and growth results from two of the most dynamic subfields of economic research. Economists now have an essentially new perspective on what financial intermediaries do and how the economic growth process works. When combined, as is taking place in ongoing research, these two new views lead us to the conclusion that financial markets can play an important role in the growth process. There is also evidence that cross-country differences in growth rates have reliable linkages to measures of the size and efficiency of the financial intermediation sector.

The traditional view of financial intermediaries was that these organizations passively funnel household saving to business investment.[1] The 'new view of financial intermediation' has a much richer vision of the nature and economic function of these organizations. Indeed, financial intermediaries are viewed as playing an active, perhaps dominant, role in the organization of industry. With their actions, they determine which economic organizations will survive and which will perish, which entrepreneurs will control organizations and which will not, which types of investment can be made and which cannot, and which new economic products can be introduced by firms and which cannot.

On the growth side, the traditional view is that for which Solow won the Nobel prize in economics and is reflected in two classic articles. First, in his theoretical work, Solow (1956) identified differences in paths of

156

physical capital accumulation as the central endogenous determinant of differences in economic growth experiences for different countries; his theoretical work also identified the resulting differences as temporary. Second, in his empirical work (1957), Solow showed that capital accumulation did not explain much of observed US growth; this finding was shown by Maddison and others to be generally true for many countries and time periods. Overall, many economists saw these two findings as producing important limits on the extent to which government policies – including financial market policies – could be potential determinants of the economic growth process. For those economists working closely with actual development experiences, this view of the relative unimportance of policy determinants of growth was essentially impossible to believe, so that development economics increasingly became a separate part of economics from the theoretical modelling of economic growth. By the end of the 1970s, each field had distinct participants and standards; there was relatively little communication between the two fields.

The new economics of growth and development of the 1980s – initiated by Romer (1986) and Lucas (1988) – is sharply different in this regard. First, the new theoretical literature suggests that a range of economic policies can have important effects on a country's growth rate over lengthy periods. In fact, within some 'endogenous growth' models, policies – particularly those that influence the private costs and benefits of investing in human capital and productivity enhancement – can *permanently* influence the growth rate of an economy. Second, the new empirical growth literature of the 1980s is closely linked to theoretical work. For example, this is very evident in the sociology of research conferences: it is common for the same economists to participate in both empirical and theoretical work. More importantly, theoretical models are used as organizing principles and sources of hypotheses in empirical investigations; empirical evidence is used to circumscribe theoretical models and to evaluate their qualitative implications.

In this paper, our objectives are threefold. To begin, we provide a detailed exposition of ongoing theoretical work that provides links between financial intermediation and economic growth. Next, we provide some empirical evidence that suggests that measures of the extent and quality of financial intermediation are reliably linked to historical differences in growth during the post World War II period. Lastly, we link our study to the monumental policy choices facing the formerly socialist economies of Europe. Our theoretical and empirical analyses suggest that financial sector reform can importantly promote economic growth in these countries by improving the efficient allocation of resources and the effectiveness of other public policies.

While theoretical and empirical research on financial intermediation and economic development is in its early stages, we think that there are now good reasons to suspect that the links may be very important. First, the independent theoretical developments in the two research areas suggest important interactions, even though developing the ties between financial intermediation and growth was not the initial objective of either research area. Second, the accumulating empirical evidence – reviewed in this paper – suggests that there has been an important historical relationship between financial intermediation and economic development. Countries with larger and more efficient financial intermediation sectors systematically outperformed other countries during the post World War II period.

2   Theoretical perspective

In this section, we first summarize why we think that there are intrinsic links between financial intermediation and the productivity of an economy, which is based on our ongoing research in this area (King and Levine, 1992b). We then discuss how variations in productivity lead to implications for (i) the long-run level of economic development or (ii) the long-term rate of growth, within some recent growth models. Lastly, we return to our working model and ask what general implications it has for (i) which types of public policy countries might have to pursue to accomplish given objectives; and (ii) which types of public policy packages would be growth promoting. The key point, which we plan to pursue further in additional work, is that there are typically important interactions across policy effects implied by our working model.

2.1   Our working model[2]

Sustained economic development originates, we believe, in a nexus that involves (i) entrepreneurship, (ii) intangible capital investment, and (iii) financial intermediation. Our working model thus involves a blending of ideas due to Frank Knight (1951) and Joseph Schumpeter (1911). In this paper, we also adopt Knight's and Schumpeter's research style by outlining the key theoretical interactions in verbal form.

At the centre of our theory is an entrepreneur contemplating an innovation, i.e. the undertaking of an economic activity in a way that is new in some dimension. From Schumpeter, we take that it is the accumulation of such innovations that is at the heart of growth. From Knight, we take the concept of entrepreneurship, which is that certain individuals have the requisite skills to turn abstract ideas into marketable products.

2.1.1 Defining innovation

From our standpoint, we want to interpret the idea of 'newness' very broadly. First, it could involve the literal invention of a new product, such as a microcomputer. Second, it could involve the enhancement of an existing product, such as the introduction of the 486 chip. Third, it could consist of adopting technology produced elsewhere, such as the production of microcomputers in Taiwan. Fourth, it could involve adapting technologies, such as creating a keyboard that could be readily used to do wordprocessing in Taiwanese. Fifth, it could involve producing an existing product using altered business methods, such as making a keyboard using a costly modification of a firm's organization of production. Among the most important of these modifications are specific investments in the human capital of the firm's workers.

2.1.2 Core elements of our model

The key aspects of our view are as follows:

(1) There is an entrepreneur who seeks to undertake an innovation, which requires finance of investment.
(2) Entrepreneurs arc heterogeneous: some have ideas that are efficient for society to undertake, others do not. Evaluating the desirability of ideas is feasible at some cost, but it is essential that the process of evaluation not reveal too much information about the nature and character of the ideas. Otherwise the ideas might be appropriated by competitors.
(3) Much of productivity-enhancing investment involves construction of an intangible capital good. By the nature of this asset, (i) it is difficult for a third party to evaluate the efficacy of the investments; and (ii) it serves as poor collateral, because it is embodied in an entrepreneur and a team of managers and production workers.
(4) The returns to intangible capital good are quasi rents that are determined by (i) the size of the market; (ii) the rates of innovation of competitors; and (iii) taxation and public regulation.

In this setting, financial intermediaries will arise endogenously as part of a market mechanism for the screening of entrepreneurs and the financing of intangible, productivity-enhancing investment by creditworthy entrepreneurs.

2.1.3 Linkages between financial intermediation and productivity

Our working model implies that countries with better-functioning financial systems will be correspondingly better at evaluating innovations and entrepreneurs. Thus, countries with superior financial systems will, *ceteris*

Figure 6.1   The traditional view

paribus, allocate savings to more efficient and productive endeavours than will countries with less effective financial systems. In our model, more efficient resource allocation translates into increased productivity and growth through physical capital accumulation, improvements in the types of intangible capital described above, and human capital development.

2.2   Financial intermediation and the development process

With financial intermediation linked to productivity, there can thus be different implications from the standard received viewpoint on the role of financial intermediaries in the economic growth process. In order to understand reasons for these differences, we begin by summarizing the traditional viewpoint and then turn to contrasting our viewpoint.

2.2.1   The traditional view

The traditional view of economic growth and its relationship to financial intermediation contains two main propositions. First, for reasons that we will detail later, the growth effects of changes in intermediation are small. Second, the effects of the level of development on a country's demand for various forms of financial services are large. Thus, the traditional view makes the prediction that most of the observed correlations would involve a causal link from development to finance: it is a corollary of the more general view that finance is the handmaiden to industry.

We begin by considering the reasons that the conventional view suggests that there are small effects of financial intermediation on the level of economic development and, even more so, on sustained economic growth. Figure 6.1 shows the linkages visually: financial intermediation was thought to have only minor effects on investment in physical capital, and investment was viewed as relatively unimportant for determining economic activity. To be more precise, it is necessary to follow Solow's analytical route and to discuss the implications of using a Cobb–Douglas production function, $y = A k^a$, with y being per capita GDP, k being the per capita stock of physical capital, and A being omitted residual elements such as general human capital and other productivity-enhancing factors. Within this type of production function, conventional estimates are that a is about 0.3, with an absolute upper bound being 0.5. This restriction

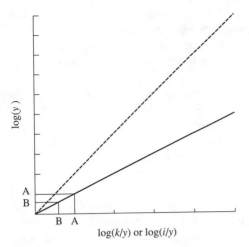

A
B

B A

$\log(k/y)$ or $\log(i/y)$

Figure 6.2   Accumulation and economic development in the physical capital (Solow) model

embodies the idea that – at a given level of exogenous technical progress – the investment process is subject to sharply diminishing returns.

Sharply diminishing returns to capital formation substantially limit the ability of the Solow model to explain cross-national differences in the level of economic development and the rate of growth. First, it implies that cross-country differences in long-run levels of the capital/output ratio (k/y) or the investment rate (i/y) can have limited effects on the level of output. Figure 6.2 graphs the long-run relationship between $\log(y)$ and $\log(k/y)$, which is a line with slope $\theta = a/(1 - a)$, such that $y = A/(1 - a)(R/y)^{\theta}$. Consequently, if country A had twice the capital/output ratio of country B, then it could have no more than twice the output level, since θ is at most $0.5/(1 - 0.5) = 1$. Hence, there is an important upper bound placed on the extent to which cross-country differences in asset stocks – including those maintained by financial intermediaries – can lead to differences in the level of economic development.[3] Second, looking at the time series of growth observations for a single country, changes in the rate of investment (i/y) within a specific sample period can lead to only relatively minor variations in growth rates. For example, an increase in (i/y) from an initial value of 0.20 to a value of 0.22 – an increase of 10 per cent – would lead to at most a 10 per cent increase in the level of output in the long run. If all of this occurred within a thirty-year period – no portion being present in the initial level of GDP and no portion being incomplete at the end – then the impact on the annual average growth rate would be at most 0.33 per cent. Third, as shown in Solow (1956), the Cobb–Douglas production function implies that physical investment and capital formation can account for only a small portion of US economic development; as may be seen from Maddison's survey (1987), this finding was strikingly confirmed for many other countries and time periods.

In addition, the traditional view circumscribed the channels through which financial intermediation could affect the level of development and the rate of growth. In particular, financial intermediaries were viewed mainly as passive conduits of funds from savers to firms undertaking physical capital investments; intermediation was important, then, only as it affected physical investment, bounding its effects. Further, a variety of evidence suggested small interest elasticities of savings rates – via financial intermediaries and in other forms – and investment so that distortions in the financial sector were viewed as relatively unimportant for investment. Consequences for the level of development and the rate of growth were thus taken to be a result of combining two empirically minor channels of influence: multiplying two small effects together produces very little.

None the less, in Goldsmith's (1969) seminal study of thirty-six countries over the period 1860–1963, he shows that there is a strong positive relationship between the ratio of financial institutions' assets to GNP and output per capita. Goldsmith also shows that periods of rapid economic growth tend to be associated with above-average rates of financial development. Goldsmith is quick to note, however, that his analysis does not establish a causal link from financial intermediary services to growth, nor does his analysis identify the channels – capital accumulation or productivity enhancements – through which growth and financial development are linked.

2.2.2 The new view

The emerging new view suggests quite a different perspective on the potential influence of financial intermediaries on the level of economic development and the rate of economic growth. This involves challenges to both the role of intermediation and the nature of the development process.

The precise nature of the links between financial intermediation and economic development will depend on which of a range of recent growth models is employed. While these models differ on the exact nature of the 'long-run' opportunities for an individual country, they all agree on some core elements. In particular, all view the relevant process of capital accumulation as much richer than that highlighted theoretically and measured empirically by Solow. In addition to physical investment, Lucas (1988) has stressed investment in general human capital, Romer (1990)

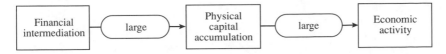

Figure 6.3 **The new view**

has stressed investments that extend the menu of products produced by an economy, and Prescott and Boyd (1987) have stressed investments in firm-specific human capital. Each of these latter ideas is an example of the investment in intangible, productivity-enhancing investments that we discussed above as 'innovation'.

Models of bounded growth. One class of models stresses the following characteristic: there is a technological frontier that is determined by the world's scientific knowledge, which it is useful to think of as growing at a constant rate. At any given level of such knowledge, there are limits to how much any individual country can achieve. Individual countries differ in the extent to which they exploit this knowledge: some utilize it poorly and others well. Rich countries are those that have high levels of three types of capital: productivity-enhancing intangible capital, physical capital and general human capital. Thus, in these models, a permanent decrease in the cost of accumulating productivity-enhancing capital increases such investments, which raises the rewards to investments in physical capital and human capital. Thus, in turn, the models set in motion the transition to a new higher growth path at which the stocks of all factors of producton are higher. Models of this form work much like the standard model of Solow but with a comprehensive capital stock – an aggregate of all social investments – that is subject only to mildly diminishing returns.

Models of perpetual growth. Another class of models views an individual country as not constrained by world scientific developments but capable of growing forever at rates that depend only on the extent of investments made by the country; investments in all of the types of capital that we discussed earlier. A range of examples of these types of model is provided by Rebelo (1991), and demonstrates that economic policies can raise or lower the growth rate of the economy forever.

2.2.3 A summary of the new view
There is a much larger potential impact of financial intermediation on economic growth in the 'new view' summarized in Figure 6.3. First, the new view suggests that there may be important connections between financial intermediation and productivity, and a range of economic growth models, new and old, indicate that productivity will have an

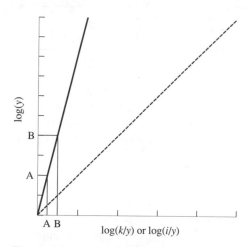

Figure 6.4   Accumulation and development in the comprehensive model

important effect on economic activity. These linkages from financial intermediation activities to productivity enhancement to economic development are the focus of our work in King and Levine (1992b). Second, in new growth models, a larger role is assigned to influences on investment – essentially by viewing more of economic activity as capitalist in nature – including physical capital accumulation, general human capital accumulation, and investment in other intangible productivity-enhancing capital goods. This suggests writing an aggregate production function of the form $y = \underline{A}(\underline{K})^{\alpha}$, where $\underline{K}$ is a comprehensive capital aggregate and $\underline{a}$ is the associated share parameter. Then, we can represent examples of these two new models of economic development very simply. First, the basic bounded growth model has $\underline{a}$ much larger than in the traditional view, but continues to have $\underline{a} < 1$. Second, the basic unbounded growth model has $\underline{a} = 1$.

Bounded growth models. Figure 6.4 shows some important implications of the bounded growth model with a comprehensive capital aggregate. First, relative to the comparable diagram in Figure 6.2, it follows that the effects of cross-national differences in $\underline{k}/y$ or $\underline{i}/y$ are much larger. For example, if we adopt the value of $a = 0.8$ that is suggested by the work of Barro and Sala-i-Martin (1992) and Mankiw, Romer and Weil (1992), then it follows that cross-national differences in output levels are related to cross-national differences in $\underline{k}/y$ or $\underline{i}/y$ levels by $\theta = 0.8/(1 - 0.8) = 4$. Thus, for example, a country with a capital/output ratio twice as high as another had double the income per capita in Figure 6.2 and $2^4 = 16$ times the income per capita in Figure 6.4. Second, the comprehensive view of capital formation implies that changes in investment rates also account for more sustained growth.[4] Reworking the example used in our discussion of the traditional view, an increase in the investment rate by 10 per cent of its base level sets off a 40 per cent increase in GDP (with $a = 0.8$). If all of this increase occurred over a thirty-year time period, then the impact on growth would average 1.33 per cent; this is four times the effect in the Solow model.[5]

Unbounded growth models. With perpetual growth ($a = 1$), there is no analogue to Figure 6.4 since there is no technological frontier toward which the economy converges. Instead, there is simply a shift to a new higher rate of growth that depends positively on the productivity of the comprehensive capital aggregate, i.e. on the value of A in the production function. Our working model suggests financial intermediation positively affects 'A' and thus permanently increases the rate of economic growth.

Implications for our empirical work. In the empirical analysis summarized below, we use specifications suggested by both the bounded and unbounded growth models. We organize our discussion as follows. First, we consider the relationship between our financial indicators and the level of development; this permits us also to provide a detailed critique of the conventional view. Second, we explore empirical linkages between the financial indicators and growth rates.

2.3 Interactions between public policies

From our standpoint, one of the most important implications of the new view is that it suggests important interaction effects among the public policy actions designed to promote long-term growth and development. Since the IMF and the World Bank have stressed openness to international trade as a growth-promoting strategy, we focus on elaborating the interactions in this area.

Consider a country – many come to mind – with substantial barriers to international trade, in the form of import/export restrictions and tariffs. We think it is important to begin by asking why such a country might have put trade restrictions in place. It seems most plausible that this is to protect the domestic monopoly position of producers – both capitalist and specialized workers – in import-competing industries. If this is so, then there are other implications of this hypothesis within the model that we have in mind: protecting the position of an existing domestic monopoly requires not only that it be isolated from international trade but that there be a restriction on the entry of potential domestic rivals. In part, this may be accomplished by public regulation of new enterprises, for example the extensive licensing requirements that include disclosure of key concepts and ideas to entrenched rivals. But, from our perspective, it also probably requires the regulation of domestic and international banking. Regulation of banking limits the ability of potential rivals to enter the protected market. Regulation of domestic banking is important, but not sufficient; there must also be an exclusion of foreign lending – either explicitly or via the threat of confiscation of returns – from domestic markets. Otherwise, domestic entrepreneurs that sought to be rivals to the domestic monopoly would have ready access to sources of venture capital. Thus, our model of finance and growth predicts that international finance restrictions would accompany trade restrictions.

Now, we want to consider what will happen if a country alters certain economic policies, specifically engaging in policies that promote exports, based on the observation that other high-export countries are high-growth countries. Inefficient domestic monopolies will not be able to compete in international markets without major government subsidies, so that changes in export policy may be of little consequence with existing capabilities. Instead, producers must adopt new technologies and products that are viable in world markets. In this regard, society must reallocate resources to a new group of producers. Consequently, the success of international trade policies may well depend on the extent to which domestic and international financial markets operate effectively.

3   Financial development and economic activity

It is useful to begin our discussion of the links between financial and economic development by asking how financial intermediation and the *level* of real economic activity are related when we look across a wide range of countries.

3.1   Some cross-country evidence

To measure the level of real economic activity, we use gross domestic product (GDP) per capita in 1987 dollars for each country in two different years, 1970 and 1985.[6] In some companion research (King and Levine, 1992a), we construct a number of measures of the extent of financial intermediation within a country and study their links to economic growth. Table 6.1 defines these measures in more detail, but the crucial types of indicators are as follows.

Money demand indicators. One of our financial indicators captures the scale of domestic currency funds held by individuals and corporations principally for transactions. The indicator M1Y is the ratio of a country's currency and demand deposits to its GDP. This indicator captures the

Table 6.1. *Financial development and real per capita GDP in 1970*

Indicators	Very rich	Rich	Poor	Very poor	Correlation with RGDP70	(*P*-value)
M1Y	0.19	0.20	0.15	0.14	0.16	(0.11)
LLY	0.48	0.38	0.21	0.19	0.43	(0.0001)
LLY-M1Y	0.31	0.18	0.06	0.05	0.56	(0.0001)
CBY	0.06	0.07	0.10	0.10	− 0.20	(0.06)
BY	0.43	0.25	0.17	0.12	0.72	(0.0001)
PRIVY	0.35	0.23	0.14	0.09	0.53	(0.0001)
BANK	0.86	0.77	0.71	0.62	0.43	(0.0001)
PRIVATE	0.72	0.71	0.56	0.48	0.42	(0.0002)
NON-MBY	0.19	0.10	0.04	0.02	0.70	(0.0001)
RGDP70	10385	1813	596	219		
N =	28	28	28	27		

Key:
Very rich: RGDP70 > 3506
Rich: RGDP70 > 799 and < 3506
Poor: RGDP70 > 362 and < 799
Very poor: RGDP70 < 362

M1Y	= M1 to GDP
LLY	= Liquid liabilities to GDP
QLLY	= LLY-M1Y
CBY	= Central bank domestic credit to GDP
BY	= Deposit money bank domestic credit to GDP
PRIVY	= Gross claims on private sector to GDP
BANK	= Deposit money bank domestic credit divided by deposit money bank + central bank domestic credit
PRIVATE	= Claims on the non-financial private sector to total domestic credit
NON-MBY	= Claims on the private sector by non-deposit money banks divided by GDP
RGDP70	= Real per capita GDP in 1970, in 1987 dollars

fraction of a year's income held for transactions purposes: in 1970, the average level is 0.18 across the 94 countries that we study; in 1985 the corresponding value is 0.19. There is some slight tendency for this financial indicator to be correlated with the level of development in the international cross-section. In fact, the finding that there is not a strong correlation is consistent with the standard view that there is close to a unit income elasticity in the demand for money: individuals and corporations hold transactions balances roughly in proportion to their income and expenditure flows.[7]

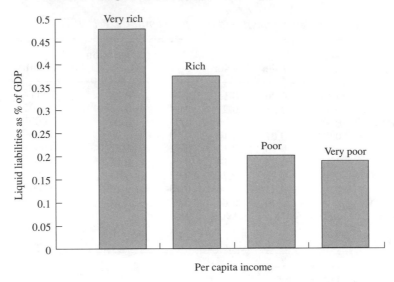

Figure 6.5   Financial size (LLY) and real per capita income, 1970

The scale of financial intermediaries. The size of the financial system is proximately measured by other financial indicators that are much more strongly correlated with the level of development. For example, as shown in Table 6.1, citizens of the richest countries – the top 25 per cent on the basis of income per capita – held about 30 per cent of a year's income in liquid assets beyond their monetary liabilities, while citizens of the poorest countries – the bottom 25 per cent – held only 5 per cent of a year's income in 1970. Figure 6.5 shows the cross-sectional relationship between GDP per capita and total liquid liabilities (including monetary and non-monetary components): we see a positive correlation, but in the poorest half of the sample there is simply little non-monetary demand for liquid liabilities and hence little correlation.

In a good portion of our empirical work, we focus on the financial indicator LLY, which measures the monetary and non-monetary liquid assets held by individuals. This is a measure long studied by development economists, so that it facilitates comparisons between our study and others; it also turns out that many other financial indicators give broadly the same results as LLY.

Central versus private bank lending. There are both public and private components of bank lending that bear distinct relations to the level of development. Private bank lending constitutes about 43 per cent of GDP in the top quarter of the world's countries and only 12 per cent of GDP in

Table 6.2. *Financial development and real per capita GDP in 1985*

Indicators	Very rich	Rich	Poor	Very poor	Correlation with RGDP85	(*P*-value)
M1Y	0.18	0.20	0.18	0.15	0.05	(0.60)
LLY	0.67	0.51	0.39	0.26	0.51	(0.0001)
LLY-M1Y	0.50	0.31	0.21	0.11	0.60	(0.0001)
CBY	0.07	0.16	0.27	0.17	− 0.27	(0.008)
BY	0.66	0.39	0.28	0.19	0.61	(0.0001)
PRIVY	0.53	0.31	0.20	0.13	0.70	(0.0001)
BANK	0.91	0.73	0.57	0.52	0.58	(0.0001)
PRIVATE	0.71	0.58	0.47	0.37	0.51	(0.0001)
NON-MBY	0.30	0.11	0.07	0.07	0.63	(0.0001)
RGDP85	13053	2376	754	241		
N =	29	29	29	29		

Key:
Very rich: RGDP85 > 4998
Rich: RGDP85 > 1161 and < 4998
Poor: RGDP85 > 391 and < 1161
Very poor: RGDP85 < 391

M1Y   = M1 to GDP
LLY   = Liquid liabilities to GDP
QLLY   = LLY-M1Y
CBY   = Central bank domestic credit to GDP
BY   = Deposit money bank domestic credit to GDP
PRIVY   = Gross claims on private sector to GDP
BANK   = Deposit money bank domestic credit divided by deposit money bank + central bank domestic credit
PRIVATE = Claims on the non-financial private sector to total domestic credit
NON-MBY = Claims on the private sector by non-deposit money banks divided by GDP
RGDP85   = Real per capita GDP in 1985, in 1987 dollars

the bottom quarter: the overall correlation is about .5. By contrast, there is a negative correlation with the extent of central bank lending.

Asset distribution. It is also possible to investigate how the level of development depends on whether the recipients of loans are principally private or public institutions. In Table 6.1, there is also a marked positive association with a measure of the extent to which loans are directed to the private sector. The richest 25 per cent of countries have 72 per cent of their loans going to private borrowers, whereas the poorest 25 per cent of countries have only 48 per cent of such loans.

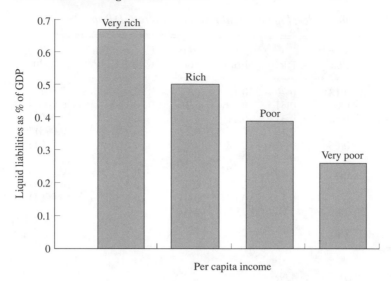

Figure 6.6   Financial size (LLY) and real per capita income, 1985

3.1.1 Robustness of findings

To gauge the stability of these cross-sectional relationships, we computed the same measures of financial development and economic development for 1985: the results for this later sample are reported in Table 6.2 and Figure 6.6. The bottom line is that these findings are largely robust to the exact year when one looks across the range of countries.

3.1.2 Summary of findings

It is useful to summarize these findings briefly before going on to interpret them. We think the main lessons are as follows. First, richer countries have more savings in liquid assets – per dollar of GDP – than do poorer countries. Second, richer countries do more lending – per dollar of GDP – via deposit banks as opposed to the central bank than do poorer countries. Third, richer countries allocate more of their lending – per dollar of GDP – to private companies as opposed to the government than do poorer countries.

Overall, this picture is consistent with the view that the health of the financial sector exerts an important positive influence on the level of development. But it is also consistent with the view that the health of the economy – measured by the level of development – exerts an important positive influence on the extent of financial intermediation.

3.2   Interpretations new and old

The traditional view is that these cross-sectional correlations are largely the result of the influence of economic development on the level of financial intermediation. The new view questions this interpretation and suggests a greater causal role for the extent of financial market development. How should we choose between these two points of view?

In situations such as this, where the direction of causality is difficult to determine, economists typically try to bring to bear other information in an effort to sort out what is going on. In the traditional view, that other information was of two sorts. First, in looking at the numbers in Tables 6.1 and 6.2, it is notable that all of the measures of financial scale are some fraction of a year's income. To take extreme values that make the point, we could view a richer country as maintaining a stock of financial intermediation assets equal to 50 per cent of its GDP and a poor country as having 10 per cent of its GDP in that form. Second, working with the aggregate production function as in section 2 above – which highlights the role of investment in physical capital – and assuming that financial intermediation is important principally via its effect on the stock of capital, it is possible to place bounds on how much this difference in the stock of assets might mean for the level of development.[8] An upper bound would be that a country with five times the rate of capital accumulation would be five times richer, but in Table 6.1 the top 25 per cent of countries have GDPs that average fifty times the GDP of the bottom 25 per cent of countries. Thus, in the traditional view, it is simply the case that direction of causality must run from development to intermediation.

From the new view of the links between financial intermediation and economic development, however, this argument misses the mark badly. From the new growth theory, it is differences in the productivity of factors – including the enhancements stemming from human capital investment, technology adoption, etc. – not differences in rates of physical capital accumulation that lie at the heart of understanding cross-national differences in the level of development. From the new theory of financial intermediation, allocation of more resources to the financial intermediary sector will enhance productivity. Combining these views, financial intermediation can lead to much stronger effects than is possible within the conventional view.

For this reason, as is explained more fully below, we try to deal with the causality issue econometrically rather than through model restrictions. This is because our working economic models have not reached the point that we can use them to produce more detailed restrictions.

Table 6.3. *Financial development and contemporaneous real per capita GDP growth, 1960–89*

Indicators	Very fast	Fast	Slow	Very slow	Correlation with growth	(*P*-value)
M1Y	0.23	0.19	0.15	0.14	0.40	(0.001)
LLY	0.60	0.38	0.29	0.22	0.62	(0.001)
LLY-M1Y	0.37	0.20	0.15	0.07	0.64	(0.001)
CBY	0.11	0.10	0.10	0.12	− 0.12	(0.27)
BY	0.46	0.33	0.24	0.17	0.55	(0.001)
PRIVY	0.35	0.27	0.20	0.13	0.44	(0.001)
BANK	0.81	0.73	0.71	0.60	0.46	(0.001)
PRIVATE	0.70	0.56	0.61	0.51	0.39	(0.003)
NON-MBY	0.10	0.18	0.06	0.05	0.14	(0.001)
GROWTH	0.045	0.026	0.014	− 0.005		
N =	29	28	29	28		

Key:

Very fast: GROWTH > 0.03
Fast: GROWTH > 0.02 and < 0.03
Slow: GROWTH > 0.005 and < 0.02
Very slow: GROWTH < 0.005

M1Y   = M1 to GDP
LLY   = Liquid liabilities to GDP
QLLY   = LLY-M1Y
CBY   = Central bank domestic credit to GDP
BY   = Deposit money bank domestic credit to GDP
PRIVY   = Gross claims on private sector to GDP
BANK   = Deposit money bank domestic credit divided by deposit money
             bank + central bank domestic credit
PRIVATE   = Claims on the non-financial private sector to total domestic
             credit
NON-MBY = Claims on the private sector by non-deposit money banks
             divided by GDP
GROWTH = Average annual real per capita growth 1960–89

4   Financial intermediation and economic growth

The extent of financial intermediation may exert a sustained effect on the rate of economic growth in theoretical models that feature linkages between productivity growth and intermediation, such as those that we discussed earlier. In this section, we provide some cross-sectional evidence on the relationship between financial development and economic growth.

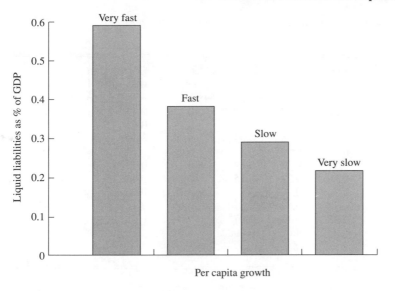

Figure 6.7 Average financial size and growth, 1960–89

4.1 Growth and financial development: some stylized facts

There is considerable dispersion in the average annual rates of economic growth over 1960–89 for the 114 countries displayed in Table 6.3. The fastest-growing countries, the top quarter of our sample, averaged a 4.5 per cent growth rate of per capita GDP and the bottom 25 per cent averaged − 0.5 per cent. While these differences may look small to some, the power of compound interest implies that this difference is very important over sustained periods: if two countries started in the same position in 1960 but had these different growth rates, then the ratio of their per capita GDPs would be 4.4 in 1990.

Interestingly, according to Table 6.3 and Figure 6.7, the stylized facts that we discussed in section 3 carry over directly to growth rates: countries that grow faster also have larger financial systems (measured by liquid assets for example), have a greater share of lending done by banks than by the central bank, and have a higher share of lending to the private sector than to the public sector.

Importantly, there is also predictive content to these relations, as documented in Table 6.4 and Figure 6.8. That is, those countries that displayed fast growth over 1970–89 had larger financial systems in 1960–9, had a greater share of lending done by banks than by the central bank in 1960–9, and had a higher share of lending to the private sector than to the public sector in 1960–9.

Table 6.4. *Initial financial development and subsequent per capita GDP growth, 1970–89*

Indicators	Very fast	Fast	Slow	Very slow	Correlation with growth	(P-value)
M1Y	0.22	0.22	0.14	0.12	0.43	(0.0001)
LLY	0.42	0.35	0.23	0.18	0.45	(0.0001)
LLY-M1Y	0.20	0.15	0.09	0.06	0.41	(0.0001)
CBY	0.08	0.10	0.07	0.06	0.14	(0.25)
BY	0.31	0.27	0.19	0.13	0.33	(0.004)
PRIVY	0.26	0.23	0.15	0.11	0.34	(0.001)
BANK	0.76	0.70	0.67	0.76	0.06	(0.64)
PRIVATE	0.67	0.57	0.57	0.60	0.18	(0.17)
NON-MBY	0.05	0.14	0.07	0.04	0.08	(0.68)
GROWTH	0.042	0.022	0.008	− 0.014		
N =	30	29	29	28		

Key:
Very fast: GROWTH > 0.03
Fast: GROWTH > 0.02 and < 0.03
Slow: GROWTH > − 0.002 and < 0.02
Very slow: GROWTH < − 0.002
All financial variables are average annual, 1960–9

M1Y   = M1 to GDP
LLY   = Liquid liabilities to GDP
QLLY   = LLY-M1Y
CBY   = Central bank domestic credit to GDP
BY   = Deposit money bank domestic credit to GDP
PRIVY   = Gross claims on private sector to GDP
BANK   = Deposit money bank domestic credit divided by deposit money bank + central bank domestic credit
PRIVATE = Claims on the non-financial private sector to total domestic credit
NON-MBY = Claims on the private sector by non-deposit money banks divided by GDP
GROWTH = Average annual real per capita growth 1970–89

4.2   Growth and financial intermediation: some regression results

There is a large and rapidly growing literature that explores the cross-country determinants of economic growth within a multivariate regression framework. We now summarize how financial intermediation fits into this setting. First, we examine the empirical importance of our measures of financial intermediation for the rate of per capita GDP

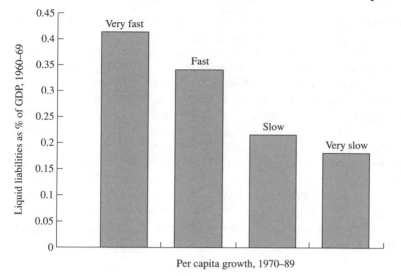

Figure 6.8   Initial financial size and subsequent per capita growth

growth, working within an empirical regression framework that is conventional in the literature (see Barro, 1991, and Levine and Renelt, 1992). Second, motivated by our theoretical discussion, we seek to explore the 'channels of influence' by which financial intermediation is linked to growth. In particular, we examine the effects of our financial indicators on (i) physical capital accumulation and (ii) a proxy for productivity growth. This proxy is based on an incomplete version of the Solow–Maddison growth accounting formula. That is, for country i, we measure productivity growth as

$$a_i = \Delta \log(Y_i) - a\, \Delta \log(K_i),$$

where $\Delta \log(Y_i)$ is annual average output growth and $\Delta \log(K_i)$ is annual average capital growth. We assume that the 'capital share' parameter a is assumed constant across time and countries (we use $a = 0.3$).

Before starting to discuss the details of the results, which are reported in various tables and figures below, we motivate the general empirical framework that we use. First, the empirical literature on cross-country determinants of growth generally includes a set of 'core' variables in regressions that are designed to capture (i) the influences of human capital accumulation and (ii) the effects of initial economic conditions on subsequent economic growth.[9] The empirical proxies used for these determinants are generally (i) the country's school enrolment rate; and (ii) the country's per capita real GDP in the starting year (1960). Second, work by

Levine and Renelt (1992) indicates that many proposed determinants of cross-country growth are individually significant in growth regressions, but that this finding disappears when additional factors are included; this finding is particularly acute for measures that seek to proxy for monetary instability, government intervention in the private economy, and government intervention in trade. In the econometric terminology of Leamer (1978), such variables are not 'robust' determinants of economic growth. Accordingly, to evaluate the 'robustness' of our financial indicators as determinants of cross-country growth, we include other policy indicators studied by Levine and Renelt (1992). Third, while we are very interested in evaluating the channels of influence by which financial intermediation is linked to economic growth, we have some concerns about the quality of the capital stock measures. Hence, we also include the investment rate – the ratio of investment to GDP – as an additional, if imperfect, measure of the extent of accumulation under way in an economy.

4.3   Results with contemporaneous financial indicators

In discussing the empirical results, we will begin by detailing the relationship between one measure of the size of the financial intermediation industry – LLY – and economic growth as displayed in Table 6.5. Subsequently, we will turn to links with other financial indicators.

4.3.1 The standard regression
The first regression in Table 6.5 is fairly representative of the standard finding in the empirical growth literature. First, there is a positive and empirically important effect of school enrolments on growth rates. Second, there is some tendency for countries that are initially rich to grow more slowly than countries that are initially poor. Barro and Sala-i-Martin (1992) and Mankiw, Romer and Weil (1992) provide recent discussions of such 'convergence' results. In most studies, however, the pace of this convergence process is found to be very slow and, in our regression, the associated coefficient on initial income is statistically insignificant.

4.3.2 Intermediation effects on economic growth
Growth is found to be significantly positively related to our financial indicator, which measures the size of the financial intermediation sector. Figure 6.9 plots the average annual per capita growth rate, net of the value predicted by all explanatory variables except LLY, against LLY. Thus, the figure shows the partial correlation between the rate of economic growth and the size of the financial intermediation industry. This figure illustrates the strong positive relationship between financial

Table 6.5. Sources of growth: links to contemporaneous financial size

Dependent variables	$N =$	Independent variables Constant	LYO	SEC	GOV	PI	TRD	LLY	R^2
GYP	88	0.02*	−0.003	0.03**				0.035**	0.43
		(0.01)	(0.002)	(0.01)				(0.006)	
GYP	88	0.02*	−0.003	0.03**	−0.04	−0.0001	0.01	0.032**	0.45
		(0.01)	(0.002)	(0.01)	(0.03)	(0.0002)	(0.01)	(0.007)	
GK	88	0.01*	−0.0004	0.003				0.014**	0.14
		(0.008)	(0.001)	(0.008)				(0.005)	
GK	88	0.01	−0.001	0.003	−0.01	−0.0001	0.0002	0.014**	0.15
		(0.009)	(0.001)	(0.008)	(0.02)	(0.0001)	(0.004)	(0.005)	
INV	88	0.12**	0.08	−0.07				0.093**	0.30
		(0.04)	(0.02)	(0.04)				(0.022)	
INV	88	0.09**	0.01	0.01	0.05	0.0001	0.06**	0.071**	0.40
		(0.04)	(0.01)	(0.04)	(0.11)	(0.0001)	(0.02)	(0.023)	
EFF3	88	0.06**	−0.005**	0.01				0.021**	0.15
		(0.01)	(0.002)	(0.01)				(0.006)	
EFF3	88	0.05**	−0.004**	0.01	−0.02	−0.0001	0.004	0.018**	0.16
		(0.01)	(0.002)	(0.01)	(0.03)	(0.0001)	(0.006)	(0.007)	

Standard errors in parentheses
*   significant at .10 level
** significant at .05 level

GYP = real per capita GDP growth rate
GK   = growth in capital stock
INV = investment share of GDP
EFF3 = real GDP growth − .3*GK
LYO = log of real GDP in 1960

SEC = secondary school enrolment rate in 1960
GOV = government consumption as share of GDP
PI   = average annual inflation rate
TRD = imports + exports as share of GDP
LLY = liquid liabilities as share of GDP

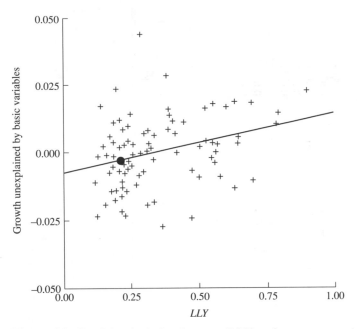

Figure 6.9   Partial association between LLY and contemporaneous per capita growth

size and growth reported statistically in Table 6.5. The estimated coefficient .04 implies that a country that increased its LLY level from the mean of the slowest-growing countries (.2) to the mean of the fastest-growing countries (.6) would raise its growth rate by 1.6 per cent per year over the thirty-year time period of our study. Since the difference between fast and slow growers is about 5 per cent in Table 6.3, this would eliminate about one-third of the growth gap. To us, this is a considerable effect.

4.3.3 Robustness
The second regression documents the fact that the significance of our financial indicator is robust to the inclusion of other public policy indicators, although there is a slight attenuation of the estimated coefficient, which would cut the effects of the experiment imagined above from 1.6 per cent to 1.2 per cent.

4.3.4 Sources of growth
The remainder of the regressions in Table 6.5 are designed to explore the channels by which variation in financial intermediation affects economic

growth. We summarize those regressions as follows. First, there are uniformly significant, positive and robust effects of the financial indicator on growth through each channel. Second, there is much more uniformity in findings with respect to the financial indicator than with respect to other determinants of economic growth.

We interpret these findings as indicating that there is some empirical support for the view that financial intermediation affects economic growth through channels that are richer than just the physical capital accumulation process that is suggested as the main linkage in the traditional view.

4.3.5 Results for other indicators

Tables 6.6 and 6.7 demonstrate that there is also a significant correlation with other financial indicators, specifically those that seek to capture (i) whether a bank or the central bank is undertaking the lending (Table 6.6); and (ii) whether a public or private institution is receiving the loan (Table 6.7). The findings are sufficiently similar to those for the size measure that they are worth only a brief summary: the financial indicators are significantly and robustly positively related to growth and appear linked through both physical and productivity channels.

While we have interpreted the preceding regressions as though the financial indicators were exogenous determinants of economic growth, as is commonplace in the empirical growth literature, these results are, of course, subject to the caveat introduced in section 3. That is, the partial correlations summarized in the tables might indicate an influence of growth on financial intermediation or a mix of causal influences between the two series. With that concern in mind, it is natural to ask whether the findings are sensitive to use of contemporaneous or initial values of our financial indicators.

4.4 Results with initial financial indicators

When we use initial rather than contemporaneous financial indicators, there are few important changes. For example, Table 6.8 reports the same regressions as Table 6.5, except that all included indicators are averaged over the 1960–9 period and related to growth over the 1970–89 period. The first regression in Table 6.8, whose counterpart we discussed in detail above, again has an LLY coefficient of .04 indicating a 1.6 per cent growth rate effect of moving from LLY = .2 to LLY = .6. The measure of the initial fraction of credit allocated by banks as opposed to by the

Table 6.6. Sources of growth: links to contemporaneous importance of banks

Dependent variables	N =	Independent variables							R²
		Constant	LYO	SEC	GOV	PI	TRD	BANK	
GYP	81	0.01	−0.004*	0.04**				0.032**	0.34
		(0.01)	(0.002)	(0.01)				(0.011)	
GYP	81	0.01	−0.003	0.04**	−0.04	−0.0001	0.002	0.032**	0.33
		(0.01)	(0.002)	(0.01)	(0.04)	(0.0001)	(0.01)	(0.012)	
GK	81	0.01	−0.0007	0.005				0.018**	0.11
		(0.01)	(0.001)	(0.008)				(0.007)	
GK	81	0.01	−0.001	0.005	0.01	0.0001	−0.0005	0.017**	0.12
		(0.009)	(0.002)	(0.009)	(0.03)	(0.0001)	(0.005)	(0.008)	
INV	81	0.08**	0.002	0.01				0.151**	0.33
		(0.04)	(0.01)	(0.04)				(0.034)	
INV	81	0.07	0.002	0.03	0.03	0.0002	0.06**	0.109**	0.41
		(0.04)	(0.01)	(0.04)	(0.12)	(0.0001)	(0.02)	(0.037)	
EFF3	81	0.05**	−0.005**	0.01				0.026**	0.12
		(0.01)	(0.002)	(0.01)				(0.0099)	
EFF3	81	0.05**	−0.005**	0.01	−0.01	−0.0001	−0.001	0.026**	0.12
		(0.01)	(0.002)	(0.01)	(0.04)	(0.0001)	(0.006)	(0.011)	

Standard errors in parentheses
* significant at .10 level
** significant at .05 level

GYP = real per capita GDP growth rate
GK = growth in capital stock
INV = investment share of GDP
EFF3 = real GDP growth − .3*GK
LYO = log of real GDP in 1960

SEC = secondary school enrolment rate in 1960
GOV = government consumption as share of GDP
PI = average annual inflation rate
TRD = imports + exports as share of GDP
BANK = deposit money bank domestic credit divided by deposit money
bank + central bank domestic credit

Table 6.7. Sources of growth: links to contemporaneous credit allocated to private sector

Dependent variables	N =	Independent variables Constant	LYO	SEC	GOV	PI	TRD	PRIVATE	R^2
GYP	80	0.02 (0.01)	− 0.004 (0.002)	0.04** (0.01)				0.024** (0.011)	0.29
GYP	80	0.02 (0.01)	− 0.003 (0.002)	0.04** (0.01)	− 0.05 (0.04)	− 0.0001 (0.0001)	0.01 (0.01)	0.022** (0.011)	0.31
GK	80	0.01 (0.01)	− 0.0003 (0.002)	0.006 (0.008)				0.011 (0.007)	0.07
GK	80	0.01 (0.009)	− 0.0002 (0.002)	0.006 (0.009)	0.01 (0.03)	− 0.0001 (0.0001)	0.002 (0.005)	0.009 (0.008)	0.08
INV	80	0.10** (0.04)	0.004 (0.01)	0.02 (0.04)				0.114** (0.035)	0.26
INV	80	0.08* (0.04)	0.004 (0.01)	0.03 (0.04)	0.04 (0.13)	0.0002 (0.0001)	0.07** (0.02)	0.078** (0.035)	0.38
EFF3	80	0.05** (0.01)	− 0.005** (0.002)	0.02 (0.01)				0.018* (0.0097)	0.08
EFF3	80	0.05** (0.01)	− 0.004* (0.002)	0.01 (0.01)	− 0.03 (0.04)	− 0.0001 (0.0001)	0.003 (0.006)	0.017** (0.011)	0.09

Standard errors in parentheses
* significant at .10 level
** significant at .05 level

GYP = real per capita GDP growth rate
GK = growth in capital stock
INV = investment share of GDP
EFF3 = real GDP growth − .3*GK
LYO = log of real GDP in 1950

SEC = secondary school enrolment rate in 1960
GOV = government consumption as share of GDP
PI = average annual inflation rate
TRD = imports + exports as share of GDP
PRIVATE = claims on the non-financial private sector to total domestic credit

central bank (BANKI) and the measure of the initial fraction of credit allocated to the private sector as opposed to the public sector (PRI-VATEI) do, however, enter less significantly.

The results in Tables 6.8–6.10 may be viewed as a simple 'proxy variable' exploration of the sensitivity of our conclusions to a particular specification of 'reverse causality', in which it is growth over 1970–89 that is linked to the variation in the financial indicators over 1960–9. There is no evidence that this form of endogeneity is important. In some companion research (King and Levine, 1992a), we use alternative, more sophisticated econometric procedures to purge growth regressions of 'reverse causality' mechanisms and find even stronger evidence that – even for the BANKI and PRIVATEI measures – measures of financial intermediary services importantly predict economic growth.[10]

5   Implications for the reconstruction of Europe

The resolution of the debate between the 'traditional' and 'new' views of the relationship between financial markets and economic development has important implications for the monumental reforms being undertaken in Europe. In general, the 'traditional' view places a low priority on financial sector reform because improvements in financial markets are viewed as having only a weak effect on the savings rate, while changes in the savings rate are viewed as having only a small, temporary effect on economic growth. This traditional view would give financial reform a particularly low priority in the reconstruction of formerly socialist econmies in Europe, because, historically, the savings and investment rates in these countries have been very high (often over 30 per cent of GDP). Thus, growth will probably come from increases in the efficiency with which resources are used not from increases in the rate of savings and investment. Since the traditional view places little weight on the role that financial markets may play in improving the allocation of resources, this view of the linkages between financial and economic development would minimize the importance of financial sector reform relative to other public policy initiatives.

In contrast, the 'new' view gives financial markets a particularly central role in stimulating economic growth in the formerly socialist countries of Europe. The new view emphasizes that financial market development can improve economic efficiency, which will probably be the engine of growth in Europe. As discussed conceptually and supported empirically above, countries with well-developed banks that allocate a relatively large share of credit to the private sector tend to enjoy more rapid economic growth over the next twenty years; and financial market development stimulates

Table 6.8. Sources of growth: links to previous financial size

Dependent variables	N =	Independent variables Constant	LYO	SEC	GOVI	PII	TRDI	LLYI	R^2
GYP	86	0.02 (0.02)	-0.002 (0.003)	0.02 (0.02)				0.035** (0.01)	0.27
GYP	86	0.02 (0.02)	-0.003 (0.003)	0.03* (0.02)	-0.04 (0.05)	0.0003 (0.0002)	0.01 (0.01)	0.036** (0.01)	0.30
GK	86	0.03** (0.01)	-0.001 (0.002)	0.002 (0.009)				0.003 (0.006)	0.01
GK	86	0.03** (0.01)	-0.001 (0.002)	0.005 (0.01)	-0.04 (0.03)	0.0001 (0.0001)	0.006* (0.003)	0.002 (0.006)	0.07
INV	86	0.18** (0.05)	0.0004 (0.01)	0.05 (0.04)				0.065** (0.028)	0.18
INV	86	0.17** (0.04)	0.0006 (0.007)	0.07 (0.04)	-0.19 (0.12)	-0.0005 (0.001)	0.07** (0.01)	0.048* (0.025)	0.38
EFF3	86	0.05** (0.01)	-0.004* (0.003)	0.001 (0.01)				0.021** (0.008)	0.08
EFF3	86	0.05** (0.02)	-0.004 (0.003)	0.004 (0.01)	-0.02 (0.04)	0.0001 (0.0001)	0.004 (0.005)	0.021** (0.009)	0.10

Standard errors in parentheses
* significant at .10 level
** significant at .05 level

GYP = real per capita GDP growth rate
GK = growth in capital stock
INV = investment share of GDP
EFF3 = real GDP growth - .3*GK
LYO = log of real GDP in 1960

SEC = secondary school enrolment rate in 1960
GOVI = government consumption as share of GDP, 1960
PII = inflation rate, 1960
TRDI = value of imports + exports as share of GDP, 1960
LLYI = liquid liabilities as share of GDP, 1960

Table 6.9. *Sources of growth: links to previous importance of banks*

| Dependent variables | N = | Independent variables | | | | | | | R² |
		Constant	LYO	SEC	GOVI	PII	TRDI	BANKI	
GYP	68	0.01 (0.02)	−0.001 (0.003)	0.03 (0.02)				0.014 (0.012)	0.16
GYP	68	0.01 (0.02)	−0.001 (0.003)	0.03* (0.02)	−0.01 (0.06)	0.0002 (0.0003)	−0.008 (0.01)	0.016 (0.013)	0.18
GK	68	0.02* (0.01)	−0.001 (0.002)	0.001 (0.01)				0.007 (0.007)	0.02
GK	68	0.02* (0.01)	0.001 (0.002)	0.002 (0.01)	−0.02 (0.03)	0.0002 (0.0002)	−0.003 (0.005)	0.010 (0.007)	0.07
INV	68	0.17** (0.04)	−0.005 (0.01)	0.07 (0.04)				0.095** (0.031)	0.28
INV	68	0.17 (0.04)	−0.01 (0.01)	0.09* (0.04)	−0.13 (0.14)	0.0001 (0.0007)	0.06** (0.02)	0.099** (0.031)	0.37
EFF3	68	0.05** (0.02)	−0.003 (0.003)	0.005 (0.01)				0.010 (0.011)	0.03
EFF3	68	0.05** (0.02)	−0.003 (0.003)	0.002 (0.01)	0.02 (0.05)	−0.0001 (0.0002)	−0.01 (0.01)	0.009 (0.011)	0.06

Standard errors in parentheses
* significant at .10 level
** significant at .05 level

GYP = real per capita GDP growth rate
GK = growth in capital stock
INV = investment share of GDP
EFF3 = real GDP growth − .3*GK
LYO = log of real GDP in 1960

SEC = secondary school enrolment rate in 1960
GOVI = government consumption as share of GDP, 1960
PII = average annual inflation rate, 1960
TRDI = imports + exports as share of GDP, 1960
BANKI = deposit money bank domestic credit divided by deposit money
bank + central bank domestic credit, 1960

Table 6.10. *Sources of growth: links to previous credit allocated to private sector*

Dependent variables	N =	Independent variables Constant	LYO	SEC	GOVI	PII	TRDI	PRIVATEI	R^2
GYP	64	0.01 (0.02)	-0.002 (0.003)	0.03 (0.02)				0.028 (0.014)	0.17
GYP	64	0.01 (0.02)	-0.002 (0.003)	0.02 (0.02)	0.01 (0.06)	0.0001 (0.0003)	-0.01 (0.01)	0.027* (0.014)	0.19
GK	64	0.02** (0.01)	-0.001 (0.002)	-0.001 (0.01)				-0.009 (0.009)	0.02
GK	64	0.02** (0.01)	-0.001 (0.002)	-0.0004 (0.01)	-0.004 (0.03)	0.0001 (0.0002)	-0.004 (0.005)	-0.009 (0.009)	0.04
INV	64	0.17** (0.05)	-0.003 (0.01)	0.06* (0.04)				0.094** (0.039)	0.24
INV	64	0.16** (0.05)	-0.006 (0.01)	0.07 (0.04)	-0.06 (0.15)	-0.0005 (0.0007)	0.06 (0.02)	0.101** (0.038)	0.34
EFF3	64	0.05** (0.02)	-0.004 (0.003)	0.002 (0.01)				0.018 (0.013)	0.05
EFF3	64	0.05** (0.02)	-0.004 (0.003)	0.003 (0.02)	0.04 (0.05)	-0.0001 (0.0002)	-0.014* (0.01)	0.018 (0.013)	0.11

Standard errors in parentheses
* significant at .10 level
** significant at .05 level

GYP	= real per capita GDP growth rate
GK	= growth in capital stock
INV	= investment share of GDP
EFF3	= real GDP growth – .3*GK
LYO	= log of real GDP in 1960
SEC	= secondary school enrolment rate in 1960
GOVI	= government consumption as share of GDP, 1960
PII	= average annual inflation rate, 1960
TRDI	= imports + exports as share of GDP, 1960
PRIVATEI	= claims on the non-financial private sector to total domestic credit, 1960

growth both by increasing the rate of capital accumulation and by increasing the efficiency with which the economy allocates resources. Since the formerly socialist economies of Europe are likely to generate growth by improving resource allocation, our conceptual framework and empirical analysis suggest that early financial market improvements should significantly enhance economic growth over the next decades. Thus, financial sector reform should be given a relatively high priority by the leaders of transitional socialist economies.

Furthermore, successful financial sector reform will promote the effectiveness of other policy reforms. Price and trade liberalization policies are designed to change relative prices, so that countries devote more resources to areas in which they have a comparative advantage. The huge relative price changes that are occurring in these countries will encourage large-scale restructuring that will require a massive reorientation of capital and labour. An improved financial system will importantly enhance the effectiveness of price and trade liberalization by expediting the efficient reallocation of capital to more productive sectors.

5.1   Qualification

Reforming the financial sector alone, however, will certainly not be sufficient to generate sustained growth. Property rights must be clearly defined and enforced, the tax system revised, and enterprises privatized. Indeed, a key aspect of financial sector reform is successfully reforming the enterprise sector. In an economy dominated by state-owned banks funding state-owned enterprises, where many of these enterprises are very unprofitable, substantial financial sector improvements will materialize and promote economic growth only when enterprises have been successfully restructured and/or privatized. Furthermore, the changing structure of the financial sector is likely to be as dynamic as the transformation of the enterprise sector. In most countries, there will probably be a declining group of financial institutions that primarily interact with state-owned enterprises and a growing group of financial institutions that primarily do business with emerging private firms. A major policy challenge will be encouraging the development of healthy, private-sector-oriented financial institutions, uncontaminated by the bad debts of deteriorating state-owned enterprises, while political pressures force some financial institutions temporarily to finance loss-making enterprises during the transition.[11]

6 Summary and conclusions

In the traditional view, the role of financial intermediaries in determining economic activity was perceived to be relatively minor, restricted by both the sense that intermediation had only minor influences on savings/investment rates and the sense that changes in physical capital accumulation had only minor effects on development.

By contrast, the emerging new view is that financial intermediaries can exert a major influence on growth and development. This new perspective involves a revision of thinking both on the nature of financial intermediaries and on the process of economic development. At the centre of each of these new modes of thought is productivity: financial intermediaries are taken to enhance the efficiency of productivity-enhancing investments and countries are taken to grow faster if they have better returns on such investments.

In this paper, we have posited the linkages between financial intermediation and economic development – in both the new and old views – and summarized some new empirical evidence. That evidence, presented in more detail in King and Levine (1992a), indicates that measures of the scale and efficiency of financial intermediation are robustly and significantly correlated with economic growth in the international cross-section. Interpreted causally, our regression estimates suggest that there is a major positive effect on economic growth of increasing the size of the financial intermediation system: roughly one-third of the gap between very fast and very slow growing countries is eliminated by increasing the scale of the financial intermediation sector (from the mean in very slow growing countries to the mean in very fast growing countries).

We conclude that financial development may well be an important determinant of economic development. We plan additional research on the channels of influence by which finance affects development, on the interaction of the effects of financial policies with those of other growth-promoting policies, and on isolating those financial policies that are particularly central to the development process.

NOTES

We thank Colin Mayer, Mark Gertler and Nouriel Roubini for comments and Sara K. Zervos for expert research assistance. Our collaborative research in this area is supported by the World Bank project, 'How Do National Policies Affect Long-run Growth?'
  1 See Chandravarkar (1992) for a discussion of the general neglect of finance in the development literature.
  2 This section summarizes the formal model under development in our manuscript, King and Levine (1992b), and hence is most closely tied to that

theoretical perspective. Other noteworthy recent contributions are Greenwood and Jovanovic (1990), Bencivenga and Smith (1991), Levine (1991), Roubini and Sala-i-Martin (1991), and Saint-Paul (1992).

3 A similar argument leads to a restriction on the influence of international differences in investment rates on economic development. In the long run of the Solow model, the investment rate (i/y) is proportional to the capital output ratio (k/y). If g is the rate of growth of population and technical progress and δ is the depreciation rate, then the relationship is $(i/y) = (g + \delta)(k/y)$.

4 In this discussion, we assume that variations in observed investment rates (i/y) are good proxies for variations in comprehensive investment rates (i/y).

5 One feature of the $a = 0.8$ models would, however, work in the opposite direction: the transitional dynamics proceed at a much slower pace, as discussed by King and Rebelo (1989). However, much of the transition would still occur within a thirty-year period.

6 The national GDP measures were converted to common international units (US$) as follows: each country's data were formed in a constant 1987 local currency series and then multiplied by the 1987 $/local currency exchange rate.

7 The departures from exact proportionality may reflect the fact that poor countries engage in inflationary policies that induce currency substitution.

8 This is a wildly optimistic upper bound becuase it assumes that fivefold differences in intermediation translate into fivefold differences in capital.

9 In contrast to some of the empirical literature, we do not use the investment rate (i/y) as an independent variable. This is because we believe that this rate depends strongly on other determinants of growth and, hence, is not an appropriate regressor.

10 In King and Levine (1992a) we consider some instrumental variables estimators that are based on initial value instruments. The results are essentially those reported in the tables because the first-stage regressions (i) have good fits; and (ii) essentially explain each individual variable by its own initial value.

11 Although every effort should be made to isolate government subsidies to lossmaking enterprises from market-based credit decisions, political economy pressures suggest that governments will attempt to 'hide' these losses in bank credit decisions. See Caprio and Levine (1992) for a general discussion of reforming the financial sector in transitional socialist economies and Levine and Scott (1992) for a detailed discussion of confronting the 'bad' debt problem in these countries.

REFERENCES

Barro, Robert J. (1991) 'Economic growth in a cross-section of countries', *Quarterly Journal of Economics* **106**, 407–44.

Barro, Robert J. and Xavier Sala-i-Martin (1992) 'Convergence', *Journal of Political Economy* **100**, 223–51.

Bencivenga, V.R. and B.D. Smith (1991) 'Financial intermediation and endogenous growth', *Review of Economic Studies* **58**, 195–209.

Chandravarkar, Anand (1992) 'Of finance and development', *World Development* **20**, 133–42.

Caprio, G., Jr and R. Levine (1992) 'Reforming finance in transitional socialist economies', PRE Working Paper, No. 898, The World Bank.

Goldsmith, R.W. (1969) *Financial Structure and Development*, New Haven, Conn.: Yale University Press.

Greenwood, J. and B. Jovanovic (1990) 'Financial development, growth, and the distribution of income', *Journal of Political Economy* **98**, 1076–107.

King, R.G. and R. Levine (1992a) 'Financial indicators and economic growth in a cross section of countries', PRE Working Paper, No. 819, The World Bank.

  (1992b) 'Finance, entrepreneurship and development: theory and evidence', manuscript in progress.

King, R.G. and S.T. Rebelo (1989) 'Transitional dynamics and economic growth in the neoclassical model', NBER Working Paper 3185, Cambridge: National Bureau of Economic Research, forthcoming in *American Economic Review*.

Knight, F. (1951) *Economic Organization*, New York: Harper Torchbooks, Harper & Row.

Leamer, E. (1978) *Specification Searches: Ad-hoc Inference with Non-experimental Data*, New York: John Wiley and Sons.

Levine, R. (1991) 'Stock markets, growth and tax policy', *Journal of Finance* **46**, 1445–65.

Levine R. and D. Renelt (1992) 'A sensitivity analysis of cross country growth regressions', *American Economic Review*, forthcoming.

Levine, R. and D. Scott (1992) 'Old debts and new beginnings', PRE Working Paper, No. 876, The World Bank.

Lucas, R.E. Jr (1988) 'On the mechanics of economic development', *Journal of Monetary Economics* **22**, 3–42.

Maddison, A. (1987) 'Growth and slowdown in advanced capitalist economics: techniques of quantitative assessment', *Journal of Economic Literature* **25**, 649–98.

Mankiw, N.G., D. Romer and D. Weil (1992) 'A contribution to the empirics of economic growth', *Quarterly Journal of Economics* **107**, 407–37.

Prescott, Edward C. and John H. Boyd (1987) 'Dynamic coalitions: engines of growth', *American Economic Review* **77**, 56–62.

Rebelo, Sergio (1991) 'Long-run policy analysis and long-run growth', *Journal of Political Economy* **99**, 500–21.

Romer, P. (1986) 'Increasing returns and long-run growth', *Journal of Political Economy* **94**, 1002–37.

  (1990) 'Endogenous technical change', *Journal of Political Economy* **98**, S71–S102.

Roubini, N. and X. Sala-i-Martin (1991) 'Financial development, the trade regime, and economic growth', NBER Working Paper 3876, Cambridge: National Bureau of Economic Research.

Saint-Paul, G. (1992) 'Technological choice, financial markets, and economic development', *European Economic Review* **36**, 763–81.

Schumpeter, J.A. (1911) *The Theory of Economic Development*; translated by Redvers Opie, Cambridge, MA: Harvard University Press, 1934.

Solow, Robert M. (1956) 'A contribution to the theory of economic growth', *Quarterly Journal of Economics* **70**, 65–74.

  (1957) 'Technological change and the aggregate production function', *Review of Economic Studies* **39**, 312–20.

World Bank (1989) *World Development Report 1989*, New York: Oxford University Press.

Discussion

MARK GERTLER

This paper is part of an ongoing research project by the authors. The objective is to provide measures of the relation between growth and the depth of the financial system. Their research updates earlier work on the problem, beginning with Goldsmith's classic treatise, *Financial Structure and Development* (1969). Their work is both comprehensive and systematic. It is likely to be a useful guide to anyone planning to study in the area.

The central theme is in sharp contrast to most of the recent work in growth theory. This new work tends to abstract from the organization and performance of markets as a factor in development, and instead focuses on endogenous technological change as the engine of growth. Financial trade is typically frictionless in these frameworks. Miller–Modigliani applies. As a consequence, these frameworks contain no predictions about the relation between financial markets and development.

I view the objective of the authors' research and related work by others as an effort to redirect some attention to studying how the evolution of markets, particularly financial markets, contributes to the growth process. In this regard, the work returns to an earlier tradition in the development literature, one associated with Gurley and Shaw (1955), Goldsmith (1969) and others. The research also follows recent work in macroeconomics which has been examining the role of financial market imperfections in the business cycle (see Gertler, 1988, for a survey). Some of the general methodology that this macroeconomics literature has used to study how credit market frictions might propagate business cycles is now being applied to consider how these frictions might affect growth.

There are a large number of obstacles present in trying to measure how financial factors may influence growth. Foremost is the problem of simultaneity. Growth and financial development are jointly determined endogenous variables. While growth may depend on financial depth, financial depth is likely to depend on the state of development of the real sector. As Goldsmith (1969, p. 48) noted long ago:

> It is difficult to establish with confidence the direction of the causal mechanism, i.e., of deciding whether financial factors were responsible for the acceleration of economic development or whether financial development reflected economic growth whose mainsprings must be sought elsewhere.

The authors clearly recognize the simultaneity issue and make no pretence about providing a definitive solution. And they do provide some results that are less easy to dismiss with the claim of simultaneity than is the typical empirical work that is seen in this literature.

The general empirical strategy is to present a set of descriptive statistics that characterize the co-movement of various financial indicators with various real variables relevant to describing growth. The growth variables include GDP growth, investment and the investment share. The financial variables include standard financial depth measures (e.g. liquid assets to income), as well as measures of the private/public mix of the financial system (e.g. ratios of privately provided to total credit).

The authors conduct two kinds of empirical exercise: first, a bivariate analysis, which provides correlations of each growth variable with each financial indicator, then a multivariate analysis, which includes a financial indicator along with the 'usual list of suspect' variables in a cross-sectional growth regression. The object of the multivariate analysis is to control for the influence of factors other than financial variables that might influence growth.

Two main conclusions arise. First, the bivariate analysis reveals a strong correlation between financial indicators and growth. Second, in the multivariate analysis, financial variables remain significant even after the inclusion of variables that normally enter as statistically significant predictors of growth.

As the authors recognize, the key consideration here is simultaneity. While the bivariate results provide a useful set of facts, they are of limited value in discriminating between competing theories. It is not difficult in each case to tell a story where causation runs the other way. The multivariate results do not automatically solve the problem either. In these kinds of regressions, variables with strong endogenous components are likely to do well, even if they are not truly causal. Financial variables surely have a strong endogenous component.

The authors address the simultaneity issue by considering a set of multivariate regressions where only beginning-of-period financial variables enter. One can interpret this strategy as using beginning-of-period financial conditions as an instrumental variable for financial conditions during the sample period. The rationale is that the beginning-of-period financial indicators are more likely to be exogenous to shocks to the real economy that occur over the sample period than are contemporaneous indicators. The authors in fact find that the beginning-of-period financial indicators are significant.

As I suggested earlier, the authors' identification strategy makes their results less easy to dismiss than those in conventional growth/financial regressions. The issue boils down to how valid are beginning-of-period financial indicators as instruments for financial conditions. The authors' position strikes me as plausible. But any more evidence that they might bring to bear on this issue could strengthen their argument considerably. Could beginning-of-period financial variables be simply responding to anticipation of growth down the road (e.g. suppose there is a lot of borrowing at the beginning of the period in anticipation of good opportunities down the road)? Could they be driven by some other omitted variable which is important at the beginning of the period? Finally, if growth prior to the sample period is correlated with growth during the sample period, beginning-of-period financial indicators could still be correlated with the error term, making them invalid instruments.

A second issue involves possible biases involved in lumping developed countries with less developed countries. Two concerns arise here. First, the *International Financial Statistics* does not give a complete picture of the financial systems of developed countries. Missing are measures of the stock and bond markets, which are of course a quite important component of the financial systems of many developed countries. The generally smooth relation between growth and financial depth could reflect undermeasurement of financial assets and liabilities in developed countries. Developed countries are not the fastest growing, but one might expect that they have the deepest financial systems. Overall, including a more accurate measure of the financial depth of the developed countries would be desirable (perhaps these data are available for the OECD countries).

The second concern has to do with whether the coefficients in the multivariate regressions are truly stable across all countries. One might expect that, owing to structural differences, the coefficient estimates might differ between developing and developed countries. For example, the impact of inflation on growth in a financially repressed economy may be different from the effect in a financially sophisticated economy. Also, one might expect diminishing returns to financial development as financial markets edge towards being perfect. If so, the marginal impact of financial conditions on growth might be stronger in less developed countries than in highly developed countries. Overall, it may be possible to exploit differences between developed and developing countries to identify the impact of financial factors. Here an analogy may be drawn with the literature that attempts to identify liquidity effects on investment by exploiting cross-sectional as well as time series predictions (e.g. Fazzari, Hubbard and Peterson, 1988).

The last issue I want to raise involves measuring the depth of the financial system. The authors do the best they can with the available data.

But caveats must apply in interpreting the results. Consider, for example, a financially sophisticated economy where businesses have access to lines of credit and households have credit cards and possibly lines of credit as well, versus one where none of these instruments exist. Holdings of liquid assets relative to GDP could possibly be greater in the latter country, but it would be incorrect to conclude that it then has greater financial depth. A measure of financial efficiency that is less susceptible to these problems (but not completely free of difficulties) is the cost of intermediation as reflected by the spread between the loan and deposit rates. It appears that the authors are analysing this variable in related work.

Overall, I enjoyed reading this paper and think that King and Levine have embarked on an interesting and important research programme.

REFERENCES

Fazzari, S., G. Hubbard and B. Peterson (1988) 'Financing constraints and corporate investment', *Brookings Papers on Economic Activity*, No. 1, 141–95.
Gertler, M. (1988) 'Financial structure and aggregate economic activity', *Journal of Money, Credit and Banking* Part 2, August, 559–88.
Goldsmith, R. (1969) *Financial Structure and Development*. New Haven, Conn.: Yale University Press.
Gurley, J.G. and E. Shaw (1955) 'Financial aspects of economic development', *American Economic Review* 45, September, 515–38.

NOURIEL ROUBINI

This paper presents a very interesting and original analysis of the relation between financial intermediation and economic growth. The paper presents some preliminary results of a much wider theoretical and empirical research project undertaken by the authors on the relation between financial markets and economic development.

The authors stress that the traditional view of economic growth did not suggest an important role for financial intermediation in the process of economic growth, whereas the importance of financial intermediation has been recognized in the recent new growth literature. It is correct to argue that the neoclassical model did not recognize a role for financial intermediation (and distortions in financial markets) in long-term economic growth: since growth was assumed to be exogenous, financial market distortions would affect only the level of output but not its rate of growth. It must also be observed, however, that even in the 1960s and 1970s a large literature on financial markets and the effects of financial repression on economic growth had recognized the importance of financial intermediation for the correct allocation of savings to investment and its effects on the productivity of capital, and found a significant negative relation between financial repression and economic growth (see the seminal studies of Cameron, 1967; Goldsmith, 1969; McKinnon, 1973; and Shaw, 1973). What was missing in the early literature were two elements. First, there was no formal theory of the links between financial development and growth (the then ruling neoclassical growth paradigm could not explain the growth rather than the level effects of financial repression on growth). Second, while this literature showed the correlation between indicators of financial deepening and economic development and the negative effects of financial repression on growth, the empirical methodology used in these studies was quite simple and did not address important econometric issues such as simultaneity, reverse causality and robustness.

The new growth literature has recently addressed both the theoretical and the empirical shortcomings of the previous studies and the work of King and Levine is an important theoretical and empirical contribution to this new wide literature on financial intermediation and growth (see Greenwood and Jovanovic, 1990, Bencivenga and Smith, 1991, Levine, 1991, and Roubini and Sala-i-Martin, 1992, for some recent theoretical contributions). Although the theoretical model of the authors is only briefly sketched in the paper, the main ideas appear to be quite appealing. The idea of a relation between the efficiency of the financial system, the quantity and efficiency of the allocation of resources to entrepreneurs and the amount of productivity-enhancing investment in intangible capital is original and very sensible.

The empirical results are also quite convincing and expand the results of other recent empirical contributions (Gelb, 1988; Roubini and Sala-i-Martin, 1991) in two directions: first, they consider a much wider range of financial development indicators; second, while most previous studies concentrate on the effects of financial development on growth, the authors consider the channels through which financial development affects growth by studying the effects of these indicators on the level of investment and its efficiency. The result that financial development is associated with higher productivity growth is particularly interesting and related to the theoretical model outlined by the authors.

While the results of this and other recent theoretical and empirical contributions suggest that financial development is good for economic development and that financial repression has serious negative effects on economic growth, a number of cautionary caveats are required.

First, although the empirical issue of causality is partly addressed in this and other studies, it is fair to say that it is not fully resolved. In particular, when the authors consider the effects on growth of initial financial conditions (in 1960) to control for endogeneity, only one of the three financial indicators appears to have significant effects on growth (see Tables 6.5–6.7). Moreover, it is well known that financial deepening partly follows economic development rather than just causing it. This suggests that one should also look at direct measures of financial repression rather than measures of financial deepening in order to analyse the specific effects of distortionary public policies on growth.

Second, available evidence on the effects of policies of financial repression on growth (see Roubini and Sala-i-Martin, 1991) is mixed: while very high degrees of repression (as proxied by highly negative real returns to savings) appear to be associated with low growth, countries with moderately negative real interest rates do not appear to suffer serious growth consequences. Moreover, protectionist trade policies and financial repression appear to be highly correlated and the introduction of variables proxying the trade regime (such as indexes of protection) seriously weakens the robustness of the financial variables in growth regressions. Lastly, financial repression in the form of capital controls does not appear to be associated with lower economic growth.

Third, consistent with the above evidence, the experience of several high-growth countries shows that they were characterized by highly repressed financial sectors and negative returns to savings. In countries such as Korea, Taiwan, Thailand and other successful developers (as well as in several West European countries such as Italy), financial markets were heavily regulated, the government had a fundamental role in the allocation of savings to particular investment purposes and severe capital controls were maintained for long periods of time. The experience of these countries suggests that one should look more carefully at specific government policies in financial markets and their effects on investment and productivity growth.

Fourth, the above evidence suggests that the relation between government intervention in financial markets and economic growth is not obvious. The theoretical literature on the relation between economic growth and public policies suggests that, in the presence of externalities and market failures, it is easy to construct models where government distortionary policies in trade, government spending and taxation and subsidization of human and physical capital might be growth and welfare enhancing. Similarly, it would not be hard to derive models where some degree of government intervention in financial markets might be growth enhancing. For example, recent theoretical and empirical work by Jappelli and Pagano (1992) suggests that borrowing constraint on households might increase the savings rate and the growth rate of an economy.

The above arguments suggest that the relation between economic growth and financial development is a complex one and, in spite of the many important recent contributions to this research area, we still have a lot to learn on this topic. The research project of King and Levine represents an important theoretical and empirical contribution to this developing subject of research.

REFERENCES

Bencivenga, V.R. and B.D. Smith (1991) 'Financial intermediation and endogenous growth', *Review of Economic Studies* **58**, 195–209.

Cameron, R. (1967) *Banking in the Early Stages of Industrialization*, New York: Oxford University Press.

Gelb, A. (1988) 'Financial policies, efficiency, and growth: an analysis of broad cross-section relationships', World Bank.

Goldsmith, R.W. (1969) *Financial Structure and Development*, New Haven, Conn.: Yale University Press.

Greenwood, J. and B. Jovanovic (1990) 'Financial development, growth, and the distribution of income', *Journal of Political Economy* **98**, 1076–107.

Jappelli, T. and M. Pagano (1992) 'Saving, growth and liquidity constraints', CEPR Discussion Paper Series No. 662, May.

Levine, R. (1991) 'Stock markets, growth and tax policy', *Journal of Finance* **46**, 1445–65.

McKinnon, R.I. (1973) *Money and Capital in Economic Development*, Washington, DC: Brookings Institution.

Roubini, N. and X. Sala-i-Martin (1991) 'Financial development, the trade regime, and economic growth', NBER Working Paper No. 3876, November.
  (1992) 'A growth model of inflation, tax evasion and financial repression', NBER Working Paper No. 4062, May.

Shaw, E.S. (1973) *Financial Deepening in Economic Development*, New York: Oxford University Press.

7 Creditor passivity and bankruptcy: implications for economic reform

JANET MITCHELL

1 Introduction

The development of financial institutions, and the establishment of capital markets in particular, is central to the transition from a centrally planned, non-market economy to a market economy. This paper concerns the importance of bankruptcy in the process of financial reform. Specifically, it focuses on a problem with the implementation of bankruptcy in the early stages of reform that has the potential for bringing financial reform to a halt. This problem is a lack of aggressiveness of creditors in the reforming socialist economies (RSEs) in seeking satisfaction of their claims.[1] That is, when debtors default on their debt, creditors passively accommodate by taking such actions as extending the payment period for loans and capitalizing unpaid interest rather than pursuing their claims through bankruptcy or other means.

Bankruptcy laws and other (non-bankruptcy) laws governing default serve crucial roles in market economies. The general purpose served by default law is that it helps to complete very incomplete debt contracts by specifying contingencies in the event of default. More precisely, default law stipulates whether control over assets is transferred in the event of default, how control is transferred, and also defines rights to future income streams either directly through provisions governing payment of creditors' claims or indirectly through the provisions on transfer of control. In brief, default law directs the reallocation of claims to a debtor's assets in the event of default.

By resolving some of the uncertainty associated with default, bankruptcy and other default laws achieve three beneficial types of outcomes. First, they define more precisely the property rights of creditors and thereby lower the cost of writing debt contracts. This should smooth the functioning of capital markets: financial contracts will take less time to write; the terms of contracts will likely be more standardized, containing

197

fewer covenants, and will, therefore, be easier to enforce. The lower cost of writing and enforcing debt contracts should also increase the supply of funds in financial markets relative to supply in the absence of default law. Second, default law limits the rights of the debtor to control the assets in all states of the world; therefore, it should improve the efficiency of resource allocation. When debtors default, creditors generally acquire some say in the question of transfer of the debtor's assets to alternative uses; hence, they may force assets to be reallocated to more productive activities. Efficient resource allocation in this context implies that firms whose values in continuation exceed their liquidation values continue in operation (despite liquidity problems) and firms whose continuation values are less than their liquidation values liquidate. Third, default law precludes the debtor from abrogating the debt contract, i.e. from appropriating all of the returns to the assets plus retaining complete control over them. As a consequence, default law should impose financial discipline on the debtor.[2] One may, therefore, cite the goals served by default law as defining more precisely the property rights of the firm's claimants, improving the efficiency of resource allocation, and imposing discipline on the debtor.

The goals that bankruptcy (or, more generally, default law) serves in a market economic system thus persuade that bankruptcy is, or should be, a keystone of reform in the post-socialist economies. Smoothly functioning capital markets require clear and enforceable definitions of property rights, and bankruptcy laws constitute an important component of property rights. Bankruptcy offers one of the only potential mechanisms for improving the efficiency of resource allocation in the reforming economies, since developed capital markets and the related mechanisms for transfer of resources across activities, such as takeovers, are not yet present. Finally, bankruptcy can be expected to exert a stronger disciplinary effect at early stages of economic reform than in developed market economies. In market economies with developed capital markets and a body of non-bankruptcy default law, the bankruptcy law does not necessarily exert an independent disciplinary effect. Its purpose is conceived more to stop the race by creditors to dismantle the firm.[3] The multiplicity of creditors with varying priorities and the ability to appeal to non-bankruptcy law achieve the necessary discipline.

In the reforming economies on the other hand, financial markets are limited, the number of major creditors is few, government regulators still exert some sway over firms, and there is a history of bail-out. The lack of development of capital markets explains the virtual non-existence of non-bankruptcy default law; therefore, bankruptcy is an important tool for hardening firms' 'soft budget constraints'.[4] Bankruptcy laws have potentially significant incentive effects at this point that they do not necessarily possess at later stages of reform, where financial markets are more extensive and multiple creditors exist. More generally, because evolving capital markets yield varying sets of owner/claimants of the firm at differing stages of financial reform, one should expect optimal bankruptcy laws also to differ at the different stages.[5]

Yet, experience in Eastern Europe to date indicates that bankruptcy has not played an important role. Even in countries such as Hungary where bankruptcy laws are on the books and where bankruptcy presents a realistic option for creditors, initiation of bankruptcy proceedings has been a rare event. Creditor passivity thus presents us with two questions: why are creditors ignoring the bankruptcy option, and what does this imply for financial reform? In later sections of the paper, I explore a number of possible explanations for creditor passivity and the associated policy implications. It is likely that several of the potential explanations are simultaneously operative in each of the reforming economies. The variety of policy implications flowing from these explanations argues for further investigation of the phenomenon.

The remainder of the paper is organized as follows. The next section presents evidence of the problem of creditor passivity, using experience with bankruptcy in Hungary as a case study of bankruptcy at early stages of economic reform. Section 3 develops a framework for analysing creditor passivity and reviews literature relevant to the analysis. Section 4 studies a number of possible explanations for the problem.[6] Section 5 discusses policy implications and the interrelation between design and enforcement of bankruptcy laws and creditor passivity. This section also concludes the paper.

2   The history of Hungarian bankruptcy

Hungary's experience with bankruptcy illustrates the problem of creditor passivity in a transforming economy. Because Hungary passed its first (modern) bankruptcy law in 1986, sufficient time has passed to observe experience with its implementation. Hungary's experience is likely to be representative of that of other reforming economies, such as Poland and Czechoslovakia. Although there exist conditions in the latter two countries that are conducive to creditor passivity, bankruptcy laws have not been on the books long enough to assess this claim fully.

The 1986 bankruptcy law in Hungary envisioned a three-stage bankruptcy procedure.[7] In the first stage, a defaulting firm or its creditors could submit a request for a conciliation procedure, where the firm and its creditors would meet and renegotiate the creditors' claims on the firm.

Lack of a conciliation agreement initiated the second stage, in which the firm's case was referred to the Reorganization Office, which decided if the firm met one of three criteria that would qualify it for rehabilitation.[8] If the firm did not qualify for rehabilitation, then it was to enter the third stage of bankruptcy, liquidation. The major features of the law, then, were voluntary initiation, no pre-specified rules for approval of a reorganization plan or priority ordering for the satisfaction of creditors' claims during the conciliation procedure,[9] and government determination of the firm's suitability for reorganization.

Given that hundreds of Hungarian firms were operating with losses, one might have expected a significant number of bankruptcy proceedings to be initiated after the law's promulgation. Yet, virtually no requests for conciliation proceedings were submitted. According to one source, whereas economists had predicted that close to 100 bankruptcies would occur annually after passage of the law, only ten requests for initiation of bankruptcy proceedings were submitted from 1986 to the end of 1989.[10] Creditor passivity came as a surprise, at least for some.

The government's initial response to the problem was to punish creditors who were not implementing the law. In 1987 a regulation required banks to create 'risk reserves' for any claims that were greater than 25 million forints and more than three months overdue. In addition, creditor firms that did not initiate claims against their insolvent debtors were to receive no further state financial support. These provisions were easily evaded, for example by a bank's rolling over overdue loans of greater than 25 million forints. Although direct evidence concerning the degree to which the banks adhered to the regulation is unavailable, indirect evidence suggests that adherence was not complete. Doubtful accounts (which included any payment greater than sixty days overdue) among the large banks grew from 2.7 billion forints in 1987 to 38.8 billion in 1990, while reserve capital grew from 8.8 billion forints in 1987 to 21.6 billion in 1990.[11] The provisions had no effect on the number of bankruptcy proceedings initiated.

The government next pursued a strategy of rewarding creditors for initiating bankruptcy proceedings. In late 1989 the government announced that financial institutions could exchange 20 per cent of their uncollectable claims for housing bonds, which functioned essentially as state securities. Institutions could also undertake this exchange for 50 per cent of any losses that they sustained after liquidation of debtor firms.

Perceived failure of all of these provisions prompted an amendment to the bankruptcy law in March 1990. This amendment stipulated that, whereas creditors may request initiation of bankruptcy proceedings, debtors who have 'discontinued making payment' must do so. Just what constituted discontinuation of payments, however, was not entirely clear and gave rise to debate regarding the actual meaning of the amendment. Meanwhile, inter-enterprise indebtedness had grown to a point where many firms were defaulting on their obligations as a consequence of their unsatisfied outstanding claims. This phenomenon had been termed in Hungary 'waiting in line' for debt repayment. Overdue credit payments had risen from 14 billion forints in 1988 to over 100 billion forints in 1990. A subsequent amendment to the bankruptcy law relieved firms whose defaults on payments to creditors were less than the value of unsatisfied claims against another firm from the legal obligation to initiate bankruptcy proceedings against themselves.

Although the latter amendment was designed to give incentives to enterprise creditors to initiate bankruptcies against their defaulting debtors, it had the potential for undermining the automatic triggering requirement, whereby defaulting debtors must declare bankruptcy. A firm expecting to default on its obligations could collude with another firm by extending a 'loan' to the latter firm in an amount equal to the former's obligations. If the latter firm delayed repayment until it became 'overdue', then the former firm would not be obliged to enter bankruptcy. The extent to which this actually occurred in practice is, of course, unknown.

The amendments to the bankruptcy law were believed to be of no avail; lawmakers felt compelled to draft a new bankruptcy law in 1991 which went into effect on 1 January 1992. This law allows for voluntary initiation of bankruptcy but also provides for automatic triggering. Any firm that fails to pay any of its debts within ninety days following the due date must declare bankruptcy within eight days of this date. Upon receipt of a petition for reorganization the court appoints a trustee, whose duties include reviewing the financial operation and management of the debtor, reporting its information to the creditors, and safeguarding the value of the debtor's assets. Once the debtor declares bankruptcy, it must prepare a programme and a proposal for settlement of its claims within thirty days. A meeting of creditors is called to vote upon the debtor's proposed settlement, and all creditors must consent to the settlement. If no consent is reached, then liquidation of the firm is to begin within fifteen days.

A creditor may also petition for bankruptcy if a debtor's claim is overdue by sixty days; however, this petition must be for liquidation of the firm. Creditors cannot petition for a debtor's bankruptcy with the debtor immediately entering reorganization. Moreover, the creditor must show that the debtor's insolvency is likely, by providing a description of the debt and why the creditor deems the debtor insolvent. The bankruptcy court then determines whether the firm is insolvent. Despite the fact that the firm must enter the liquidation procedure in this case, it may propose a settlement at any time during the liquidation proceedings. Only half of the creditors whose claims represent two-thirds of those of all creditors need approve a settlement proposed once liquidation is under way.

Whereas the initial bankruptcy law in 1986 provided for voluntary initiation of bankruptcy, government determination of the firm's suitability for rehabilitation, and no bargaining rules for design of a reorganization plan, the new law requires automatic triggering, appointment of a bankruptcy trustee, and determination on the part of the firm and the creditors of the nature of reorganization. The automatic triggering mechanism is designed to set the bankruptcy process in motion. On the other hand, the period for determining and approving a reorganization plan is short, and the requirement of unanimous consent by the creditors to a reorganization plan is much more restrictive than bankruptcy laws of most industrialized, market economies.

Hungary's experience with bankruptcy illustrates a problem that appears general to the reforming socialist economies: creditors' lack of aggressiveness in seeking satisfaction of their claims. Whereas the need to rely on creditors to initiate bankruptcy proceedings was a result of the original bankruptcy law's design, creditors' passiveness in seeking satisfaction of their claims was not directly related to the provisions of the law. The reluctance of creditors to pursue their claims nevertheless had a drastic impact on the success of bankruptcy and was in large part responsible for the law's ineffectiveness. This problem with application of bankruptcy fed back into the design of the law: the law was adapted to the prevailing financial conditions.

That the degree of creditor passivity is influenced by the financial environment is illustrated by data on bankruptcies in Hungary in late 1990 and in 1991.[12] The number of bankruptcy proceedings filed in the Budapest Court (which handled roughly 65 per cent of all Hungary bankruptcy filings in 1990) grew steadily during this period, in spite of the problems with the existing bankruptcy law. By mid 1990, 772 of the 3,299 enterprises required to file mid-year balance sheets (those with annual returns greater than 250 million forints, or $4–5 million) reported a total loss of 30.1 billion forints.[13] A total of 425 bankruptcy proceedings were initiated in the Budapest Court in 1990, and 884 were initiated from 1 January to 31 October 1991. Of the bankruptcy proceedings in the first ten months of 1991, 681 were initiated by creditors. Yet, closer examination reveals that most of these bankruptcies were small, private firms, and most of the aggressive creditors appear to be trade creditors. Small cooperatives accounted for 352 bankruptcies; limited companies for 243; and state enterprises for only 168. Social security agencies initiated seventeen of the bankruptcy proceedings; the tax authority (APEH) fifty-one; and banks initiated only nine. Trade creditors appear to have been responsible for the remainder of the creditor-initiated cases.

The only creditors who appear to have become truly aggressive, then, are trade creditors, and more information needs to be obtained regarding the characteristics of these creditors. Government agencies initiated few proceedings relative to their non-performing claims, and banks were almost completely inactive. Creditor passivity thus remains a serious issue.

At this point it is useful to enquire how general is the phenomenon of creditor passivity. Much anecdotal evidence exists to suggest that the phenomenon is not confined to Hungary and is in fact common to the RSEs. For example, the reluctance of banks to collect outstanding claims in Yugoslavia resulted in 1990 in widespread liquidity and solvency problems in the banking sector and a call to reform the banking system before proceeding further with economic reform.

Anecdotal evidence from Poland and Czechoslovakia also indicates that many creditors are not making visible attempts to collect outstanding debt. As an illustration, the component of reported losses of Polish enterprises associated with interest charged on invoices and overdue bank credits rose from 2.5 trillion zlotys at the end of the first half of 1991 to 9 trillion zlotys by November 1991. In addition, approximately 17 per cent of the total amount of bank loans outstanding in Poland in November 1991 was held by enterprises that had fallen into the category of non-creditworthy. Of the 2,403 Polish enterprises designated as non-creditworthy by November 1991, only 115 were facing liquidation.[14] Promissory notes appear to have become a medium of exchange in Poland in some circumstances. One Polish bank attempted to purchase firms' promissory notes at a discount, with the intention of collection on the notes. After a few months of this activity and some apparent success at it, the bank found that firms were no longer willing to sell their notes to the bank.[15]

Vaclav Klaus, Czechoslovakia's finance minister, has declared that a high level of business debt and low bank capitalization are an economy-wide problem that is severely hampering the effectiveness of monetary policy.[16] An article in the Czech press describing a decision to channel 50 billion korunas into the banking system to bolster commercial banks' capital begins with the statement, 'Enterprise insolvency, the most serious problem of our economy, finally found a solution.'[17]

Creditor passivity not only plagues the reforming economies, but has also appeared in developing economies. The World Bank (1989) notes that, in the decade preceding 1989, twenty-five governments came to the aid of distressed financial institutions, many of which had disguised their non-performing debt. This observation suggests that creditor inaction is not obligatorily a transitory phenomenon that will disappear once reforms have been instituted. There appear to exist conditions in a variety of settings that induce the behaviour. The risk with creditor passivity appears to be that it may grow to the point where its resolution will entail large costs for the government and threaten the progress of reform. The possible causes and consequences of creditor passivity thus warrant closer scrutiny.

3   The design of bankruptcy laws and decisions to liquidate

This section presents a framework for analysing the phenomenon of creditor passivity and reviews some of the literature relevant to the analysis. Other related literature is cited in section 4. Before addressing the problem of creditor passivity, however, it is useful to note that no actual bankruptcy law can perfectly achieve the goals for bankruptcy (and other default law) cited in section 1. In practice, provisions of bankruptcy laws temper the degree to which property rights are optimally allocated and unambiguous, resources are efficiently reallocated, and discipline is enforced. Furthermore, experience with bankruptcy in any economy depends not only upon the terms of bankruptcy statutes but also upon financial institutions and political constraints. These latter factors may be just as critical as the provisions of the bankruptcy law itself.

These observations suggest a framework for analysing bankruptcy in an economy. Determinants of experience with bankruptcy may be classified into three areas: design, or the provisions of the bankruptcy law; implementation, which refers to experience with the law given that it is honoured; and enforcement, which refers to the degree to which bureaucratic officials attempt to circumvent laws that are on the books. The provisions of bankruptcy laws may have a strong effect on the extent and type of utilization of the law; therefore, the law's design is an important determinant of experience with bankruptcy. Implementation refers to actions that are taken by creditors or the debtor outside of or during a bankruptcy proceeding that are not a direct response to provisions of the law yet that affect experience with application of the law. Factors that influence the degree to which implementation is successful include the history of operation of the economy and the general financial environment, described by the level of development of capital markets, the nature of regulation of banks, and the degree of aggregate uncertainty. Successful implementation of bankruptcy may require adapting provisions of bankruptcy laws to prevailing financial conditions and/or modifying financial institutions to render them more compatible with the application of bankruptcy laws. Enforcement problems arise when bureaucratic officials with the power to enforce bankruptcy laws have a vested interest in continuation of insolvent firms.

Two major issues that appear in the literature on design of bankruptcy laws are whether or not the law should contain a reorganization as well as a liquidation phase and the effects of the priority ordering of creditors upon application of the law. Much of the discussion of bankruptcy design is concerned with the law's effectiveness in allocating resources efficiently: does the law permit firms whose continuation values exceed their liquidation values to survive and force firms whose liquidation values exceed their continuation values to liquidate?[18] The US bankruptcy law, like many Western bankruptcy laws, allows the debtor to choose between reorganization and liquidation; however, the US debtor's management and stockholders gain significant bargaining power in US reorganization that debtors in other Western countries do not enjoy.[19]

Critics of the US reorganization procedure argue that the bargaining powers gained by management in Chapter 11 (reorganization) relative to their bargaining powers outside of bankruptcy lead to a bankruptcy law that allows firms that should be liquidated to stay in operation (see, for instance, Baird, 1986). Additional criticisms of US reorganization are that it permits transfers of wealth from creditors to debtors (Miller, 1977), and that it relies on administrative valuations of the firm (Baird, 1986; Jackson, 1986). Consequently, a number of authors have proposed changes in the US bankruptcy procedure. Roe (1983) proposes selling a portion of new equity of the reorganized firm in order to obtain a market valuation of the firm. Bebchuk (1988) suggests an exchange of new equity and equity options for cancellation of the creditors' claims. He devises a scheme for distributing and pricing the equity and equity options that maintains the absolute priority rule of creditors.[20] Baird (1986) and Jackson (1986) propose eliminating the reorganization procedure, arguing that there is nothing in the US bankruptcy code that prevents the firm's being sold as a going concern rather than piecemeal in the liquidation procedure.

One potential advantage of a reorganization procedure, pointed out by White (1989), is that it may provide the incentive to the firm's managers to declare bankruptcy before the value of the firm's assets is driven to zero. If liquidation were the only option, then managers might undertake risky actions as the firm's financial position deteriorated in order to avoid liquidation at all costs. Reorganization, then, if properly designed, might prevent an inefficient delay in the declaration of bankruptcy.

A proposal for the design of East European bankruptcy laws has been made by Aghion, Hart and Moore (1992). These authors begin with the scheme proposed by Bebchuk (1988), which would eliminate a bankrupt firm's debt and previous stock and distribute new equity and equity options to the creditors according to a particular pricing scheme. The authors then add the option for anyone to make a (cash or non-cash) bid for the firm. Bids would be voted upon by the firm's new owners, who comprise the previous creditors who chose to exercise their new equity options and perhaps old stockholders who purchased the equity options from the creditors. This bankruptcy procedure is designed to eliminate several problems with bankruptcy that appear in the West: costly bargaining by creditors during the reorganization phase; a bias for maintaining the firm as a going concern; a bias towards the incumbent management if the firm is reorganized.

The proposal of Aghion, Hart and Moore has tremendous merit for an economy with developed capital markets. Indeed, it addresses a number of the design problems that have been cited for US bankruptcy and that also exist to a greater or a lesser extent in the laws of major Western economies. Its reliance on distributing equity, however, poses problems in the reforming post-socialist economies, which do not yet have broadly functioning equity markets. The problems redressed by the proposed scheme are also more characteristic of experience with bankruptcy in developed market economies. I argue below that the principal problems with bankruptcy in the reforming economies appear to be inducing creditors to invoke the procedures at all and valuing the firm in an environment with a large amount of aggregate uncertainty, where information is extremely limited and costly to obtain, and where agents have little experience with markets. As I discuss below, there are a number of arguments to be made for passing a bankruptcy law in the reforming economies that is biased towards reorganization in order to encourage implementation and enforcement of the law. In addition, appointment of a neutral party such as a bankruptcy trustee to value the firm's assets and to propose a reorganization plan may avoid serious free-rider problems among creditors in bearing the costs of devising a plan. These free-rider problems may be much greater in the reforming than in the developed market economies because of the costs of acquiring information in the former. I use these observations to illustrate a claim that the level of development of capital markets is a determinant of the optimal form of bankruptcy laws.

Literature concerning the creditor's decision to refinance or liquidate a firm can also be applied to the analysis of creditor passivity; it implicitly identifies some of the potential explanations for the behaviour. One question that a number of authors have explored is the willingness of a new lender, such as a bank, to extend a loan to a debtor in default, thereby obviating the need for a bankruptcy proceeding. The willingness of the new creditor to extend the loan and the efficiency of the decision depend upon the priority ordering of creditors foreseen in the bankruptcy law. Models of this decision assume a coalition of equity holders and the new creditor.[21]

Another potential explanation for the reluctance of creditors to use bankruptcy is the high costs associated with bankruptcy. Potential sources of bankruptcy costs are explicit costs, such as administrative costs, which include payments to lawyers and accountants, and implicit costs, such as management's undertaking of risky investment and the loss of valuable employees or customers during the bankruptcy period. Studies of administrative costs of bankruptcy in the US (e.g. Ang, Chua and McConnell, 1982) suggest that administrative costs account for only a small portion of the value of the debtor's assets. White (1989), however, reports estimates of implicit bankruptcy costs that are ten times as great as administrative costs.

4   Creditor passivity: an implementation problem

I argue that the problem of creditor passivity is an implementation problem, although considerations of design and enforcement are also important in contributing to the problem. After first treating the problem as primarily one of implementation, I discuss the interaction of design and enforcement issues with creditor passivity.

Creditor passivity may take a host of forms. Among the common means of accounting for bad debt are for enterprise creditors to record their bad loans as accounts receivable and for banks to roll over loans and record their overdue interest payments as increases in the outstanding principal. Several plausible explanations for these actions appear below. Each is capable of yielding creditor passivity and may accurately describe some of the circumstances in at least one of the reforming or developing economies. It is likely, however, that several explanations are operating in many cases. After listing the possible explanations, I consider each explanation in turn and its policy implications or predictive power with respect to financial reform.

The explanations for creditor passivity may be grouped into three categories: those relating to the value of the debtor or, equivalently, of the creditors' claims; those relating to the solvency of the creditor; and those relating to regulation of creditors or of the relations between the government and creditors. Table 7.1 lists the explanations by category, as well as the remedies suggested by the discussion that follows.

Which of these explanations actually applies to particular economies and creditors will depend upon a number of conditions, some of which

Table 7.1. *Explanations and remedies for creditor passivity*

Category	Explanation	Remedies
1. Value of creditors' claims	Expected value of creditors' claims, net of bankruptcy costs, is zero	●None necessary if revenues > variable costs ●Automatic triggering if revenues < variable costs ●Need for restructuring policy for large firms ●Simple bankruptcy procedure. May need government subsidization
2. Value of creditors' claims	Illiquid but not insolvent firms	●May need automatic triggering
3. Creditors' solvency	Signalling of non-performing claims may entail negative consequences for creditor	●Improve auditing and regulatory infrastructure
4. Creditors' solvency	Large quantities of non-performing, inherited debt render creditor insolvent	●Clean banks' and firms' balance sheets of inherited bad debt
5. Regulation of creditors	Assured bail-out	●Improve prudential regulation and enforcement
6. Regulation of creditors	Implicit collusion, or coordination failure in creditors' choices of action	●Alter beliefs of creditors

can be empirically identified. Identification of the conditions supporting particular explanations is important, since several of the explanations have differing policy predictions.

4.1   Zero value of claims

Factors that would lead to an expected zero value of assets from a creditor's point of view, perhaps net of the costs of bankruptcy, are the poor state or vintage of the capital stock of a debtor firm, the absence of a market for capital, high bankruptcy costs, or the priority assigned to a creditor in bankruptcy relative to the ordering of other creditors. There is reason to believe that the capital of many, though not all, firms in the reforming economies is indeed worth very little. Moreover, markets for capital are still quite undeveloped. This explanation, then, is likely to apply in at least some cases.

4.1.1 Low resale value of assets

The first two of these factors may be considered in tandem. If the value of the firm's capital stock were it to be put up for sale is zero, either because of the nature of the capital or because of the absence of buyers, then the relevant question to consider is whether the firm is able to cover its variable costs if it continues in operation. Whereas there is no need for bankruptcy if revenues exceed variable costs, the firm should be closed down if variable costs exceed revenues. Note that if the firm cannot cover its variable costs and initiation of bankruptcy proceedings is left up to the creditors, then they have no incentive to push the debtor into bankruptcy, especially if so doing involves some costs on their part.[22] The problem that may arise is a type of free-rider problem: it may be costly for an individual creditor to initiate bankruptcy although the total expected value of the firm's operating losses is greater than the total costs of initiating bankruptcy. Whereas bankruptcy should be playing a role in forcing the exit of firms, it does not do so because of faulty design. Automatic triggering of bankruptcy could obviate this problem.

Although creditors may have no strong incentive to push the debtor into bankruptcy when the value of the debtor's capital stock is very low, they should have a strong incentive not to increase their lending to the debtor, unless the credit is for acquiring new capital that will render the firm profitable. This type of restructuring, however, would seem to require a large investment and the cooperation of several creditors. One should not observe creditors continuing to lend to defaulting firms for such items as working capital if the explanation of zero value of the capital stock is the sole cause of creditor passivity. Observation of continued lending by a creditor to its defaulting debtors would thus be inconsistent with this explanation.[23]

Allowing the firm that can cover its variable costs to continue in operation represents the economically efficient decision. At the same time, the government may believe that allowing the firm that cannot cover its variable costs to continue in operation is also a socially desirable decision because it avoids the political problems of abruptly closing the firm. While this strategy may be politically convenient, it is socially undesirable. Permitting such a firm to continue to function may have strong negative repercussions in the financial system. As long as the firm continues in operation, the amount of non-performing loans that it generates grows. If the firm can take advantage of measures such as issuing promissory notes to prolong its life, then the amount of extra non-performing debt that it produces may be large. Yet, as some of the above posited explanations suggest, the accumulation of non-performing loans may alter creditors' behaviour in a way that adversely affects the functioning of the financial system. For example, creditors who are on the brink of insolvency due to high quantities of non-performing loans will have incentives to undertake risky or even speculative projects. If liquidation of insolvent firms is politically infeasible, then at least the financing of these firms should be removed from the financial system. This would eliminate the negative externalities arising from the accumulation of non-performing debt.

An example of this problem appears in Hungary, where some policy makers have asserted that a small number of loss-making firms were largely responsible for the problem of massive inter-enterprise indebtedness and default. For example, although 772 Hungarian firms reported mid-year losses in 1990, 61 per cent of the total amount of losses was accounted for by only seventy-four firms.[24] The apparent intent of the automatic triggering amendment to the bankruptcy law introduced in 1990 was to single out the large debtor firms, estimated at thirty to forty in number, and remove them from the inter-enterprise credit system.[25]

That a significant proportion of firms in the RSEs may be operating with assets of zero value and that governments deem it currently unacceptable to close down these firms raises the need for an explicit policy of restructuring during the transition. This policy must be implemented simultaneously with other reform measures in order to avoid the distortions in economic decisions that arise from the externalities created by these firms. Hungary is addressing the restructuring problem by establishing organizations specializing in firm reorganization. One such organization is a holding corporation whose purpose is to restructure firms and to prepare them for privatization. The holding corporation will be run by Coopers and Lybrand and will be financed through grants from the World Bank and from private capital. Its mission is to restructure firms by altering their operations and investing in new technology so that the firms can avoid liquidation and be privatized. This process is obviously time consuming and more than one holding corporation will be required to undertake economy-wide restructuring. Of a list of 150 firms that were identified as good prospects for restructuring, Coopers and Lybrand chose 12.[26] A second organization that will deal with restructuring in Hungary is a specialized financial institution that has been established for the purposes of managing liquidations of firms and of reorganizing firms.

4.1.2 Bankruptcy costs

Creditors in the RSEs face a number of potential sources of high bankruptcy costs that do not exist to the same degree in developed market economies. These include a high degree of aggregate uncertainty, which renders valuation of firms extremely difficult; the risk of lengthy proceedings due to the primitive state of legal systems; and uncertainty regarding the outcome of bankruptcy proceedings due to lack of experience with bankruptcy and ambivalence of government officials towards dismantling state-owned firms. The greatest perceived cost associated with the difficulty of valuing firms appears to be the risk that solvent firms will be forced to liquidate and that the proceeds from liquidation will not cover creditors' claims. I address this problem below in the discussion of illiquidity versus insolvency.

The risks of lengthy bankruptcy proceedings with uncertain outcomes may encourage creditors to bide their time until the uncertainty surrounding bankruptcy is resolved. Two types of remedies, one relating to design of bankruptcy laws and the other relating to enforcement, may be called for in this case. First, the bankruptcy procedure should be made as simple and predictable as possible. This would facilitate more rapid resolution of the procedure. Second, if creditors are uncertain of the government's commitment to enforce the bankruptcy law, the government may need to initiate a number of bankruptcies in order to signal that commitment. Subsidization of the early bankruptcy proceedings might also be required.

4.2 Illiquid but not insolvent debtor

The explanation that debtors may be illiquid but not insolvent describes a situation where rescheduling or renegotiation of claims is warranted if the firm's value in continuation is greater than its value in liquidation. Two special problems in this regard arise in the RSEs. First, a restrictive monetary policy combined with undeveloped capital markets may lead to credit rationing and may raise the number of illiquid debtors, including solvent as well as insolvent firms. Second, it may be extremely difficult to determine continuation and liquidation values of firms owing to the high degree of uncertainty concerning the progress and outcome of economic reform and the limited development of capital markets.[27] Creditors may adopt a 'wait-and-see' attitude.[28] This observation suggests that, given the large degree of institutional uncertainty associated with reform, one might expect a lower rate of bankruptcies than in economies where such uncertainty is not present. Automatic triggering of bankruptcy may be necessary to generate collectively financed valuation of firms, even at the risk of forcing some viable firms to liquidate.

Although creditors who believe that a debtor is illiquid but not insolvent might be willing to increase their lending to the debtor, one should not expect that all defaulting debtors are in such positions. Increased lending to some debtors but not others would be consistent with this explanation; increased lending across the board would not be consistent. Furthermore, if creditors are refraining from pursuing defaulting debtors because they deem these debtors to have positive option values, there is no need to alter provisions of bankruptcy laws.

It is conceivable that the degree of uncertainty in the RSEs is so great that it is impossible to value any firm; therefore, the decision to liquidate a firm or to allow it to continue in operation will necessarily be arbitrary. That is, the probability of a type II error is just as great as or greater than that of a type I error, and it is undesirable to force what may be viable firms into bankruptcy. Bankruptcy may not be feasible to implement until capital markets are developed.

A number of problems are associated with this argument. First, bankruptcy is not synonymous with liquidation; most bankruptcy laws contain provisions for reorganization as well as liquidation. Designing a law with a bias towards reorganization of claims or of production operations might be desirable when a large proportion of firms have particularly uncertain liquidation or continuation values. Second, a significant moral hazard problem among firm managers and workers has been created in the privatization processes of the RSEs that could be mitigated if the threat of bankruptcy were real. Specifically, one of the first steps in the privatization process in the RSEs has been to separate ownership from control: control over firms has devolved from central authorities interested in fulfilling plans to firm managers, who may pursue individual goals at the expense of the firm's future value. Moreover, given that the ownership rights of these firms are ill defined, managers have become *de facto* owners in the sense of possessing residual rights of control over assets, though not necessarily rights to residual income streams. The right of control over assets without the right to residual income streams creates incentives for managers to divert resources or profits from the firm. The only potential threats to a manager's control over a firm are managerial replacement or bankruptcy. Separation of ownership and control has likely weakened the threat of managerial replacement. In the absence of bankruptcy, there is little threat; hence, firms' values may fall significantly relative to what they would have been if bankruptcy posed a threat. The costs created by the absence of bankruptcy may well exceed those arising from an imperfectly implementable law.

A third problem with the argument that capital markets should be operative before a bankruptcy law is imposed is that the fact that investment in firms is ongoing and resources are limited implies that implicit estimates of relative firm values are currently being made. Yet, those 'making' the estimates, such as firm managers or bureaucrats with vested interests in a particular firm, may have incentives to overvalue the firm. Bankruptcy proceedings would serve the purpose of allowing an estimate to be agreed upon either by all of the firm's claimants or by a neutral party. Moreover, if the 'wrong' firms are claiming the resources in the absence of such a forum for a formal valuation of the firm, not only will there be a direct effect due to lower social product but there will also likely be an indirect effect deriving from distortions in creditors' actions due to accumulation of non-performing debt.

4.3   Signalling of non-performing claims

Creditors may not wish to signal that they have non-performing claims. By engaging in accounting tricks to disguise non-performing debt, a creditor can overstate its profits and may therefore maintain the ability to pay higher bonuses to workers or to continue a level of borrowing that would not be possible at lower reported profit levels. More generally, a signal of financial problems may cause a creditor's owners or claimants to initiate actions that would entail negative consequences for the creditor. For example, a creditor may fear that pushing a defaulting debtor into bankruptcy may force its own entry into bankruptcy.

That creditors may engage in activities designed to mask their financial standing suggests the existence of costly state verification. It is costly, for example, for authorities to verify the true financial state of a firm or bank.[29] Whether costly state verification and the information that seeking satisfaction of claims conveys will result in creditors' reluctance to pursue their claims will depend upon their own financial standing and upon the probability that they may be forced into bankruptcy as a result of failure to collect claims. Creditors who refrain from being aggressive in order not to signal financial difficulties must weigh the current benefits of not revealing their financial state against the future risk of not having enough cash to cover obligations. If the auditing system for banks is poor, if banks can borrow at the central bank's discount window to eliminate liquidity problems, and if financial distress carries with it penalties, then bank managers may have an incentive to roll over non-performing debt in order to disguise their financial problems.

Several arguments attest to the plausibility of the assumption of costly state verification and, hence, to this explanation as, if not the most likely current one, then one that is likely to hold in the near future. First, the absence of Western accounting practices combined with the complex network of inter-enterprise credit renders the assessment of firms' financial positions costly. Second, the rudimentary level of banking supervision in economies with relatively large numbers of banks renders costly the task of valuing banks' net assets. Although Western accounting firms have audited large state banks in Czechoslovakia and Hungary, the audits provide only a picture of the banks' assets at the beginning of reform. These audits are being used to determine policies for removing non-performing inherited debt from banks' balance sheets; however, debt that becomes non-performing after the audits have been conducted will be more difficult to detect.

Evidence suggests that supervisory systems are inadequate and that some banks in all of the RSEs are in financial difficulty. Some of the difficulty derives from large quantities of inherited, non-performing debt, which constitute the source of the fourth explanation of creditor passivity; however, banks will be undercapitalized by Western standards even with the bad debt eliminated. Moreover, government budgetary needs have influenced the quantities that banks have been able to add to their reserves. For example, Hungarian banks were able to apportion 20 and 30 per cent, respectively, of their after-tax profits in 1987 and 1988 to reserves; they were allowed no additions to reserves in 1989.[30] The growth of doubtful accounts relative to reserves of Hungarian banks cited in section 2 suggests deteriorating balance sheets of the commercial banks. In Czechoslovakia as of April 1992, over forty banks were operating, and the bank supervisory body had not yet formulated the definition of a bad loan.

That the training of one bank examiner in the West requires five to six years further supports the claim that adequate prudential supervision in the RSEs is lacking. The Polish experience illustrates this claim. Poland's General Inspectorate for Banking Supervision (GIBS) employs around seventy people, which is half the number of employees of the Warsaw branch of Price Waterhouse, and supervises over eighty banks. Whereas the rules and guidelines for bank examiners in the US comprise over one hundred pages, the guidelines in Poland derive from 'a few articles of law and a couple of pages of internal rules'.[31] The GIBS has difficulty holding on to its better employees, who are attracted by commercial banks paying much higher salaries. Furthermore, there appear to be too few sanctions available to the GIBS. Unlike in the West, the board cannot impose fines on banks. It can recommend replacement of bank management or revocation of a bank's licence; these appear to be sanctions of last resort, however. One reason for this is likely that the small market for bank management renders managerial replacement costly. In the three years that the inspectorate has been in operation, it has required two banks to draw up programmes to remedy financial violations and forced one bank to replace its board of governors. It has also notified a number of banks in writing of irregularities in their operations.

Costly state verification, together with weak bank balance sheets and poor banking supervision, render this explanation of creditor passivity on the part of banks in the RSEs highly plausible. In this case, imposition of an automatic triggering mechanism in the bankruptcy law, as was undertaken in Hungary, will not correct the implementation problem. Banks will still have the incentive to roll over debt for their debtors for whom the law is about to be triggered, since the debtor's entry into bankruptcy may well signal the creditor's financial difficulties. The solution to the problem lies in structuring bank regulation and auditing systems so that bank managers' incentives are compatible with the goals of the bankruptcy law. This will entail a large investment of resources in legal and regulatory infrastructure.

4.4 Inherited debt

Large amounts of non-performing debt create a number of potential problems in the RSEs. First, given the structural changes taking place in the economy, default on this debt may occur with equal frequency for 'good' firms and for 'bad'. Default does not send an unambiguous signal of poor performance or management; rather, it may indicate large levels of historical debt arising from arbitrary prices in the previous regime.[32] Enforcing bankruptcy laws when debtors hold inherited debt raises the already large risk in the RSEs of forcing solvent firms to liquidate, and may thereby lower willingness to enforce bankruptcy laws. This will further increase incentives to disguise non-performing debt and to refrain from pushing defaulting debtors into bankruptcy. The second problem arising from the inherited debt is the additional difficulty that it adds to the valuation of firms. Third, default on inherited debt may encourage creditors to continue lending to the debtor, throwing good money after bad in many cases, since the inherited debt appears on creditors' balance sheets as assets. Finally, large quantities of non-performing, inherited claims on a creditor's balance sheet may create incentives that are similar to those of US managers (of firms and the S & Ls) to undertake risky investment once bankruptcy becomes imminent. The probability of this response in the RSEs, however, is greater owing to the vulnerability of these economies to large, aggregate shocks and the resulting inability of the banks to diversify their risks. There may be strong incentives on the part of banks to roll over non-performing loans and to engage in speculative investment.

Policy makers in the reforming economies are well aware of the problem associated with the quantities of non-performing inherited debt on the banks' balance sheets. Two types of measures have been adopted in Czechoslovakia to purify banks' balance sheets. The first was to remove long-term loans associated with inventory accumulation to a special bank, the Consolidation Bank. The second measure involved an infusion of 50 billion korunas into the banking system via bonds issued by the State Property Agency. These bonds will be served by revenues from privatizations. Hungarian policy makers have provided state guarantees for half of the non-performing, inherited debt on the banks' balance sheets.[33] Neither Czechoslovakia nor Hungary has attempted to remove bad debt from the balance sheets of enterprises.

4.5   Assured bail-out of creditors

The explanation of assured bail-out for creditors illustrates the crucial role of bank regulation and ownership. Most banks in the RSEs are currently state owned, which implies that deposits are fully guaranteed. In Poland and in Czechoslovakia, as is probable in the other countries, deposits of state banks are guaranteed by the state budget. In contrast, private banks have no deposit insurance. While deposit insurance has both advantages and disadvantages, one of its advantages is that it encourages depositors to monitor the bank's activities. Depositors in Poland and Czechoslovakia have much greater incentives to monitor private banks than state banks, and the risk of a bank run is virtually non-existent with a state-owned bank. The absence of incentives for depositors of state-owned banks to monitor bank management and the weakness of bank supervisory functions create an environment in the RSEs that imposes almost no discipline on bank management. The only disciplinary mechanism that exists for state-owned banks may be the prospect of privatization: bank management will have an incentive to perform well in order to increase the probability of retaining their positions once the bank is privatized.

The scenario depicted here is suggestive of the US savings and loan crisis: behaviour of bank creditors will be a function of the regulations affecting them and of the nature of bank ownership. A question of interest is what similarities and differences exist in the environments of banks in the RSEs with respect to that of the S & Ls. One similarity is that the US government turned out to be the implicit owner of the S & Ls, whereas governments in the current stage of reform in the RSEs are the explicit owners of most banks. Furthermore, even if at later stages banks are privately owned, they will be regulated and monitored by government regulators. Another similarity is that the US regulators attempted to avoid the problems of liquidation of too many S&Ls by simply ignoring the oncoming crisis. Explanations for this passivity (or 'forbearance' as labelled by Kane, 1989) resemble arguments put forth in Mitchell (1990b) with respect to regulators in the RSEs: when regulators who are charged with enforcing liquidation rules suffer costs of liquidating firms under their direction, they may choose to ignore these rules.[34]

One notable difference in the environments of the S&Ls and the banks in the RSEs is that in the latter banks are the primary external providers of long-term investment finance. The potential thus exists for a much greater impact on the productive sector in these economies if problems of the order of those with the S&Ls were to arise with the banks.

A second difference, with equally negative implications, in the environments of the S&Ls and the banks in the RSEs is that macroeconomic conditions in the RSEs are more adverse than were the conditions in which the S&Ls operated. There is a greater probability that banks in the RSEs will suffer financial distress than existed for the S&Ls, and one can expect that regulators will be more favourably disposed towards bailing out banks in periods of recession than in periods of boom.[35]

In brief, the issue of banking regulation is of central importance to the implementability of bankruptcy laws and, hence, to financial and economic reform. The negative effects of bank passivity are magnified in the reforming economies because of the dominant role that banks play in credit markets. Although the recent surge of trade credit in the RSEs has caused problems in controlling money supplies, it may have the beneficial side-effect of causing the bankruptcy process to function if trade creditors are more aggressive than banks.

4.6   Implicit collusion

Suggestion of the explanation of implicit collusion often appears in the popular press in the West and in the East, yet policy makers have perhaps accorded little attention to it. One such intimation of implicit collusion among creditors is provided by the *New York Times* (3 June 1991). In describing the operation of a large Polish chemical factory, the *Times* asserts that executives 'amass[ed] huge debts among themselves that were never collected. They sent workers on unpaid holidays, built up inventories and played for time, in the hope that the Government would be forced by rising social discontent to give up.' The *Economist* (6 April 1991) offers another version of creditor collusion. In describing the failed efforts of the Polish bank to purchase firms' promissory notes at a discount and recover the claims, the author asserts that firms became reluctant to turn over their notes to the bank 'because it meant turning over their mates as well'.

The implications of creditor collusion are several. First, passiveness as a form of collusion requires the belief that the government will not be willing to force 'too many' creditors (or banks) into liquidation. Second, in order for collusion to succeed, enough creditors must be passive. If creditors believe that other creditors are going to be aggressive, then they, too, may find it in their interest to be aggressive, since the benefits from remaining passive may have been drastically reduced. This suggests that creditor collusion represents a coordination failure generated by a strategic complementarity in creditors' choices of action.[36] There may exist multiple equilibria in the game in which creditors with defaulting debtors decide to be active or passive. As long as players believe that others will be passive, then they may have an incentive to remain passive, but if players believe that others will choose to be active, it may be optimal to become active.

A problem that arises in the collusive equilibrium is that creditors' beliefs are self-fulfilling. If all creditors believe that the government will bail everyone out if everyone is insolvent, then the government will be obliged to undertake this action. Moreover, such beliefs constitute rational 'priors' for creditors to hold at early stages of reform, since the history of the RSEs has been one in which bail-outs were guaranteed. Vaclav Klaus aptly describes creditor behaviour in Czechoslovakia as resulting from 'continued adherence to past management principles, of living in the present at the expense of the future'. These arguments suggest that one of the government's tasks at the earliest stage of reform is to influence the beliefs of creditors in order to prevent a collusive equilibrium from occurring.

This explanation allows for two types of equilibria: one where creditors are aggressive, and one where they are passive. The multiple equilibria arise because of strategic complementarities and a set of beliefs inherited from past behaviour and experience. The legacies of the past thus include not only institutions that are poorly suited for market economics but also beliefs that must be revised.

5   Towards a link between financial institutions and bankruptcy

This paper argues that a functional bankruptcy process is an essential ingredient of a market economy, and it demonstrates that utilization of bankruptcy is not automatic in all economies. It identifies a number of conditions that 'solve' the puzzle of creditor passivity in the reforming economies, i.e. that lead to avoidance of the bankruptcy process. Whereas most of these conditions exist to a certain degree in every economy, the characteristics of the RSEs exacerbate them. The characteristics include a high degree of aggregate uncertainty, a low level of development of capital markets and prudential supervision, a legacy of financial obligations from a previous regime, and a history of governmental paternalism. These observations raise two questions: how easy is it to alter the conditions leading to creditor passivity, and what are the implications for financial reform if the conditions are not alleviated?

The analysis of section 4 reveals that some of the conditions (explanations 1 and 2) may be mitigated by tailoring bankruptcy laws to the prevailing financial environment, but other conditions (explanations 3–6) are unaffected by design changes. Hence, the form of bankruptcy laws can affect the operation of credit markets, but conditions in credit markets can also determine the operation of bankruptcy.

Bankruptcy design is important when the expected value of creditors' claims is low. Yet, the proposed remedies differ from those discussed in the literature on bankruptcy design cited in section 2. Automatic triggering in this case will help ensure that firms that should be liquidated are liquidated. At the same time, a bias in bankruptcy laws towards reorganization can encourage implementation by mitigating creditors' fears that solvent but illiquid firms will be liquidated, and it can also aid enforcement by reducing the political risk associated with excessive liquidation of firms. Automatic triggering of bankruptcy and a bias towards reorganization thus balance a trade-off between mistakes in resource allocation that occur with bankruptcy because of the uncertainty of valuation of the debtor's assets and the lack of discipline that prevails in the absence of bankruptcy.

Appropriate bankruptcy design, however, will not be sufficient if enforcement of liquidation poses a problem. Stated differently, if continuation of enterprise operation is part of a politically or socially optimal restructuring programme, then an explicit restructuring policy must be devised. Such a policy will be needed to minimize the negative financial externalities generated by large, loss-making firms that are difficult to liquidate. The long period required for completion of restructuring, however, demands that a functioning bankruptcy process be put into place in order to apply to those firms that do not need restructuring and to those that have been restructured.

The bankruptcy law is unimportant when creditors ignore the bankruptcy option for the following reasons: they do not want to signal that they have non-performing claims; they will have to write off 'large enough' quantities of past debt; they are assured of bail-out. Redesigning bankruptcy laws will not change creditor behaviour in these circumstances; rather, the building of regulatory infrastructures and broadening of capital markets will. Until capital markets are developed, however, the network of trade credit may have the beneficial effect of creating a class of creditors who are willing to employ the bankruptcy procedure against their defaulting debtors. In any event, given the time needed for accomplishing either of the policy objectives of building financial infrastructure or broadening capital markets, a greater understanding of the functioning of credit markets in the absence of bankruptcy would be useful for aiding determination of the optimal path of financial reform.

It is clear that development of sound banking and financial regulatory systems is a prerequisite for successful implementation of bankruptcy if any of the explanations 2–6 is the primary condition generating passivity. Moreover, permitting bank competition through entry of new banks without adequate regulatory oversight may actually exacerbate problems in the financial system. Managers of financial institutions must also face some threat of replacement. If the small size of the market for bank managers or if the state ownership of banks impedes the government's ability to impose the threat of replacement, then scarce resources should be allocated from other uses (such as development of fledgling stock markets) to increase the managerial pool, and banks should be privatized quickly. The construction of banking and regulatory systems should assume high priority in the sequencing of reform measures.

The multiplicity of potential explanations for creditor passivity and the long time needed for eliminating all of the underlying conditions generating it suggest the need for both empirical and theoretical research to understand the problem better. Theoretical modelling, of which Mitchell (1992) is an example, could provide insight into creditor behaviour in the conditions of the RSEs. Empirical work will aid identification of the explanations prevailing in different reforming economies. For example, observation of accommodation to default with no additional extension of credit would lend support to the explanation that creditors believe the value of their claims to be zero. Observation of increased lending to some debtors but not to others would allow for the explanation that creditors believe that some of their debtors are solvent while others are not. Determining the characteristics of the debtors to whom creditors continue to lend would help to validate or to rule out this explanation. The extent to which creditors attempt to disguise their non-performing debt would provide information regarding the perceived negative consequences of acquiring non-performing debt. Calculation of the proportion of non-performing debt in creditors' portfolios and comparison with normal levels for creditors in the West would help assess the merits of the explanation regarding the negative incentive effects of the non-performing debt.

Section 3 asserted the analytical convenience of separating issues relating to bankruptcy into the categories of design, implementation and enforcement. The analysis of creditor passivity illustrates the usefulness of the approach, although issues of design, implementation and enforcement here are clearly related. For example, some of the conditions for creditor passivity could be alleviated if bankruptcy laws were designed with automatic triggering mechanisms. On the other hand, unwillingness of public officials to permit firms to be dismantled – a problem of enforcement – would be sufficient to cause passivity among creditors in initiating bankruptcy proceedings. Yet, the analysis of section 4 demonstrates that, whereas problems of enforcement or design may be sufficient to generate creditor inaction, they are not necessary. Creditor passivity may pose a serious problem even where governments are committed to enforcing bankruptcy laws. Implementation problems are likely to arise independently of problems of design or enforcement.

NOTES

I would like to thank Larry Blume, Charles Kahn, Ken Koford, Colin Mayer, Bruce Smith and participants at the Jerome Levy Economics Institute conference 'Moving to a Market Economy: Economic Reform in Eastern Europe and the Soviet Union' for helpful discussions and comments. Rimjhim Mehra provided excellent research assistance. I also gratefully acknowledge the financial support of NSF Grant SES–9109696.

1 This phenomenon has also been observed widely in developing economies. For an extensive discussion of financial distress in developing economies, see World Bank (1989, Ch. 5).
2 A number of papers have noted the disciplinary effect of bankruptcy. Examples include Grossman and Hart (1982) and Jensen (1986), who consider the incentive effects of bankruptcy, and the consequences for the firm's choice of financial structure, on managers' willingness to divert productive resources to non-productive uses. Harris and Raviv (1990) also emphasize the disciplinary function of debt contracts resulting from the investigation that is triggered and the information gained by creditors when debtors default on debt repayments. Legros and Mitchell (1991) study the effect of bankruptcy in an economy at an early stage of financial reform on managers' choices of productive effort and the amount of investment. The government in this economy provides investment finance and determines the optimal bankruptcy rule.
3 Jackson (1986) presents a detailed exposition of this problem.
4 This term was coined by Kornai (1980).
5 In other works (Mitchell, 1990a, 1990b) I develop an argument that the links between bankruptcy statutes and the development of capital markets work in two directions. On the one hand, bankruptcy statutes define a set of property rights that form a foundation for the operation of capital markets and, hence, that influence the development of these markets. On the other hand, the focus

of bankruptcy laws is likely to differ at differing stages of development of capital markets.

6 Mitchell (1992) presents a theoretical model of creditor behaviour in the RSEs incorporating some of these explanations.

7 In Mitchell (1990b) I provide a more detailed description of the original Hungarian bankruptcy provisions as well as provisions of the Yugoslav bankruptcy law, which was significantly amended in 1986.

8 The criteria for rehabilitation were: (i) that the firm's continuing operation was necessary for national security; (ii) that liquidating the firm would risk non-fulfilment of an international contract; and (iii) that the firm's liquidation would have a significant impact on regional unemployment.

9 There did exist a priority ordering for creditors in the event of liquidation. This priority ordering resembled those observed, with minor variations, in Western bankruptcy laws: administrative expenses; wages, allowances, social security benefits, and the like; other claims by private persons such as problems due to product defects; secured claims; all other debts. One might argue that this priority ordering implicitly determined the reservation values of creditors and their bargaining powers during conciliation; however, this argument holds only if creditors believed that the threat of liquidation was real.

10 'Government tries to enforce bankruptcy law', *Joint Publications Research Service (JPRS)*, 23 January 1990.

11 *Market Letter*, National Bank of Hungary, September 1991. In computing reserve capital I have added the categories of reserve capital and tax-free reserves.

12 'Bankrupt enterprises, proceedings analyzed', *JPRS*, 12 August 1991, and 'Over 1000 bankruptcies in progress', *JPRS*, 2 January 1992.

13 'Semiannual report on enterprise performance', *JPRS*, 13 November 1990.

14 'Analysis of earning capacity, profitability noted', *JPRS*, 14 November 1991.

15 'East European banks in red braces', *Economist*, 6 April 1991.

16 'Bank recapitalization, debt reduction viewed', *JPRS*, 5 November 1991.

17 'Kcs fifty billion bond issue for bank improvements', *JPRS*, 28 October 1991.

18 White (1989) provides a detailed discussion of the efficiency of resource allocation of the US liquidation and reorganization procedures.

19 See Johnston (1988) for a detailed discussion of the powers gained by management relative to creditors in reorganization.

20 The absolute priority rule is a priority ordering of creditors that holds in US liquidation and requires that creditors be paid in the following order: administrative expenses of the bankruptcy procedure; priority claims such as taxes, social security payments, unpaid salaries, etc.; unsecured creditors.

21 See Bulow and Shoven (1978), White (1980, 1989) and more recent references cited in Gertner and Scharfstein (1991).

22 For example, it may be costly to Hungarian creditors to have to make a case that the debtor who has defaulted on payment is likely to be insolvent. On the other hand, if creditors need only document that the default occurred, then initiating a request for a bankruptcy proceeding is not costly.

23 It should be remarked, however, that an initial creditor's refusal to increase lending to an insolvent debtor does not rule out lending to the debtor by a new creditor. In fact, other creditors may be willing to lend to a debtor for the purpose of allowing the debtor to service previous debt if the new creditors are granted seniority in the repayment of the debtor's claims. References cited in section 2 above take into account this fact.

24 'Semiannual report on enterprise performance', *JPRS*, 13 November 1990.
25 'Parliament acts to reduce enterprise mutual indebtedness', *JPRS*, 3 July 1990.
26 'Upgrading holding corporation progress report', *JPRS*, 18 October 1991.
27 It is clear that, in the absence of price reform, estimation of liquidation and continuation values is meaningless. All of the discussion of this paper presumes that price reform has already been undertaken and that market prices prevail.
28 An increase in uncertainty in the distribution of the firm's revenues alone will not give creditors the incentive to postpone collecting their claims; on the contrary, an increase in uncertainty (through a mean-preserving spread) reduces the expected value of a creditor's claim and provides the incentive to collect sooner rather than later. What is necessary to induce creditors to roll over debts is a belief that a change in institutions, such as imposition of market-clearing prices, will alter the expected value of the firm's assets.
29 Townsend (1979) and Gale and Hellwig (1985) use the assumption of costly state verification to derive the use of debt as an optimal contract in a relation between an entrepreneur and an investor.
30 'Banks without cash soon to be privatized', *JPRS*, 28 September 1990.
31 'Need for improvement of bank supervision voiced', *JPRS*, 23 October 1991.
32 Calvo and Frenkel (1991) emphasize the difficulties of assessing the credit-worthiness of firms with large levels of inherited debt. Brainard (1991) argues that the reason that all attempts to the present at financial reform in the RSEs have failed to increase financial discipline is that they have not addressed the problem of the balance sheet losses arising from non-performing debt.
33 'State guarantee on bad enterprise debt', *JPRS*, 30 July 1991.
34 When stock and bond markets are absent and firms are publicly owned, the relevant owner/claimants of firms include government regulators. These regulators often serve in a dual capacity, with vested interests in the firm and as enforcers of bankruptcy laws. This dual role introduces a conflict of interest: regulators are in prime positions to avoid enforcing bankruptcy statutes. Automatic triggering of bankruptcy may be necessary to obviate the enforcement problem.
35 This assertion is corroborated for regulators of US banks in Calomiris (1990).
36 See Cooper and John (1988) for a study of coordination failures due to strategic complementarities.

REFERENCES

Aghion, P., O. Hart and J. Moore (1992) 'The economics of bankruptcy reform', manuscript.
Ang, J., J. Chua and J. McConnell (1982) 'The administrative costs of corporate bankruptcy: a note', *Journal of Finance* 11 (March), 219–26.
Baird, D. (1986) 'The uneasy case for corporate reorganizations', *Journal of Legal Studies* 15 (January), 127–47.
Bebchuk, L. (1988) 'A new approach to corporate reorganization', *Harvard Law Review* 101 (4), 775–804.
Brainard, L. (1991) 'Strategies for economic transformation in Central and Eastern Europe: role of financial market reform', in Hans Blommestein and Michael Marrese (eds.), *Transformation of Planned Economies: Property Rights Reform and Macroeconomic Stability*, Paris: OECD.

Bulow, J. and J. Shoven (1978) 'The bankruptcy decision', *Bell Journal of Economics* **9** (Autumn), 437–56.

Calomiris, C. (1990) 'Is deposit insurance necessary?: An historical perspective', *Journal of Economic History* **50**, 283–95.

Calvo, G. and J. Frenkel (1991) 'Credit markets, credibility, and economic transformation', *Journal of Economic Perspectives* **5** (Fall), 139–48.

Cooper, R. and A. John (1988) 'Coordinating coordination failures in Keynesian models', *Quarterly Journal of Economics* **103** (August), 441–63.

Gale, D. and M. Hellwig (1985) 'Incentive-compatible debt contracts: the one-period problem', *Review of Economic Studies* **52**, 647–63.

Gertner, R. and D. Scharfstein (1991) 'A theory of workouts and the effects of reorganization law', *Journal of Finance* **46** (September), 1189–222.

Grossman, S.J. and O.D. Hart (1982) 'Corporate financial structure and managerial incentives', in John McCall (ed.), *The Economics of Information and Uncertainty*, Chicago: University of Chicago Press.

Harris, M. and A. Raviv (1990) 'Capital structure and the informational role of debt', *Journal of Finance* **45** (June), 321–49.

Jackson, T. (1986) *The Logic and Limits of Bankruptcy*, Boston: Little, Brown, and Company.

Jensen, M.C. (1986) 'Agency costs of free cash flow, corporate finance, and takeovers', *American Economic Review* **76** (May), 323–9.

Johnston, B.J. (1988) 'The bankruptcy bargain', Working Paper No. 7 (December), Stanford Center on Conflict and Negotiation, Stanford University.

Kane, E. (1989) 'The high cost of incompletely funding the FSLIC's shortage of explicit capital', *Journal of Economic Perspectives* **3** (Fall), 31–48.

Kornai, J. (1980) *The Economics of Shortage*, Amsterdam: North-Holland.

Legros, P. and J. Mitchell (1991) 'Control and bankruptcy under budgetary constraints and risky investment', CAE Working Paper No. 91–01, Economics Department, Cornell University.

Miller, M. (1977) 'The wealth transfers of bankruptcy: some illustrative examples', *Law and Contemporary Problems* **41** (Autumn), 39–46.

Mitchell, J. (1990a) 'The economics of bankruptcy in reforming socialist economies', Final Report to the National Council for Soviet and East European Research, October.

(1990b) 'Managerial discipline, productivity, and bankruptcy in capitalist and socialist economies', *Comparative Economic Studies* **22** (Fall), 93–197.

(1992) 'Strategic creditor passivity' (in progress).

Roe, M. (1983) 'Bankruptcy and debt: a new model for corporate reorganization', *Columbia Law Review* **83** (April), 527–602.

Townsend, R. (1979) 'Optimal contracts and competitive markets with costly state verification', *Journal of Economic Theory* **13**, 137–51.

White, M.J. (1980) 'Public policy toward bankruptcy: me-first and other priority rules', *Bell Journal of Economics* **11** (Autumn), 550–64.

(1989) 'The corporate bankruptcy decision', *Journal of Economic Perspectives* **3** (Spring), 129–51.

World Bank (1989) *World Development Report*, New York: Oxford University Press.

Discussion

DAVID M. NEWBERY

Janet Mitchell has given us a fascinating account of the evolution of the institution of bankruptcy in Hungary. She raises an important question. There are good reasons to expect large numbers of state-owned enterprises (SOEs) in Eastern Europe to be insolvent. In Hungary the banking system has been restructured to enable the commercial banks to take over the task of financing long-term loans for investment, and they have been allocated debts in SOEs. Why do these banks not force insolvent firms into bankruptcy? Why have only 9 out of 681 (less than 2 per cent) bankruptcy proceedings in 1991 been initiated by banks? Janet has given a variety of convincing explanations, and I shall concentrate on the question of the urgency of action to remedy this failure. It is useful to distinguish two cases: firms that have positive cash flow but cannot fully service the debt, and those that can. Those that can service their debt either can have their debt written down, if their assets are best used in their current form, in which case bankruptcy is not necessary (but capital restructuring may be), or their assets should be reallocated if they have higher value in alternative use. If their assets are best reallocated, then they should be sold. If they are SOEs, this process is proceeding as fast as possible through the State Property Agency (SPA), and it is not clear that bankruptcy proceedings usefully alter priorities. They might, but might not – the main problem is the scarcity of administrative capacity to reorganize and restructure, and the problem of finding a buyer or new management. So, in either case of firms with positive cash flow, passivity is not obviously harmful, providing new loans are carefully assessed.

What about firms with negative cash flow? These should evidently be liquidated. But now we have a puzzle. If they have negative cash flow, then they cannot survive without extra cash inflows.

Trade creditors would be unwise to lend to them, though, if they believed that the absence of bankruptcy proceedings was a signal that all was well, the passivity is costly. But one suspects that trade creditors are aware of this problem, and should naturally insist on cash for at least the operational cost element of their sales. Apparently many do so insist. Surely the banks, knowing the negative cash flow situation, should not advance further loans and, if no one lends, then the firm will not be able to survive.

However, there is a suggestion that such firms do survive, for a variety of reasons. It has been claimed that one strategy is to sell valuable assets to create cash flow, thereby essentially defrauding the state budget. Often this is with the approval of the SPA, which presumably believes that continuing the enterprise is preferable to termination. Again, perhaps this is because they do not have the resources to devote to reorganization, so doing nothing is the least socially costly activity. Reorganization takes scarce resources, though perhaps there are better solutions, such as spontaneous privatization. This would, however, perhaps send the wrong signals in an environment in which the government is trying to realize as much value as possible from the privatization of the SOEs.

A second possible reason for not forcing bankruptcy is that cross-holding is now extensive in Hungary: banks hold enterprise debt, but enterprises hold stock in banks, and might therefore be able to force the banks to continue lending to insolvent firms. It is not clear whether this happens, but if it does the obvious answer is to swap bank equity for enterprise debt, and perhaps reallocate some fraction of that equity to the SPA (to avoid the banks owning themselves).

One interesting question that is suggested by the coexistence of state and private banks is whether or not a refusal by a private bank to advance loans might be taken as a signal of non-creditworthiness that would foreclose any enterprise debt. This might happen if all inter-enterprise debt was discounted by private banks. This would put pressure on state-owned banks to tighten up their monitoring.

To summarize, one defence of apparent passivity is that the country is restructuring as fast as possible, and nothing is gained by precipitating further bankruptcies. This implies, however, that banks are not partici-pating in the process of restructuring perhaps because they lack expertise. If so, then equipping them with such expertise is of high priority, though it may not affect the diagnosis in the short run.

The other explanation is that banks can and should bankrupt insol-vent firms, to avoid further misallocation of resources and to create confidence for investors and lenders, but they choose not to do so because there are private costs that outweigh the benefits – it might cause them to lose their clients and hence their reason for the current size and staffing, which might lead to job losses. They might then rapidly lose market shares to new private and foreign banks. If so, then maintaining freedom of entry to foreign banks would seem very important, as is strengthening bank surveillance.

The final explanation is that there is so much uncertainty about what might happen over the next few years that banks genuinely do not know whether any enterprise is irredeemably insolvent; the best strategy is to wait and see, presumably whilst not advancing further loans or only those sufficient to increase the option value of further waiting. This ignorance is exacerbated by the lack of skilled staff able to evaluate loans, and the hope that others will take on the job. 'Don't just do something, stand there' may be the best advice in such cases, especially in the face of the threat of the domino effect of multiple bankruptcy precipitating a financial crash that would leave all worse off than now. Passivity then becomes collectively rationalizable, even if not privately rational.

What are the policy implications? The first is to make sure that banks have something to lose if they do not act in the public interest. This suggests privatization, which requires recapitalization, and supervision, as well as encouraging competition from foreign banks. The second is to make sure that banks are *able* to act, which requires training, equipping them with teams competent to restructure enterprises and, again, allowing in foreign banks that possess such abilities. Finally, and more speculatively, some of the problems might be reduced if firms were easier to restructure. This would be the case if all enterprises were automatically broken up into autonomous establishments. This would alter the balance of power of firms vis-à-vis banks, as well as having desirable pro-competitive implications for industry.

PHILIPPE AGHION

This paper provides a relevant and up-to-date account of the difficulties involved in enforcing bankruptcy procedures and hard budget constraints in Eastern European countries. The author attributes these difficulties to three types of considerations.

First, the *design* of bankruptcy legislation: this should be improved so as both to avoid excessive liquidation of firms during the transition period (characterized by a high degree of macroeconomic and systematic uncertainty) and to maintain a threat (or a disciplinary device) upon the incumbent managers in the absence of alternative mechanisms for transferring corporate control (such as takeovers or proxy fights).

Second, structural reforms in Eastern Europe such as the reduction (or writing-off) of inherited enterprises' debts, the setting up of sound banking supervisory institutions and the development of a private banking sector (partly through the privatization of existing state banks) will help mitigate the creditors' passivity and thereby facilitate the *implementation* of bankruptcy procedures. Such reforms will indeed reduce the risks of contagious insolvencies, thereby allowing creditors to become tougher on insolvent debtors, especially with properly recapitalized banks that will no longer need to cover up their client enterprises' badly performing loans.

Third, *enforcement* considerations, which refer to the role that the state should play so as to favour (or at least not impede) the implementation of bankruptcy procedures. There, the author has in mind the governments' commitment to restructuring policies that involve closing down loss-making state enterprises.

I agree on most grounds with the author, especially regarding the desideratum of a good bankruptcy procedure, which should seek to maximize the *ex post* net present value of assets (and in particular avoid excessive liquidation of viable companies) while imposing a bonding device on managers *ex ante*. The Aghion–Hart–Moore scheme referred to in section 3 of the paper was designed precisely with that purpose in mind: it involves removing the incumbent management team as in Chapter 7 of the US Bankruptcy Law (thereby preserving the bonding device of debt) but at the same time it allows for both cash and *non-cash bids* to be solicited or made after bankruptcy has been declared. Non-cash bids typically involve incumbent or new management teams proposing to maintain the firm as a going concern by exchanging shares in the present firm not for cash but for shares in the reorganized firm. A relatively quick and efficient decision by claim-holders to select the best cash or non-cash bid can in turn be achieved *by vote*, provided their heterogeneous claims have already been transformed into equity claims. This is precisely what the A.H.M procedure recommends, referring to various mechanisms for transforming the debt claims into uniform equity claims. Here, not surprisingly, I do not share the author's concern about the absence of equity markets being a problem for our procedure to be applied in Eastern European countries. Indeed, the new shareholders can always decide to select a cash bid or a non-cash bid involving positive debt–equity ratios.

Overall, I share the author's view that the main difficulties in enforcing bankruptcy procedures in Eastern Europe have more to do with structural and institutional loopholes or deficiencies than with the particular design of bankruptcy laws throughout the region. I would still like to add the following remarks:

First, the macroeconomic dimension of restructuring policies should be kept in mind when dealing with the governments' attitude vis-à-vis inefficient (or loss-making) state enterprises. In particular, it is unrealistic to believe that Eastern European governments will be able to accommodate (from both a political and also a budgetary point of view) high unemployment rates (e.g. more than 20 per cent of the labour force). These governments will thus have to maintain most of the existing state firms in activity until the new private sector has grown sufficiently large to absorb the bulk of the labour force. (Growth of the private sector is currently limited by credit constraints, in particular those imposed by state banks for reasons mentioned above and in the paper and also by the macroeconomic and institutional uncertainties which tend to discourage risk taking by new private investors.)

Restructuring policies by state governments should thus involve the maintenance of a large number of state activities, in the prospect either of their future privatization or of their progressive phasing out. Such maintenance policies should naturally be accompanied by various measures aimed at improving regulation and incentives in the state sector.

Second, following from the previous remark, a strong case should be made for dealing separately with public and private firms. *Stricto sensu*, the new bankruptcy procedures should apply to private firms only, even though several features of these procedures could be adapted to deal with both the debt restructuring and commercialization of state-owned enterprises (see van Wijnbergen, 1992, on this latter point).

REFERENCE

van Wijnbergen, S. (1992) 'Economic aspects of enterprise reform in Eastern Europe', mimeo, World Bank.

8 Enterprise debt and economic transformation: financial restructuring in Central and Eastern Europe

DAVID BEGG and RICHARD PORTES

1 Introduction

In this paper we discuss a problem that is not confined to the transitional economies of Central and Eastern Europe (CEE) but that is now acute in these countries. Unless it is overcome quickly, successful transition to the market may be in jeopardy. The problem is the widespread failure of enterprise debtors to make scheduled payments of principal and interest to creditors, whether to banks or other enterprises. In such circumstances, enterprise budget constraints no longer bite, and the price mechanism loses much of its significance in the reallocation of resources. Restructuring may be greatly delayed or halted completely. Not only has the normal process of exit in a market economy been suspended, entry is impeded by the disproportionate share of bank credit being allocated as refinancing of incumbents. For some time to come, this 'crowding out' threatens to confine the emerging private sector to small-scale activities such as retailing.

The failure of banks to enforce debt contracts with their long-standing customers should not be viewed simply as a perpetuation of the previous regime, in which finance adjusted passively to targets for the real economy. Nor is it simply a failure of political will or of management expertise. We argue that in current circumstances there may be powerful incentives for banks not to enforce debt contracts. This has three implications. First, enactment of bankruptcy laws is not sufficient for initiation of bankruptcy proceedings; there must also be appropriate incentives for creditors to foreclose. Second, until incentives are altered, the government cannot successfully delegate credit allocation in general and associated control rights over closure in particular. Centralized policy will be required. Third, when there are major credit market failures, privatization alone, whether of banks or state-owned enterprises (SOEs), is unlikely to promote substantially greater efficiency.

Poor microeconomic incentives perpetuate inefficiency and inhibit struc-

230

tural adjustment. Such imperfections in the credit market raise the cost or reduce the efficiency of monetary policy as a macroeconomic tool. Failure to enforce credit obligations may even render orthodox monetary policy ineffective or perverse. This is unfortunate since fiscal policy remains fragile until reforms of tax structure are implemented and a tradition of taxpaying established. Thus macroeconomic considerations reinforce the priority for structural reform of credit markets to enhance their efficiency. In this paper we set out how this might be done and propose a sequencing of reforms likely to be robust and credible.

The 'bad debts' problem (often linked to financial repression) is familiar from the experience of many LDCs (see World Bank, 1989) and middle-income industrializing countries (for Greece, Portugal and Spain, see Bliss and Braga de Macedo, 1990). There are three major difficulties in CEE: the debts inherited from the period of central planning have little relation to real assets or future profitability; weak banks and a concentrated industrial structure mean that most SOEs are 'too big to fail'; but the debtors and creditors are state owned, so the problem can be attacked by operations that are still entirely within the public sector and have no effect on its consolidated balance sheet.

The problem has also been discussed in the literature on economic transformation (e.g. Brainard, 1991; Portes, 1991). But, aside from partial, delayed and in our view inadequate measures to deal with it in Czechoslovakia and Hungary, little has been done. Action is urgent not just in the Central European countries already well along the road of transition, but also at earlier stages in CEE and the former Soviet Union.

The paper is organized as follows. Section 2 documents the credit problem in CEE, discussing its extent and the reasons why creditors fail to collect from their enterprise debtors. Section 3 analyses the costs to which such behaviour gives rise. Section 4 considers the possible policy responses to credit market failures: recapitalizing banks, SOEs, or both; allowing banks to widen profit margins to strengthen their balance sheets; selective controls on bank credit; and privatization. Section 5 proposes a sequencing of reforms designed to be credible and robust to the incentive failures identified. Section 6 considers the implications for macroeconomics and monetary policy.

2 Identifying the problem

2.1 Documenting the CEE credit problem

Enactment of bankruptcy laws has not been sufficient to achieve the implementation of bankruptcy procedures in CEE. Banks seem to have

Table 8.1. *Credit to enterprises and households, CSFR, 1989–91 (Kcs bn)*

End period:	1989	1990				1991			
		I	II	III	IV	I	II	III	IV
Bank credit to:									
SOEs	531	524	532	540	530	558	587	600	611
Private firms				1	3	9	25	41	67
Households	47	45	47	47	50	51	52	53	54
Inter-enterprise	7	11	14	28	54	77	123	147	155

Notes: Bank credit to SOEs excludes a government-funded Kcs 38 bn write-off of enterprise bad debts. Inter-enterprise data combine two data series, one from bank data (until 1991 I, unavailable thereafter), the other from enterprise data (available since end 1990).

Source: Dyba and Svejnar (1992).

Table 8.2. *Money supply, interest rates and prices in the CSFR, 1989–91*

	1989	1990				1991			
		I	II	III	IV	I	II	III	IV
% growth since previous December:									
M0	9	3	6	8	8	−1	3	9	20
M1	1	−7	−3	−5	−6	−4	1	12	23
CPI	1	2	3	14	18	41	49	50	53
PPI	−1	0	0	0	19	45	52	49	51
Nominal interest (%):									
Loans	5	5	5	5	6	15	15	14	14
Deposits	3	3	3	3	3	8	8	9	8

Source: Dyba and Svejnar (1992).

had little difficulty keeping control of credit to households (see Tables 8.1 and 8.3). In marked contrast, enterprises have frequently failed to make scheduled payments both to their banks and to one another.

Data on enterprise debts and bank balance sheets are not easily obtained. Table 8.1 reports balance sheet data for the Czech and Slovak Federal Republic (CSFR), and Table 8.2 provides corresponding background macroeconomic data. Table 8.3 shows similar, though less detailed, data for Hungary.

Tables 8.1–8.3 illustrate some typical features of CEE economies during

Table 8.3. *Domestic credit, interest rates and prices in Hungary, 1989–91*

	1989	1990	1991	1989	1990	1991
				% of total credit		
Domestic credit (Ft bn):						
Working capital loans	321	404	486	21	24	28
Investment credit	132	143	143	9	9	8
General government	726	730	784	48	44	45
Loans to individuals						
& small entrepreneurs	332	374	318	22	23	19
Consumer price inflation (%)	17	29	35			
Discount rate	14	20	29			

Note: 1991 data for January–October.

Source: Market Letter, National Bank of Hungary, November 1991.

the early phase of economic reform. First, bank lending to households, tightly controlled in nominal terms, has fallen sharply in real terms. Second, bank lending to SOEs has increased substantially in nominal terms, and been squeezed less in real terms than might have been expected. Much bank credit has traditionally financed working capital. As market forces and recession took hold, many SOEs found themselves producing not for sale but for unsold inventories: circumstances in which their demand for real bank credit tended to rise. Putting it differently, without sales and cash flow, many SOEs had little option but to suspend payment on existing bank loans. By the end of 1991, there were 2,880 'entities which had lost their creditworthiness' in Poland, up from 548 at end 1990 (National Bank of Poland, *Monthly Review*). Since few SOEs have been forced into liquidation in CEE, in many instances the response of the banks must have been to roll over the loan and capitalize the interest that should have been paid.

2.2 Why banks do not enforce credit

Inadequate credit control may be a legacy from the past, because of surviving relationships between those running banks and those running SOEs, or because state banks still feel social responsibility for SOEs. Such failures of corporate control within banks are appropriately treated in the long run by privatization of banks and development of a market in corporate control.

But such changes are not sufficient. There are many reasons why a well-run private bank might take similar decisions. In Chapter 7 of this volume, Mitchell discusses arguments for 'creditor passivity'. First, banks may not initiate bankruptcy because the expected value of the debtor's assets is less than the costs of enforcing bankruptcy, or because there is an option value in waiting. In the former case, there is no incentive for new lending, whereas the latter may justify rescheduling debt: a sufficiently favourable outcome may work wonders for existing non-performing debt (see also Perotti, 1992).

Second, taking action against creditors may signal the extent of the bank's existing non-performing loans, prompting a run on the bank. In CEE a run is unlikely, because of implicit 100 per cent deposit insurance, but the bank may nevertheless be reluctant to signal its problems to regulatory authorities. Third, there may be free-rider problems when there are multiple creditors: if each bank foresees that a government bail-out will become necessary because other creditors take no action, such an expectation may become self-fulfilling.

Note that these arguments embody an element of hysteresis. Initial portfolios matter. Banks that do not begin in trouble may act very differently from banks that inhabit a landscape in which everyone knows banks are severely undercapitalized, have extensive non-performing loans, and face political pressure to maintain a lifeline to struggling SOEs.

2.3   Inter-enterprise credit

Having focused on banks, we conclude this section by examining the proliferation of inter-enterprise credit. Table 8.1 gives data for the CSFR, where during 1989–91 inter-enterprise credit grew from Kcs 7 bn to Kcs 155 bn, while bank credit to SOEs as a whole increased only from Kcs 531 bn to Kcs 611 bn. Bofinger (1992) paints a similar picture elsewhere in CEE: in Poland the ratio of inter-enterprise credit to bank credit increased from 70 per cent at end-1988 to over 150 per cent in 1990.

At first sight, the data on inter-enterprise credit look dramatic, yet its significance can be overstated. Many statistics refer to *gross* credits before any attempt is made to net out bilateral and multilateral credits among firms.[1] Nor should we forget that in mature Western economies interfirm credit is very substantial in scale. In part, CEE is simply adjusting to the market economy. Table 8.4 compares UK data on interfirm credit and bank loans to industrial and commercial companies (ICCs). In a mature market economy these two categories of credit are of roughly equal size. Viewed in this light, the so-called explosion of inter-enterprise credit in CEE is less remarkable.

When the price of bank credit is high, firms try to economize on this

Table 8.4. *UK bank lending and inter-enterprise credit, industrial and commercial companies, 1980–90 (£ bn)*

	Inter-enterprise credit: domestic ICCs	Bank lending to ICCs
1980	44.1	32.6
1981	44.7	36.0
1982	48.7	41.8
1983	59.0	42.9
1984	66.2	49.8
1985	71.1	55.0
1986	72.6	64.2
1987	79.5	74.1
1988	83.3	97.8
1989	87.5	123.5
1990	91.5	139.8

Source: Bank of England.

expensive commodity. Those enterprises with liquid assets, and perhaps low costs of monitoring other enterprises in their own sector, may even join the banking business by extending credit to their customers rather than pressing for payment on delivery. It is useful to distinguish such credit, which we shall call voluntary, from that which we shall call involuntary. By the latter we mean loans that it is optimal to extend only because of creditor passivity. The arguments of section 2.2 used to explain bank behaviour apply also to inter-enterprise transactions. For example, a supplier will be reluctant to provoke the closure of a major customer.

SOEs did have some bank deposits when embarking on the transition to the market. Initially, these may even have been augmented: countries such as Poland and the CSFR had deep devaluations whose effect was to increase the profitability of SOEs in the traded goods sector. With the collapse of CMEA export markets and domestic recession, however, any such period of enterprise prosperity was short lived.

It is therefore implausible that the explosion of inter-enterprise credit should be attributed primarily to SOEs' cash surplus in search of solvent customers to whom voluntary credit was extended. As with bank credit, we view the stylized facts as being a proliferation of credit involuntarily extended through creditor passivity.

There is a significant relationship between bank credit and interfirm credit. The greater the creditor passivity of banks, the more probable is creditor passivity in interfirm credit. Conversely, when banks press vigorously for bankruptcy of those unable to service bank loans, it is optimal for enterprises to take a tougher line with their customers in order to secure their own cash flow. This causal connection will play an important role when we discuss how to tackle the underlying causes of credit market failures. If the growth of inter-enterprise credit in CEE has been unusually rapid, we regard this primarily as a symptom of underlying credit problems not as a cause. It is a response to tight monetary policy and expensive bank credit, and the symptom of a second problem, inadequate incentives for banks to keep their loans performing.[2]

However, the proliferation of interfirm credit serves to make matters worse when debtors are already financially weak. First, it increases uncertainty about the liquidation value of individual enterprises, thereby increasing the costs of implementing bankruptcy. Second, it increases systemic risk by creating an interlocking network of enterprise commitments. Such outcomes may be not innocent but strategic: enterprises that, individually, are not 'too big to fail' may be able to create networks with that characteristic by making use of inter-enterprise credit, thereby raising the political cost of restructuring. Third, it redistributes liquidity from sound to potentially unsound enterprises, which may impede exit and restructuring.

Having examined microeconomic implications of inter-enterprise credits, we briefly discuss their macroeconomic effect. First, such attempts to economize on expensive bank credit affect the demand for bank deposits and the velocity of money. Designing the target ranges for monetary growth is difficult when money demand is uncertain, but inter-enterprise credit is only one of many factors tending to generate this uncertainty.

Second, inter-enterprise credit should not be confused with money creation. It is banks that create money. Inter-enterprise credit can force banks to create more money, but only through a roundabout route. For example, when firm A reluctantly accepts a delay in payment for delivery of goods to firm B, firm A may be able to use this to persuade its bank to extend a further bank loan. But money is created only if the bank accedes to that request.

We do not believe that it will be easy for policy directly to restrict inter-enterprise credit. It is hard to monitor and enterprises may see a pressing need to extend such credit to their principal customers. Fortunately, policy need not intervene through such a channel. Indeed, it would be a mistake to do so. Instead, policy should address the financial health of banks and enterprises. With that restored, inter-enterprise credit will take care of itself as in Western economies. For that reason, it is on bank credit that we now focus.

Table 8.5. *Real interest rates in Chile, 1975–83 (% per annum)*

	Loan rate	Deposit rate	Margin
1975–77	68	8	60
1978–80	21	9	12
1981–83	30	18	12

Source: Griffith-Jones (1987).

3   Implications of credit market failures

3.1   Costs of creditor passivity of banks

When banks are driven to refinance too much credit to incumbent SOEs, either total bank lending rises or the composition of a given quantity of lending is altered. We defer macroeconomic considerations until section 6. Here we focus on changes in the composition of bank lending. This distortion is costly for several reasons.

Consider first the effect on households. They are crowded out of the bank credit that would let them pursue intertemporal consumption smoothing through domestic borrowing. This may not be the most costly distortion: it is partly offset by the additional wages and employment facilitated by loans to SOEs that would otherwise close. Even so, deadweight losses arise, most visibly where enterprises generate negative social value added (see Hare and Hughes, 1991).

A second deadweight loss arises when banks and their regulators recognize the potential or actual insolvency of banks themselves. It is tempting then to allow banks to raise the spread between loan rates and deposit rates to enable gradual recapitalization of the banks. To date, some countries, such as the CSFR, have kept margins down (Table 8.2). However, as an indication of what may yet emerge, Table 8.5 shows data from Chile at a comparable stage in its liberalization. High real intermediation margins drive a huge wedge between the incentive to save and the cost of investment. One lesson of the LDC literature is that such financial repression is extremely costly. Table 8.6 shows that CEE countries such as Poland are already incurring that cost.

Overextension of credit to SOEs has further costs. It crowds out lending to new private businesses, through two distinct routes. The first is an inadequate quantity of credit, the second is unduly expensive credit. Credit is unduly expensive because the 'tax base' for high interest rates is unnecessarily restricted. If interest rate policy is designed to achieve a

Table 8.6. *Interest rates and bank margins in Poland, 1990–1 (% per annum)*

	1990	1991			
	Dec.	March	June	Sept.	Dec.
Interest rate on:					
Credit from main banks					
(i) lowest risk loans	54–68	72–90	59–72	40–62	40–58
(ii) overdue credits	80–100	115–150	102–140	72–100	70–120
Deposits in main banks					
(iii) sight deposits	18–23	20–30	18–25	9–20	9–20
(iv) 3-month deposits	45–55	60–72	45–60	30–42	30–41
Average margin on					
sight deposits (i–iii)	40	56	45	36	34
3-month deposits (i–iv)	11	15	13	15	13

Source: National Bank of Poland, *Monthly Review.*

desired level of aggregate demand, the soft budget constraint on SOEs means the pain on others – households and the private sector – must be correspondingly increased.

One insight on how much new private firms are being impeded is the survey evidence in Webster (1992). In each of Poland, Hungary and the CSFR, she chose a random sample of 125 private manufacturing firms from registered, limited liability enterprises with at least seven employees. Her results are summarized in Table 8.7.

In Poland, 65 per cent of the firms surveyed had a short-term bank loan; indeed only four firms in her sample had been turned down when applying for credit. However, 28 per cent had not applied for credit because interest rates were too high. Thus, in Poland credit distortions may be more significant for their induced effect on the price of credit than for any direct quantity effect.

In Hungary, a much smaller percentage (about 30 per cent) of the surveyed private firms had bank loans. Hungarians reported many more problems in obtaining bank credit even when the private firm could show considerable business success. Such financial distortions have induced second-best responses. For example, capital goods producers resort much more to leasing rather than sale (Webster, 1992).

The CSFR has very high private sector dealings with the banking system: 80 per cent of respondents had a bank loan, many had several

Table 8.7. *Bank loans to private manufacturing firms (survey of 125 firms in each country)*

	Poland	CSFR	Hungary
% of firms with a bank loan	65	80+	30
Significant % deterred by cost of loan	yes	no	no
Significant % had trouble obtaining loan	no	no	yes

Source: Webster (1992).

loans. Forty per cent of loans to these private enterprises had been made in connection either with successful restitution claims for businesses or for purchase (or multi-year lease) of businesses under the Small Privatization Law.

Thus, although credit control is a problem throughout Eastern Europe, it appears that its extent varies importantly across individual countries. To date, new private business borrowing has perhaps been impeded less in the CSFR than in Poland and especially in Hungary. But such snapshot evidence can be overstressed. At present the private sector in a country such as the CSFR is really very small. If these countries continue to set tight overall monetary targets and if SOE bank debt is allowed to cumulate at close to the interest rate under circumstances where real interest rates are positive,[3] the share of bank lending to SOEs will inevitably *increase* unless something is done. The something could be either an end to positive real interest rates (whose other effects would be undesirable) or measures to change the relationship between banks and enterprises, to which we return shortly.

Credit market failures inhibit the price mechanism not only from providing incentives for new entry, but also from enforcing exit. Some enterprises that survive ought to go. Restructuring is inefficiently slow.

Yet another cost arises from the effect on management incentives within SOEs. Some SOEs that, under threat of closure, might improve sufficiently to survive, can delay such upheavals into the distant future. Since SOEs will form a very large share of the economy of all CEE economies for many years to come, these problems are too important to neglect.

4   Tackling the problem

We now discuss possible policies that might be employed to alleviate credit market failure in CEE. These are: (i) selective credit controls, (ii) widening bank margins, (iii) recapitalizing banks, (iv) recapitalizing enterprises, and (v) privatization. Essentially, the first two policies operate through changes in regulation of conduct; the last three aim to change the structure of markets or of the institutions operating in them. We shall argue that none of the five policies alone is sufficient; nor is it desirable to implement them simultaneously. This analysis will lead in section 5 to a reform proposal designed to introduce the appropriate aspects of policy in an appropriate order.

4.1   Selective credit controls

Selective credit controls seek to place a ceiling on particular categories of bank lending. Poland, we understand, has since 1991 required that one-third of all new bank credit go to the private sector.[4] Such regulation of quantities is in this instance preferable to intervention through prices (taxation of bank lending to SOEs) for two reasons. First, until banks are privatized and an active market in corporate control established, banks may not maximize profits and may not respond to taxation of lending in the desired manner. Second, to the extent banks themselves are insolvent or expected to become so, the prospect of a future bail-out may diminish the sensitivity of current decisions to profit incentives.

Credit controls may be a useful stop-gap. They can be implemented quickly. But precisely because they deal with the symptom not the cause of the problem, they cannot represent an efficient long-run solution.

4.2   Widening bank margins

We believe that making wider margins the primary solution to weak balance sheets of banks is inappropriate. First, if banks initially have very weak balance sheets, it will take a long time to restore their financial health, and in the meantime credit failures will continue. Spreads may widen but SOEs will simply cumulate unpaid debts at even higher interest rates than before. Second, and consequentially, the burden of this strategy will be focused on those debtors who do pay, namely the new private firms and those SOEs beginning to make a success of the market economy. Selecting those two groups for what is effectively penal interest for borrowing is not a promising strategy for restructuring. CEE should learn from the damage that financial repression has caused in many LDCs.

4.3   Recapitalizing banks

Early recapitalization of banks is vital to re-establish credit control.[5] First, it prevents banks' solvency fears from inhibiting their attempts to pursue debtors. Second, it paves the way for the early privatization of banks to place corporate control of banks on a sounder footing. Third, in agreeing that banks' existing loan books should first be 'marked to market' and then made good, the government's commitment to the transition is enhanced: it is forced to acknowledge the extent of the problem with SOEs. Fourth, it opens the way for competition between domestic and foreign banks. This last point bears some emphasis. Expertise in financial services, particularly banking, may be *the* most important commodity the West can supply; cleaning up the domestic banks will be a prelude to transfer of technology and human skills through both joint ventures and direct competition.

Calvo and Frenkel (1991) discuss briefly the choice between *debt cancellation* and *debt socialization*. The former is little more than the reality of marking to market. The latter is a debt-for-debt swap in which the government takes over ownership of non-performing assets, issuing creditors with 'good' assets to replace them. For our present discussion we can think of these as government bonds.

Since most activities in Central and Eastern Europe were in the public sector, it must be possible, with the stroke of a pen, to cancel debts of one public agency to another without affecting the consolidated wealth of the public sector. Contrary to the frequently held view that action on debts may have adverse consequences for the public finances, it is simple arithmetic to demonstrate that its impact effect is zero *provided the public finances were being properly measured.*

In itself, however, this observation does not lead to the conclusion that cancellation is the appropriate course of action. Disaggregation of the public sector matters. Cancelling SOE debts to banks leaves banks insolvent (more accurately, it makes explicit the current reality by marking to market). Recapitalization of banks requires debt socialization. Nor are debts and credits entirely confined within the public sector. Begg (1991) reports that in Czechoslovakia two-thirds of enterprise debt in 1990 was in effect owed to households, whose deposits in the savings bank had then been lent on to the commercial bank making loans to enterprises. In such circumstances, mere bookkeeping is impossible: recapitalizing the banks can be achieved only by a government injection on the asset side or by default on household deposits on the liability side. Since these countries implicitly have 100 per cent deposit insurance, it must be an injection of assets.

Recapitalization must be thought to be a once-and-for-all occurrence, not a government pledge to underwrite banks in perpetuity. Privatization will help here, but it must be accompanied by much closer banking supervision, which generally has been conspicuous by its absence.[6] Once the financial system has been cleaned up, such supervision will be easier to carry out. There is one immediate trap into which the government should not fall, however; namely, doubt about the quality of the assets with which banks have been recapitalized.

CEE countries face a period of fiscal fragility until output and profits stop falling and until more soundly based tax structures can be put in place. With domestic markets for government securities also in their infancy, future pressure to monetize deficits cannot be excluded. Since a sound banking system is necessary for successful transition, it is unwise to threaten the solvency of banks by recapitalizing them with long nominal bonds vulnerable to expropriation through future inflation. Recapitalization with indexed bonds would be the clearest commitment to a sound banking system and would raise the credibility of monetary policy. A future government in fiscal difficulties would then be forced to seek its savings elsewhere.

Wall Street and London are scarcely awash with indexed bonds. Whether because of risk, tax treatment or unfamiliarity, financial markets seem to be averse to such bonds and to prefer nominal securities. Three-month Treasury bills are almost invulnerable to expropriation through inflation unanticipated at their date of issue and have the advantage that injection into bank portfolios would be an important stimulus to the development of a well-functioning domestic market for government paper. Such a market, by breaking the automatic link between fiscal deficits and monetization, would also have important macroeconomic benefits. Thus bank recapitalization using Treasury bills lies at the heart of the reform package we present in the next section.

Recapitalization of banks is not sufficient to solve credit failures. First, the costs of enforcing bankruptcy may still exceed the proceeds that can be realized from an enterprise; policy must also address SOEs. Second, corporate control cannot be taken for granted in state banks. Third, and critically, having recapitalized or bailed out the banks once, the government needs to take what action it can to diminish the prospect that such bail-outs can be expected again in the future. To some extent, privatization of banks can be viewed as an attempt to meet these last two points.

4.4   Recapitalization of SOEs

Unless the insolvency of SOEs is addressed, even solvent banks may find it unprofitable to institute bankruptcy and closure. In this section we discuss what this implies for the recapitalization of enterprises. We approach the issue from two viewpoints: control rights and credibility.

New theories of capital structure (e.g. Dewatripont and Tirole, Chapter 2 in this volume) emphasize that some mixture of debt and equity is generally efficient in a market economy in which monitoring of managers is costly. When profits are high, there is some presumption that managers have done well. High profits easily allow debt repayments and vest control rights with the managers, who are free to get on with the job without external interference. When profits are low, there is some presumption that management is failing. Difficulties in meeting debt repayments act as the trigger for a transfer of control to creditors (banks), who can use the opportunity to restructure the enterprise and change the management team. How might these ideas be applied in Central and Eastern Europe, and have they any implication for any proposal to write off some or all SOE debts as part of a recapitalization?

Viewing the capital structure as a control device, three issues are likely to be of greatest relevance: (i) the correlation of individual enterprise performance with the ability of its management team, (ii) the ability of incumbent managers relative to the managers who feasibly could be brought in to replace them, and (iii) the relative effectiveness of managers and their bank monitors. The more the fate of an enterprise depends on factors outside its managers' control, the less important is capital structure as a device to alleviate moral hazard. The benefits to potential external control also depend on the realistic possibility of being able to find alternative management talent with which to displace failed managers. Finally, the control structure depends critically on the willingness of external monitors to play the role assigned to them.

Thus, whereas the literature on capital structure emphasizes the moral hazard of managers within SOEs, creditor passivity argues that it may not be optimal for banks to discharge their monitoring role effectively. Since the focus of our paper is correcting the latter deficiency, we do not see the literature on capital structure as providing any justification for rejecting per se the recapitalization of SOEs through some form of debt write-off.

Turning to the implications for credibility of policy, where the moral hazard issue is the temptation to repeat such bail-outs in the future, it is important to distinguish two sources of current enterprise debts. First, there is the legacy from state planning, in which debts were partly the counterpart to working capital, much of which is now unsaleable inventories. But debts incurred under the old quantities and prices convey little information about the current prospects of an enterprise; these debts are random endowments, which should not be allowed to get in the way of anything important (Portes, 1990, 1991). If government and banks take a similar view, that may help explain why some SOEs have been allowed to reschedule these debts repeatedly.

Such debts should be distinguished from those that have been accumulated through operating deficits since reform began. In the latter case, it is much harder credibly to convey any write-off as a once-off event.

The relative importance of the two types of debt in practice depends in part on the extent of inflation during the stabilization programme (more accurately, on the behaviour of real interest rates while extreme price adjustment was occurring). Thus, for example, in Poland substantial price increases since 1990 have partly deflated the real value of initial enterprise debts; in the CSFR, where the monetary overhang was small and price stability quickly re-established, the legacy of debts incurred under state planning is more important.

Thus it may be argued that it is already too late to write off enterprise debt: there was no clean break at the beginning of the transition, so any write-offs call into question the legitimacy and authority of monetary policy in the new regime. But bygones are bygones, even if an early clean break might have minimized moral hazard. Without action by the government, the problem will not disappear.

But the danger of moral hazard and the weaknesses of micro policy now argue for some *further delay* in implementing write-offs until credible rules and structures can be established. While there remain significant problems of corporate control in enterprises and banks and until government attitudes to lame ducks are clearer, debt write-offs for enterprises are likely to deal with a symptom not a cause: further debts are likely to emerge rapidly. Easing the burden on enterprises that should be coming under pressure is counterproductive. Hence, in sequencing the steps towards re-establishing credit control, debt relief for enterprises' debt to the banks should *not* be an early step.

Many of these arguments resemble those arising in the treatment of the debt overhang of sovereign borrowers. Historically, the resolution has usually involved substantial write-offs, which have led to renewed access to voluntary lending (Eichengreen and Portes, 1989); recent experience with Brady Plan debt reduction suggests that write-offs should not come until a serious reform programme is in place, but that then the danger of moral hazard is small (van Wijnbergen, 1991).

4.5   Privatization

Although privatization is an essential component of reform, it is no panacea and will not be sufficient for success. Indeed, without accompanying reform, it may not even be feasible. It is harder to privatize firms if their balance sheets are encumbered by inherited debt – indeed, their accounting net worth may be negative, even if they can be expected to make operating profits. Mayer and Carlin (1992) document the slow pace of privatization to date in Central and Eastern Europe.

Early privatization of banks should not be an isolated policy. Not only is privatization facilitated by cleaning up banks' balance sheets – both in restoring solvency and in transparency that reduces risk for potential investors – privatization is also required as a precommitment by government: it reduces the likelihood of continuing bail-outs. Of course, no watertight commitment is possible. Chilean banks, privatized in the 1970s, were extensively bailed out in 1982 after a financial crisis. Even so, the present situation in CEE is so alarming that reform is imperative. Governments must use what limited devices they can to achieve the maximum possible credibility.

4.6   Summing up

In this section we analysed possible policies to deal with the CEE credit market failure. Since we argued that inter-enterprise credit was primarily a symptom of the failure, we focused on proposals to reform the relationship between bank-creditors and SOE-debtors. Reforms of conduct regulation – selective credit controls and wider margins – can be implemented quickly but fail to deal with the root causes of the problem and themselves have large costs in deadweight losses.

Recapitalizing banks and SOEs is useful, as is privatization. But credibility and transparency are needed, so that the prospect of future bail-outs does not impede alteration of current behaviour. An incentive-compatible reform package must pay careful attention to the sequencing of its individual components. We now discuss such a design.

5   Reforming credit relations in Central and Eastern Europe

5.1   Steps to be taken at once: selective credit controls not wider margins

Until more fundamental reform is under way, we advocate the imposition of selective credit controls specifying a minimum share of bank lending to be allocated to private firms. Should this quota not be taken up, banks should be allowed to offer credit at cheaper rates to private firms until the quota is exhausted. Such credit controls must be of only temporary duration, and we shortly explain how their withdrawal should be tied to other aspects of the sequencing of reforms.

This policy meets the immediate need of providing a more efficient incentive for entry (new private firms) and exit (fewer SOEs being sustained by banks). From the outset the controls would apply only to commercial banks in the state sector. This stop-gap legislation would therefore be self-liquidating: it would end when banks were privatized.

New entry will become easier since a larger share of bank credit will be devoted to new private firms. If this is to occur, exit will also be enhanced by the change in composition in bank lending. This forces us to confront the issue of whether or not it will really be possible for existing banks to decline credit to incumbent SOEs. If existing creditor passivity is really a profit-maximizing calculation by banks, and if banks' decision problem has an interior solution, even a small change in the constraints on banks should alter their behaviour; it will now be profitable to close some SOEs previously unprofitable to pursue. In contrast, if banks were at a corner solution, or are simply uninterested in profit maximization, even credit controls may have little effect. In the next section, we discuss a policy that alters more fundamentally the incentives of banks.

A change in bank regulation is the one type of policy that can be introduced overnight, and that is why it begins our discussion of sequencing. In favouring credit controls as the overnight measure, we unequivocally reject the alternative, a substantial widening of spreads within the banking system. The costs of the latter are prohibitive – whereas credit controls foster creation of new private businesses, wider margins further inhibit it – and the strategy of recapitalizing the banks through this route is unlikely to succeed. Given the initial weakness of their balance sheets, it will simply take too long to correct this by distortion of flows. Stock adjustment is required.

5.2   Fiscal subsidies and cash limits

Many problems discussed in this paper stem from a reluctance to force rapid adjustment on the SOEs with least chance of survival. It is appropriate for governments to wish to smooth the transition: they should simply do so more transparently. This means converting a monetary problem into a fiscal issue, though the distinction between fiscal and monetary policy is greatly exaggerated when the fiscal authorities have residual liability for debts accumulated in the monetary system.

We suggest two changes in fiscal policy. When governments wish to keep loss-making SOEs going, they should do so by explicit fiscal subsidy, not by conniving in open-ended rescheduling of credit and capitalization of interest arrears. When banks cannot cope with the pressures of delegated credit monitoring, it is impossible to avoid a resumption of government control. Second, subsidies themselves should avoid any open-ended character. Rather, they should be for an immutable amount, enterprise by enterprise, for those explicitly assigned to a 'lame ducks' category, fixed annually in advance, and fully budgeted in the aggregate fiscal projections which are the subject of conditionality in international loans from the IMF and others.

Such a system of cash limits on state enterprises was operated in the UK in the late 1970s and early 1980s. Its success in controlling the public finances and improving public sector performance paved the way both for UK disinflation and for privatization.

It may be objected that such a system is vulnerable to rent seeking and makes heavy demands on the government and public officials. Both assertions are true. But these activities are already occurring and are part of the cause of the underlying problem. Greater transparency, and the need to consider all subsidy claims simultaneously in framing budget projections, is likely to stiffen resistance compared with a situation in which individual credit deals can be done with banks in circumstances that are much harder to monitor. Putting it differently, if badly performing SOEs required explicit fiscal subsidies for which the government was then called to account, restructuring would be less likely to grind to a halt.

Subsidies must be matched by fiscal retrenchment elsewhere or by additional borrowing, probably from abroad. Since CEE countries are already subject to IMF conditionality, this would have to be approved by these external monitors. Such conditionality offers a realistic prospect that subsidies will not become perpetual. Indeed, by making the transfer from state to SOEs transparent (through fiscal subsidies) rather than obscure (through refinancing of dubious loans from banks) the task of the monitor is made easier. For that reason, there should be no objection to this proposal from international agencies. It cannot be implemented overnight, but it can and should be implemented quickly.

5.3   Recapitalizing banks

With the largest source of unprofitable SOE refinancing thus removed, the most serious remaining obstacles to the development of efficient credit allocation through the banking sector are the solvency of banks and the incentives for those who control banks. The solution is to recapitalize banks and then privatize them.

Recapitalization is required to prevent an inherited stock problem from continuing to distort flow decisions that could otherwise be taken more efficiently. Recapitalization must not get bogged down in disputes about the valuation of non-performing loans; the government should take over all such assets of banks and replace them at par with Treasury bills. Uncertainty about the government's net worth is less damaging than uncertainty about that of banks about to be privatized. Whether or not there is a general case for voucher privatization or other forms of discounted sale, we believe it unlikely and undesirable that major banks should be handled in this way. Joint ventures that bring in foreign management expertise in this key sector may be a better solution. In any case, here we simply note that recapitalizing banks, to the extent it increases their net worth, will be partly recouped by the state revenues when the banks are privatized.

5.4   What to do with the enterprise debts taken over

When the government, perhaps through some holding company, assumes the non-performing loans from the banks, should it now cancel these debts? The advantage of cancellation is that enterprises themselves are cleaned up and therefore more transparent. This simplifies monitoring by banks when new requests for credit are made. The disadvantage of cancellation is that the old structure of corporate control of enterprises still remains in place; there is a real danger this will be seen as a signal that lossmaking can continue. Recapitalization of banks can be clearly linked to privatization. The SOEs with the greatest thirst for credit are precisely those that cannot quickly be privatized. For such firms, privatization cannot serve as the precommitment not to undertake further bail-outs in future. This reinforces the logic of our proposal in section 5.2 that, for such SOEs, visible fiscal subsidies must supplant covert lending as the mechanism of government control.

It is useful to set out a hypothetical example showing how balance sheets are altered at each stage in the reform process (see Table 8.8). Initially, banks' assets are loans to SOEs with a book value of 100, their liabilities are deposits of 95, and their residual net worth of 5 is ultimately owned by the government not banks themselves. It is shown as a liability of 5 for government equity.

SOEs have physical assets whose book value is 150. The spirit of the example, however, is that these assets are really worth much less. To fix ideas, suppose they are really worth only 50. SOEs' liabilities are the 100 owed to banks and the government equity in SOEs, reflecting public ownership. This has a book value of 50.

Finally, at the outset the government's assets are its ownership of banks and SOEs, whose joint book value is 55. This appears to be the net worth of the public sector, but of course it is based only on book values. It has no relation to reality.

In period 2, the banks are recapitalized. The government takes over at par the bank debt to SOEs and replaces it with Treasury bills. Thereafter, banks are privatized (though this is not shown in Table 8.8).

Table 8.8. *Recapitalization of banks and cancellation of SOE debt*

	Banks		SOEs		Government	
Period 1: now						
Assets	loans to SOEs	100	plant & equip	150	equity in SOEs	50
					equity in banks	5
Liabilities	deposits	95	due to banks	100		
	govt equity	5	govt equity	50		
Net worth		0		0		55
Period 2: bank recapitalization						
Assets	T-bills	100	plant & equip	150	equity in SOEs	50
					equity in banks	5
					due from SOEs	100
Liabilities	deposits	95	due to govt	100	T-bills	100
	govt equity	5	govt equity	50		
Net worth		0		0		55
Period 3: marking SOEs to market						
Assets	T-bills	100	plant & equip	50	equity in SOEs	50
					equity in banks	5
Liabilities	deposits	95	govt equity	50	T-bills	100
	govt equity	5				
Net worth		0		0		−45

Note: We are grateful to Thomas Huertas of Citibank for suggesting that we lay out an example in this fashion.

In period 3, the SOE debt held by the government is marked to market. Since we began by postulating that SOE assets were 100 below book value, in this example marking to market happens to imply complete debt cancellation; more generally, it will imply writing down the debt to some degree. Thus government assets (loans + equity) with a book value of 150 have a market value of 50. The book value of the loss shows up in the government accounts. In Table 8.8 this converts government net worth in periods 1 and 2 to a net worth of − 45 in period 3. This is the present value of the future taxes which will be necessary to finance the debt write-offs.

Or is it? When were the losses actually incurred? Before the start of period 1, when the market value of SOE assets fell 100 below their book value. Thus even at the start of period 1, SOEs are in effect bankrupt. In turn this means they cannot repay their bank loans, rendering banks also insolvent. One way or another, the government is eventually going to have to pick up the tab for the missing 100: at market value, the consolidated net worth of the public sector is − 45 even as period 1 begins.

It cannot be emphasized too strongly that it is not the act of marking to market – at whatever stage – that gives rise to an adverse movement in the public finances, with a corresponding need at some date for higher taxes[7] or lower government expenditure; the public sector liability is incurred when the SOEs first lose the money.

We return to the public finances in the next section. We conclude this section by discussing at what stage marking to market should be undertaken. In section 5.3 we explained why it is desirable that debt be removed from banks without any disputes about valuation. The remaining decision is whether the government should write down SOE debts before privatization of SOEs, or whether SOEs should be privatized 'with debts'. When SOEs are sold, the latter course simply invites the bidder to do the marking to market. Where bidders are scarce, as in specialized sectors, the government, like the Treuhand in Germany, may find itself negotiating with only one or two bidders. In such circumstances, bidding tactics may dictate whether or not the government wishes to reveal *ex ante* an aspect of its implicit valuation of the enterprise. When there are many potential bidders, however, cleaning the balance sheet prior to sale should be preferred. Bygones are bygones, and it is for its future operating profits that an enterprise should be valued, not how its debt position may fit for tax purposes in the financial engineering of the bidder.

5.5   Can the public finances really stand it?

> Peck observed that the tremendous debts accumulated under central planning are a special problem making it difficult to value enterprises properly. He noted that cancelling the old debts . . . would create new macro problems because these debts are so large. Enterprise debts in the Soviet Union are about 300 billion roubles whereas financial assets are 100 billion roubles, so that cancelling the debts would eliminate the assets of the state banking system and require in turn the write-down of some of its liabilities, which are the deposits of individual citizens. Implicit deposit insurance means that state bonds could be substituted for the eliminated assets, but this would add to the deficit.
>
> (*Brookings Papers on Economic Activity*, 1991, 2, p. 364)

> [In Chile in 1982] the government nationalised the bad loans by buying them back with long-term bonds carrying a realistic interest rate. However the fiscal position of the government obviously deteriorated.
>
> (Tanzi, 1992)

The two quotations above are representative of a widely held view that write-offs are bad for the public finances. Individuals and companies in mature market economies reckon their solvency by a comparison of assets and liabilities. We should do the same for the public sector, but problems in valuing the asset side of the balance sheet lead most of the public discussion into statements purely about liabilities (e.g. debt/GDP ratios). This clearly has little logical basis except under some heroic 'other things equal' assumption about public sector assets (see e.g. Buiter, 1985; Begg, 1987). This is very misleading when valuable state assets are being privatized, or when SOEs are merrily cumulating losses that are being ignored by state banks. It makes little difference whether a lossmaking SOE is credited with a bank deposit or given a fiscal transfer of the same amount, creating a budget deficit that is then monetized. By making explicit a fiscal problem currently being concealed, we increase the urgency of tax reform, which we take to be desirable.[8]

In fact, the only serious argument against what we propose is a version of the argument Mitchell (Chapter 7 in this volume) applies to individual creditors, but now extended to the government as a whole: namely, that in cleaning things up, the government may reveal the extent of its own insolvency, thereby provoking a crisis of confidence.

It would be helpful to know the size of the fiscal burden involved. In Poland at end-1991, 'credits to the socialized sector' stood at Zl 151 trillion, about 16 per cent of GDP (National Bank of Poland, *Monthly Review*). That is the estimate of the once-and-for-all cost to the public finances. It is not particularly large. And it is definitely an overestimate, since it assumes *all* SOE debts taken over by the government are *completely* worthless, which will surely not be true.

What about the impact effect on the budget deficit? The National Bank was paying 12 per cent interest on demand deposits, and 30 per cent on six-month deposits. Commercial banks were charging at least 38 per cent on bills of exchange and paying 30–40 per cent on three-month deposits. National Bank of Poland ninety-day bills paid 19 per cent. This range of interest rates suggests that 20–30 per cent might be appropriate as the interest rate on government debt issued to finance the recapitalization. On this basis, the maximum that would be added immediately to the budget deficit by debt interest would be 5 per cent of GDP. In practice, 2–3 per cent seems more likely as an impact effect. Persisting inflation, by raising nominal GDP, will reduce even this percentage in subsequent years.

5.6   *A role for the international community?*

In our view, this is where external agencies can play a key role. The prime objective of the change we propose is to facilitate restructuring and obtain the supply-side benefits of much-improved credit allocation.[9] If our argument has been accepted to this point, it should not be allowed to fall because of the prospect of a confidence crisis.

International agencies (IMF/World Bank/EBRD) already play a vital role as external lenders imposing conditionality. These agencies should first indicate their clear support for such a programme; and, second, should endorse some relaxation in declared budget deficit targets, precisely because the asset side of the public sector balance sheet has now been tackled. In our judgement, these measures should be sufficient to avert any significant confidence crisis.

6   Monetary policy after credit reform

The measures we have set out would place credit control on a much sounder footing. Without such a foundation, the costs of monetary austerity are likely to impinge symmetrically but severely. It is particularly unfortunate that, in present circumstances, the sector bearing the heaviest burden is the emerging private sector.

Of equal importance, a world in which budget constraints continue to be flouted calls into question the commitment of the government to reform and its capacity to implement it. These are unhelpful signals. The microeconomic changes for which we call not only place the transition on a safer footing, encouraging rather than impeding the development of appropriate incentives, they also allow a more informed judgement about the stance and wisdom of macroeconomic policy.

Any statement about the sustainability of the public finances is questionable given the enormous uncertainty about the value of public sector assets. In such circumstances, it is unwise to focus too closely on an honest declaration of some recently incurred liabilities. Rather the focus of policy should be to take steps now that enhance to the maximum extent the supply side of the economy, and thereby the value of many state assets. Part of the job of the rest of the world is to encourage the long view when it is constructive.

The steps we propose do not in themselves have the consequence of making the public sector worse off, or of fostering a profligate monetary policy. They cannot, since they merely come clean about what is happening in any case. Therefore their only possible downside is through adverse effects on expectations.

That is why we propose that current debt write-offs should be tied to structural changes (e.g. bank privatizations), and that binding ceilings be put on any fiscal subsidies that the government then wishes to retain for a period. These changes would liberate both monetary and fiscal policy, making it easier not harder then to build reputation.

One consequence will be that financial statistics become more transparent. The macroeconomic significance of this is that judgements about the stance of monetary policy will be more reliably based. In turn this makes it easier for market participants to distinguish an accidental misjudgement of monetary policy and the engineering of a little inflation to help with the public finances. In short, it reduces the cost of monitoring the government, and increases the incentive for governments to invest in a reputation for sound policy. Such a reputation will be especially valuable as the countries of Central and Eastern Europe attempt simultaneously to bring inflation under control and to correct structural weaknesses in fiscal policy, both in tax design and in expenditure control.

NOTES

For helpful discussions we thank, without implication, Sudipto Bhattacharya, Patrick Bolton, Ramon Caminal, Brian Henry, Thomas Huertas, Dwight Jaffee, Colin Mayer, Janet Mitchell, David Newbery, Joan Pearce, Lionel Price, Rafael Repullo, Jacek Rostowski, Xavier Vives, Leila Webster, and Rutger Wissels. This work is part of a CEPR research programme on the Economic Transformation of Eastern Europe, supported by the Ford Foundation and the ACE and SPEC programmes of the Commission of the European Communities.

1 Begg (1991) reports an early attempt by the Commercial Bank of Czechoslovakia to clear inter-enterprise credits and debts in 1991 which reduced estimates of the stock by over 20 per cent. In contrast, a similar attempt in Hungary cleared only 2 per cent.
2 In some countries, banks have participated more directly in the build-up of inter-enterprise credits. OECD (1991) reports that, in the CSFR, until March 1991 banks were required to accept all bills presented for payment against an enterprise that held an account with that bank. If the relevant account had insufficient funds, these bills were put into a queue, to be paid off when funds were available. Since March 1991 banks can refuse to accept bills for payment.
3 Bofinger (1992) emphasizes that the initial price increase following liberalization tends to slash the outstanding real level of enterprise debt to banks. During such a period real interest rates are hugely negative. But this does not persist. For example, Table 8.2 documents the large positive real interest rate in the CSFR during the second half of 1991.
4 Jacek Rostowski drew this to our attention.
5 Some countries have already begun to do so. For example, the CSFR allowed its banks to write off Kcs 38 bn in 1991 in exchange for government bonds. Banks were allowed to write off their 'worst' debts. In addition, a new Consolidation Bank took over Kcs 110 bn of loans by banks to enterprises for 'perpetual credits for inventories' that had no fixed maturity and a low fixed interest rate (6 per cent).
6 Since the start of the Polish reforms, around sixty private banks have been created. Most are now bankrupt, not because of the portfolios they initially

inherited, or because of established links with loss-making enterprises, but because they appear to have been managed with some ineptitude.

7 This 'taxation' could take the form of default on bank deposits or a drastic widening of bank margins. Since we have argued that a sound and reputable banking system is vital, we remain flatly opposed to recapitalization through either of these channels.

8 Tanzi (1992) puts the matter rather well: 'Technically, these loans are fiscal subsidies that, if justified, should be made through and financed by the budget. By being made through the banking system, they do not swell the fiscal deficit and, thus, distort the fiscal accounts giving an inaccurate view of the tightness of the country's fiscal policy.'

9 This should not be confused with the claim in Calvo and Coricelli (1992) that a temporary squeeze on real credit can have substantial supply-side effects by reducing firms' access to working capital.

REFERENCES

Begg, D. (1987) 'UK fiscal policy since 1970', in P.R.G. Layard and R. Dornbusch (eds.), *The Performance of the British Economy*, Oxford: Oxford University Press.

—— (1991) 'Economic reform in Czechoslovakia: should we believe in Santa Klaus', *Economic Policy* **13**.

Bliss, C. and J. Braga de Macedo (eds.) (1990) *Unity with Diversity in the European Economy*, Cambridge: Cambridge University Press.

Bofinger, P. (1992) 'The experience with monetary policy in an environment with strong microeconomic distortions', in *Economic Consequences of the East*, London: Centre for Economic Policy Research.

Brainard, W. (1991) 'Strategies for economic transformation in central and eastern Europe: the role of financial market reform', in H. Blommestein and M. Marrese (eds.), *Transformation of Planned Economies: Property rights reform and macroeconomic stability*, Paris: OECD.

Buiter, W. (1985) 'A guide to public sector debt and deficits', *Economic Policy* **1**.

Calvo, G. and F. Coricelli (1992) 'Stabilizing a previously centrally planned economy: Poland 1990', *Economic Policy* **14**.

Calvo, G. and J. Frenkel (1991) 'Credit markets, credibility and economic transformation', *Journal of Economic Perspectives* **5**(4).

Dyba, K. and J. Svejnar (1992) 'Stabilization and transition in Czechoslovakia', presented at NBER Conference on 'Transition in Eastern Europe', Cambridge, Mass., February.

Eichengreen, B. and R. Portes (1989) 'Dealing with debt: lessons from the 1930s for the 1980s', in I. Husain and I. Diwan (eds.), *Dealing with Debt*, Washington, DC: World Bank.

Griffith-Jones, S. (1987) *Chile to 1991: The End of an Era?* London: Economist Intelligence Unit.

Hare, P. and G. Hughes (1991) 'Competitiveness and industrial restructuring in Czechoslovakia, Hungary and Poland', in R. Portes (ed.), *The Path of Reform in Central and Eastern Europe*, special issue of *European Economy*, Brussels: CEC.

Mayer, C. and W. Carlin (1992) 'Restructuring enterprises in Eastern Europe', *Economic Policy* **15**.

OECD (1991) *Economic Survey, Czech and Slovak Federal Republic*, Paris: OECD.

Perotti, E. (1992) 'Bank lending in transition economies', mimeo, Financial Markets Group, London School of Economics.

Portes, R. (1990) 'Introduction', *Economic Transition in Hungary and Poland*, special edition of *European Economy*, Brussels: CEC.

(1991) 'Introduction', *The Path of Reform in Central and Eastern Europe*, special edition of *European Economy*, Brussels: CEC.

Tanzi, V. (1992) 'Financial markets and public finance in the transformation process', in *Economic Consequences of the East*, London: Centre for Economic Policy Research.

van Wijnbergen, S. (1991) 'Mexico's external debt restructuring 1989–90', *Economic Policy* **12**.

Webster, L. (1992) 'Private manufacturing in Eastern Europe', mimeo, World Bank.

World Bank (1989) *World Development Report*, Washington, DC: World Bank.

Yarrow, G. (1986) 'Privatisation in theory and practice', *Economic Policy* **2**.

Discussion

RAFAEL REPULLO

The purpose of the paper by Begg and Portes is to discuss the problem of enterprise debt in the context of the transformation of the economies of Central and Eastern Europe, and to propose a sequencing of reforms designed to tackle it.

In these comments I will first consider the stylized facts documented in the paper, then I will propose a simple model of banking that captures some of the costs of increased bank lending to state-owned enterprises, to conclude with some comments on the policy proposals set out in the paper.

1   The facts

The paper starts with a section in which the problem is identified. I have two comments on this section. First, I do not find the evidence on the magnitude of the problem entirely convincing. In particular, Tables 8.1

and 8.3 do not show a very significant pattern of increased bank credit to state-owned enterprises in Central and Eastern Europe. Second, I think that the discussion of the causes and consequences of the explosion of inter-enterprise credit is much weaker than what would be required to support the line of argument in the paper. In this respect, I would have liked to see a serious effort to model the relationship between bank and interfirm credit. At any rate, I basically agree with the conclusion that 'policy should address the financial health of banks and enterprises [and that] with that restored, inter-enterprise credit will take care of itself'.

2   The costs

The next section of the paper discusses the costs of the increase in bank credit to state-owned enterprises. Leaving aside its effects on households, two main costs are singled out, namely an increase in the spread between loan and deposit interest rates and a reduction in the amount of lending to new private businesses (and/or an increase in its price). Both effects could be easily derived from a simple model of banking along the following lines.

Consider a partial equilibrium model with four types of economic agent, called households, state-owned enterprises, private firms, and banks, which are described as follows:

(a)   Households have a deposit demand function $D(i_D)$, which is assumed to be increasing in the deposit rate i_D.

(b)   State-owned enterprises have an outstanding level of bank loans, LS, which is simply rolled over, capitalizing interest arrears.

(c)   Private firms have a loan demand function $LP(i_L)$, which is decreasing in the loan rate i_L.

(d)   Banks are modelled as (local) monopolies setting the deposit rate i_D and the loan rate i_L but taking the central bank discount rate i_W as given. Thus, without loss of generality, we can think of a representative monopoly bank.

The balance sheet of this bank is given by

$$LS + LP = D + W, \tag{1}$$

where W denotes the amount of discount window borrowing from the central bank. Given the discount rate i_W, the bank is assumed to choose the deposit rate i_D and the loan rate i_L in order to maximize its profits, which are given by

$$i_L LP(i_L) - i_D D(i_D) - i_W W.$$

Substituting W from the balance sheet identity (1) into this expression yields the following objective function:

$$(i_L - i_W)\, LP(i_L) + (i_W - i_D)\, D(i_D) - i_W\, LS.$$

Thus, the profits of the bank are the sum of three terms. The first is the net revenue from the bank's private loans, which is equal to the difference between the loan and the discount rate multiplied by the total volume of private loans. The second is the net revenue from the bank's deposits, which is equal to the difference between the discount and the deposit rate multiplied by the total volume of deposits. The last term, with a negative sign, subtracts the costs of financing the lending to state-owned enterprises from the other two terms.

As is well known in these kinds of models, the exogeneity of the discount rate brings independence between the bank's deposit and loan rate decisions. In particular, assuming that the elasticity of the demand for deposits ϵ_D and the elasticity of the demand for loans ϵ_L are both constant (with $\epsilon_L > 1$), one can easily show that

$$i_L = \left[\frac{\epsilon_L}{\epsilon_L - 1}\right] i_W, \tag{2}$$

and

$$i_D = \left[\frac{\epsilon_D}{\epsilon_D + 1}\right] i_W, \tag{3}$$

so that equilibrium loan and deposit rates are determined by (constant) mark-ups applied to i_W.

In order to close the model, we can assume that the central bank fixes the discount rate i_W in order to keep the amount of discount window borrowing constant, which from the balance sheet identity (1) gives the equilibrium equation:

$$LS + LP(i_L) - D(i_D) = \bar{W}. \tag{4}$$

Equations (2)–(4) constitute a system of three equations which can be solved for the equilibrium values of the deposit rate i_D, the loan rate i_L, and the discount rate i_W.

We can now use this model to analyse the effects on the equilibrium interest rates of an exogenous increase in the lending to state-owned enterprises, LS. In particular, one gets the following results:

$$\frac{di_L}{dLS} > 0 \quad \text{and} \quad \frac{d(i_L - i_D)}{dLS} > 0,$$

as claimed by Begg and Portes in section 3 of their paper (although here the second effect works through a different channel).

3   *The proposals*

Turning next to the policies discussed in the paper to tackle the problem of state-owned enterprises' debt, the authors single out two bank regulation proposals, namely selective credit controls (specifying a minimum share of bank lending to be allocated to private firms) and widening bank margins. I believe that the argument in favour of the former overlooks the considerable administrative costs involved in setting up and monitoring such a system, as well as the distortions in the allocation of financial resources that it may generate. In addition, I have two queries about the proposal. First, I think that, in the cases where the prescribed quota is not taken up, banks should be allowed to buy government debt until the quota is exhausted (rather than 'offer credit at cheaper rates to private firms'). Second, I do not see the rationale for applying the controls only to commercial banks in the state sector, and not to all banks.

The proposal for widening bank margins is, on the other hand, not well specified, since there is no discussion of how margins are to be widened. In particular, I see no reason for ruling out deposit interest rate ceilings as a way of increasing banks' profits. (Incidentally, note that in the monopoly bank model described above deposit rate ceilings would not help, but this would not be the case in models with monopolistic or perfect competition.)

I have little to say about the remaining three policy proposals. Concerning the recapitalization of banks, I am against using indexed bonds for two reasons. First, I think that in setting up efficient domestic markets for public debt one should avoid complex debt instruments (like indexed bonds) and favour simple ones (like Treasury bills). Second, any policy of financial indexation runs the risk of inducing wage indexation through demonstration effects, which would not be desirable.

As for the proposals for the state-owned enterprises whose bank debt is transferred to some holding company, I have two worries, one micro and one macro. The first is that the transfer implies decoupling the banks from the restructuring of these enterprises, which might have negative consequences for the restructuring process. The second worry is that I have the impression that the authors are not sufficiently aware of the risks for public finances involved in their debt write-off proposals. While it is clear that write-offs per se do not add to the budget deficit, they may allow unprofitable enterprises to obtain new fresh lending, which would not only reduce the pressure for restructuring but also (eventually) add to the deficit.

To conclude, I think that this is an interesting paper on a topic of critical importance for the transformation of the economies of Central and Eastern Europe. The proposed sequencing of reforms appears to be reasonable, although I am a bit concerned about the possible fiscal implications of some of the proposals. In particular, I feel that too much emphasis on (very exciting) structural changes and too little on (rather boring) macroeconomic balances is not the recipe for a successful transition to a market economy.

RAMON CAMINAL

The starting point of the paper is the following empirical observation: in some Eastern European countries, state-owned enterprises (SOEs) fail to repay their loans to commercial banks (or to other enterprises); banks more or less automatically extend credit to include unpaid principal plus interest; and, apparently, the central bank implicitly accommodates this credit expansion. This observation raises four broad questions:

(1) Why are banks willing to extend credit automatically to insolvent or illiquid borrowers?
(2) What are the effects of such a situation on allocative efficiency?
(3) What are the implications for macroeconomic policy?
(4) What should and can be done about it?

On the first question the authors borrow heavily from Mitchell's paper in this volume. However, one particular explanation of banks' behaviour does not look very plausible. It is argued that banks may not take any action against debtors because this might signal to the market (or to the government) that the bank is in trouble and this new information might induce a bank run, or alternatively a regulatory agency might step in.

Presumably, the model behind such a claim looks as follows. Each bank is better informed than depositors or regulatory agencies (and perhaps than other banks as well) about the realization of its assets (which include the amount of unpaid loans). After observing such a realization, individual banks must choose whether or not to take action against insolvent or illiquid borrowers (initiate bankruptcy procedures or not). These actions are publicly observable. Depositors and/or regulatory agencies must then choose whether to withdraw their funds and/or take action against banks.

The outcome of the game has the characteristics of a pooling equilibrium in which banks, independently of their observation, never initiate bankruptcy proceedings (in particular, they extend credit to hide a low realization of the return on their assets). Depositors and/or regulatory agencies choose to withdraw their money and/or take legal action against the bank only if the bank has initiated legal action against a significant subset of borrowers. And, finally, a crucial ingredient of such an equilibrium is that the *ex ante* beliefs held by depositors and/or regulatory agencies include a low probability of a bad realization of the return on the banks' assets, otherwise it would not be optimal for them to stay put. This last ingredient seems particularly implausible, and clearly in contradiction with the general picture being drawn in the paper. The debt problem seems so general that it is difficult to believe that banks can hide it by passively extending credit to bad borrowers.

The answers given to the second question seem quite appropriate and I do not have any relevant comments.

With respect to the third question, the discussion in the paper is somewhat disappointing. It is clear that in such a context setting aggregate monetary targets may not be of much significance if the central bank is supposed to accommodate any credit extension to SOEs. Moreover, a tight monetary policy is likely to have very negative welfare effects, since it worsens the crowding-out effect on households and private businesses. Given this situation, the central bank should conduct a more expansive monetary policy. This sounds reasonable, but the question is what is actually happening in these countries? Given the trade-off between the macroeconomic benefits of a tight policy (namely price stability) and the microeconomic costs (huge distortions in the allocation of credit), have these governments chosen the right policies or they have overlooked the micro problem? Although this question is raised in the introduction, it is not discussed at all. The paper also advocates selective credit controls to reduce the microeconomic effects of a tight macro policy. This policy is usually very costly to implement and, moreover, it requires a complex system of bank supervision, which does not seem to be feasible in the short run.

The paper becomes much more interesting when it discusses how governments should approach the problem and how this interacts with the general process of economic reform. One important recommendation is the achievement of greater transparency by replacing implicit 'monetary' subsidies (through automatic credit extension) by explicit 'fiscal' subsidies. This should significantly reduce monitoring costs and improve overall efficiency.

Another important issue is the potential credibility problem associated with debt cancellation. It is argued that at some point the government will have to face the decision to cancel the debt of at least a subset of SOEs. The reason is that the debt inherited from the previous regime is an irrelevant signal of the viability of the enterprise in a market system. The debt was not, however, cancelled at the beginning of the economic reform, and the authors are concerned about the possibility that any decision taken afterwards may give rise to a credibility problem. That is to say, the optimal policy may be subject to a time consistency problem. If the debt is cancelled at an arbitrary date, SOEs' managers may believe that, since it has been optimal to do so, it will be optimal to do it again at some future date. Thus, managers may still act under the belief that the budget constraint remains soft.

In order to overcome the credibility problem, it is suggested that debt cancellation should be linked to some structural change, like privatization. The rule would be like this: the debt accumulated up to period t of enterprises privatized at period $t + s$, able to meet all their obligations from t to $t + s$, will be cancelled in period $t + s$. If the rule is believed, it creates the right incentives for managers. The problem is that it is not clear why such a rule is more credible than any other arbitrary rule. Managers can still act under the belief that, given the time inconsistency problem, the government will find it optimal to cancel all previous debt even when the enterprise has performed badly between t and $t + s$. The role of international institutions as a commitment device is mentioned but not spelled out in detail.

9 Bank regulation, reputation and rents: theory and policy implications

ARNOUD W.A. BOOT and
STUART I. GREENBAUM

1 Introduction

US bank regulation, and more particularly the government deposit insurance system, is widely believed to be obsolete and substantially to blame for hundreds of billions of dollars of taxpayers' losses stemming from the recently deteriorating performance of the US banking system. With the Federal Deposit Insurance Corporation's Bank Insurance Fund nearing exhaustion, a sense of urgency has gripped Washington and the banking community, prompting a variety of proposals for banking reform. In this paper, we derive implications for bank regulation from a reputational model of financial intermediation. En route, we examine the various reform proposals that are part of the debate on US banking reform. Our ideas, however, transcend the specifics of US banking and therefore allow us to discuss contemporary developments in European banking.

Most analyses of banking regulation focus on deposit insurance that permits banks to finance risky assets with governmentally insured liabilities. The moral hazards created by a fixed-rate, risk-insensitive deposit insurance system are widely acknowledged; any increase in the underlying asset risk benefits the banks' shareholders to the detriment of the deposit insurer (see Merton, 1977). Recently, John, John and Senbet (1991) have argued that these moral hazards are induced simply by the presence of risky debt, and represent just another example of the conflict of interest between debt and equity holders. This suggests that the benefits to shareholders of increasing asset risk may have little to do with deposit insurance per se. However, as we will see, this conclusion is unwarranted.

The extant literature has for the most part overlooked the effect of regulation on the reputation-building incentives of financial institutions. We will demonstrate how, in the context of a *dynamic* model of financial intermediation, reputational considerations have become increasingly important with the erosion of monopoly rents previously available in a less competitive setting. Reputation allows banks to lower their market-determined funding costs. We show that banks may have an incentive to avoid risk by expending greater effort on monitoring in order to create these funding-related reputational benefits. This benefit is, however, available only to banks that are uninsured. Several results follow. First, funding-related reputational benefits and (monopolistic) rents are substitutes in that both encourage banks to monitor. Second, by fixing the banks' future funding costs, deposit insurance destroys the funding-related benefits of reputation. We argue that, in a less competitive environment, risk-insensitive deposit insurance might be viable since monopolistic rents alone may encourage optimal monitoring. This would explain why fixed-rate deposit insurance might have worked tolerably well in the past.

Another finding is that funding-related reputational benefits are strictly increasing in the observable risk of the banks' assets, and negligible for safe assets. This supports the various narrow bank proposals for banking reform. A distinguishing feature of the narrow bank proposals is that they restrict the use of insured deposits, but allow greater freedom in the banks' usage of uninsured deposits. This dichotomy is also suggested by our results. Limited insured deposits to the funding of safe assets ensures that the sacrifice of funding-related reputational benefits is minimized. For most other activities of the banks, prudent behaviour is motivated by the use of uninsured deposits that preserve funding-related reputational benefits. This approach to reform contrasts with that proposed by the US government (US Treasury, 1991).

The remainder of the paper is organized as follows. Section 2 presents our theoretical results. Section 3 discusses changes in the competitive environment of US banking and examines implications for the effectiveness of proposed reforms. The paper concludes with a discussion of the lessons of the US experience for European banking.

2   The formal analysis

2.1   Moral hazard in banking

We consider a model of financial intermediation in which banks invest in assets with partially observable credit risk characteristics. A bank's assets consist of loans extended to entrepreneurs to fund projects.[1] By construction, banks have inherently different monitoring abilities, and they also choose the intensity of their monitoring effort. Monitoring ability as well as actual monitoring are unobservable to all save the bank itself. The monitoring of the bank influences the borrower's choice of project and therefore the bank's risk. For simplicity, we assume that the bank lends to a single entrepreneur and that the entrepreneur's choice of project affects the project's risk, but not the expected return. Thus, all projects offer the same (positive) expected net present value but differ in mean-preserving spread of returns. The project choice is unobservable to the lender, but, given (partial) debt financing, the entrepreneur will optimally maximize risk in the absence of monitoring.[2] Moreover, at any loan interest rate, the bank's expected payoff is strictly *decreasing* in the risk choice of the entrepreneur.[3] The bank's cost of monitoring depends on its monitoring *ability*. A bank with greater ability has lower costs for any chosen level of monitoring effort. Monitoring ability varies across banks and, like monitoring effort, is unobservable to all save the bank. A bank monitors with intensity $m \in (\underline{m}, \bar{m})$, and the risk of an entrepreneur's project is strictly decreasing in m. Let τ^* be the entrepreneur's choice of risk, then $\partial \tau^* / \partial m < 0$. Note that, absent considerations of costs, monitoring always improves a bank's expected (gross) returns from lending, in the sense of first-order stochastic dominance. Given the positive costs of monitoring, a bank will choose the first-best monitoring effort only if fully self-financed.

In several recent papers, the banks' moral hazard problem is described as one where the banks' returns are subject to a mean-preserving spread (see Chan, Campbell and Marino, 1991, and Merton, 1977). This characterization is isomorphic to the incentive conflict of our entrepreneurs in that banks are assumed to choose the mean-preserving spread of their assets directly. Given partial debt financing, banks will then optimally maximize risk. As in our formulation, the moral hazard problem requires that the banks' behaviour is only privately observed.[4] Mean-preserving moral hazard, however, is problematic. Bank assets are principally debt and a mean-preserving spread is possible therefore only if banks quote higher interest rates for riskier loans.[5] Since the agency problem is generally rooted in the unobservability of risk choices, however, loan interest rates should then be unobservable. Otherwise they could be used to infer the banks' risk-choices.[6] If loan interest rates are observable and reflect asset risk, binding contracts could be written on the loan interest rates, and the banks' risk-seeking incentives could thereby by mitigated. For example, interest loan rates could be used *ex post* to determine the correct risk premium for the banks' debt or the deposit insurance premium.[7]

Hence, the banks' debt-type assets distinguish their asset-substitution problem from that of firms that hold physical assets or equity claims. The bank–depositor conflict therefore seems more likely to be expressed in terms of the unobservable choice of effort of the bank that influences the riskiness of a borrower's project.

2.2   The model

At the beginning of each of two periods a bank chooses a one-period loan asset. The loan amount is $1. Let $x(\theta)$ denote the payoff to the bank; the payoff is either $\bar{x}(\theta) > 0$, or 0. In the state $x = \bar{x}(\theta)$ the project succeeds and the entrepreneur fulfils the terms of the loan contract; in the state $x = 0$ the entrepreneur defaults totally. The parameter θ is an index of *observable* risk characteristics, with $\theta \in (\underline{\theta}, 1)$, where higher values of θ imply less risk. Since a safer loan pays a lower interest rate, we have $\partial \bar{x}(\theta) / \partial \theta < 0$. We let $m \in (\underline{m}, \bar{m}) \subset (0, 1)$ be the bank's choice of monitoring. The probability distribution of the bank's return in each period is as follows:

$$x = \begin{cases} \bar{x}(\theta) & \text{with probability } \theta + m[1 - \theta] \\ 0 & \text{with probability } [1 - m][1 - \theta] \end{cases} \tag{1}$$

The representation in (1) has the following properties (see Appendix):

(i)   monitoring improves the bank's return in a first-order stochastic dominance sense, and

(ii) the marginal benefit of monitoring decreases in θ (monitoring is less beneficial for safer projects).

The bank's moral hazard is rooted in its choice of m. We examine this problem in the context of a model where the bank's reputational concerns could ameliorate the moral hazard problem. For tractability, we employ a two-period model wherein a bank is privately informed about its monitoring costs. This construction follows Boot, Greenbaum and Thakor (1992), Chemmanur and Fulghieri (1991) and Milgrom and Roberts (1982), and incorporates an incentive for reputation acquisition in a finite-period model.

A bank is one of two types. A type Z has zero monitoring costs, while a type C faces a strictly positive and convex monitoring cost schedule, $V(m)$. By assumption, $V(m)$ is twice continuously differentiable in m over the interval $(\underline{m}, \bar{m})$. The bank knows its own type; others have only a prior belief π at date 0, where $\pi \in (0, 1)$ is the probability that the bank is of type Z.

The type C bank is to all appearances identical to a type Z bank at date 0. Owing to cost considerations, a type Z bank will always choose $m = \bar{m}$. Type C's choice of monitoring will depend on $V(m)$, the effect of monitoring on the bank's expected return, and also on the *future* benefits of monitoring. These more remote benefits have two aspects. First, monitoring reduces the probability of loan default and thus enhances the present value of future rents. Note that, if $x = 0$, the bank is terminated and future rents are lost. Second, a positive first-period return provides reputational benefits in the form of lower second-period funding costs. The funding advantage is linked to the market's date-1 posterior belief about the bank's type. Since a type Z bank enjoys a higher probability of realizing $x = \bar{x}(0)$, any bank realizing that state will be favoured. Therefore, in the second period we have two types of banks: *de novo* banks with reputation π, and surviving banks with a better reputation.[8]

2.3   *Capital regulation and moral hazard*

The question we pose in this section is whether capital regulation can mitigate the bank's moral hazard. We will show that, in this respect, capital regulation may be counterproductive. While this result is not derived in full generality, it is argued that this result is supported by a large body of theoretical research. Moreover, our intention in this paper is *not* to analyse capital regulation in detail, but rather to emphasize that a market-rooted reputation-preserving design of the regulatory environment of banks is desirable.

Consider first a single-period version of our model. The bank has $1 in assets. Let $a be the equity contribution of the owner/manager. Capital regulation then determines how much of the remaining $[1 - a]$ is contributed by outside equity holders or depositors.[9] The monitoring cost, $V(m)$, can be thought of as the monetary equivalent of the monitoring effort devoted by the bank's owner/manager. This interpretation seems natural for a small institution, but less so for larger banks. Alternatively, we can view $V(m)$ as monitoring costs paid by existing shareholders. With these preliminaries, we have the following (see Appendix).

Lemma 1: A capital requirement reduces the monitoring effort and hence the asset quality of the bank.

The intuition is that capital regulation dilutes ownership and therefore reduces monitoring incentives. Although Lemma 1 depends on the standard agency theory assumption of disproportionate sharing of monitoring costs between new and existing shareholders (see Jensen and Meckling, 1976), it is readily generalized.[10]

Lemma 1 casts doubt on the effectiveness of capital regulation for containing moral hazard in banking. Others who have modelled moral hazard in banking also find no beneficial incentive effect of capital requirements on asset quality. For example, in a mean-variance framework with utility-maximizing banks, both Kahane (1977) and Koehn and Santomero (1980) show that capital requirements increase asset risk.[11] Others who have focused on banks that maximize the value of equity find that banks seek to maximize (mean-preserving) risk to exploit deposit insurance (see Kareken and Wallace, 1978). In that environment, however, the benefit of increasing risk decreases with the capital requirement (see Furlong and Keeley, 1989). Nevertheless, maximizing risk remains optimal unless the capital requirement is 100 per cent.[12, 13]

Like any corporation, a bank may have an incentive to choose an interior capital structure. Maximizing leverage may be suboptimal because of the losses of informational and deposit rents associated with insolvency. Also off-balance sheet activities involving unfunded *contingent* obligations may impose *dissipative* costs on a bank's clientele in the event of bank default (e.g. it may disrupt trade that depends on *credible* letters of credit). Hence, banks may not be competitive in these activities unless adequately capitalized.[14] Thus, maximizing leverage is unlikely to be privately optimal for a bank. Why then might capital regulation be needed? The traditional answer is that banks and the payment system serve a special role in the economy and bank defaults produce negative externalities. The government might then wish to compel banks to hold capital beyond their privately optimal choices.[15] Another possible reason for capital requirements is the risk of bank runs deriving from the *liquidity role* of banks (see Diamond and Dybvig, 1983). Since the bank-run argument is based on costs associated with the liquidation of the bank's assets, higher capital requirements may convince the public that the value of assets net of liquidation costs will not fall below the value of deposits.

Our analysis focuses on moral hazard in the bank's choice of monitoring. We have emphasized that capital regulation might have little beneficial effect on moral hazard, or may even aggravate it. In the next sections, we will show that reputational considerations, and in particular the benefits associated with an enhanced reputation, may mitigate moral hazard.

2.4   The main results

2.4.1 The bank's choice of monitoring in the absence of deposit insurance
The next step is to analyse the bank's choice of monitoring in a two-period model. We ignore capital requirements, and let the $1 asset be funded by deposits.[16] We first consider the case where deposits are uninsured. Thus, the cost of deposits will reflect the market's perception of the bank's type, thereby subsuming the anticipated choice of monitoring. We assume that the supply of deposits is perfectly elastic; thus depositors require an expected return equal to the risk-free interest rate, r. Let $\bar{r}$ be the nominal return that guarantees an expected return r. The

second-period choice of monitoring of a type Z bank is $\bar{m}$, but a type C bank chooses m_2 to solve,

$$\underset{m_2}{\text{Max}} \ \{0 + m_2[1 - 0]\}[\bar{x}(0) - \bar{r}] - V(m_2). \tag{2}$$

The incentive for a type C bank to exploit moral hazard and reduce monitoring is most compelling in the final period, since in that period monitoring does not provide reputational benefits, nor are any future rents at stake. Therefore, we may assume, without loss of generality, that (2) is maximized for $m_2^* = \underline{m}$.[17] With these preliminaries, we can derive the second-period funding cost of a bank with reputation ϕ, where ϕ is the probability that the bank is perceived to be of type Z at the outset of the second period. The correct second-period funding cost for a type Z bank is $r_Z = r\{0 + \bar{m}[1 - 0]\}^{-1}$, and for a type C bank it is $r_C = r\{0 + \underline{m}[1 - 0]\}^{-1}$, Thus, for a bank with reputation ϕ, the second-period funding cost is

$$\begin{aligned} r_\phi &= \phi r_Z + [1 - \phi]r_C \\ &= \phi r\{0 + \bar{m}[1 - 0]\}^{-1} + [1 - \phi]r\{0 + \underline{m}[1 - 0]\}^{-1}. \end{aligned} \tag{3}$$

Given the bank's choice of first-period monitoring, $\bar{m}$ for a type Z and $m_1 \in (\underline{m}, \bar{m})$ for a type C, we can derive the following expression for the date-1 reputation.[18] We focus on the state realization $x = \bar{x}(0)$.[19] Then,

$$\phi_1 = \frac{\pi\{0 + \bar{m}[1 - 0]\}}{\pi\{0 + \bar{m}[1 - 0]\} + [1 - \pi]\{0 + m_1[1 - 0]\}}. \tag{4}$$

Define $R(\phi_1) \equiv r_\pi - r_{\phi_1}$, where $R(\phi_1)$ measures the reduction in second-period funding costs due to a gain in reputation of $[\phi_1 - \pi]$. A type C bank faces the following maximization problem at date 0:

$$\begin{aligned} \underset{m_1}{\text{Max}} \ H &= \{0 + m_1[1 - 0]\}\{\bar{x}(0) - r_\pi \\ &\quad + \{0 + \underline{m}[1 - 0]\}\{\bar{x}(0) - r_\pi + R(\phi_1)\} - V(\underline{m})\} - V(m_1). \end{aligned} \tag{5}$$

The first-order condition of (5) is

$$\begin{aligned} [1 - 0]\{\bar{x}(0) - r_\pi\} &+ [1 - 0]\{\{0 + \underline{m}[1 - 0]\}\{\bar{x}(0) - r_\pi\} - V(\underline{m})\} \\ &+ [1 - 0]\{0 + \underline{m}[1 - 0]\} R(\phi_1) = V'(m_1^*). \end{aligned} \tag{6}$$

This shows that the first-period choice of monitoring depends on the effect of monitoring on current returns as well as on the expected rents, $\{0 + \underline{m}[1 - 0]\}\{\bar{x}(0) - r_\pi\} - V(\underline{m})$, and on the expected reputational benefits $\{0 + \underline{m}[1 - 0]\} R(\phi_1)$ in the second period.[20] The last term represents the funding cost advantage of a surviving institution. We can now derive the following result.

Proposition 1: The bank's choice of first-period monitoring is strictly increasing in the expected second-period rents and funding-cost related reputational benefits.

From Proposition 1, rents and reputational benefits are *substitutes* in that both reduce the moral hazard associated with the bank's choice of monitoring.

2.4.2 Deposit insurance and the bank's choice of monitoring

In many countries, bank depositors are governmentally insured. Generally, the insurance is limited to deposits below a pre-specified amount. However, regulators often have responded to bank crises by protecting virtually all depositors. Although the design of deposit insurance differs across countries, nearly all Western countries have some variant. In some, it is an industry arrangement with a narrowly restricted governmental role, as in Germany for example, while in others the insurance system is more substantially governmental, as in the US. The insurance premia, where levied, tend to be independent of the riskiness of the insured institution.

Risk-insensitive deposit insurance premia encourage risk taking (see Ronn and Verma, 1986, and Merton, 1977). In our setting, they discourage monitoring. John, John and Senbet (1991) correctly note that the moral hazard incentives that previous authors have attributed to deposit insurance are induced by the presence of debt. Deposit financing creates a convexity in the levered equity payoff and the standard agency conflict between debt and equity holders leads to distortions that have little to do with deposit insurance or its pricing. All these authors have, however, focused on single-period models. This is important because the arguments of John *et al.* are valid only in a *static* setting. In a dynamic setting, we will show how deposit insurance affects the bank's moral hazard independently of the distortion associated with debt financing.

Fixed-rate (risk-insensitive) deposit insurance in effect freezes the bank's funding costs. With complete (and credible) deposit insurance, the bank obtains deposits at the risk-free interest rate. Its total cost of funds is the sum of the insurance premium and the risk-free interest rate. Thus, the bank's total cost of funds is independent of the reputation of the bank. In our model, the expected reputational benefit, $\{\theta + \underline{m}[1 - \theta]\}R(\phi_1)$, in the bank's second-period funding cost (see equation (6)) disappears. Assuming that the deposit insurance premium is set so that the deposit insurer breaks even across all banks and that we hold the number of banks fixed across time periods, we have the following:

Proposition 2: The bank's choice of first-period monitoring is strictly lower with a system of fixed-rate deposit insurance than in the absence of deposit insurance.

Hence, fixed-rate deposit insurance aggravates the bank's moral hazard problem. Since the bank knows that with deposit insurance it cannot lower its future funding costs, there is no reputational benefit to monitoring and it is therefore discouraged. If we assume additionally that fixed-rate insurance is provided below cost, the discouragement of bank monitoring may be offset by the additional expected rents earned by the bank.[21] Only upon default would these rents be lost, and monitoring reduces the probability of default. Subsidies are formally identical to the rents mentioned in Proposition 1, and, as stated there, improve the bank's choice of monitoring. Deposit subsidies have been imbedded in deposit insurance, historically, but these subsidies are an independent instrument whose impact should be analysed separately from that of deposit insurance.

2.4.3 Deposit insurance and the competitiveness of the financial system

It does not follow from the observation that fixed-rate deposit insurance aggravates the bank's moral hazard problem that such deposit insurance is not incentive compatible. For example, sufficient rents in the banking system may entice banks to monitor optimally (see Proposition 1). Such rents substitute for the reputational benefits that a fixed-rate deposit insurance system subverts. A more intrusive monitoring role of the government may further constrain moral hazard.

The question of incentive compatibility is important because the banking systems in most Western countries have displayed remarkable stability for decades, despite fixed-rate deposit insurance. We will argue that the stability was rooted in the legal and regulatory restrictions on competition in the US and in intra-industry cartel agreements in Western Europe. Monopoly rents therefore induced low-risk strategies, and the attendant suppression of funding-related reputational benefits – an artefact of deposit insurance – proved inconsequential. Recent increases in competition, particularly in the USA, have dissipated banking rents (see Keeley, 1990) and thereby reduced the banks' incentives to monitor. Asset quality has therefore deteriorated (see Chan, Greenbaum and Thakor, 1986).

2.4.4 Observable risk, reputation and bank monitoring

We have thus far ignored θ, the measure of *observable* risk characteristics, either the risk of a specific asset category, or the average risk of bank assets. Proposition 3 states the main result of this section.

Proposition 3: The funding-related expected reputational benefits of a surviving institution, $\{\theta + \underline{m}[1 - \theta]\}R(\phi_1)$, are *strictly increasing* in observable risk (decreasing in θ).

The reputational benefits attainable in the absence of deposit insurance are greater for riskier assets.[22] Thus, the reputational value of monitoring, destroyed by a system of fixed-rate deposit insurance, is strictly greater for riskier assets.[23] Given that monitoring is more important for riskier assets, Proposition 3 shows that it is potentially costly to let banks fund *risky* assets with insured deposits. Given that the asset risk faced by banks has increased in the past decade, in the sense of a decline in θ, Proposition 3 then suggests that deposit insurance has become increasingly costly in terms of the losses of funding-related reputational benefits.

3 The changing environment of banking: the US experience and its implications for Western Europe

3.1 The competitive environment of US banking

Bank failures and loan losses have reached alarming levels in the US. With the near exhaustion of the FDIC's Bank Insurance Fund, a sense of urgency has gripped the banking community, and the government too. Many believe that the current regulatory structure, including the deposit insurance system, is obsolete. This has prompted a plethora of reform proposals, including those of the US Treasury (1991).[24]

In the quarter century following World War II, US banking displayed historically abnormal stability. The regulatory structure was then, as it is today, largely based on banking legislation enacted during the 1930s. In particular, the Banking Act of 1933, better known as the Glass–Steagall Act, was a direct reaction to a series of banking panics during 1930–3. Glass Steagall (modified in the Banking Act of 1935) consisted of three basic elements. First, it created the Federal Deposit Insurance Corporation (FDIC) to insure deposit accounts up to a maximum of $2,500 for a flat insurance premium of less than 10 basis points. Participation in the FDIC insurance system was mandatory for all Federal Reserve member banks. Others, including state-chartered banks that chose not to join the Federal Reserve, could participate if approved by the FDIC. Second, Glass Steagall restricted the operations of insured banks. The restrictions included limitations on deposit interest payments and a strict separation between investment and commercial banking that prohibited the latter from originating, trading or holding securities other than those of the US Government and general obligations of state and local governments.[25] Finally, together with the McFadden–Pepper Act of 1927, Glass–Steagall elevated entry barriers that reduced competition among banks. Foremost it affirmed the individual states' authority to restrict *de novo* bank charters, inter-state banking and bank holding companies, as well as other means of consolidation and entry. Further restrictions were introduced with the Bank Holding Company (BHC) Act of 1956, which established the Federal Reserve's hegemony over multi-bank holding companies. The 1970 Douglas Amendments to the BHC Act extended these controls to one-bank holding companies.

The combination of ceilings on deposit interest rates and functional and spatial barriers to entry created an environment in which banks faced only limited competition, and consequently earned substantial rents, most especially on deposits. These monopolistic benefits provided banks with compelling incentives to pursue low-risk strategies, *despite the presence of deposit insurance*. In exchange for these benefits, banks accepted restrictions on their activities and intrusive governmental supervision. As a result, the US has a peculiarly fragmented banking industry with many thousands of small, undiversified banking institutions; i.e. geographically local and functionally specialized institutions.

The redefining event of this story was the stubborn inflation, record-setting interest rates and soaring volatility of the 1970s. With inflation exceeding 10 per cent annually towards the end of the decade, nominal interest rates rose to unprecedented levels, and the opportunity costs of holding interest-rate-constrained deposits exploded. Depositors withdrew from the banking system and invested in largely unregulated mutual funds that offered more competitive returns. This was the cash management revolution that swept both the consumer and corporate sectors. Banks were forced to cope with destabilizing endogenous product innovation and advances in information technology; developments that made it easier for the banks' best customers to gain access to the capital markets and abandon their banks. Adverse selection left the banks with the weaker customers and impaired asset quality.[26]

In their weakened condition, the banks discovered a variety of new competitors. Credit card issuers built a presence in the retail market. Insurance companies entered money management with guaranteed investment contracts and a variety of annuities and also expanded their offering of financial guarantees. At the same time, foreign banks expanded in US markets, concentrating on wholesale banking. Non-bank competitors were not subject to the banks' regulatory restrictions. As a result, the percentage of financial assets held by commercial banks dropped from 35 per cent in 1975 to 27 per cent in 1990 (Mishkin, 1992).

Changes in the US competitive environment dissipated the rents that had sustained the Glass–Steagall design. In particular, latent incentive problems of the fixed-rate deposit insurance system were no longer contained by the risk-abating incentives of the rapidly eroding monopoly rents (see Propositions 1 and 2). In addition, the macroeconomic instability and adverse shifts in the quality of the banks' clientele added to the observable risk of the banks' assets.[27] As indicated in Proposition 3, this inflated the cost of the fixed-rate deposit insurance by destroying more substantial funding-related reputational benefits.

3.2 The governmental response

The Treasury's proposal (1991) addressed both the latent flaws of the deposit insurance contract and the declining competitiveness of US banks. No one knows whether the government's programme will become law. It has failed passage once, but has been resubmitted to Congress in somewhat modified form.

First and foremost, deposit insurance reform seeks to realign the divergent incentives of banks and the deposit insurer. The Treasury characterizes the problem in terms of overextension of deposit insurance, weakened financial strength of banks, and fragmentation of regulation. It therefore proposes to reduce deposit insurance coverage, to enhance the role of bank capital, and to intensify supervision.

Clearly, reduced deposit insurance coverage could contain the insurer's exposure, and enhance the potential for funding-related reputational benefits that address the banks' moral hazard incentives. The scope for reduced coverage may, however, be limited. As presently construed, the doctrine of too-big-to-fail (TBTF) weakens the distinction between explicitly insured and uninsured deposits.[28]

The effectiveness of an expanded role for bank capital is unclear. As shown, capital may be counterproductive in combating moral hazard. However, capital does act as a deductible from the viewpoint of the deposit insurer. The Treasury proposes to calibrate deposit insurance premia on the basis of bank capital and also to adjust bank empowerments and frequency of examinations on the basis of the banks' accounting capital.

First, note that the measurement of bank capital is imprecise. Some would address this problem by replacing GAAP (Generally Accepted Auditing Principles) accounting with current value accounting (see White, 1991). This suggestion is, however, misleadingly simple. Banks exist for the purpose of producing liquidity. This means holding non-traded or infrequently traded assets. For these, current value is not well defined. Moreover, the disparate bid–ask spreads of assets are magnified in the capital account as a result of leverage. The problem of measuring capital is further aggravated by problems of deposit and contingent liability accounting. Discounting cash flows, as suggested by some, merely substitutes the difficulties of estimating cash flows and discount rates for those of identifying a market price. This should not be read as a defence of GAAP accounting, or as a rejection of capital-based regulation. We merely wish to emphasize that bank capital is a fragile construct tied up with the banks' production of liquidity and its warehousing of non-traded assets. Any reform programme that relies heavily on capital-based incentives therefore deserves a wary response.

Were it possible to calibrate deposit insurance premia on the perceived reputation of a bank, the funding-cost-related reputational benefits could be reinstated, and the negative incentive effects of deposit insurance would be mitigated. However, linking premia to capital is tricky at best. Linking bank empowerments to GAAP capital is similarly questionable. Regulators might then be put in a position where they would feel compelled to force a divestiture when the bank suffers a capital impairment. All of this presupposes an informed and time-consistent regulator of a type not widely in evidence.

If one shares our scepticism of capital-related measures, the inference is that the Treasury's principal weapon for controlling moral hazard is increased supervision. It is difficult to quarrel with the calls for improved monitoring. At the same time, it is difficult to think of improved supervision as the centrepiece of a programme to correct the deposit insurance incentive problem. There are at least two problems. First, the rapidly changing banking environment, with an explosive growth of trading, interest-rate, exchange-rate, payments and off-balance-sheet risks, creates an ambience where examiners are perpetually trying to catch up. This severely limits what supervision can achieve. Second, and perhaps more important, supervision is a *discretionary* form of regulation. As such, it relies upon regulatory judgement and ambiguity to ameliorate incentive problems (see Boot and Thakor, 1991). Discretionary regulation introduces a form of non-diversifiable sovereign risk in the market for bank capital. Bankers and bank investors eventually learn that the regulator employs situational standards in implementing closure and more limited sanctions, and the banks' cost of capital is elevated. This may help explain the relatively low price/earnings ratios of US banks in comparison with European competitors.[29, 30]

Elsewhere, we have characterized these proposed legislative changes as relying on *indirect regulation* (see Boot and Greenbaum, 1992). The distinction between indirect and direct regulation is that indirect regulation does *not* explicitly prescribe the activities that a bank can undertake, but rather establishes calibrated incentives designed to promote socially desired activities. The Treasury's proposal falls largely into this category. Direct regulation, on the other hand, explicitly limits permitted activities.

The product and geographic restrictions included in the Glass–Steagall Act illustrate direct restrictions. In line with the shift to indirect regulation, the Treasury proposes to expand bank powers for the 'adequately' capitalized to enhance their competitiveness. For the well endowed, geographic restrictions on branch banking and on investment banking activities would be lifted as well.

By contrast, deposit insurance reform based on direct regulation would restrict the asset choices of banks offering insured deposits. Narrow bank is the name recently attached to this proposal (see Litan, 1987). This idea goes back to the 1930s when proposed as '100 percent reserve banking' by Henry Simons (1948). The narrow bank idea restricts banks to holding 'safe' assets with the proceeds of insured deposits. Numerous variants have been articulated, differing mostly in terms of the definition of safe assets. The narrow bank would trivialize the exposure of the deposit insurer. Advantages include less dependence on regulatory monitoring and supervision, and increased flexibility for banks in their usage of uninsured deposits. The latter would improve the competitiveness of US banks globally as well as vis-à-vis less-regulated domestic non-bank financial institutions. The narrow bank also restores the funding-related reputational benefits for all activities that are uninsured, and thus weakens moral hazard incentives. Moral hazard might still be present with insured funds. By restricting their use to safe assets, however, the moral hazard is narrowly circumscribed, and for these assets only few funding-related reputational benefits are at stake (see Proposition 3). A criticism of the narrow bank proposal is that it would isolate the credit from the deposit creation operations of intermediaries. Less restrictive variants (see Benston et al., 1989, and Boot and Greenbaum, 1991), however, permit banks to finance higher-quality, securitized, private credits with insured deposits while retaining much of the certitude of the narrow bank.

Another potential criticism is that banks may not be able to obtain uninsured funding to finance their risky assets. Given the unobservability of monitoring, this problem may arise because the actual riskiness of the banks' (observably) risky assets is unknown. How then would the market be willing to provide uninsured funding to banks that hold these assets? The important underlying question is, therefore, whether the narrow bank type reform proposals would preserve the role of banks in funding these assets. Our answer is that precisely the reputation-building incentives that we have emphasized in this paper should overcome this 'lemon's problem'. In other words, financial intermediaries that have their reputation at stake facilitate the funding of risky monitoring-sensitive assets.

3.3   *Lessons for an integrating Europe*

American banking illustrates the most important pitfall in regulation, i.e. the futility of structural designs that fly in the face of the economics of financial intermediation. The anomalies of US bank regulation have cost taxpayers hundreds of billions of dollars directly and untold additional sums in terms of forfeited competitiveness. And there is still no clear understanding in the public domain of the issues. Deposit insurance has become an entitlement in the US, a political sacred cow, even now that the need for it is less than ever. Given the difficulty of eliminating deposit insurance, the issue becomes one of minimizing the distortions it can be expected to produce. We have argued that the choice is between indirect controls that motivate the bank to choose safe assets and direct controls that require that insured deposits be secured with safe assets. This choice dictates the design of the rest of the banking enterprise. Ultimately, the choice affects the banks' ability to innovate and remain competitive.

What are the implications of our analysis for European banking? Like the US, most West European countries have some type of deposit insurance and regulators also seem reluctant to let individual banks fail. Our analysis indicates that, unless contained by monopoly rents, moral hazard will distort bank decisions in order to exploit the insurer. Here European banking still differs from banking in the US. Protective legislation and intra-industry cartel arrangements, together with the less developed financial markets, continue to provide a supportive environment in which substantial rents are still available. While protected, European banks were less restricted within their home country. Hence, *universal banking* is dominant in Europe, and banks tend to be well diversified. This has undoubtedly contributed to the stability of banking in Europe.

Two major developments will threaten this cosy environment. First, the European integration, based on the principles of *home-country control* and *mutual recognition*, allows unrestricted branching across national borders and thus heralds pan-European banking (see Fitchew, 1990). Second, the European financial markets have lagged behind those in the US, but should be expected to develop quite rapidly. The latter development will allow more corporations to gain access to the financial markets directly and bypass the banks. European banks will not necessarily lose customers, but interest-spread income will be replaced by fee income, although not necessarily unit for unit. Competition will put increasing pressure on cost structures. It should therefore be expected that profitability will diminish, prompting a potentially painful process of exit. Public regulation in the US has inhibited the process of exit and therefore inflated its cost and prolonged the necessary adjustment. The same principal–agent and time consistency problems can be expected to challenge European bank regulation.[31]

If we are right about the imminent dissipation of monopoly rents, Europe will be confronted with the same difficult choices currently facing the US. In particular, as we have shown, an extensive safety net may not be compatible with a competitive banking industry. We believe that it is critical to reintroduce incentives for reputation-building. For this, it seems necessary to reform the regulatory structure along the lines suggested in the previous sections. The importance of a cross-border payment system in an integrated Europe would suggest a European-wide system of deposit insurance, based, however, on strict asset restrictions. Other activities of the banks would not be insured and would be only weakly regulated. Prudent behaviour would be assured by the desire of banks to maintain their reputation. Indeed, this would put banks on a level playing field with their less regulated non-bank competitors, fostering healthy competition between 'market-disciplined' financial institutions.

Our lessons for Europe can be summarized in terms of Dire Straits, Joni Mitchell, as well as Boot and Greenbaum:

From Dire Straits, we have: 'Denial is not only a river in Egypt.'
From Joni Mitchell we have: 'Don't it always seem to go, you don't know what you've got till it's gone.'
And finally, from our own work: 'Sometimes a little more restraint locally can provide much more freedom globally.'

Appendix

Proof of properties of expression (1)

(i) With a two-state distribution, first-order stochastic dominance holds if the bank's expected output is increasing in m. The bank's expected output is:

$$E(x) = \{0 + m[1 - 0]\}\bar{x}(0). \tag{A.1}$$

Obviously $\partial E(x)/\partial m > 0$. (ii) Next we show that the marginal benefit of monitoring is decreasing in 0. This holds if $\partial\{\partial E(x)/\partial m\}/\partial 0 < 0$. From (A.1) we get $\partial E(x)/\partial m = [1 - 0].\bar{x}(0)$, thus

$$\partial\{\partial E(x)/\partial m\}/\partial m = -\bar{x}(0) + [1 - 0]\{\partial\bar{x}(0)/\partial 0\}. \tag{A.2}$$

Since $\partial\bar{x}(0)/\partial 0 < 0$, (A.2) is strictly negative. $\quad\square$

Proof of Lemma 1

Let $a[1 - a]$ be the capital contributed by external equity holders. The amount $[1 - a][1 - a]$ of the funds is contributed by depositors. Note that

a represents the capital requirement; higher values of a imply a more stringent capital requirement. The bank maximizes

$$\text{Max}_m \; L = \frac{a}{a + a[1 - a]} \{0 + m[1 - 0]\}\{\bar{x}(0)$$
$$- [1 - a][1 - a]\hat{r}\} - V(m), \tag{A.3}$$

where $\hat{r} = r\{0 + m[1 - 0]\}^{-1}$. The first-order condition is

$$\frac{a[1 - 0]}{a + a[1 - a]}\{\bar{x}(0) - [1 - a][1 - a]\hat{r}\} = V'(m^*). \tag{A.4}$$

Next, we show that $\partial m^*/\partial a < 0$. We take the implicit differential of (A.4) with respect to a. This gives,

$$\frac{-a[1 - 0][1 - a]}{\{a + a[1 - a]\}^2}\{\bar{x}(0) - [1 - a][1 - a]\hat{r}\}$$
$$+ \frac{a[1 - 0]}{a + a[1 - a]} a[1 - a]\hat{r} = V''(m^*)[\partial m^*/\partial a]. \tag{A.5}$$

The LHS of (A.5) can be written as

$$\frac{-a[1 - 0][1 - a]}{a + a[1 - a]}\left\{[1 - a]\hat{r} + \frac{\bar{x}(0) - \hat{r}}{a + a[1 - a]}\right\}$$
$$= V''(m^*)[\partial m^*/\partial a]. \tag{A.6}$$

We know that $\bar{x}(0) > \hat{r}$, thus the LHS of (A.6) is strictly negative. Also $V''(m^*) > 0$. Therefore (A.6) implies that $\partial m^*/\partial a < 0$. From (1), we now observe that an increase in a leads to an adverse shift in the bank's output distribution, and thus reduces asset quality.   □

Proof of Proposition 1

The proof follows immediately from (6). Note that $V''(m_1) > 0$, thus, if the LHS of (6) increases, m_1^* is positively affected.   □

Proof of Proposition 2

We will prove this proposition by assuming that the insurer sets the insurance premium such that it breaks even in each period across all banks. Since the cross-section of banks has a different reputation on average across periods, the insurance premium in the first period is different from that in the second period. However, the deposit insurance has a fixed-rate premium, which implies that in a given period the premium is constant across banks. In the first period, the average reputation of a bank is π. The bank's all-in cost of funds (i.e. insurance premium plus the interest rate promised on deposits) is therefore r_π; for details see also note 21. The second-period population of banks consists of a proportion $\eta = \pi\{0 + \bar{m}[1 - 0]\} + [1 - \pi]\{0 + m_1[1 - 0]\}$ of banks with reputation ϕ_1, and a proportion $[1 - \eta]$ of *de novo* banks with reputation π. The fixed-rate fairly priced deposit insurance leads to an all-in second-period funding cost $\tilde{r}(\phi_1)$, with $r_{\phi_1} < \tilde{r}(\phi_1) < r_\pi$. The intertemporal improvement in funding costs (induced by the cross-sectional improvement in bank quality between date 0 and date 1) equals $\tilde{R}(\phi_1) = r_\pi - \tilde{r}(\phi_1)$. The first-order condition (6) now becomes

$$[1 - 0]\{\bar{x}(0) - r_\pi\} + [1 - 0]\{\{0 + \underline{m}[1 - 0]\}\{\bar{x}(0) - r_\pi\} - V(\underline{m})\}$$
$$+ [1 - 0]\{0 + \underline{m}[1 - 0]\}\tilde{R}(\phi_1) = V'(m_1^*). \quad (6')$$

Since $\tilde{R}(\phi_1) < R(\phi_1)$ and $V(m_1)$ is strictly positive and convex, we observe from (6') and (6) that the bank's choice of monitoring is strictly lower with fixed-rate deposit insurance than without. This completes the proof of the proposition. $\square$

Proof of Proposition 3

The funding-related expected reputational benefits equal

$$T \equiv \{0 + \underline{m}[1 - 0]\} R(\phi_1). \quad (A.7)$$

We can use (3) and the definition $R(\phi_1) \equiv r_\pi - r_{\phi_1}$ to write $R(\phi_1)$ as,

$$R(\phi_1) = r[\phi_1 - \pi] \left\{ \frac{1}{0 + \underline{m}[1 - 0]} - \frac{1}{0 + \bar{m}[1 - 0]} \right\}. \quad (A.8)$$

From expression (4) we can derive

$$[\phi_1 - \pi] = \frac{\pi[1 - \pi][1 - 0][\bar{m} - m_1]}{\pi\{0 + \bar{m}[1 - 0]\} + [1 - \pi]\{0 + m_1[1 - 0]\}}. \quad (A.9)$$

Next, substitute (A.9) in (A.8), and the resulting expression in (A.7), to get

$$T \equiv \left\{ \frac{\pi[1 - \pi][1 - 0][\bar{m} - m_1]}{\pi\{0 + \bar{m}[1 - 0]\} + [1 - \pi]\{0 + m_1[1 - 0]\}} \right\}$$
$$\left\{ 1 - \frac{0 + \underline{m}[1 - 0]}{0 + \bar{m}[1 - 0]} \right\} \quad (A.10)$$

From (A.10) we can show immediately that $\partial T/\partial 0 < 0$. (Both expressions in (A.10) are strictly positive, and their first derivatives with respect to 0 are negative.) $\square$

NOTES

We gratefully acknowledge the comments of Pierre-André Chiappori, Bill Emmons, Gary Gorton and Xavier Vives.

1 We take the details of the debt contract between the entrepreneur and the bank as given. As shown in the costly-state-verification literature, in the absence of asset-selection moral hazard, debt is optimal if the output realization is not costlessly observable to the lender (see Townsend, 1979; Diamond, 1984; and Gale and Hellwig , 1985). Mookherjee and P'ng (1989) show, however, that the optimality of debt depends on the assumption of deterministic monitoring (which is made in these papers). With both asset-selection and 'output-representation' moral hazard, the optimal contract cannot be characterized in general (see Williams, 1989). Boot, Thakor and Udell (1991) show that secured lending can resolve these moral hazard incentives.

2 Let $f(x|\tau)$ be the density function of the return on the entrepreneur's project, where $x \in (0, \infty)$ denotes return and $\tau \in (\underline{\tau}, \bar{\tau})$ the mean-preserving risk parameter; $f(x|\tau_1)$ is a mean-preserving spread of $f(x|\tau_2)$ for $\tau_1 > \tau_2$. Let $\hat{r}$ be the entrepreneur's repayment obligation on the \$1 bank loan. Then τ will be chosen so as to maximize

$$\max_{\tau} L = \int_{\hat{r}}^{\infty} [x - \hat{r}] f(x|\tau) dx.$$

Given the specification of $f(x|\tau)$, it now follows immediately that L is maximized for $\tau = \bar{\tau}$.

3 The bank's expected payoff is

$$G = \int_{0}^{\hat{r}} x f(x|\tau) dx + \hat{r}[1 - F(\hat{r}|\tau)],$$

where

$$F(\hat{r}|\tau) = \int_{0}^{\hat{r}} f(x|\tau) dx.$$

Given the specification of $f(x|\tau)$, it is straightforward to show that the bank's expected payoff is strictly decreasing in τ.

4 The agency problem is rooted in the unobservability of the bank's actions and leads to incomplete contracting.

5 With interest-earning assets of identical default risk, banks could affect the variance of their return by creating duration gaps. However, a maturity mismatch presumably is *observable*. Undoubtedly, off-balance sheet *contingent* liabilities are also subject to moral hazard. Boot and Thakor (1991) show that these liabilities actually may weaken the bank's incentive to choose more risk.

6 Yoon and Mazumdar (1991) explicitly use observed loan interest rates to design a risk-based deposit insurance pricing system.

7 It is true, however, that regulators have done little to adjust their actions to *observable* differences in risk. They have thereby created incentives that go beyond exploiting the unobservability of a bank's actions.

8 The return distribution generalizes quite naturally to one with more than two states, and where default occurs only with the worst realization. Then, surviving banks display a variety of reputations and *de novo* banks would all have 'average' reputations. Likewise, it is easy to show that our *qualitative* results are

robust with respect to alternative specifications of the closure rule. Our closure rule, i.e. close the bank if state $x = 0$ is realized, is as stringent as possible. As such, it provides the bank with a strong incentive to monitor in the first period (i.e. all future rents are at stake). If, alternatively, it had been assumed that an institution is *never* closed, the bank would have less incentive to monitor. However, even with a more lax closure rule, there would be future benefits of first-period monitoring. That is because the bank's return realization has an effect on its second-period reputation and funding costs. For papers that examine the closure rule as a regulatory instrument see Mailath and Mester (1991) and Davies and McManus (1991). Boot and Thakor (1992) show that regulatory self-interest (i.e. self-serving behaviour by regulators that are concerned about their perceived ability) distorts their closure decision. An implication of the latter is that a closure rule may not be a credible regulatory instrument.

9 Other papers in this area assume that banks earn liquidity rents on deposits, and that therefore, in the absence of bankruptcy costs, deposits are the preferred funding mode (see Giammarino, Lewis and Sappington, 1991). Deriving the bank's optimal capital structure is *not* the focus of our analysis. However, since analysing capital regulation is of interest only if such regulation affects the bank's endogenous choice of capital, we will assume that the bank's capital constraint is binding, and that banks would not otherwise seek external capital.

10 Besanko and Kanatas (1991) analyse the announcement effects of new capital issues. They also distinguish between owner-equity and external capital, but do not focus on the effect of capital on moral hazard. However, it can be shown that, even in their model, capital regulation aggravates moral hazard incentives.

11 They also claim that, depending on relative risk aversion, the *default risk* of a bank increases with required capital. Keeley and Furlong (1990), however, argue that Kahane and Koehn and Santomero mis-characterize the risk–return frontier and therefore that their conclusion regarding default risk is unwarranted.

12 As emphasized earlier, we do not believe that moral hazard based on mean-preserving risk is an appropriate characterization of the bank's incentives.

13 Avery and Berger (1991) analyse risk-based capital requirements and find that asset risk may be negatively related to capital requirements.

14 This argument is implicit in recent discussions of the competitiveness of US banks. Kraus and Evans (1990) argue that US banks are losing market share to European competitors owing to their weak capitalization.

15 Lemma 1 indicates that this might be counterproductive in that monitoring and elevated default probabilities could result. Whereas the negative effect of capital requirements on monitoring is robust with respect to alternative specifications of the return distribution, the link between the default probability and the capital requirement is *not*. With a continuous return distribution, the effect of capital requirements on default risk is ambiguous. Generally, we would expect default risk to be negatively related to the capital requirement; only with extreme distributions of asset returns could the opposite result be obtained. Avery and Berger (1991) show empirically that risk-based capital requirements might be effective in ensuring the negative correlation between default risk and the level of capital requirements.

16 The analysis does not change qualitatively if the owner/manager contributes

equity. The objective of the bank is to maximize the value of the bank to the owner. The net return, if positive, is paid to the owner at each date.

17 This assumption sacrifices no generality because we can easily show that (taking the endogenously determined funding costs into account) a *de novo* bank of type C with future reputational benefits and rents will choose a higher level of monitoring than a surviving bank of type C without future reputational benefits and rents.

18 Consistent with the arguments given in note 17, we focus on interior solutions for the bank's choice of first-period monitoring.

19 Only if the state $x = \bar{x}(0)$ is realized at date 1 can the bank continue. We can therefore ignore the bank's reputation after realizing $x = 0$.

20 While it is true that in equilibrium ϕ_1 depends on the anticipated choice of monitoring m_1 (see (4)), the first-order condition (6) may *not* include the factor $\partial R(\phi_1)/\partial m_1$.

21 In this note we will show that the *timing* of payments of premia for the deposit insurance has *no* effect on the bank's choice of monitoring. Deposit insurance reduces the cost of first-period deposits from r_π to r. From (6) we might be tempted to conclude that this enhances the marginal value of monitoring; i.e. the end-of-period payoff in the good state is $\bar{x}(0) - r$ with deposit insurance, which is higher than the payoff $\bar{x}(0) - r_\pi$ without deposit insurance. Thus, monitoring seems more valuable *with* deposit insurance. This is, however, true only if the bank treats the deposit insurance premium as a sunk cost. While this may be true for most insurance, it is *not* true for deposit insurance. Consider the bank's maximization problem with and without deposit insurance in a single-period setting. Without deposit insurance, the bank maximization problem is

$$\max_m S = [0 + m(1 - 0)]\{\bar{x}(0) - \hat{r}\} - V(m),$$

where $\hat{r} = r\{0 + m[1 - 0]\}^{-1}$. The solution follows from the f.o.c. With deposit insurance the bank obtains deposits at cost r. The bank now needs to raise *more* than \$1 of deposits in order to pay for the insurance. Assume that the bank has to raise D deposits, then the fair-priced deposit insurance premium is $p = \{1 - \{0 + m[1 - 0]\}\}D$. Note that $D \equiv 1 + p$. Thus the bank's repayment obligation to depositors is $[1 + p]r = \{1 + \{1 - \{0 + m[1 - 0]\}\}[1 + p]\}r$. This can be rearranged to $[1 + p]r = r\{0 + m[1 - 0]\}^{-1}$. Observe that this is precisely the same repayment obligation as for the bank in the absence of deposit insurance. Thus, banks face the same maximization problem with or without (fairly priced) deposit insurance. For further details and extensions of these arguments, see Emmons (1991). The feasibility of fairly priced deposit insurance is analysed in Chan, Greenbaum and Thakor (1992).

22 The effect on first-period monitoring is more striking yet. The marginal reputational benefit of first-period monitoring is $[1 - 0]\{0 + \underline{m}[1 - 0]\} R(\phi_1)$, which decreases in 0 more rapidly than $\{0 + m[1 - 0]\} R(\phi_1)$.

23 It can be shown that the expected rents, $\{0 + \underline{m}[1 - 0]\}\{\bar{x}(0) - r_\pi\} - V(m)$, are higher for riskier assets only if $\partial\{\bar{x}(0) - r_\pi\}/\partial 0$ is *sufficiently* negative. Therefore, the greater loss of reputational benefits on riskier assets is not necessarily offset by higher rents earned on these assets.

24 To date, numerous competing proposals have surfaced. The Congressional Budget Office (1990) summarizes a non-exhaustive list of twenty-two proposals.

25 This created a distinction between investment and commercial banks built on a tenuous and increasingly artificial distinction between loans and securities.
26 The weaker remaining customers were further impaired when forced to accept floating-rate loans in place of the previous fixed-rate term loans that hedged their interest-rate risk.
27 The quality of the banks' clientele deteriorated for two reasons, both tracing to the shortened duration of bank deposits that resulted from the spread of consumer and business cash management practices. Rising bank interest-rate risk forced the banks from fixed-rate term to indexed (e.g. prime-plus) lending. This prompted the migration of better clients to the capital markets and impaired the weaker remaining customers by increasing their interest-rate risk and the banks' consequent credit risk (see Boot and Greenbaum, 1991).
28 TBTF is a code word for situations where bank regulators consider the implications of a large bank failure unacceptable, and therefore opt to bail out all depositors.
29 The issue of the desirability of regulatory discretion is analysed in recent game-theoretic models of public utility regulation. For example, Blackmon and Zeckhauser (1992) argue that, once a regulated utility has made an irreversible capital investment, that investment becomes vulnerable to expropriation by a regulator. As a result, the cost of attracting capital may rise, and the utility may abstain from desirable investments.
30 The Federal Deposit Insurance Corporation Improvement Act of 1991 attempts to establish rules that limit regulators' discretion. However, it is unlikely that a satisfactory set of rules can be found (see *The Economist*, 15 February 1992).
31 A development that may prolong the cosy competitive environment of European banking is the consolidation that is occurring *within* many European countries. While this might preserve rents in the short run, we are sceptical about its long-term consequences. There is little empirical evidence that mergers between *large* financial institutions create value. On the contrary, diseconomies of scale might be present.

REFERENCES

Avery, R.B. and A.N. Berger (1991) 'Risk-based capital and deposit insurance reform', *Journal of Banking and Finance* **15**, 847–74.
Benston, G.J., R.D. Brumbaugh, Jr, J.M. Guttentag, R.J. Herring, G.G. Kaufman, R.E. Litan and K.E. Scott (1989) *Blueprint for Restructuring America's Financial Institutions*, Washington, DC: Brookings Institution.
Besanko, D. and G. Kanatas (1991) 'Moral hazard, hedging and incentive compatible bank capital regulation', Working Paper, Northwestern University.
Blackmon, G. and R. Zeckhauser (1992) 'Fragile commitment and the regulatory process', *Yale Journal on Regulation* **9**, 73–105.
Boot, A.W.A and S.I. Greenbaum (1991) 'Deposit insurance reform', BRC Working Paper No. 176, Northwestern University, April.
    (1992) 'American banking legislation, recent', forthcoming, *New Palgrave Dictionary of Money and Finance*.
Boot, A.W.A, S.I. Greenbaum and A.V. Thakor (1992) 'Reputation and con-

structive ambiguity in financial contracting', Working Paper, Northwestern University, October.

Boot, A.W.A and A.V. Thakor (1991) 'Ambiguity and moral hazard', BRC Working Paper, Northwestern University, August 1991.

(1992) 'Self-interested bank regulation', Working Paper, Northwestern University, February.

Boot, A.W.A, A.V. Thakor and G. Udell (1991) 'Secured lending and default risk: equilibrium analysis, policy implications and empirical results', *Economic Journal* **101**, 458–72.

Chan, Y.-S, T.S. Campbell and A.M. Marino (1991) 'An incentive-based theory of bank regulation', Working Paper, University of Southern California, September.

Chan, Y.-S., S.I. Greenbaum and A.V. Thakor (1986) 'Information reusability, competition and bank asset quality', *Journal of Banking and Finance* **10**, 243–53.

(1992) 'Is fairly priced deposit insurance possible?', *Journal of Finance* **47**, 227–45.

Chemmanur, T.J. and P. Fulghieri (1991) 'Investment banker reputation, information production and financial intermediation', Working Paper, Columbia University, September.

Congressional Budget Office, Congress of the United States (1990) *Reforming Federal Deposit Insurance*, September.

Davies, S.M. and D.A. McManus (1991) 'The effects of closure policies on bank risk-taking', *Journal of Banking and Finance* **15**, 917–38.

Diamond, D. (1984) 'Financial intermediation and delegated monitoring', *Review of Economic Studies* **51**, 393–414.

Diamond, D. and P. Dybvig (1983) 'Bank runs, deposit insurance, and liquidity', *Journal of Political Economy* **91**, 401–19.

Emmons, W. (1991) 'Some equivalence results in a model of bank regulation', PhD thesis in progress, Northwestern University, August.

Fitchew, G. (1990) 'Overview: European financial market – The Commission's proposals', in J. Dermine (ed.), *European Banking in the 1990s*, Oxford: Basil Blackwell.

Furlong, F.T. and M. Keeley (1989) 'Capital regulation and bank risk-taking: a note', *Journal of Banking and Finance* **13**, 883–91.

Gale, D. and M. Hellwig (1985) 'Incentive compatible debt contracts: the one period problem', *Review of Economic Studies* **52**, 647–63.

Giammarino, R.M., T.R. Lewis and D. Sappington (1991) 'An incentive approach to banking regulation', Working Paper, University of British Columbia, October.

Jensen, M. and W. Meckling (1976) 'Theory of the firm: managerial behavior, agency cost, and capital structure', *Journal of Financial Economics* **3**, 305–60.

John, K., T. John and L. Senbet (1991) 'Risk-shifting incentives of depository institutions: a new perspective on Federal deposit insurance reform', *Journal of Banking and Finance* **15**, 895–916.

Kahane, Y. (1977) 'Capital adequacy and the regulation of financial intermediaries', *Journal of Banking and Finance* **2**, 207–18.

Kareken, J. and N. Wallace (1978) 'Deposit insurance and bank regulation', *Journal of Business* **51**, 413–38.

Keeley, M.C. (1990) 'Deposit insurance and market power in banking', *American Economic Review* **80**, 1183–201.

Keeley, M.C. and F.T. Furlong (1990) 'A reexamination of mean-variance analysis of bank capital regulation', *Journal of Banking and Finance* **14**, 69–84.

Koehn, M. and A.M. Santomero (1980) 'Regulation of bank capital and portfolio risk', *Journal of Finance* **35**, 1235–50.

Kraus, J.R. and J. Evans (1990) 'U.S. and Japanese surrender edge in global bank growth to Europe', *American Banker*, 27 December.

Litan, R.E. (1987) *What Should Banks Do?* Washington, DC: The Brookings Institution.

Mailath, G.J. and L.J. Mester (1991) 'When do regulators close banks? When should they?' Working Paper, University of Pennsylvania, November.

Merton, R.C. (1977) 'An analytic derivation of the cost of deposit insurance and loan guarantees', *Journal of Banking and Finance* **1**, 512–20.

Milgrom, P. and J. Roberts (1982) 'Predation, reputation and entry deterrence', *Journal of Economic Theory* **27**, 253–79.

Mishkin, F.S. (1992) 'An evaluation of the Treasury plan for banking reform', *Journal of Economic Perspectives* **6**, 133–53.

Mookherjee, D. and I. P'ng (1989) 'Optimal auditing, insurance, and redistribution', *Quarterly Journal of Economics* **104**, 399–416.

Ronn, E.I. and A.K. Verma (1986) 'Pricing risk-adjusted deposit insurance: an option-based model', *Journal of Finance* **41**, 871–95.

Simons, H.C. (1948) *Economic Policy for a Free Society*, Chicago: University of Chicago Press.

The Economist (1991) 'America's banks: living, and dying, by the rule books', 15 February, 97–8.

Townsend, R. (1979) 'Optimal contracts and competitive markets with costly state verification', *Journal of Economic Theory* **21**, 265–93.

United States Treasury (1991) *Modernizing the Financial System: Recommendations for Safer, More Competitive Banks*, Washington, DC: US Government Printing Office.

White, L.J. (1991) *The S & L Debacle: Public Policy Lessons for Bank and Thrift Regulation*, Oxford: Oxford University Press.

Williams, J. (1989) 'Ex-ante monitoring, ex-post asymmetry and optimal securities', Working Paper, University of British Columbia.

Yoon, S.H. and S. Mazumdar (1991) 'Fairly priced deposit insurance, incentive compatible regulations and bank asset choice', Working Paper, McGill University, October.

Discussion

PIERRE-ANDRÉ CHIAPPORI

The paper by Boot and Greenbaum provides a careful and interesting analysis of bank regulation, and specifically of the moral hazard problems associated with deposit insurance. As such, it is especially welcome, and provides useful insights in the perspective of the forthcoming European Monetary System.

I shall first discuss the main issues that arise in this class of models and the way they are dealt with in the present paper. Then I shall briefly comment on policy implications.

1   Models of deposit insurance

A widespread conclusion, drawn in particular from the crisis of US Savings and Loan, is that fixed-rate deposit insurance creates perverse incentives favouring excessive risk-taking behaviour. This 'moral hazard' explanation of the crisis, at least in its current version, is however not fully convincing at first sight, and deserves further elaboration. Moral hazard arises whenever some insurance scheme, by protecting an agent against the consequences of inappropriate behaviour, alters the agent's incentives in an undesirable direction. The case of deposit insurance is clearly more complex, because the people insured – depositors – do not decide on the bank's portfolio composition, while the decision maker – the banker – is not insured. Perverse incentives, if any, must thus be indirect: the insurance provided to one party results in excessive risk taking by the other party.

The question, of course, is by which mechanism such incentives are transmitted. An obvious candidate is the price system. Specifically, should the market operate without regulation, excessive risk taking should raise the bank's funding costs, since depositors will exact a risk premium. Fixed-rate deposit insurance destroys this mechanism, since depositors bear no risk. The price to pay for excessive risk taking is reduced, hence the perverse incentive.

Prevalent as this explanation may be, two questions still remain. For one thing, why are banks willing to take excessive risks at all – and how sensitive is the corresponding motive to funding costs? Secondly, to what extent is the bank's level of risk observable by third parties (including depositors and regulation agencies) – a necessary condition for the existence of risk premia?

2   Limited liability

The traditional answer to the first question relies on limited liability. Since the banker's loss is bounded, his payoff function will be convex (in the absence of risk aversion), and he will consequently maximize risk for a given return. Together with the traditional assumption that risky assets (or loans) pay larger mean returns, this provides a sensible (and probably quite realistic) story that accounts for excessive risk taking. The problem with this explanation is however that it is extremely robust, in particular to cost-funding considerations. It turns out, in fact, that, even without deposit insurance, the risk premium required to attract (risk-neutral) depositors is not sufficient to discourage excessive (and actually maximum) risk taking. Should this be the case, deposit insurance would have no effect upon banks' behaviour, simply because the level of risk would be maximum anyway.

Of course, several arguments can be invoked to mitigate this conclusion. Depositors are risk averse, and may demand a very large premium; bankers themselves may not be risk neutral, etc. Still, constructing a convincing explanation along these lines is not an easy task. The trick, in the present model, is to assume away the trade-off between safety and return. Here, lower risk is associated with *higher* return, the interpretation being that the bank can engage in costly monitoring activities that *simultaneously* decrease risk and increase expected return. Hence, technically speaking, the model replaces the usual assumption of second-order dominance by a first-order dominance hypothesis. Finally, since monitoring is costly, the level of monitoring effort chosen by the bank will be sensitive to the gain generated by the reduction of risk, including lower funding costs.

I believe this framework does capture important components of the situation. But it should be emphasized that it does not apply to the (somewhat more traditional) representation where the bank composes its portfolio of assets by choosing between more or less risky assets.

3   Observability

A second question is whether the level of risk chosen by the bank is observable (and possibly verifiable). The problem here is that we may assume that banks' choices are not observable – but then the moral hazard story essentially vanishes, since depositors cannot react at all to banks' behaviour, whether deposit insurance exists or not. Or we may alternatively suppose that banks' decisions can be observed and contracted upon – in which case, however, an immediate solution would be to make both deposit contracts and insurance schemes contingent upon risk. (A last possible situation is when banks' behaviour is observable but not verifiable, which would typically require more sophisticated contracts and insurance schemes. The authors rightly point out that a bank cannot, in general, face a safety/return trade-off for its loan portfolio. The idea is that higher return can be obtained only through higher interest rates; but the latter are verifiable, and would then be contracted upon. This argument would however not apply to German and French banks, which hold equities.)

The answer proposed in the paper goes through reputation effects. Though banks' portfolios (or rather, in this case, monitoring efforts) are not observable, survival acts as a signal, because banks that survive are more likely to have behaved cautiously in the past. They thus acquire a 'good' reputation, which will in turn be translated into lower funding costs. The key point with this explanation is, of course, that *cautious behaviour yesterday must be correlated with cautious behaviour today*, at least in people's minds. In the model, this effect is obtained through the convenient fiction of an adverse selection setting, in which some banks have a zero monitoring cost; a good reputation then means being perceived as a zero-cost bank with higher probability. But this assumption is rather ad hoc. It implies, for instance, that deposit insurance premia should be lower for old banks than for new ones – a conclusion that a regulator may be reluctant to accept, given the number of old and well-known institutions that have gone bankrupt in the past. In other words, I am not fully convinced by the story given in the model – though I do accept that reputation may matter, which is after all the point the authors wanted to make.

4   Policy implications

Let me now briefly comment on the policy implications of the model. The main message is that the drop in profits that follows deregulation of banking has a double impact on the stability of the financial system. On the one hand, fat margins are decreased, and banks become more vulnerable to fluctuations in their environment. On the other hand – and, I believe, more importantly – future expected profits shrink as well; then the cost of bankruptcy, i.e. of being driven out of business, is reduced. In consequence, banks are likely both to take more risks and to be more exposed to the risk they take.

This is certainly a very serious problem, the solution to which is not clear. The authors support narrow banking, on the grounds that, in the case of uninsured deposits, the market mechanism will efficiently operate through reputation-based funding costs – while insured deposits would fund only safe assets anyway. I must confess that I am not totally convinced that the prospect of higher funding cost will be sufficient to deter risky behaviour, especially from banks that are already in an unsafe situation. In my view, the solution also entails much strengthened direct supervision by monetary authorities. In any event, the paper has the merit of stressing an important fact, namely that the future stability of the European monetary system may be much more difficult to achieve than past experience may suggest.

GARY GORTON

Professors Boot and Greenbaum consider a model of banking in which the role of banks is to monitor borrowers, that is, to reduce the risk-increasing asset substitution that leveraged borrowers will otherwise undertake, at the expense of the bank. There are two types of bank: those that can monitor at zero cost and those that can monitor at a positive cost. Banks with positive monitoring costs will tend to monitor less and, consequently, will have riskier portfolios. In this context the authors stress two results. First, that a capital requirement for banks will reduce banks' monitoring efforts and hence decrease their asset quality. Thus, capital requirements can be counterproductive. Second, the existence of fixed-rate deposit insurance will prevent bank depositors from charging a higher interest rate to those banks that are revealed (at least partially) to be riskier banks (i.e. those with positive monitoring costs). Consequently, the prospect of lower future funding costs cannot be an inducement for these banks to monitor more. The authors discuss a number of policy implications of these results.

The first result concerning capital requirements seems counter-intuitive since, as the amount of equity is increased, the residual claimants are more at risk and might be expected to monitor more intensely as a result. This does not happen in this model because the capital requirement increases the amount of *outside* equity. But inside equity holders (the original equity holders) bear the monitoring costs. The *inside* equity holders do not maximize the value of the bank, but maximize the value of their own holdings net of the monitoring costs. More capital dilutes their holdings, but the new equity holders do not share in the monitoring costs. Consequently, the insiders choose to monitor less.

This view of the agency relation between inside and outside equity holders is somewhat peculiar. Usually we think of insiders as receiving private benefits from control of the firm, benefits that they want to protect. Since insiders have large amounts of human capital invested in the firm, and receive private benefits of control, they behave more conservatively than they would in the absence of agency costs, that is, they are more risk averse than outsiders would like them to be. There is a great deal of empirical evidence supporting this view. For example, empirically, the motivation for bank mergers seems to be risk reduction.

In this model the insiders bear a cost, but receive no benefit from control. This drives the result. If we were to believe this result, the problem could easily be rectified by designing a compensation scheme for the insiders that offsets their loss when outside capital is raised. For example, the insiders could be given stock options or performance bonuses that offset the loss due to dilution when new capital is raised.

To see the second result, suppose that there is no deposit insurance and that bank depositors can observe the borrowers' payoffs to the bank at the end of the first period. Then depositors learn something about the bank type (positive or zero monitoring costs), and the cost of funds in the second period will reflect their updated beliefs. Since banks with positive monitoring costs will be riskier, they will have to pay depositors a higher interest rate. Banks with zero monitoring costs will (on average) have the lower cost of funds. Anticipating that good performance during period one will result in lower funding costs in period two, the banks with positive monitoring costs are induced to monitor more than they otherwise would in period one. Clearly, if there is fixed-rate deposit insurance then there can be no such incentive effect. Deposit insurance thus destroys the possibility of incentive effects from learning.

This idea of reputation is based on depositors being able to observe outcomes at the end of period one. The problem with this assumption is that the theoretical justification for bank existence, as opposed to direct issuance of securities by firms to households, is that households cannot observe outcomes. If households can observe outcomes then they can hire monitors, who do not make loans and condition their fees on their performance. Banking would be completely unbundled. Alternatively, the same arguments about future funding costs affecting current performance can be applied directly to the borrowing firms. For the same reasons that bank performance is affected, the performance of borrowers will be affected. Firms can form reputations directly and banks are not needed. So, to the extent that bank actions are observable, banks are needed in this economy.

Is there empirical evidence that bank (uninsured) depositors or outside equity holders can, in fact, observe outcomes to the extent that such reputations can be formed? Attempts to find such evidence have taken the form of examining the prices of bank uninsured liabilities for signs that they differentially reflect bank risk. The results of this research have been mixed at best.

Since, as the authors stress, world banking is changing dramatically, it is important to understand these changes in order to formulate appropriate public policies. It is difficult to model these changes theoretically and, at this point, it is perhaps premature to draw strong implications from such analyses.

10 Relationship banking, deposit insurance and bank portfolio choice

DAVID BESANKO and ANJAN V. THAKOR

1 Introduction

The purpose of this paper is to examine the consequences of interbank competition and bank–capital market competition on the portfolio choices of banks and the welfare of borrowers in a regulatory environment of (*de facto*) complete deposit insurance. Our focus is on an industry characterized by 'relationship banking', i.e. a setting involving repeated, bilateral credit transactions between banks and borrowers. A key feature of relationship banking is the intertemporal accumulation of proprietary borrower-specific information in the hands of the bank, and the consequent creation of informational rents (see Sharpe, 1990). To the extent that these rents are shared by the bank and the borrower, *both* parties see a value in continuing their relationship. The desire to protect such relationships affects the bank's asset portfolio choice.

A second factor that affects the bank's asset portfolio choice is deposit insurance. As is well known, risk-insensitive deposit insurance pricing induces socially wasteful risk taking by banks (see Merton, 1977).[1] Partially mitigating this fondness for risk is the threat of bank charter termination by the insurer, but this threat is effective only if bank charters are sufficiently valuable (see Chan, Greenbaum and Thakor, 1992).[2] We show that relationship banking provides one source of value for the bank charter.[3] Relationship banking diminishes in value, however, as the banking industry becomes more competitive, so that increased interbank competition accentuates the attractiveness of risk pursuit initially engendered by deposit insurance. The same holds true for increased competition from the capital market.

This framework provides a useful cognitive link between bank market structure, the capital market, relationship banking, deposit insurance and bank portfolio choice. It thus allows us to explore simultaneously a rich set of issues related to the consequences of relaxing barriers to entry into

292

banking and improving borrowers' access to the capital market. We are particularly interested in the manner in which deregulated entry into banking impinges on *borrower* welfare.

The question of optimal market structure in banking has dominated regulatory thinking (especially in the US) for decades. Prior to 1980, the focus in the US was on safety and thus bank charters were issued rather selectively. As a result, despite the presence of numerous banks owing to interstate and intrastate branching restrictions, the banking industry in the US was an oligopoly like its counterparts in Canada, Japan, the UK, etc. Since then, however, the focus has shifted to the virtues of competition, and entry restrictions have been relaxed. The putative rationale for this regulatory shift is that borrowers and savers are made better off by increased interbank competition.

This assertion was formally verified by us using a spatial model of oligopolistic banking (see Besanko and Thakor, forthcoming). We showed that increased competition would make depositors and borrowers better off and banks' shareholders worse off. However, that model did not analyse potentially interesting interactions between the bank's portfolio choice and the market structure of the banking industry. Moreover, the static nature of the model precluded consideration of relationship banking issues.

In this paper we show that this conventional wisdom is not quite correct when the impact of market structure on banks' portfolio choices is accounted for. It may *not* be a good thing for some borrowers if banks compete more fiercely for their business. This seemingly counter-intuitive result is based on two conflicting effects that increased interbank competition has on borrowers' welfare. The direct effect is that their borrowing cost is lowered in the current period as well as in future periods, which is good for them. But this increase in the borrowers' surplus causes a concomitant reduction in the value of the bank–customer relationship to the bank. This weakens the pivotal countervailing force to the bank's desire to maximize the value of the deposit insurance put option in the *current* period by appropriately increasing risk. The resulting reduction in the bank's survival probability jeopardizes the bank–customer relationship and creates an indirect effect of increased interbank competition, which is not good for borrowers.

Similar reasoning applies to improved capital market access. Although a given borrower is unambiguously better off owing to greater access to the capital market, this creates a negative externality for *other* borrowers who have poorer access. For such borrowers, relationship banking is valuable, but there is an asymmetry in the way they assess relationship banking and the way the bank assesses it. Each of these borrowers is concerned solely with the value of that borrower's *bilateral* relationship with the bank, whereas the bank takes a *multilateral* portfolio approach and considers the cumulative value of all its relationships. A lowering of the value of this 'relationship portfolio' due to improved capital market access for a *subset* of its borrower pool distorts the bank's asset portfolio choice in the direction of greater risk. This hurts the borrowers whose capital market access has not improved.

Our work is related to three distinct strands of the contemporary financial intermediation literature. One strand is related to exploring the efficiency connotations of market structure in banking. Apart from our earlier work (Besanko and Thakor, forthcoming), Wong (1991), Winton (1991) and Matutes and Vives (1991) have recently taken up different aspects of this issue. Wong (1991) argues that a less competitive banking system may be less harmful than pro-competition advocates suggest, if borrowers possess sufficiently strong bargaining power in dealing with banks. Winton (1991) suggests that deposit insurance leads to banking industry fragmentation – smaller and more numerous banks – and thus strengthens regulatory incentives to limit charters and permit collusion. Matutes and Vives (1990) focus on banking instability arising from the multiplicity of equilibria attributable to the usual coordination problem between depositors. They find that competition per se is not responsible for banking instability, even though it is 'socially excessive'. They also make a case for deposit insurance and deposit interest rate regulation. Our intended contribution on this score is the finding that regulating entry to create an imperfectly competitive banking industry is not only good for stability but *may also make borrowers better off*.

A second strand of the literature is concerned with relationship banking. Sharpe (1990), von Thadden (1990) and Rajan (1991) have all examined the implications of bank–customer relationships in informationally constrained settings. Sharpe (1990) focuses on subgame perfect Nash equilibria in which the incumbent bank is tempted opportunistically to raise its loan interest rate to successful borrowers about whom it knows more than competing banks. *Ex ante* interbank competition results in banks bidding away these anticipated *ex post* expected profits by sufficiently lowering the initial loan interest rate. With a downward-sloping demand schedule for loans, this results in new borrowers being allocated *too much* credit and older borrowers being allocated too little credit relative to the first best. A different sort of second-best inefficiency arises in von Thadden (1990). In that model, a privately informed borrower can choose between a short-term project that reveals its 'type' to all early, and a socially preferred long-term project that resolves the informational asymmetry later. The incumbent bank is assumed to be able to learn the borrower's type early at a cost. The subgame perfect strategy for the incumbent bank is then to exploit its informational advantage in pricing its second-period loan. Anticipation of this future surplus extraction may induce the borrower to prefer the short-term project that would deny the incumbent bank any future informational monopoly. Rajan (1991) shows that borrowers may sometimes prefer 'arm's-length' borrowing (capital market access) to bank borrowing because the latter involves an extraction of borrower surplus that can be avoided with the former. While it is true that the incumbent bank's informational advantage can create distortions, our focus in this paper is on its *beneficial* effects. In this regard, our paper can be distinguished from the earlier research on the basis of its focus on the effect of relationship banking on the bank's portfolio choice rather than on the borrower's investment decisions.

A third strand of the literature to which our work is connected is that on deposit insurance. This literature is too voluminous to cite exhaustively, but in most models that rationalize governmental deposit insurance the role of deposit insurance is to enhance banking stability and improve the liquidity of depositors' claims.[4] Moreover, borrowers also benefit because deposit insurance eliminates banking panics that could disrupt borrowers' projects. We abstract from the coordination failures that cause panics in these models. Given this abstraction, the only beneficial role of deposit insurance is to provide depositors a riskless claim. But deposit insurance has the disadvantage of inducing excessive risk taking by banks, a disadvantage that is magnified with increased interbank competition for borrowers. We assume that regulators expeditiously close banks that fail, so that an increase in bank portfolio risk jeopardizes relationship banking even with governmental deposit insurance. Hence, deposit insurance creates costs even for borrowers.

The rest of the paper is organized as follows. In section 2 we develop a model of dynamic asset portfolio choice for a bank operating over two time periods spanning three points in time. We examine the dependence of the bank's portfolio choice on its anticipated future informational advantage as well as credit market structure. Section 3 contains the analysis. Section 4 discusses the policy implications of the analysis. Section 5 concludes with a summary of the main results.

2   The model

2.1   Preferences, endowments and time horizon

We consider an environment with universal risk neutrality. There are three points in time, $t = 0$, 1 and 2, and two time periods, the first beginning at $t = 0$ and ending at $t = 1$, and the second beginning at $t = 1$ and ending at $t = 2$. There are five types of players: banks, borrowers, depositors, the deposit insurer and the capital market. At the start of each period, each borrower is endowed with a project requiring a $1 investment, but does not have the necessary investment funds. Each borrower can either approach a bank for a loan or access the capital market directly for funds. Borrowers have no terminal wealth so, if a borrower's project produces insufficient cash flow to repay the lender, the borrower defaults and surrenders the cash flow to the lender. Realized cash flows are costlessly observable to all.[5] In the first period, the bank raises D of deposits. Deposit insurance is complete, so that depositors must be repaid Dr_f at $t = 1$, where r_f is one plus the riskless interest rate. If the bank can fully repay depositors on its own at $t = 1$, it stays in business for a second period and raises D in new deposits. If not, the deposit insurer pays off the depositors and closes the bank.[6] Also, for simplicity, we assume that the bank has no equity capital, so that D is the total amount available for lending in each period. As an alternative to lending, any bank can invest in a marketable security which yields R with probability $\delta \in (0,1)$ and zero with probability $1 - \delta$ for every dollar invested. This marketable security is priced to preclude arbitrage (i.e. $\delta R = 1$ and the net present value from purchasing this security is zero). The availability of this investment opportunity implies that, despite deposit insurance, the bank will not price its loan to earn a net expected return less than that available on the marketable security.

In what follows, we will assume that each borrower has an effort choice in the second period (but not in the first period, because first-period effort choice has no bearing on the analysis), with negative utility for effort.

2.2   Borrowers' investment opportunities

At $t = 0$, each borrower can invest $1 in a project that will pay off at $t = 1$. The payoff will be either $R_1 > r_f$, or zero. In the first period, there are two observationally distinct risk classes of borrowers, A and B. These two classes are distinguished by success probability, with $\delta_A \in (0,1)$ denoting the success probability of class A borrowers, and $\delta_B \in (0,1)$ the success probability of class B borrowers. The higher-quality (lower-risk) borrowers are in class A, so $\delta_A > \delta_B$. Borrower types are common knowledge at $t = 0$.

The evolution of a borrower's investment opportunities and risk class is depicted in Figure 10.1. If a borrower's first-period project succeeds, then the borrower's second-period project (which also requires a $1 investment) is riskless and yields S at $t = 2$. If the borrower's first-period project

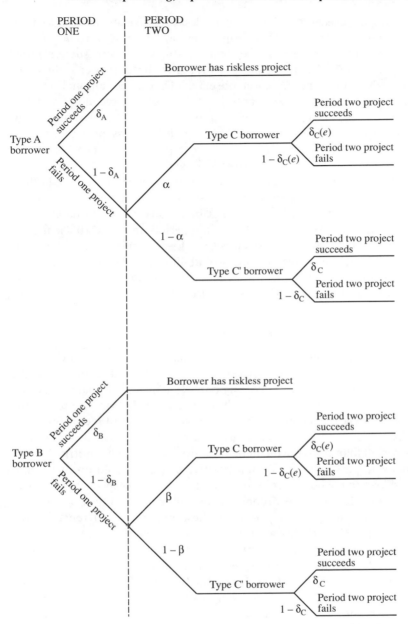

Figure 10.1   Evolution of borrower types

fails, then their second-period project is less lucrative and more risky than the first-period project. This project has a return $R_2 \in (r_f, R_1)$ in the successful state and zero in the unsuccessful state, with success probability $\delta_i(e)$, $i \in \{C, C'\}$, $e \in \{0, 1\}$, where e is the borrower's choice of effort, which only the borrower observes. That is, conditional on first-period failure, the borrower can fall into one of two second-period risk classes, designated by C and C'. We assume that $\delta_C(1) > \delta_C(0) \equiv \delta_C = \delta_{C'}(0) = \delta_{C'}(1)$. Since the success probabilities for type C' do not depend on e, we will write $\delta_{C'} \equiv \delta_{C'}(e)$. The borrower's effort disutility for choosing effort e is with We, $W > 0$. In this first period, a borrower does not know what class they will be in should their project fail, although transition probabilities are common knowledge. Given that a borrower is in risk class A in period one, the probability that they are in risk class C should they fail in period one is $a \in (0, 1)$, and the probability that they are in risk class C' is $1 - a$. If they are in risk class B in period one, the corresponding probabilities are $\beta \in (0, 1)$, and $1 - \beta$, respectively. We assume that $\beta < a$. Thus, there is imperfect intertemporal correlation of risk classes for risky projects.

2.3   Information structure and market structure

At $t = 0$, a borrower's 'type' (their risk class) is common knowledge, as are all the exogenous parameter values. We assume that, at this stage, the borrower is already with an existing bank (the incumbent bank) and that the banking industry is imperfectly competitive. Let M_{1l} represent the 'mark-up' over the incumbent bank's breakeven interest factor (one plus the loan interest rate) that is charged to a borrower of risk class l on their first-period loan from the incumbent bank. We will argue shortly that the incumbent bank stands to earn a positive expected profit on its second-period loan to the borrower in some states and a zero expected profit in all other states. *Ex ante* (date 0) competition will then affect the pricing of the first-period loan, in anticipation of these second-period rents for the incumbent bank. If there was perfect competition at the outset, M_{1l} would be negative (see Sharpe, 1990, for a verification). With imperfect competition, M_{1l} could be positive, zero or negative. The point is that the incumbent bank will set M_{1l} such that the borrower is indifferent between staying with that bank and switching to a competitor, but M_{1l} will not dissipate all of the incumbent bank's expected future rents.

Now, if a borrower fails in period one, the incumbent bank learns the borrower's period-two risk class perfectly. Outside banks know that the borrower has failed *and* also receive an additional imperfect signal about the borrower's period-two risk class. The commercial paper market knows only that the borrower failed in the first period. For borrowers who succeeded in period one, all parties know that such borrowers have access to a riskless project. We assume that, at the start of the second period, the borrower simultaneously solicits bids from all credit sources and selects the cheapest source. An outside bank's screening technology can be described as follows. A bank observes a signal σ about a borrower's type, where $\sigma \in \{C, C'\}$, i.e. the signal tells the bank either that the borrower is of risk class C or that they are of risk class C'. Assume $\Pr(\sigma = C \mid \text{true type is } C') = \Pr(\sigma = C' \mid \text{true type is } C) = \phi \in (0, 0.5)$. Thus, ϕ is the probability of an erroneous identification by a competing bank. The incumbent bank's second-period interest factor will depend on two considerations: the magnitude of the error in screening by a competing bank and credit market structure. As $\phi \to 0$, the competing bank's information set converges with that of the incumbent bank. If, in addition, the credit market is also perfectly competitive, then incumbent banks cannot earn any second-period profits.

3   The analysis

3.1   The second-period problem

3.1.1 Interest factors charged by competing banks

To ensure subgame perfection, we adopt the usual dynamic programming approach and start with the second period. By Bayes rule, the posterior probabilities, as assessed by a competing bank, are:

Pr (true type is $C \mid \sigma = C$, failure in first period, true type was A in period one) =

$$a' = a[1 - \phi][a(1 - \phi) + [1 - a]\phi]^{-1} \in (a, 1)$$

Pr (true type is $C \mid \sigma = C'$, failure in first period, true type was A in period one) =

$$\hat{a} = \phi a[\phi a + (1 - \phi)(1 - a)]^{-1}.$$

Pr (true type is $C \mid \sigma = C$, failure in first period, true type was B in period one) =

$$\beta' = \beta[1 - \phi][\beta(1 - \phi) + [1 - \beta]\phi]^{-1} \in (\beta, 1)$$

Pr (true type is $C \mid \sigma = C'$, failure in first period, true type was B in period one) =

$$\hat{\beta} = \phi\beta[\phi\beta + (1 - \phi)(1 - \beta)]^{-1}.$$

It is clear that $a' > \hat{a}$ and $\beta' > \hat{\beta}$.

Given this screening technology, we can compute the minimum interest factor an outside bank can charge a borrower who failed in the first period. Consider first a borrower whose first-period risk class was A, who failed in the first period and for whom $\sigma = $ C. If an outside bank assumes that a borrower of second-period risk class C will choose $e = 1$, then the bank's breakeven rate $i'_{\min}(A, \sigma = $ C) will make it just indifferent between making bank loans and investing in the risky marketable security. Given that the marketable security is priced to prevent arbitrage, the breakeven rate satisfies

$$i'_{\min}(A, \sigma = C)[a'\delta_C(1) + (1 - a')\delta_C] = r_f.$$

That is,

$$i'_{\min}(A, \sigma = C) = \frac{r_f}{a'\delta_C(1) + [1 - a']\delta_C}. \tag{1}$$

If $\sigma = $ C' for such a borrower, then

$$i'_{\min}(A, \sigma = C') = \frac{r_f}{\hat{a}\delta_C(1) + [1 - \hat{a}]\delta_C}. \tag{2}$$

Similarly, if the borrower's first-period risk class was B, they failed in the first period, and the bank's screening reveals $\sigma = $ C, the bank's breakeven rate (assuming that $e = 1$ will be chosen by a borrower of risk class C) $i'_{\min}(B, \sigma = $ C) is

$$i'_{\min}(B, \sigma = C) = \frac{r_f}{\beta'\delta_C(1) + [1 - \beta']\delta_C}. \tag{3}$$

And, if the screen reveals $\sigma = $ C', it is

$$i'_{\min}(B, \sigma = C') = \frac{r_f}{\hat{\beta}\delta_C(1) + [1 - \hat{\beta}]\delta_C}. \tag{4}$$

Since $a' > \hat{a}$ and $\delta_C(1) > \delta_C$, it is clear that $i'_{\min}(A, \sigma = $ C) $< i'_{\min}(A, \sigma = $ C'). Likewise, $i'_{\min}(B, \sigma = $ C) $< i'_{\min}(B, \sigma = $ C').

Now, the expected utility of a borrower of risk class C is

$$\delta_C(e)[R_2 - i] - We,$$

where i is the interest factor on the borrower's \$1 loan. Suppose there exists a value of ϕ, call it ϕ^*, such that if the 'error probability' associated with the signal σ is ϕ^*, i.e. the signal is $\sigma(\phi^*)$, then

$$\delta_C[R_2 - i'_{\min}(j, \sigma(\phi^*) = C)]$$
$$= \delta_C(1)[R_2 - i'_{\min}(j, \sigma(\phi^*) = C)] - W. \tag{5}$$

It follows then that the left-hand side (LHS) of (5) will exceed the right-hand side (RHS) if $\phi > \phi^*$ and the LHS will be less than the RHS if $\phi < \phi^*$. We will assume henceforth that $\phi > \phi^*$.

Given this assumption, the outside bank's belief that the borrower of risk class C will choose $e = 1$ is incorrect, regardless of whether the borrower was of risk class A or B in the first period. Hence, the minimum interest factors an incumbent bank can charge a borrower in the second period if the borrower failed in the first period are based on the belief that the borrower of risk class C will choose $e = 0$, and are as follows:

$$i_{\min}(A, \sigma = C) = i_{\min}(A, \sigma = C') = i_{\min}(B, \sigma = C)$$
$$= i_{\min}(B, \sigma = C') \equiv i_{\min} = r_f[\delta_C]^{-1}. \qquad (6)$$

It is transparent that

$$\delta_C[R_2 - i_{\min}] > \delta_C(1)[R_2 - i_{\min}] - W, \qquad (7)$$

so that the borrower of risk class C will indeed choose $e = 0$ when faced with $i_{\min}$.

3.1.2 Interest factors charged by incumbent banks

We now wish to examine the interest factors that the incumbent bank would charge the different borrowers in the second period. We denote these interest factors by i_{2j}^k, where k denotes the borrower's first-period risk class and j denotes their second-period risk class. Since the incumbent bank knows the borrower's second-period risk class precisely, it can compute the maximum interest factor it can charge the borrower before he switches to effort $e = 0$. For the borrower whose risk class is C, this interest factor, $i_{\max}$, is given by

$$\delta_C[R_2 - i_{\max}] = \delta_C(1)[R_2 - i_{\max}] - W. \qquad (8)$$

Now, the expected second-period profit of the incumbent bank if it charges this interest factor is $\delta_C(1)[i_{\max} - r_f]$. Note that $i_{\max} < i_{\min}$. If the bank charges a higher interest factor, then it might as well set the rate as high as $i_{\min}$. Thus, its expected profit will be $\delta_C[i_{\min} - r_f]$. We now assume that

$$\delta_C(1) > \frac{\delta_C[i_{\min} - r_f]}{[i_{\max} - r_f]}, \qquad (9)$$

with $i_{\min}$ given by (6) and $i_{\max}$ given by (8). Given (9), the incumbent bank will find it optimal to set

$$i_{2C}^A = i_{2C}^B = i_{\max} = \frac{R_2[\delta_C(1) - \delta_C] - W}{[\delta_C(1) - \delta_C]}. \qquad (10)$$

The incumbent bank's optimal pricing strategy will be to charge the borrowers in risk class C′ a rate that leaves them indifferent between borrowing from the incumbent bank and an outside bank. The incumbent bank knows that, if such a borrower approaches an outside bank, they will be offered a rate of i_{min}.[7] If the banking industry were perfectly competitive (with its competitiveness constrained only by the incumbent bank's informational advantage), then the incumbent bank would set $i^A_{2C'} = i_{min}$ and $i^B_{2C'} = i_{min}$. But with an imperfectly competitive banking industry, the incumbent bank may set $i^A_{2C'}$ and $i^B_{2C'}$ higher.[8] Let M_{2A} and M_{2B} represent the positive second-period 'mark-ups' over i_{min} for borrowers of first-period risk classes A and B respectively such that the incumbent bank can charge these mark-ups and still leave the borrower in risk class C′ indifferent between staying with the incumbent bank and switching to an outside bank. Thus, the incumbent bank will set

$$i^A_{2C'} = i_{min} + M_{2A} \tag{11}$$

$$i^B_{2C'} = i_{min} + M_{2B} \tag{12}$$

With this set-up, all borrowers who are successful in the first period go to the commercial paper market in the second period. All borrowers who default on first-period loans solicit offers simultaneously from all sources. Those who belong to risk class C accept offers from their incumbent banks, whereas those who are in risk class C′ are indifferent between borrowing from their incumbent banks and from competing banks.

The assumptions made thus far fix the outcome in period two. Imperfect competition at date 0 will determine the mark-ups M_{1A} and M_{1B} of the first-period interest rates offered by the incumbent bank over the respective one-period breakeven rates. That is, borrowers in risk class A will receive loans priced at $r_f/\delta_A + M_{1A}$ and borrowers in risk class B will receive loans priced at $r_f/\delta_B + M_{1B}$.

3.2   Banks' portfolio decisions

The focus of the remaining analysis is on a bank's first-period portfolio decision. Each bank must choose the fraction λ of its $\$D$ in deposits to be loaned to type A borrowers and the fraction $1 - \lambda$ to be loaned to type B borrowers. For simplicity, we set $D = 1$ and focus our analysis on the polar case in which borrower returns are perfectly correlated *within* risk classes but are independent *across* risk classes.

The assumption of perfect correlation within risk classes implies either all of a bank's type A borrowers succeed or all fail. Similarly, type B borrowers all succeed or fail. This means that, for a given bank, there are

Table 10.1. *Financial states of the world for the bank at the end of the first period*

State	Description	Probability of state	Bank's first-period cash flow	Bank's survival
I	Both types succeed	$\delta_A \delta_B$	$\lambda\left(\dfrac{r_f}{\delta_A} + M_{1A}\right) + (1-\lambda)\left(\dfrac{r_f}{\delta_B} + M_{1B}\right) - r_f$	Bank survives
II	Type As succeed Type Bs fail	$\delta_A(1-\delta_B)$	$\max\left[\lambda\left(\dfrac{r_f}{\delta_A} + M_{1A}\right) - r_f, 0\right]$	Bank fails if $\lambda < \delta_A r_f(r_f + \delta_A M_{1A})^{-1}$
III	Type As fail Type Bs succeed	$\delta_B(1-\delta_A)$	$\max\left[(1-\lambda)\left(\dfrac{r_f}{\delta_B} + M_{1B}\right) - r_f, 0\right]$	Bank fails if $\lambda < 1 - \delta_B r_f(r_f + \delta_B M_{1B})^{-1}$
IV	Both types fail	$(1-\delta_A)(1-\delta_B)$	0	Bank fails.

four relevant states in period one, which we denote I–IV. Table 10.1 describes the relevant properties of these states as a function of the portfolio decision λ.

It is useful to summarize the information in Table 10.1 graphically. This is done in Figures 10.2 and 10.3. Figure 10.2 shows first-period cash flows as a function of λ from low- and high-risk borrowers, respectively. When the cash flows from a given borrower class are positive, the bank survives in the states in which that borrower class succeeds while the other fails. For example, if $\lambda > \delta_A r_f(r_f + \delta_A M_{1A})^{-1}$, the bank will survive if the type As succeed but the type Bs fail. Note that there are two cases, depending on whether $\delta_A r_f(r_f + \delta_A M_{1A})^{-1} + \delta_B r_f(r_f + \delta_B M_{1B})^{-1} > 1$ or $\delta_A r_f(r_f + \delta_A M_{1A})^{-1} + \delta_B r_f(r_f + \delta_B M_{1B})^{-1} < 1$. Henceforth, to simplify notation, let $a \equiv r_f(r_f + \delta_A M_{1A})^{-1}$ and $b \equiv r_f(r_f + \delta_B M_{1B})^{-1}$.

Figure 10.3 shows the bank's survival probability as a function of λ. As before, there are two cases. When $a\delta_A + b\delta_B < 1$, the bank's survival probability is maximized over an interior range $[a\delta_A, 1 - b\delta_B]$. When $a\delta_A + b\delta_B > 1$, the bank's survival probability is maximized over the end range $[a\delta_A, 1]$. A discussion of the economics of these relationships will be deferred until we discuss the bank's profit-maximizing portfolio choice.

Table 10.1 in conjunction with the figures enables us to calculate the bank's first-period expected profit per dollar of deposits, $E\Pi_1(\lambda)$. For the case of $a\delta_A + b\delta_B < 1$, we have

$$E\Pi_1(\lambda) = \delta_A \delta_B(\varDelta + \varLambda - 1)r_f$$
$$+ \begin{cases} \delta_B(1 - \delta_A)(\varLambda - 1)r_f & \lambda \in [0, a\delta_A] \\ \left\{ \begin{matrix} [\delta_B(1 - \delta_A)(\varLambda - 1)r_f + \\ \delta_A(1 - \delta_B)(\varDelta - 1)r_f] \end{matrix} \right\} & \lambda \in [a\delta_A, 1 - b\delta_B] \\ \delta_A(1 - \delta_B)(\varDelta - 1)r_f & \lambda \in [1 - b\delta_B, 1] \end{cases}$$

where $\varDelta \equiv \lambda/a\delta_A$ and $\varLambda \equiv (1 - \lambda)/b\delta_B$. For the case of $a\delta_A + b\delta_B > 1$, we have

$$E\Pi_1(\lambda) = \delta_A \delta_B(\varDelta + \varLambda - 1)r_f$$
$$+ \begin{cases} \delta_B(1 - \delta_A)(\varLambda - 1)r_f & \lambda \in [0, 1 - b\delta_B] \\ 0 & \lambda \in [1 - b\delta_B, a\delta_A] \\ \delta_A(1 - \delta_B)(\varDelta - 1)r_f & \lambda \in [a\delta_A, 1] \end{cases}$$

The expected first-period profit function is displayed in Figure 10.4 for the case in which $M_{1A} = M_{1B} = 0$. In this case, first-period expected profit is maximized by choosing the riskiest portfolio, $\lambda = 0$. In general, it is straightforward to establish that $E\Pi_1(\lambda)$ either has the shape shown in Figure 10.4 (i.e. has an interior minimum) or it is strictly monotone in λ. Thus, the portfolio that maximizes first-period expected profit is either

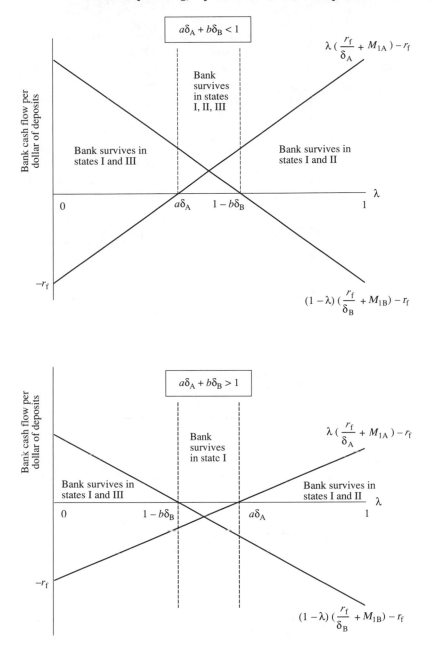

Figure 10.2 Bank's cash flow per dollar of deposits as a function of portfolio choice λ

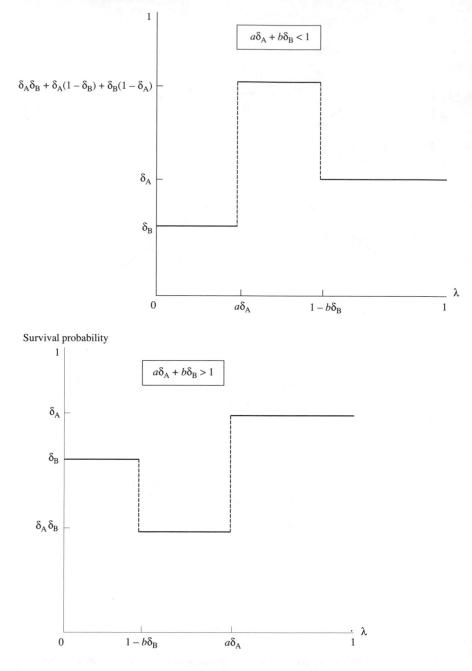

Figure 10.3   **Bank's survival probability as a function of portfolio choice** λ

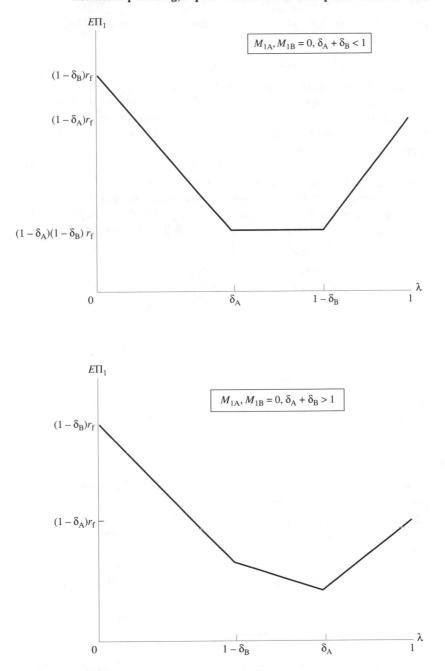

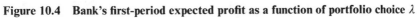

Figure 10.4 Bank's first-period expected profit as a function of portfolio choice λ

$\lambda = 0$ or $\lambda = 1$. In general, $\lambda = 0$ maximizes first-period expected profit if and only if

$$(\delta_A - \delta_B) r_f \geq \delta_A M_{1A} - \delta_B M_{1B}. \tag{13}$$

Hereafter we assume that condition (13) holds.

The bank's second-period cash flow is also dependent on the four states identified in Table 10.1. In states I and IV, the bank's second-period cash flow is zero. In state IV, this occurs because the bank fails. In state I, this occurs because both borrower types succeed and can thus gain access to the commercial paper market at the riskless rate. In states II and III, the bank's period two cash flows are positive because the bank has survived but is faced with at least one type of borrower who failed and must therefore rely on the bank to finance the risky second-period project. The bank's second-period expected profit per dollar of deposits, $E\Pi_2(\lambda)$, is given as follows. For $a\delta_A + b\delta_B < 1$,

$$E\Pi_2(\lambda) = \begin{cases} \lambda J_2 & \lambda \in [0, a\delta_A] \\ \lambda J_2 + (1 - \lambda) K_2 & \lambda \in [a\delta_A, 1 - b\delta_B] \\ (1 - \lambda) K_2 & \lambda \in [1 - b\delta_B, 1], \end{cases}$$

where

$$J_2 \equiv (1 - \delta_A) \delta_B \{ a\delta_C(1)[i_{2C}^A - r_f] + (1 - a)\delta_{C'}[i_{2C'}^A - r_f] \}.$$

$$K_2 \equiv (1 - \delta_B) \delta_A \{ \beta\delta_C(1)[i_{2C}^B - r_f] + (1 - \beta)\delta_{C'}[i_{2C'}^B - r_f] \}.$$

If, by contrast, $a\delta_A + b\delta_B > 1$, then

$$E\Pi_2(\lambda) = \begin{cases} \lambda J_2 & \lambda \in [0, 1 - b\delta_B] \\ 0 & \\ (1 - \lambda) K_2 & \lambda \in [a\delta_A, 1]. \end{cases}$$

Period two expected profits as a function of λ are displayed in Figure 10.5 for the case in which $M_{1A} = M_{1B} = 0$.

The bank will make its portfolio decision to maximize the present value of first- and second-period profits. The solution to this problem is difficult to characterize because the discontinuous piecewise linearity of the objective function gives rise to a host of different cases. What is clear, however, is that there are only four possible solutions to the bank's portfolio problem: $\lambda = 0$, $\lambda = a\delta_A$, $\lambda = 1 - b\delta_B$, and $\lambda = 1$. But given (13), we can immediately rule out $\lambda = 1$. This is because $E\Pi_1(0) > E\Pi_1(1)$ and $E\Pi_2(0) = E\Pi_2(1) = 0$. Thus, it is never optimal for a bank to lend solely to the low-risk borrowers. The reason for this is that if $\lambda = 1$ and the bank survives in period one, it can only be because the type A borrowers succeeded in period one. But in that case these borrowers will gain access

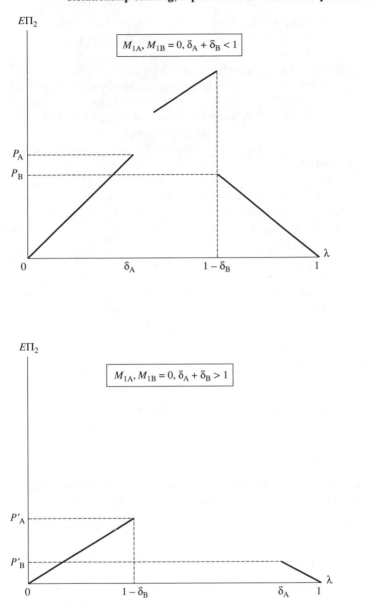

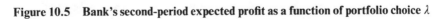

Figure 10.5   Bank's second-period expected profit as a function of portfolio choice λ

to the commercial paper market and the bank earns nothing in period two. Thus, there is no second-period gain to offset the deposit insurance put option effect in period one.

The bank's first-period portfolio choice will be interior if either $\lambda = a\delta_A$ or $\lambda = 1 - b\delta_B$ dominates $\lambda = 0$. Setting $\lambda = 0$ gives the bank an expected profit $(1 - \delta_B)r_f + \delta_B M_{1B}$ in period one and zero in period two (period two profit is zero because all borrowers either succeed or fail; if they succeed, the bank loses them to the commercial paper market; if they fail, the bank fails). When $a\delta_A + b\delta_B < 1$, setting $\lambda = 1 - b\delta_B$ gives the bank a period one expected profit of $(1 - \delta_A)[1 - b\delta_B]r_f + \delta_A(1 - b\delta_B)M_{1A} + \delta_A b\delta_B^2 M_{1B}$ and a period two expected profit given by $(1 - b\delta_B)J_2 + b\delta_B K_2$. The corner solution will be dominated if J_2 and K_2 are sufficiently large, which will be true if the period two interest factors i_{2C}^A, i_{2C}^B, $i_{2C'}^A$, $i_{2C'}^B$ are sufficiently large, δ_C and $\delta_C(1)$ are sufficiently large, or a and β are sufficiently large.

If $a\delta_A + b\delta_B > 1$, and the bank chooses $\lambda = 1 - b\delta_B$, it achieves first-period profit equal to $\delta_B(1 - b\delta_B)r_f + (b - 1)\delta_A \delta_B r_f + \delta_A \delta_B(1 - b\delta_B)M_{1A} + \delta_A b\delta_B^2 M_{1B}$ and a second-period expected profit equal to $(1 - b\delta_B)J_2$. The corner solution will be dominated if J_2 is sufficiently large, which is true if i_{2C}^A, $i_{2C'}^A$ are large, δ_C and $\delta_C(1)$ are large, and a is large.

To summarize this discussion, we state:

Proposition 1: A bank's first-period portfolio problem will have an interior solution ($\lambda \in (0,1)$) if one or more of the following conditions hold:

(i)   the period two interest factors, $i_{2C'}^A = i_{2C}^B$, $i_{2C'}^A$, and $i_{2C'}^B$, are sufficiently large,
(ii) δ_C and $\delta_C(1)$ are sufficiently high,
(iii) a and β are sufficiently high.

Proposition 1 confirms the intuition that the prospect of second-period rents counteracts the perverse risk incentives created by deposit insurance in period one.

3.3   Perfect competition

When the banking industry is perfectly competitive, the second-period mark-ups M_{2A} and M_{2B} are zero so that $i_{2C'}^A = i_{2C'}^B = i_{min} = r_f/\delta_C$ and the first-period mark-ups M_{1A} and M_{1B} must be such that a bank's two-period profit is zero, given its optimal first-period portfolio choice. That is, M_{1A} and M_{1B} must be such that

$$0 = \underset{\lambda}{\text{Max}} \ \{E\Pi_1(\lambda)|M_{1A}, M_{1B}) + E\Pi_2(\lambda|M_{1A}, M_{1B})\}, \tag{14}$$

where $E\Pi_2$ is evaluated at $i_{2C'}^A = i_{2C'}^B = i_{min}$ and $i_{2C}^A = i_{2C}^B = i_{max}$. Because $E\Pi_2(\lambda \,|\, M_{1A}, M_{1B}) \geq 0$ for all M_{1A}, M_{1B}, it follows that M_{1A} and M_{1B} must be such that expected profits in period one are less than or equal to zero. In particular, it is straightforward to show that either M_{1A} or M_{1B} must be non-positive. Because (14) is a single equation in two unknowns, the mark-ups are not determined uniquely. Thus, (14) describes a locus of equilibrium mark-ups, M_{1A} and M_{1B}.

An important issue is whether there are conditions under which the bank has a unique interior portfolio choice when there is perfect competition. The next proposition shows that there are constellations of parameter values under which an interior optimum exists.

Proposition 2: There exist constellations of parameters under which, given perfect competition, the bank's optimal first-period portfolio choice is interior.

Proof: Suppose $\delta_A \approx 1$, and let $M_{1A} = 0$ so that $a = 1$ (recall M_{1A} and M_{1B} are not unique so that this is without loss of generality). Since $\delta_A \approx 1$, the relevant case is thus $a\delta_A > 1 - b\delta_B$.

Let λ^* be a candidate equilibrium portfolio choice, and note that λ^* will be an interior optimum if there exists M_{1B}^* such that

$$E\Pi_1(\lambda^* \,|\, M_{1B}^*) + \lambda^* J_2 = 0 \tag{15}$$

and

$$E\Pi_2(0 \,|\, M_{1B}^*) < 0.$$

This last condition is equivalent to:

$$M_{1B}^* < \frac{-(1 - \delta_B)}{\delta_B} r_f. \tag{16}$$

We now show that (15) implies (16). Suppose (15) holds but $M_{1B}^* \geq [-(1 - \delta_B)r_f]/\delta_B$. Note that λ^* must equal either δ_A or $1 - b\delta_B$. In either case, given $M_{1A} = 0$,

$$E\Pi_1(\lambda^* \,|\, M_{1B}^*) = \delta_A \delta_B \left[\frac{\lambda^*}{\delta_A} + \frac{(1 - \lambda^*)}{\delta_B} + \frac{(1 - \lambda^*)}{r_f} M_{1B}^* - 1 \right] r_f.$$

Thus, if $M_{1B}^* \geq [(1 - \delta_B)/\delta_B] r_f$, then

$$0 = E\Pi_1(\lambda^* \,|\, M_{1B}) + \lambda^* J_2$$

$$\geq \delta_A \delta_B \left[\frac{\lambda^*}{\delta_A} + \frac{(1 - \lambda^*)}{\delta_B} - \frac{(1 - \lambda^*)(1 - \delta_B)}{\delta_B} - 1 \right] r_f + \lambda^* J_2$$

$$\geq \delta_A \delta_B \left[\frac{\lambda^*}{\delta_A} - \lambda^* \right] r_f + \lambda^* J_2 > 0,$$

a contradiction. Thus, the equilibrium portfolio choice cannot be at a corner in this case.   QED

3.4   *Implications for borrower welfare*

We now turn to an analysis of borrower welfare. A first-period borrower has an *ex ante* interest in the incumbent bank's survival because of the possibility of sharing the gains from the informational surplus generated by their relationship with the bank.

A borrower who is in risk class A in the first period computes their expected utility, conditional on receiving bank financing in the first period, as

$$U_A = \delta_A\{R_1 - r_f\delta_A^{-1} + S - r_f\}$$

$$+ [1 - \delta_A]\left\{\begin{matrix} \xi[a\{\delta_C(1)[R_2 - i_{2C}^A] - W\} + (1 - a)\delta_C[R_2 - i_{2C'}^A]] \\ + [1 - \xi]\delta_C[R_2 - i_{2C'}^A] \end{matrix}\right\} \quad (17)$$

where S is the payoff on the borrower's second-period project if they succeed in the first period and is thus riskless in the second period, and ξ is the probability that the incumbent bank survives after the first period. Note that, if the incumbent bank survives, the borrower gets their second-period loan at i_{2C}^A (and they choose $e = 1$) if they are in risk class C, and $i_{2C'}^A$ if they are in risk class C'. If the incumbent bank fails, the borrower must rely exclusively on outside banks. If they are in risk class C or C', they will receive a loan at the interest factor $i_{\min}$, and borrowers in risk class C gaining access to outside banks will choose $e = 0$.

In similar fashion, we can write the expected utility of a borrower who is in risk class B in the first period, as follows

$$U_B = \delta_B\{R_1 - r_f\delta_B^{-1} + S - r_f\}$$

$$+ [1 - \delta_B]\left\{\begin{matrix} \xi[\beta\{\delta_C(1)[R_2 - i_{2C}^A] - W\} + (1 - \beta)\delta_C[R_2 - i_{2C'}^B]] \\ + [1 - \xi]\delta_C[R_2 - i_{2C'}^B] \end{matrix}\right\}. \quad (18)$$

We can now see the impact of ξ on the borrower's welfare. We know that

$$\delta_C(1)[R_2 - i_{2C}^l] - W = \delta_C[R_2 - i_{2C}^l] > \delta_C[R_2 - i_{2C'}^l], \quad l \in \{A, B\},$$

since $i_{2C}^l < i_{2C'}^l$. Thus, the term multiplying ξ in (17) is strictly greater than the term multiplying $1 - \xi$. Thus, $\partial U_l/\partial\xi > 0$ for $l \in \{A, B\}$, i.e. both types of borrower are better off as one improves ξ, the survival probability of the bank, holding everything else fixed.

Any factor that increases the likelihood of an interior optimal solution to the bank's portfolio problem will enhance the bank's survival probability and work to increase borrower welfare. One such factor is *bank market structure.* As market structure becomes less competitive, there is an increase in the bank's mark-ups M_{2A} and M_{2B} on loans to borrowers in risk class C' in the second period and hence the bank is more likely (i.e. for a larger set of exogenous parameter values) to make interior optimal portfolio choices, as indicated in Proposition 1. Of course, making the market structure less competitive also hurts borrowers directly because the risk class C' borrowers pay higher interest rates. Thus, it is not obvious that the overall impact on borrower welfare is positive. However, one can assert that there are parameter shifts that do result in an improvement in borrower welfare. Suppose $a\delta_A + b\delta_B < 1$, and assume that exogenous parameter values are such that the bank is just below the point at which it is indifferent between $\lambda = 0$ and $\lambda = 1 - b\delta_B$. In this case, the bank's optimal portfolio choice is $\lambda = 0$ and its survival probability is $\xi = \delta_B$. Now suppose the banking market becomes slightly less competitive so that $i_{2C'}^A$ and $i_{2C'}^B$ increase by infinitesimal amounts. The bank's optimal portfolio choice switches from $\lambda = 0$ to $\lambda = 1 - b\delta_B$. From Figure 10.3, we see that this increases the bank's survival probability from δ_B to $\delta_B + \delta_A[1 - \delta_B]$. The increases in $i_{2C'}^A$ and $i_{2C'}^B$ have a negative, but infinitesimal, impact on the borrower's *ex ante* expected utility, but the positive effect of the discrete jump in the bank's survival probability implies an increase in overall borrower welfare.

When $a\delta_A + b\delta_B > 1$, the bank's survival probability is maximized with a portfolio choice of $\lambda = a\delta_A$. In this case, the welfare implications of making banking less competitive are not clear because whether $\lambda = a\delta_A$ or not depends on the relative magnitudes of $i_{2C'}^A$ and $i_{2C'}^B$, among other things. Making bank market structure less competitive has an ambiguous effect on the bank's survival probability and a directly negative effect on the borrowers through an increase in their expected borrowing cost. We summarize this discussion in the following proposition.

Proposition 3: (a) If $a\delta_A + b\delta_B < 1$, making bank market structure less competitive works to enhance the bank's survival probability, which may benefit the borrowers. (b) If $a\delta_A + b\delta_B > 1$, making bank market structure less competitive has an ambiguous effect on the bank's survival probability.

We can also use this framework to analyse the implications of improving capital market access to a given set of borrowers. Suppose, in contrast to the above analysis, that a type A borrower who fails in period one and becomes a type C' borrower in period two can be distinguished as such by the commercial paper market. Thus, unlike the above situation in which a borrower of this sort was captive to an imperfectly competitive banking market, now this borrower can gain access to the commercial paper market in period two. This means that the interest rate charged by banks,

$i_{2C'}^\Lambda$, can no longer exceed the competitive level, r_f/δ_C. Thus, the effect of improving capital market access to a given subset of borrowers is analogous to a decrease in the second-period interest rates for these borrowers. This directly benefits these borrowers, but it may also exert a negative externality on the other class of borrowers. Specifically, for the case in which $a\delta_A + b\delta_B < 1$, a reduction in $i_{2C'}^\Lambda$ makes an interior solution to the bank's portfolio problem less likely to occur (recall Proposition 1). If improved capital market access causes a switch from $\lambda = 1 - b\delta_B$ to $\lambda = 0$, then, from Figure 10.3, the bank's survival probability will drop, and this will reduce the *ex ante* welfare of type B borrowers who receive bank loans. In effect what has happened here is that improved capital market access for a subset of a bank's borrower pool reduces the value of the bank's relationship portfolio and distorts the bank's asset portfolio choice in the direction of greater risk. This hurts borrowers whose capital market access has not improved.

4   Policy implications

Our analysis produces a number of implications for various banking issues that are being currently debated. We discuss each in turn below.

4.1   Banks' portfolio choices

When relationship banking is important, we have shown that commercial banks' asset portfolio choices depend on a variety of factors: the size of the deposit insurance subsidy, banking market structure, and the size of an incumbent bank's informational advantage relative to competing banks and the capital market. The deposit insurance subsidy effect raises interesting regulatory issues, which we discuss shortly. We have shown that, conditional on the assumed closure policy, the prospect of dealing repeatedly with borrowers has a potentially significant effect on the bank's *ex ante* portfolio choice. In general, of course, the bank's optimal portfolio choice will depend also on the regulatory closure policy and will deviate further from the risk-minimizing solution if the bank is faced with something less severe than the most draconian bank closure policy of certain charter termination upon failure that we have assumed here. But the broader point remains valid: a concern with protecting rents that arise from relationship-specific informational advantages will work to offset the distortionary effects of the deposit insurance put option and will thus improve bank safety.

Banking market structure and the size of an incumbent bank's informational advantage will also impinge on the bank's portfolio choice.

Greater competition and/or a smaller informational advantage in dealing repeatedly with borrowers will induce greater portfolio risk. Intertemporal linkages in borrowers' risk classes are important as well. If borrowers' future risk classifications are extremely sensitive to cash flow realizations, so that poor realizations lead to borrowers becoming poor credit risks and good realizations lead to relatively easy access to alternative credit sources, then too will banks be induced to choose high levels of portfolio risk.

From a policy standpoint, this suggests that regulators face a complex task in coming up with reforms aimed at improving banking stability. Restricting entry into banking to retard interbank competition will enhance stability, and this is a choice variable for regulators. However, this regulatory initiative will be of limited help if capital markets become more efficient in processing credit information and/or the interbank flow of borrower-specific information itself improves so much that incumbent banks cannot retain significant proprietary rights to information about their borrowers. Apart from relaxed barriers to entry into US banking, these other factors also appear to have played a contributing role in increasing the fragility of US depository institutions. For instance, commercial paper issues in the US have grown sixfold in dollar volume in the last two decades. It is difficult to visualize much regulatory control over these developments.

4.2   Borrower welfare and banking deregulation

Our analysis exposes the fallacy of the 'common wisdom' that the lowering of the price of credit due to increased competition in banking will be good for all borrowers. Increased competition leads to lower bank charter values, which in turn leads to riskier (endogenously determined) asset portfolio choices by banks. With relationship banking, one can expect banks and borrowers to share the informational surplus arising from their relationship. Hence, the higher bank insolvency probability resulting from riskier loans increases the likelihood of disruption of bank–customer relationships and the associated destruction of valuable information. The cost of this for some borrowers may exceed the benefit of lower loan interest rates.

From the vantage point of regulators, this implies that striking a delicate balance between the cost of reduced bank safety for borrowers and the benefit of lower loan interest rates for borrowers must be a consideration in determining whether banking should be made more competitive. Of course, by choosing not to close failed institutions, regulators can protect the sanctity of bank–borrower relationships. But this comes at a cost. As the probability of closing a failed bank declines, banks will find the pursuit of risk more attractive. This raises a fundamental *time consistency* issue in bank closure policy, and is at the heart of the debate on the 'too big to fail' controversy in the US.

Another interesting issue has to do with the manner in which improved capital market access for *some* borrowers affects *other* borrowers. Suppose that a subset of the bank's currently profitable borrowers now find it preferable to go to the capital market. This depletes banks' charter values and induces greater portfolio risk. The borrowers who do not enjoy capital market access still have something to gain from relationship banking, but find that the higher risk in banking reduces the value of relationship banking to them. Hence, these borrowers are worse off even though some other borrowers are better off owing to their own improved access to the capital market. This implies that the welfare implications of reducing the *uniqueness* of banks are ambiguous.

4.3 The role of regulatory subsidies

One implication of our analysis is that regulators may wish to adopt a deposit insurance pricing scheme that links the premium charged to the bank's performance. As the number of periods over which the bank has survived without regulatory assistance grows larger, the bank's premium per dollar of insured deposits should decline. Indeed, a point should be reached beyond which the premium is subsidized. The enticement of access to future regulatory subsidies (which could go beyond just deposit insurance subsidies) will be a powerful deterrent to risk taking for the bank.

If the banking industry is highly imperfectly competitive, the importance of regulatory subsidies as a risk deterrent is diminished because bank charters have high value without subsidies. Subsidies grow in importance, however, as banking becomes more competitive and/or capital markets provide access to more firms. The irony is that *financing* subsidies through general tax revenues becomes increasingly expensive as greater competitiveness is achieved through an increase in the number of banks.

4.4 Post-unification European banking

What European unification means for banks in Europe will depend on three factors: the impact of unification on the competitiveness of European credit markets, the impact of unification on the political/economic feasibility of government subsidies for banks, and the evolution of (integrated) European capital markets in the post-unification era. As for the first effect, it is not obvious to us what the overall impact of unification will be on competition. In some parts of Europe, it is reasonable to expect unification to increase competition as new arrivals – encouraged by unification – begin to develop 'toe-holds' in previously unexplored markets. But in other parts of Europe, it may well be that unification leads to *consolidations* that *reduce* competition. If unification indeed leads to greater competition, then its effect will be to increase banking industry risk in Europe.

As for the second effect, it is likely that unification will make it more difficult for governments to subsidize banks headquartered in their own countries because of the obvious political ramifications of endowing these banks with an 'unfair' advantage relative to their European competitors. This will result in greater portfolio risks being chosen by European banks.

Finally, a big question mark hangs over the issue of what unification will entail for European capital markets. Because of the traditional dominance of banks in Europe, capital markets in European countries are generally not as well developed as in the US. It is possible that the increased mobility of capital facilitated by unification will lead to a growth in the scope/sophistication of European capital markets. Our analysis implies that this is likely to induce banks to choose riskier asset portfolios.

5   Conclusion

We have examined a host of issues related to interbank competition and competition between banks and the capital market in a setting of relationship banking. Our focus has been on banks' asset portfolio choices and their consequences for *borrowers'* welfare. We have shown that increased interbank competition *may* actually make *all* borrowers worse off. Moreover, improved capital market access for some borrowers may make other borrowers worse off. These observations raise fundamental issues related to bank market structure and the relationship between the bank credit market and the capital market that deserve further study.

NOTES

We thank Richard Gilbert, Carmen Matutes and Xavier Vives for their comments. Only the authors are responsible for any remaining infelicities.
1 Chan, Greenbaum and Thakor (1992) show that *risk-sensitive* deposit insurance pricing may not be feasible in a competitive banking environment.
2 Keeley (1990) provides empirical support for the hypothesis that a sufficiently large bank charter value restrains risk taking.
3 Sharpe (1990) and Rajan (1991) also show that informational rents can arise from bank–customer relationships. See the discussion of this in Bhattacharya and Thakor (1991).

4 See, for example, Bryant (1980), Diamond and Dybvig (1983) and Chari and Jagannathan (1988).
5 This means we do not endogenize the debt contract as, for example, in Townsend (1979).
6 We do not address the time consistency issues this raises. In this respect, our set-up is similar to the rationing policy in Stiglitz and Weiss (1983).
7 One possible strategy for an outside bank would be to try and use the result of its screening to distinguish among various borrower types. The lowest rate that the bank could charge a borrower with first-period type j and a signal σ about the borrower's second-period type is $i'_{min}(j,\sigma)$. If this rate were lower than i_{max} for some $(j,\sigma = C)$ combination, then the outside bank would be able to offer a rate between $i'_{min}(j,\sigma = C)$ and i_{max} to those borrowers, screen out other borrowers and make a profit. To preclude this, we assume

$$r_f[\sigma_C(1)]^{-1} < i_{max} < i'_{min}(A,\sigma = C).$$

Since $i'_{min}(A,\sigma = C) < i'_{min}(B,\sigma = C)$, the above inequality ensures that outside banks cannot bid away borrowers who are being offered i_{max} by the incumbent bank, recalling that outside banks cannot see the offers made by incumbent banks. Thus, the outside bank can only attract borrowers with success probability δ_C, and hence its equilibrium rate is i_{min}. We thank the discussant, Carmen Matutes, for raising this issue with us.
8 The excess of $i_{2C'}^A$ and $i_{2C'}^B$ over i_{min} respectively may be due to spatial considerations as in Besanko and Thakor (forthcoming).

REFERENCES

Besanko, D. and A.V. Thakor (forthcoming) 'Banking deregulation: allocational consequences of relaxing entry barriers', *Journal of Banking and Finance*.
Bhattacharya, S. and A.V. Thakor (1991) 'Contemporary banking theory', Working Paper 504, Indiana University, November.
Bryant, J. (1980) 'A model of reserves, bank runs, and deposit insurance', *Journal of Banking and Finance* **4**, December, 335–44.
Chan, Y.-S., S.I. Greenbaum and A.V. Thakor (1992) 'Is fairly priced deposit insurance possible?', *Journal of Finance*, forthcoming.
Chari, V.V. and R. Jagannathan (1988) 'Banking panics, information, and rational expectations equilibrium', *Journal of Finance* **43**, July, 749–61.
Diamond, D.W. and P. Dybvig (1983) 'Bank runs, deposit insurance, and liquidity', *Journal of Political Economy* **91**, June, 401–19.
Keeley, M.C. (1990) 'Deposit insurance, risk, and market power in banking', *American Economic Review* **80**, December, 1183–200.
Matutes, C. and X. Vives (1991) 'Competition for deposits, risk of failure, and regulation in banking', Working Paper, CSIC, Universitat Autònoma de Barcelona, September.
Merton, R.C. (1977) 'An analytic derivation of the cost of deposit insurance loans guarantees', *Journal of Banking and Finance* **1**, June, 3–11.
Rajan, R. (1991) 'Insiders and outsiders: the choice between relationship and armslength debt', Working Paper, MIT, April.
Sharpe, S.A. (1990) 'Asymmetric information, bank lending, and implicit contracts: a stylized model of customer relationships', *Journal of Finance* **55**, September, 1069–87.

Stiglitz, J.D. and A. Weiss (1983) 'Incentive effects of terminations: applications to the credit and labor markets', *American Economic Review* **73**(5), 912–27.

Townsend, R.M. (1979) 'Optimal contracts and competitive markets with costly state verification', *Journal of Economic Theory* **21**, 1–29.

von Thadden, E. (1990) 'Bank finance and long-term investment', WWZ Discussion Paper No. 9010, University of Basel.

Winton, A. (1991) 'Competition among financial intermediaries when diversification matters', Working Paper, Northwestern University, December.

Wong, K.P. (1991) 'Efficiency and banking structure under product market competition', Working Paper, UBC, November.

Discussion

RICHARD J. GILBERT

In most industries, competition benefits consumers by encouraging firms to reduce costs and improve service. Besanko and Thakor join a growing chorus of academics who argue that the banking industry is different. Deposit insurance is a key element that distinguishes the impact of competition in banking. Competition in the financial market benefits borrowers in the short run by lowering the price of loans, but competition also causes banks to operate on thinner margins and deposit insurance may tempt banks to hold risky portfolios, knowing that they are shielded from down-side risk. Thin margins and risky portfolios increase the risk that a bank may fail, which is bad for borrowers who have developed valued relationships with the failed bank.

Deposit insurance is a 'put option' that allows the bank to sell its assets at a zero price if liabilities exceed assets. If a bank faces two alternative loan prospects, both with a zero expected return, the alternative with a higher variance (the more risky loan) would offer an insured bank a higher expected profit. Reducing the extent of competition would have (roughly) the effect of increasing the returns to the bank in every state of nature, so the bank would be less likely to exercise the deposit insurance put option. A less competitive environment would diminish the value of deposit insurance and make the bank more accountable for the hazards as well as the benefits of a risky loan. In the absence of competition, the bank would accept the more risky prospect only if the expected returns compensated the bank for its higher risk of loan losses.

Besanko and Thakor undertake the ambitious task of rigorously demonstrating the link between imperfect competition and the composition of banking portfolios in an environment with deposit insurance. Imperfect competition in their model arises from competition among banks for customers in a known risk class and from private information that banks have about customers with whom they have had prior banking relationships. Both elements of imperfect competition are important to the results in this paper. Imperfect competition for loans of known risk permits each bank to achieve higher expected cash flow from a given loan portfolio. High cash flow reduces the probability of bank failure and may discourage risk taking, because the bank would not want poor loan performance to trigger a failure and consequently jeopardize future profits. Imperfect competition that arises from private information about borrowers allows Besanko and Thakor to explore the benefits of long-term relationships to the bank and its customers, and to investigate how these benefits are affected by portfolio risk.

Borrowers differ in this model in their risk classes in the first period, before they take out a loan, and in the second period, after they experience the results of their investments. Before any borrowing takes place, borrowers can be either low (type A) or high (type B) risk, where risk is the probability that the borrowers will default. In the second period, if the investment is a success, the borrower is declared to be riskless. If the investment fails, both types are assumed to fall into one of two risk classes in the second period, both risky. These classes differ in that one is assumed to respond to the borrower's effort, while the other does not. The two types of borrower, A and B, differ in the probabilities of becoming one of the two risk classes in the second period conditional on failure.

This is obviously a complex model structure. Add to it competition among banks for customers in both periods, the actions of depositors and the deposit insurer, and the capital market, all of which influence the possible equilibria, and this is a model that mirrors only too well the intricacies of actual financial markets. The authors don't give the reader much coaching into why all their apparatus is necessary, but the multiplicity of risk classes in the second period appears central to the paper's emphasis on relationship banking. Besanko and Thakor assume that a borrower's first-period bank has perfect knowledge of its borrower's risk class in the second period. Other banks know the borrower's risk class imperfectly, because the borrower's actual risk depends on his effort, which only the incumbent bank knows. Unsuccessful borrowers split into two groups in the second period, with borrowers in one group (where risk depends on effort) accepting offers from their incumbent banks and borrowers in the second group accepting offers from either their incumbent banks or other banks. The private information possessed by incumbent banks benefits those borrowers who fall in the first camp.

Having derived the equilibrium interest rates for each risk class, the paper next takes a step backwards and determines the composition of bank portfolios between low (type A) and high (type B) risk customers in the first period. They show that, if first-period competition is sufficiently intense, banks will have a tendency to load their portfolios with high-risk customers. Intense competition limits banking profits to the rents that can be earned from private information in the second period. In this model, the bank has private information only if borrowers in one of the risk classes fail in the first period. If both types of borrowers succeed, they can borrow from the credit market at a riskless rate. (If both fail, the bank has no cash flow in the first period and is assumed to fail.) The bank would not want to load its portfolio with only low-risk customers, because the bank would earn nothing if they succeeded, and would go out of business if they failed. High-risk customers can be more valuable to the bank because, conditional on the bank remaining in business, they have a higher probability of becoming a source of private information that the bank can exploit. Deposit insurance limits the down-side risk of failure and therefore makes the banks willing to absorb these borrowers' greater risk.

The authors argue that the tendency of banks to weight their portfolios towards high-risk borrowers can be bad for all borrowers. Borrowers have a personal interest in the survival of their banks, because they share with their banks the value of private information about their risk characteristics, at least in some outcomes. Yet if the bank loads up on high-risk customers, the bank has a higher probability of failing after the first period, and thus denying its customers the benefits of private information.

The results in this paper depend on the degree of competition in each period, as indicated by the mark-ups on each risk class. These mark-ups are taken as exogenous, but they should be computed as equilibria in the financial market. Some of the results in the paper are derived under the assumption of zero mark-ups. The authors acknowledge, however, that zero mark-ups are not a natural outcome, even in the case of perfect competition, as competition could drive first-period mark-ups below zero when banks face expected profits in the second period. Conclusions about banks' optimal loan portfolios depend on these mark-ups, and there is little reason to believe that banks' margins for different borrowers should be the same. Although the combination of deposit insurance and relationship banking may encourage banks to lend to risky customers when customer mark-ups are similar, competition for risky loans is likely to lower their profit margins and cause a change in the banks' optimal portfolios. The authors need to close the loop. In effect, what is needed is a version of the capital asset pricing model that would generate prices for risky loans in this market.

Besanko and Thakor take a useful step towards a general theory of bank portfolio choice. Their goal is ambitious and consequently fraught with obstacles. The model in this paper is complex, perhaps more than it has to be in some respects. Yet it is also an oversimplification, because it does not close the loop and derive equilibrium prices for loans. None the less, there is no doubt that this endeavour, though risky itself, should be part of an optimal portfolio of knowledge in this important field, and the authors should be commended for their contribution.

CARMEN MATUTES

This paper explores the effects of interbank competition and competition from the capital market on borrowers' welfare in a framework where the incumbent bank has an informational advantage ('relationship banking') over outsiders. Its main conclusion is that borrowers may benefit from *imperfect* competition in banking. The authors argue that competition affects banks' optimal portfolio: with perfect competition banks cannot appropriate the benefits of 'relationship banking', which induces a more risky portfolio. Competition from both rival banks and the capital market may result in low-risk individuals not getting credit.

There are two consequences of this main conclusion. First, since relationship banking enhances profitability from the low risks, it mitigates the moral hazard problems associated with limited liability through its effect on portfolio choice. Second, to the extent that it enhances the limited liability problem and thus induces a more risky portfolio, deposit insurance may damage borrowers.

I think that the paper addresses interesting issues in a field that deserves more attention than it has had in the past. I have various concerns, however, about the validity of some of the assumptions and hence the empirical relevance of its policy conclusions. Before discussing these criticisms, I will summarize the main features of the model.

1   Summary

There are two time periods. It is assumed that banks raise D from depositors each period and pay these deposits the risk-free rate r_f. There are two types of borrowers, A (low risk) and B (high risk), and both banks and the capital market know to which class each individual belongs. At the beginning of period one, borrowers have the opportunity to undertake an investment that yields R at the end of the period in the event of success and zero otherwise; the project requires borrowing $1. The outcome of the investment is observable by everyone. If an individual succeeds, he can undertake a new riskless project in period two. Investors who failed can be in either class C or C'. Thus, at the end of period one there are four types of risky individuals: AC, AC', BC and BC'. Those in class C' are riskier than those in class C. Furthermore, the latter can increase the success probability with costly effort. Only the *incumbent bank* has information about which class an individual who failed in period one belongs to. *Outside banks* get a signal s such that:

$$\Pr(s = C'/\text{true type is } C) = \Pr(s = C/\text{true type is } C') = \phi.$$

That is, ϕ is the probability that the outside bank receives a misleading signal. The *capital market* has no information about individuals who failed in period one except for the fact that they failed.

Banks can set different rates for different individuals depending on their information about the riskiness of various types; the outside bank cannot, however, see the specific offer made by the incumbent to a particular customer. The capital market is assumed to be perfectly competitive.

The timing of the game is as follows. In period one, banks set first-period rates for each borrower class (A and B) and select a portfolio (percentage of borrowers in each class), and individuals apply for loans to various banks. In period two, banks set rates for various borrowers in their customer base and for outsiders. Individuals apply for funds to undertake the second-period project to the incumbent bank, outside banks and the capital market.

When a bank fails, the regulator collects the revenue, pays depositors r_f, and closes the bank. Parameters are constrained to be such that in period two the equilibrium is as follows:

The incumbent bank sets a lower rate than the rival for the C types, whether they are in class A or B, so as to keep them as customers and induce them to undertake costly effort. C types generate a positive expected profit to the incumbent bank

The incumbent bank sets the same rate to the C' types as the outside bank (except for an exogenous mark-up that reflects the extent of competition). This rate is of course higher than the one offered to the C types.

Once second-period equilibrium rates are determined, the authors solve for the first-period outcome of the game. First-period rates are set ignoring the expected future benefits that various borrower types will yield; the portfolio choice, on the other hand, is chosen taking into account its consequences for future profitability. The authors focus on the case of perfect correlation within risk classes and independence across classes and show that, under some conditions, (a) the equilibrium portfolio is interior so that both types get loans, and (b) an increase in banking competition may hurt the borrowers. The intuition is that in period two the incumbent bank can exploit individuals who failed in period one but who are relatively good risks, and hence it does not pay to specialize in high risks.[1] An increase in competition limits the profitability from these relatively low-risk types, however, and as a result may induce the bank to focus on high-risk individuals.

2   Comments

My main criticism of the paper is that competition for loans is not modelled explicitly, it is embodied in *exogenous* margins. Furthermore, banks ignore future profits when setting first-period interest rates. I find the combination of these two simplifications particularly problematic. It is not true that the consideration of first-period profits can be embodied in *exogenous* period one margins above the perfect competitive rates of a single-period model. This is because the equilibrium margins in period one should decrease with the expected profits in period two. Not only is it inconsistent that for some purposes (namely, portfolio choice) banks consider the future and for others they ignore it, but, in fact, full consideration of intertemporal issues might affect the conclusion. Indeed, intuition suggests that the higher the second-period expected profits from one class of borrowers, the more willing banks are to lower rates in period one for these borrower types. Hence, relationship banking may conceivably increase the likelihood that a bank fails in period one, precisely because it competes with rivals for the low-risk individuals: those who generate larger expected profits in period two. Thus, it appears that relationship banking may affect overall profits and survival probabilities in ways opposite to those claimed in the paper.

A related issue is that the information structure is completely exogenous. I find this somewhat restrictive both on the part of banks and on the part of borrowers. With respect to the former, there is a literature which explores oligopolists' incentives to share information and finds that in a wide variety of circumstances these incentives exist (see, for instance, Vives, 1984; Gal-Or, 1985, 1986; and Shapiro, 1986). Pagano and Japelli

(1991) address the issue of information sharing in the context of financial intermediation. They argue that banks may be willing to give up their informational advantage relative to competitors in order to get the benefits of more accurate information about potential borrowers. In fact, 'information brokers' such as the credit bureaus in the US or UK collect, file and distribute the information voluntarily provided by their members; they also make sure that the information is accurate, and deny further access to members that attempt to free-ride. The existence of credit bureaus indicates that there are forces driving banks to give up their informational advantages. These forces cannot be understood within the equilibrium analysed by Besanko and Thakor where there is no trade-off: the larger the informational advantage of the incumbent bank, the better off it is. On the other hand, if the implications of informational advantages were taken into account when setting first-period lending rates, banks might be willing to commit to share information to decrease competition in period one (even though in period two competition will be tougher and profits lower).

With respect to borrowers, it is assumed that they maintain a unilateral relationship with banks, that is, they do not borrow from more than one bank. It is clear, however, that, in the setting studied, entrepreneurs do have incentives to patronize more than one bank so as to avoid being (partially) exploited if they turn out to be relatively good risks. Whether entrepreneurs borrow from several banks is an empirical question; the extent to which they do jeopardizes the policy conclusions of this paper. In this sense, I would find empirical evidence supporting unilateral relationships between banks and borrowers reassuring. Moreover, the assumption that individuals cannot go to a rival bank and reveal what rate the incumbent is offering plays exactly the same role as unilateral relationships with banks. Therefore, additional evidence would be needed.

A further criticism is that the authors appear to reach conclusions that go far beyond the actual implications of the model. The paper shows that any policy measure that induces banks to undertake a more risky portfolio may hurt the borrowers, simply because the low risks may end up without credit. This applies to deposit insurance because it enhances the limited liability problem. On the other hand, it should be clear that deposit insurance does not play a role in this model, the reason being that depositors are not players in the game and competition for deposits is assumed away: $D are deposited each period in each bank and get the risk-free interest, r_f, whether or not the banks fail. Since neither the utility of depositors nor their strategies are considered, however, the solution of the model would not be affected if depositors lost everything in the event of bankruptcy. In models of competition for deposits (see for instance Matutes and Vives, 1991), equilibrium rates do depend on whether or not there is deposit insurance; and, in a world with insurance, depositors are guaranteed to earn the posted rates, not an exogenous rate, r_f. (The fact that regulators close banks that fail may be true with or without deposit insurance.)

Likewise, the statement that more competition from the capital market may be detrimental for borrowers' welfare is not substantiated. The reason is twofold. First, no comparative statics exercise is performed in the paper; throughout it is simply assumed that those borrowers who become riskless have access to a perfect capital market. A possible way to proceed is as follows. If those borrowers who become riskless at the end of period one have only a probability p of getting access to the perfect capital market (e.g. the informational advantage of the incumbent bank is larger than is assumed in the paper), does an increase in p bias the portfolio against the A types? The answer seems to be positive: an increase in p implies that the capital market is more likely to serve successful types (whether they are an A or a B type) and the probability of success is higher for low-risk types (A types). On the other hand, and this leads us to the second point, the assumption that the capital market 'does not make mistakes' and never finances high-risk individuals may be misleading. If there were a positive probability, q, that the capital market served an entrepreneur who failed in period one, an increase in q would probably modify the portfolio choice in favour of the low risks. Therefore, the implicit definition of 'competition from the capital market' is rather biased.

Overall, I find that the model explores a promising field of research and points out interesting issues relative to borrowers' welfare. On the other hand, my impression is that the empirical validity of the points raised is rather limited. In particular, I do not have many doubts that, if European unification brings about more interbank competition and competition from the capital market, the benefits from this additional competition will outweigh its costs in terms of the number of projects not undertaken because they are low risk.

NOTE

1 If the incumbent bank survives period one, it will earn most profit from individuals in class A who fail in period one and turn out to be in class C; this makes A types more attractive than B types. On the other hand, individuals in class A are more likely to succeed in period one, which makes them less desirable since they will have access to the capital market.

REFERENCES

Gal-Or, E. (1985) 'Information sharing in oligopoly', *Econometrica* **53**, 329–43.
(1986) 'Information transmission – Cournot and Bertrand equilibria', *Review of Economic Studies* **53**, 85–92.
Matutes, C. and X. Vives (1991) 'Competition for deposits, risk of failure, and regulation in banking', mimeo, Institut d'Anàlisi Econòmica.
Pagano, M. and T. Japelli (1991) 'Information sharing in the consumer credit market', Working Paper 91-5, Programa de Estudios Bancarios y Financieros, Institut d'Anàlisi Econòmica.
Shapiro, C. (1986) 'Exchange of cost information in oligopoly', *Review of Economic Studies* **53**, 433–66.
Vives, X. (1984) 'Duopoly information equilibrium: Cournot and Bertrand', *Journal of Economic Theory* **34**, 71–94.

11 Competition and bank performance: a theoretical perspective

MICHAEL H. RIORDAN

1 Introduction

Banks serve as financial intermediaries between borrowers and lenders. More precisely, banks borrow from depositors and lend to investors. In this financial intermediation role, banks perform (at least) two important functions. First, banks insure depositors, who could in principle lend directly to borrowers, against the risk of default. Second, in the process of approving loans and setting terms, banks screen investment projects. This paper is concerned with how well banks perform this second function, and with how performance depends on market structure.

In a capitalist economy most investment projects are owned and managed by private entrepreneurs and firms. Generally these investors lack enough equity fully to finance their projects and consequently seek loans to complete financing. Banks, on the other hand, aggregate deposits to make these loans. In choosing which loans to make, banks play a crucial role in determining the investment portfolio of the economy.

The loan-making decisions of banks depend on many factors. Among these are banks' assessments of the creditworthiness of a borrower and the intrinsic merit of an investment project. Banks screen loans to reduce the risk of default. The loan approval practices of banks are endogenous, however, depending on the structure of loan markets, and in particular on the nature and degree of competition.

The performance of the banking system also depends on many factors. Among these are (1) how well the banking system utilizes information about investment risks in making loans, and (2) to what extent the loan-making incentives of banks are aligned with society's interest. The analysis that follows demonstrates how these two factors are crucial for an understanding of how competition matters for bank performance.

The issue is policy relevant for Europe. The financial integration of Europe is now guided by the EC's Second Banking Directive. The centre-

328

Table 11.1. *European banking structure, 1988*

Country	No. of banks	Assets ($bn)	Concentration ratios (% of market assets)	
			5-firm	3-firm
Belgium	86	228.3	84.7	57.1
France	367	1012.6	63.0	42.3
Greece	n.a.	48.4	n.a.	n.a.
Ireland	43	22.1	n.a.	71.0
Italy	980	529.2	55.1	35.2
Luxembourg	120	198.1	22.4	16.7
Netherlands	81	272.3	n.a.	71.3
Portugal	40	43.3	n.a.	49.7
Spain	349	332.3	34.7	21.9
United Kingdom	661	1337.8	32.6	26.5
West Germany	4465	1465.0	31.2	21.2
Total EC	7192	5489.4	17.0	10.7

Source: Country data are from Gardner and Molyneux (1990, p. 33), who use data from *The Banker* (data for Greece are deposits). Concentration ratios for total EC are based on data from *The Banker* (1989).

piece of this agreement is a 'single banking licence' which makes it very easy for member country banks to expand into markets of other member countries (Devinney, 1989). The potential implications of this change are indicated in Table 11.1, which presents market structure statistics on banking for individual EC countries and for the whole EC. Both concentration ratios tell the same story. For example, the three-firm concentration ratio varies from 71.0 for Ireland to 16.7 for Luxembourg. If, however, the relevant market were the entire EC, the three-firm concentration ratio would drop to 10.7.[1]

The point is that a single banking licence for Europe could significantly increase the competitiveness of banking markets. Of course, European banking is a multimarket industry, and the single banking licence will affect some market segments more than others. The large-firm corporate loan market is already highly competitive internationally, so not much effect is expected here. On the other hand, markets for small and medium-sized loans are relatively concentrated. In these market segments, as well as in retail banking, the single banking licence is likely to have the most significance (Vives, 1991).

Is more competition in loan markets a good thing? The issue is addressed in the context of a simple screening model of lending that draws on the theory of common value auctions (Milgrom and Weber, 1982). The model suggests two reasons why more competition in loan markets might damage market performance. First, the statistic the market uses to select loans may become less informative about the quality of the loan. Second, the loan approval practices of individual banks may be too conservative, and more competition may make them even more so.

In the model, a borrower seeks a loan for an investment project that might be either productive or wasteful. Each of several lenders observes a signal about loan quality, i.e. the probability of repayment. In equilibrium, the market selects loans based on the best signal observed by any prospective lender. An increase in the number of lenders increases the number of signals observed. This may or may not improve the informativeness of the best signal. It is possible that an increase in bad loans resulting from more competition has an overwhelming negative effect on welfare. This is the first reason why more competition may damage market performance.

The second reason comes from a misalignment of social and private incentives for loan-making. In general, an entrepreneur is not willing to invest in a productive project without some anticipation of earning rents from the project. Because of this incentive problem, a lender cannot fully appropriate the returns of even a marginal loan. This failure to internalize all the benefits of a marginal loan leads lenders to adopt loan approval practices that are too conservative from a social welfare standpoint. Moreover, because of the 'winner's curse', more competition leads lenders to be even more conservative. This greater conservativeness can also reduce welfare by a significant amount.

The importance of the winner's curse in loan markets has been discussed before. Broecker (1990) takes a similar game-theoretic approach to modelling loan market competition, focusing on how the extensive form matters for equilibrium. Broecker assumes lenders observe a binary signal about loan quality, and proves the existence of a unique equilibrium in mixed strategies when lenders cannot react to each other. In contrast, I assume a continuous signal, and characterize a unique equilibrium in pure strategies. Broecker does not address normative issues, which is my main focus.[2]

Matutes and Vives (1992) also argue that competition can harm banking market performance, but for very different reasons. They focus on retail banking competition for deposits, and point out that lower margins resulting from more competition might harmfully increase the probability of a bank's insolvency. There is also an informal literature on why rents might discourage excessive risk taking by financial institutions (*Journal of Economic Perspectives*, 1989).

2 A simple model of lending

The following simple model is not intended to describe an actual banking system. It is intended only to illustrate some of the basic theoretical issues raised in the Introduction. Towards this end, the model focuses narrowly on the equilibrium incentives for lenders to screen loans in a competitive environment.

There are n lenders and one borrower. The borrower is either a good type or a bad type. The prior probability of a good type is λ, $0 < \lambda < 1$. A good type earns a return R by investing \$1 of borrowed money and repaying P. The bad type squanders the \$1, getting a private value Q, with $0 \leq Q \leq 1$, and repays nothing. The good type has the option of squandering too, and will do so unless $P \leq R - Q$. If $Q > 0$, bad borrowers have nothing to lose and something to gain by seeking a loan, so the adverse selection problem is clear. However $Q = 0$ is an interesting limiting case.

Each lender observes a signal S, $0 \leq S \leq 1$. For a good type, S has a density $f(S)$ and a cumulative distribution function $F(S)$. For a bad type, S has density $g(S)$ and distribution function $G(S)$. Conditional on type, lenders' signals are independent and identically distributed. Moreover, these densities are assumed to satisfy the strict Monotone Likelihood Ratio Property (MLRP), so a higher value of S is 'good news' (Milgrom, 1981).

Assumption 1: $f(S)/g(S)$ is strictly increasing.

By Bayes Rule, the probability of a good type conditional on S is

$$\mu(S) \equiv \frac{\lambda f(S)}{\lambda f(S) + (1 - \lambda)g(S)}. \tag{1}$$

Therefore, strict MLRP is equivalent to saying $\mu(S)$ is increasing. A high value of the signal makes a lender more confident of a good type.

There are several implications of strict MLRP that are important later for proving results. An unapparent implication is that $f(S)/F(S) > g(S)/G(S)$ for $S > 0$, which follows from integration.[3] This property implies $F(S)/G(S)$ is strictly increasing. Since $F(1)/G(1) = 1$ by definition, it must be that $F(S) < G(S)$ for $0 < S < 1$. That is, $F(S)$ first-order stochastically dominates $G(S)$.

Strict MLRP also has implications for the maximum order statistic, $\max\{S_1, S_2 \ldots S_n\}$. Conditional on observing S, the probability that the loan is good and all rivals have observed $t \leq T$ is $\mu(S)F(T)^{n-1}$. The conditional probability that the loan is bad and all rivals have observed $t \leq T$

is $[1 - \mu(S)]G(T)^{n-1}$. Setting $T = S$, the ratio of these conditional probabilities is

$$\frac{f(S)}{g(S)} \left(\frac{F(S)}{G(S)}\right)^{n-1}, \tag{2}$$

which must be increasing also by strict MLRP. Note that $nf(S)F(S)^{n-1}$ is the density of the maximum order statistic for n independent and identically distributed signals for a good type, and $ng(S)G(S)^{n-1}$ is the corresponding density for a bad type. Therefore, strict MLRP extends to the maximum order statistic. A higher value of the most favourable signal observed by any lender indicates that a good type is more likely. This property is important because, as we shall see, the market selects loans based on the maximum order statistic.

This model of a loan market has a broader interpretation. The prospective borrower can be thought of as a member of a particular class, e.g. a small business. Each lender understands that within this class a fraction λ of loans are good and the remainder are bad, but no lender knows which is which. Nevertheless, lenders get more information by evaluating the characteristics of the investment project and of the borrower using standard procedures. Moreover, even though different lenders evaluate essentially the same data, they may arrive at different evaluations simply because of human fallibility (Sah, 1991). Inevitably, some lenders will be more optimistic than others. This heterogeneity is captured in the model by the idiosyncratic signals $\{S_1, S_2 \ldots S_n\}$.

It remains to describe how lenders compete with each other. After observing a signal, each lender must decide whether to offer a loan and on what terms. The incentives of an individual lender depend on expectations about rivals' behaviour. These expectations in turn depend on beliefs about what signals rivals have observed and how rivals' actions depend on these signals. This is modelled in a standard way as a Bayesian–Nash equilibrium of a game of incomplete information.[4]

Assume (for simplicity) that the best alternative to lending earns zero interest. Consider the problem of a lender, having observed signal S, whose rivals offer to lend for repayment $P(t)$ upon observing a signal $t \geq X$, and refuse to lend if $t < X$. Assume that $P(t)$ is differentiable and decreasing and $P(X) = R - Q$. Deciding to offer a loan, the deviant lender will demand repayment $P(T)$ such that T maximizes

$$\mu(S)F(T)^{n-1}[P(T) - 1] - [1 - \mu(S)]G(T)^{n-1} \tag{3}$$

subject to $X \leq T \leq 1$.

The maximand (3) is the sum of two components: the expected return from good and bad loans. The first component multiplies the posterior probability of a good loan, $\mu(S)$, the probability that rivals offer less favourable terms, $F(T)^{n-1}$, and the margin on a \$1 good loan, $P(T) - 1$. The expected loss from a bad loan equals the posterior probability of a \$1 bad loan, times the probability that rivals offer less favourable terms.

This formulation of the deviant lender's problem requires some further explanation. The deviant observing a signal S is choosing a repayment $p \in [P(1), P(X)]$; it is apparent that the deviant has no reason to consider repayments outside this interval.[5] This decision is equivalent to choosing $T \in [X, 1]$ and setting $p = P(T)$. This repayment is a winning one if other lenders observe signals worse than T. The solution to this formulation of the deviant lender's problem yields a choice of T as a function of S, say $t(S)$. The deviant's optimal price is therefore $P(t(S))$.

The first-order condition for an interior solution to the deviant lender's problem is

$$\mu(S)(n-1)f(T)F(T)^{n-2}[P(T)-1]$$
$$- [1-\mu(S)](n-1)g(T)G(T)^{n-2} + \mu(S)F(T)^{n-1}P'(T) = 0. \quad (4)$$

Moreover, at a symmetric equilibrium, it must be that $t(S) = S$. Setting $T = S$, and simplifying, equation (4) becomes

$$\lambda(n-1)f(S)^2F(S)^{n-2}[P(S)-1]$$
$$- [1-\lambda)(n-1)g(S)^2G(S)^{n-2} + \lambda f(S)F(S)^{n-1}P'(S) = 0. \quad (5)$$

This is a necessary condition for a symmetric equilibrium. It is a first-order linear differential equation with variable coefficients.

The boundary condition for the differential equation is

$$P(X) = R - Q, \quad (6)$$

with X determined by

$$\lambda(R - Q - 1)f(X)F(X)^{n-1} - (1 - \lambda)g(X)G(X)^{n-1} = 0. \quad (7)$$

These are additional necessary conditions for a symmetric equilibrium.

The value of X satisfying equation (7) is a cut-off value for the signal. A lender refuses to offer a loan if $S < X$. In this case, the lender is simply too pessimistic about repayment to be willing to risk the \$1 principal. Condition (6) says that the repayment required for a marginal loan is the highest possible amount that would induce a good type of borrower to undertake a productive investment. Condition (7) says that conditional on having observed the cut-off signal X, the expected value of a loan at the maximum repayment, and conditional on other lenders observing worse signals, is exactly zero. Therefore, a lender is indifferent about making the marginal loan.

There is a simple intuition for the boundary condition (6). At symmetric equilibria, a lender who observes a marginal signal X knows that he will win the loan only if every other lender observes a worse signal. In this case, however, rival lenders will not offer a loan. Knowing this, the lender observing X views himself essentially as a monopolist, and demands a monopoly repayment, $R - Q$.

It is straightforward to find a sufficient condition under which equation (7) has a unique interior solution in X for each value of n. Since strict MLRP implies that (2) is strictly increasing, equation (7) has at most one interior solution. Moreover, if

$$\frac{\lambda}{1-\lambda}(R-Q-1)\left[\frac{f(0)}{g(0)}\right]^{n} < 1 < \frac{\lambda}{1-\lambda}(R-Q-1)\frac{f(1)}{g(1)}, \qquad (8)$$

such a solution necessarily exists. Given the first inequality of condition (8), the left-hand side of equation (7) is negative, while under the second inequality of (8) the right-hand side of (7) is positive. Since the left-hand side of (7) is continuous, a solution must exist, and since it is increasing this solution must be unique. Moreover, since $f(0) \leq g(0)$ by strict MLRP, the left-hand side of the first inequality of (8) is non-increasing in n, and is at a maximum when $n = 1$. Therefore if (8) holds for $n = 1$, it must hold for all positive integers. Hence the following assumption guarantees a unique interior cut-off for all n.

Assumption 2:

$$\frac{f(0)}{g(0)} < \frac{1-\lambda}{\lambda(R-Q-1)} < \frac{f(1)}{g(1)} . \qquad (9)$$

The necessary conditions for a symmetric equilibrium, equations (5)–(7), imply $P(S)$ is differentiable and decreasing, as hypothesized. The argument follows from strict MLRP. First, note from (5) that $P'(S)$ has the same sign as

$$(1 - \lambda)g(S)^2 G(S)^{n-2} - \lambda f(S)^2 F(S)^{n-2}[P(S) - 1]. \qquad (10)$$

Second, setting $S = X$, and using boundary conditions (6) and (7), it follows that $P'(X)$ has the same sign as

$$\frac{g(X)}{G(X)} - \frac{f(X)}{F(X)}, \qquad (11)$$

which is negative by strict MLRP. Third, suppose there exists T such that $P'(T) = 0$ and $P'(S) > 0$ for $S > T$ in the neighbourhood of T. It must be that

$$(1 - \lambda)g(T)^2 G(T)^{n-2} - \lambda f(T)^2 F(T)^{n-2}[P(T) - 1] = 0 \tag{12}$$

and

$$(1 - \lambda)g(S)^2 G(S)^{n-2} - \lambda f(S)^2 F(S)^{n-2}[P(S) - 1] > 0 \tag{13}$$

with $P(S) > P(T)$ and $S > T$, but this implies a contradiction of MLRP. Therefore, $P'(S) \leq 0$ for $S \geq X$.

To solve the differential equation for equilibrium repayments, define

$$\psi(S) \equiv F(S)^{n-1}[P(S) - 1]. \tag{14}$$

The differential equation (5) becomes

$$\psi'(S) = \frac{(1 - \lambda)(n - 1)g(S)^2 G(S)^{n-2}}{\lambda f(S)}, \tag{15}$$

and boundary conditions (6) and (7) become

$$\psi(X) = F(X)^{n-1}[R - Q - 1] = \frac{(1 - \lambda)g(X)G(X)^{n-1}}{\lambda f(X)}. \tag{16}$$

Therefore, by integration,

$$\psi(S) = \frac{(1 - \lambda)g(X)G(X)^{n-1}}{\lambda f(X)} + \int_X^S \frac{(1 - \lambda)g(t)}{\lambda f(t)} \, dG(t)^{n-1}. \tag{17}$$

Dividing by $F(S)^{n-1}$, and adding 1, yields an equilibrium expression for $P(S)$.

It remains to check that, with this expression for $P(S)$, the first-order condition is sufficient for an optimum of the individual lender's problem. Using expressions (14) and (17), the individual lender's first-order condition (4) can be written as

$$\left\{ \frac{\mu(S)(1 - \lambda)g(T)}{\lambda f(T)} - [1 - \mu(S)] \right\} \frac{dG(T)^{n-1}}{dT} = 0. \tag{18}$$

By strict MLRP, the left-hand side is positive if $T < S$, zero if $T = S$, and negative if $T > S$. Therefore, $T = S$ is the unique solution to the individual lender's maximization problem.

Proposition 1. (Under Assumptions 1 and 2) there exists a unique symmetric equilibrium. A lender refuses to lend upon observing a signal $S < X$, and demands repayment $P(S)$ otherwise. The cut-off X is defined uniquely by equation (7) and satisfies $0 < X < 1$. The repayment function is

$$P(S) = 1 + \frac{\dfrac{(1-\lambda)g(X)G(X)^{n-1}}{\lambda f(X)} + \displaystyle\int_{X}^{S} \frac{(1-\lambda)g(t)}{\lambda f(t)}\, dG(t)^{n-1}}{F(S)^{n-1}}, \qquad (19)$$

and satisfies $P(X) = R - Q$ and $P'(S) \leq 0$.

The equilibrium probability that a loan is made depends only on the loan approval decision, i.e. the cut-off X. Indeed, this loan market performs exactly as a polyarchy (Sah and Stiglitz, 1986). Each of n lenders independently evaluates an investment project based on a screening function $\{F(X), G(X)\}$. Given the equilibrium cut-off X, this gives the probability of acceptance as a function of the borrower's true type. The cut-off value X determines the tightness of the screen. Any one lender can approve the project unilaterally.

On the other hand, the division of rents from a successful project depends on the equilibrium loan repayment terms as a function of the best signal $P(S)$. Only the cut-off X has allocative significance in this model.

3   Comparative statics of more competition

Recall that strict MLRP implies $F(X) < G(X)$. It follows from equation (7), which defines X, that more competition induces tighter screening by individual lenders.

Proposition 2. The equilibrium cut-off for offering a loan, $X(n)$, is strictly increasing in n.

The reason for this is the familiar 'winner's curse' of common value auctions (Milgrom and Weber, 1982). A lender who observes the cut-off signal $X(n)$ successfully wins a loan only if all other lenders observe a worse signal. This is bad news, which becomes worse with more lenders. Therefore, a Bayesian lender becomes more conservative about marginal loans the greater the number of competing lenders.

Clearly, equilibrium loan selection involves two types of error: some bad loans are made (Type II error), and some good loans are not (Type I error). The respective probabilities of Type I and Type II errors are

$$\lambda f(X(n))^{n} \qquad (20)$$

and

$$(1 - \lambda)[1 - G(X(n))^{n}]. \qquad (21)$$

In view of Proposition 2, it appears ambiguous *a priori* whether more competition raises or lowers these two types of errors. Although individual lenders become more conservative, there are more lenders making evaluations. Put another way, it is not obvious whether a larger polyarchy performs better. Nevertheless, it is possible to say much about the welfare consequences of changes in market structure.

4 Welfare results

Given the existence of a unique interior cut-off, the social return from lending is

$$W(n) = \lambda(R - 1)[1 - F(X(n))^n] \\ + (Q - 1)((1 - \lambda)[1 - G(X(n))^n]. \tag{22}$$

Notice that this welfare criterion can be understood as a linear function of the probabilities of Type I and Type II errors. In fact, maximization of social welfare is equivalent to minimizing the social costs of both types of error.

How does social welfare depend on n? Does a larger polyarchy perform better? Insights are obtained by considering special cases that illustrate particular effects.

For the limiting case $Q = 0$, the equilibrium cut-off is socially optimal, i.e. the value of X solving equation (7) maximizes

$$\lambda(R - 1)[1 - F(X)^n] - (1 - \lambda)[1 - G(X)^n]. \tag{23}$$

The reason is that with $Q = 0$ the monopoly repayment fully extracts the rents from a productive investment project. Therefore lenders fully internalize the costs and benefits of a marginal loan. It follows from the envelope theorem that

$$W'(n) = -\lambda(R - 1)\ln[F(X(n))]F(X(n))^n \\ + (1 - \lambda)\ln[G(X(n))]G(X(n))^n. \tag{24}$$

Using the boundary condition (7), this expression has the same sign as

$$-\ln\left[F(X(n))\frac{F(X(n))}{f(X(n))}\right] + \ln\left[G(X(n))\frac{G(X(n))}{g(X(n))}\right]. \tag{25}$$

From this, the following proposition follows immediately.

Proposition 3. If $Q = 0$, $W(n)$ is increasing (decreasing) in n if the elasticity of $\ln(F(S))$ is weakly less (greater) than the elasticity of $\ln(G(S))$ for all $S \in [0, 1]$.

These are sufficient conditions. It is only necessary for the conclusions that the appropriate elasticity property holds in a sufficiently large neighbourhood of $X(n)$.[6]

This result is explained as follows. The market selects loans based on the maximum order statistic for the n signals. Moreover, if $Q = 0$, the cut-off rule the market uses is socially optimal, as discussed above. Therefore, the welfare effect of competition hinges on the informativeness of the maximum order statistic. Does the maximum order statistic become more informative about the type of project with an increase in the number of underlying signals? Proposition 3 provides sufficient conditions for affirmative and negative answers.

The proposition can also be understood with reference to the Sah–Stiglitz theory of polyarchy. For a fixed screening rule X, a higher n decreases the probability of Type I error and increases the probability of Type II error. If X is set optimally, the elasticity conditions of the proposition determine which of these two effects is the more important. Moreover, since $X(n)$ is optimal when $Q = 0$, any induced change in the screening rule is of second-order importance in the neighbourhood of this optimum and thus can be ignored. Therefore, the direct effect of a change in n dominates, leading to Proposition 3. When $Q > 0$, the indirect effect on $X(n)$ must be taken into account also.

The $Q = 0$ case illustrates the first important reason why more competition can hurt market performance. With more potential lenders, each becomes more conservative about approving loans (Proposition 2). However, the market as a whole makes loans more aggressively. Type I error decreases, but Type II error increases. The market's greater propensity for bad loans can have an overwhelming negative effect on social welfare.

Now consider another special case. Suppose $F(S) = S^\alpha$ and $G(S) = S^\beta$ with $\alpha > \beta > 0$. Assumption 1 is satisfied and Assumption 2 becomes

$$R - Q - 1 > \frac{(1 - \lambda)\beta}{\lambda a}. \tag{26}$$

Moreover

$$-\ln(G(X))\frac{G(X)}{g(X)} = -\ln(F(X))\frac{F(X)}{f(X)} = -\ln(X)\,X \tag{27}$$

for any X. Therefore, by Proposition 3, if $Q = 0$, $W'(n) = 0$.[7] Market structure is irrelevant for expected performance.[8]

On the other hand, if $Q > 0$, we have, for this special case, using equations (7) and (23),

$$W'(n) = -nQ[\lambda a X^{a(n-1)} + (1 - \lambda)\beta X^{\beta(n-1)}]\frac{dX}{dn} < 0. \tag{28}$$

The sign of this expression follows from Proposition 2. More competition is unambiguously bad.

Proposition 4. If $F(X)$ and $G(X)$ are power functions and $Q > 0$, $W(n)$ decreases with n.

The intuition for this result is clear. In deciding whether to offer a loan, lenders do not internalize the private benefits that a 'bad' borrower gets from squandering the funds. Neither does the lender internalize the rents that a good borrower must get to motivate a productive investment. For these reasons, lenders set a cut-off value which is too stringent from a social welfare standpoint. By aggravating the winner's curse, more competition makes this cut-off even more stringent, which has a first-order negative effect on social welfare.

It may not seem compelling that a social planner should worry about the welfare of charlatans who take out loans and squander funds. But this criticism misses the mark. Private gains from a bad loan are (in the model) only a transfer payment, with no intrinsic allocative significance. The key point is that the private cost of a bad loan to a lender may exceed the social cost, leading to overly conservative lending criteria. This has harmful allocative consequences: too few good loans are made.

Incidentally, the conclusion that $X(n)$ is too high might provide a rationale for some deposit insurance or bail-out policies, which in effect subsidize more aggressive lending. By subsidizing the private cost of bad loans, deposit insurance would make individual lenders more aggressive, resulting in a lower equilibrium value of $X(n)$. If $F(S)$ and $G(S)$ are power functions, and $Q > 0$, then a small subsidy would unambiguously increase welfare. On the other hand, too large a subsidy (e.g. full deposit insurance) might raise $X(n)$ above its optimal level. Banks would then be too lenient in making loans, leading to an excessively high default rate.

5   Other issues

5.1   Moral hazard and adverse selection

Loan markets, like insurance markets, have problems of both adverse selection and moral hazard. With regard to adverse selection, banks would like to attract good loans and discourage bad ones, and accordingly set terms to induce self-selection. Equity requirements, such as collateral, can play this role (Leland and Pyle, 1977). The above simple model ignores such self-selection possibilities, implicitly assuming that borrowers have no financial resources at all, or do not learn their types until after receiving the loan.

The model also treats moral hazard in a very crude way, by allowing the possibility of squandering borrowed funds. Other subtler forms of moral hazard might be important. For example, the success of an investment project might depend on how hard an entrepreneur works to organize it, and the entrepreneur's incentive might depend on loan terms. If more competition makes good loans available on more favourable terms, this might spur the entrepreneur to work harder. On the other hand, Hermalin (forthcoming) suggests that the 'income effect' of more favourable terms might discourage managerial effort.

5.2   Endogenous screening

The simple model assumes that the signals observed by lenders have exogenous statistical properties. This might be justified by supposing banks follow standard loan evaluation practices independent of the degree of market competition. On the other hand, it seems reasonable to suppose that the effort banks devote to screening is at least partly endogenous.[9]

The effort devoted to screening loans can be expected to depend positively on the probability of winning a loan and on the return from a successful loan. Competition is discouraging in both respects. First, in symmetric equilibria, more potential lenders reduces the probability of winning for any single lender. Second, more competitive repayment terms reduces the return from a successful loan. Both effects are likely to undermine equilibrium incentives for information acquisition.

Less information acquisition means that screening by individual lenders is less accurate. This might decrease the informativeness of the maximum order statistic, and lead lenders to adopt even more conservative screening practices. Both effects are likely to harm social welfare, by arguments along the lines of those developed in the simple model.

5.3   Internal organization of banks

The screening procedures of banks obviously relate to their internal organization. In a series of articles, Sah and Stiglitz (1986, 1988, 1991) have analysed alternative ways of organizing the selection of projects, and some of this work might be applicable to screening in loan markets. Two issues are relevant. First, the internal organization of loan screening will depend on the amount of resources devoted to this activity. Therefore, internal organization issues must relate to the endogenous screening issues mentioned above. Second, for a given level of expenditures, banks presumably optimize internal organization. There might be interesting issues surrounding the relationship between internal bank structure and external market structure. However, it is doubtful that hierarchy, as defined by Sah and Stiglitz (1986), is a good way to model the internal organization of banks, because of its inefficient aggregation of information. Perhaps what they call committees (Sah and Stiglitz, 1988) is a better characterization.

5.4 Application costs

A possibly important extension of the model would allow banks to charge application fees. This is natural if banks incur screening costs in processing a loan, but might play a role even if screening is costless. Application costs may limit the number of banks from which a borrower seeks a loan. Consequently, an increase in the number of potential lenders does not necessarily increase the equilibrium number of loan applications. In an extended model along these lines, the appropriate question to ask is: How does an increase in the number of potential lenders affect the informativeness of the maximum order statistic for the equilibrium number of loan applications?

5.5 Incumbency advantage

Even if a single banking licence did encourage entry into European loan markets, incumbent banks, particularly in regional and local markets, are likely to retain substantial information advantages about the credit-worthiness of borrowers. This might be captured in an extended model by supposing that a subset of the n lenders observes a more informative signal, i.e. one that yielded lower probabilities of Type I and II errors. With this modification, incumbents would keep significant market power, and be more successful at winning good loans. However, there is no apparent reason why more competition (in the form of new entry) would not have effects similar to those in the basic model. Market loan selection decisions might be less informed, and loan approval practices might become more conservative, for similar reasons. This extension is worth exploring formally.

6 Concluding remarks

Loan markets are examples of markets for which one side of the market screens the characteristics of a transaction prior to contracting. Labour markets are another example. Hiring decisions are preceded by interviews, and workers might even be tested prior to employment (Guasch and Weiss, 1980). Markets for services, such as health care, provide still other examples (Glazer and McGuire, 1991).

In all of these markets, competition matters not only because of its effect on prices, but also because of its effect on the market's screening decisions, which also have allocative consequences. In general, the normative implications of this latter effect are ambiguous, so more competition might harm market performance, even as prices draw closer to marginal cost.

NOTES

This paper was written while I was a Visiting Professor at the University of California at Berkeley. I thank the Universitywide Energy Research Group for hospitality and research support, and Richard Gilbert, Kenneth Hendricks, Benjamin Hermalin, David Pyle, Paul Ruud, Raaj Sah, Anthony Santomero, Pablo Spiller and Xavier Vives for useful conversations and comments.

1 This calculation is only suggestive, and in fact slightly misleading because some banks are foreign owned. For example, in Luxembourg most banks are foreign owned.
2 Broecker's analysis does suggest that my normative conclusions about market structure could depend on the assumption that individual lending decisions are made simultaneously and independently. Matters might be different if banks could in some way react to each other.
3 By strict MLRP, $s > t$ implies $f(s)g(t) > g(s)f(t)$. Integrating over t from zero to s gives the result.
4 The game has the structure of a common value auction in which the borrower can be understood as the 'seller' and the lenders as 'buyers'. The object being sold is the right to lend \$1. There is no price per se. Instead, lenders 'bid' required loan repayments.
5 A repayment demand above $P(X)$ results in even good loans being squandered. A repayment demand below $P(1)$ is less profitable and decreases the probability of getting the loan.
6 Bagnoli and Bergstrom (1989) discuss the mathematics of log probability and its applications, but they do not mention the elasticity of log probability.
7 A generalization is $F(S) = S^{\alpha + aS}$ and $G(S) = S^{\beta + bS}$. Then, if $Q = 0$, Proposition 3 implies the sign of $W'(n)$ may be positive or negative depending on the sign and magnitudes of parameters a and b.
8 This example contrasts sharply with the conclusions of Wilson (1977) and Milgrom (1979) that the winning bid converges to the true value as the number of bidders gets large, implying no welfare loss at all. The explanation lies in the fact that loans can be unprofitable. This gives rise to an allocative issue. In the parlance of auction theory, the valuation of the bidders (i.e. lenders) might be less than the reserve value of the seller (i.e. the borrower, who has a payoff of zero if the loan is not made). This feature undermines the Wilson–Milgrom result.
9 Matthews (1984) studies the endogenous acquisition of information in common values auctions.

REFERENCES

Bagnoli, M. and T. Bergstrom (1989) 'Log-concave probability and its applications', University of Michigan working paper, 7 September.

The Banker (1989) 'Top 500 European Banks by Country', October, pp. 100–15.

Broecker, T. (1990) 'Credit-worthiness tests and interbank competition', *Econometrica* **58**, 429–52.

Devinney, T. (1989) '1992: what will it mean for financial institutions?' *Banking Administration Institute: Issues in Bank Regulation* **12**(4).

Gardner, E. and P. Molyneux (1990) *Changes in Western European Banking*, London: Unwin Hyman.

Glazer, J. and T. McGuire (1991) 'The economics of referrals', Industry Studies Program Discussion Paper No. 20, Boston University.

Guasch, J.L. and A. Weiss (1980) 'Wages as a sorting mechanism in competitive markets with asymmetric information: a theory of testing', *Review of Economic Studies* **47**, 653–64.

Hermalin, B. (forthcoming) 'The effects of competition on executive behavior', *RAND Journal of Economics.*

Journal of Economic Perspectives (1989) 'Symposium on federal deposit insurance for S&L institutions', 3, 3–49.

Leland, H.E. and D.H. Pyle (1977) 'Information asymmetries, financial structure and financial intermediation', *Journal of Finance* **32**, 371–87.

Matthews, S. (1984) 'Information acquisition in discriminatory auctions', in M. Boyer and R.E. Kihlstrom (eds), *Bayesian Models in Econometric Theory*, Amsterdam: North-Holland.

Matutes, C. and X. Vives (1992) 'Competition for deposits, risk of failure, and regulation in banking', working paper, Universitat Autònoma de Barcelona.

Milgrom, P.R. (1979) 'A convergence theorem for competitive bidding with differential information', *Econometrica* **47**, 679–88.

   (1981) 'Good news and bad news: representation theorems and applications', *Bell Journal of Economics* **12**, 380–91.

Milgrom, P. and R.J. Weber (1982) 'A theory of auctions and competitive bidding', *Econometrica* **50**, 679–88.

Sah, R.K. (1991) 'Fallibility in human organizations and political systems', *Journal of Economic Perspectives* **5**, 67–88.

Sah, R.K. and J.E. Stiglitz (1986) 'The architecture of economic systems: hierarchies and polyarchies', *American Economic Review* **76**, 716–27.

   (1988) 'Committees, hierarchies and polyarchies', *Economic Journal* **98**, 451–70.

   (1991) 'The quality of managers in centralized versus decentralized organizations', *Quarterly Journal of Economics* **106**, 289–96.

Vives, X. (1991) 'Banking competition and European integration', in A. Giovanni and C. Mayer (eds), *European Financial Integration*, Cambridge: Cambridge University Press.

Wilson, R. (1977) 'A bidding model of perfect competition', *Review of Economic Studies* **44**, 511–18.

Discussion

DAVID H. PYLE

In this paper, Professor Riordan has provided a model of lending that he relates to the desirability of a 'single banking licence' for Europe. The comments that follow stress the relevance of this model for drawing inferences about the effects of more competition in banking markets.

The bank objective function, maximizing the expected loan payoff, misses at least three trade-offs that are important in the single banking market context. First, the bank's price-setting mechanism must depend on the number of banks in the market in ways other than the effect on the conditional probability of borrower quality. In his conclusion, Riordan clearly recognizes this point. It is repeated here for emphasis and as a suggestion that explicit treatment of the direct price effects of more competition would be a valuable extension of the model.

A second advantage of opening European bank markets is the added scope for loan diversification that this could afford banks. Might not the value of an additional Spanish loan to a French bank be greater, all else equal, than the value of that loan to a Spanish bank? To capture this effect, the objective function must include an expected return/risk trade-off.

A third consideration is comparative advantage in information processing, which, presumably, is part of what Riordan is getting at in his section on the internal organization of banks. If some banks have superior information collection and processing skills, but limited capacity for exercising those skills (or diminished ability as a function of portfolio size), competition can help. The banks with best abilities will take on the best projects and increase the liquidity of good projects. Gennotte (1992) contains a model used to analyse the effects of differential information-processing abilities across banks. This approach to information modelling might provide useful insights into the analysis of a single banking market.

Finally, Riordan's idea of incorporating the role of collateral or other forms of borrower commitment in the model is a good one. The borrower in the current model is too passive. A related point is the dependence of Riordan's results on the absence of any competitive pricing information. Good borrowers, in particular, have an incentive to provide information on other banks' bids. Unfortunately, bad borrowers will also want to suggest the presence of lower loan rate bids. If the reliable signals can be sorted out, this will affect the equilibrium and perhaps reduce or eliminate the adverse effects of competition that Riordan emphasizes.

REFERENCE

Gennotte, G. (1992) 'Deposit insurance and bank competition', unpublished manuscript, Haas School of Business, University of California, Berkeley.

ANTHONY M. SANTOMERO

Michael H. Riordan has offered the banking literature a perspective of the loan market that is quite distinct from our usual constructions. Rather than examining the lender–borrower relationship as a bilateral transaction, or one in which a bank unilaterally offers a price conditional on quantity (see Santomero, 1984, for a review), the present paper uses auction theory to analyse lending behaviour. In the process the reader is presented with a somewhat alien view of bank loan activity.

This novel approach is both the paper's strength and its weakness. There are many interesting insights to be gained. Likewise, however, there are areas and results that strain the credibility of the formal model as one representing bank lending. In the end, it leaves the reader with many questions as well as a rich research agenda to prove or disprove the perspective suggested. As such it challenges us to investigate the market on its terms and makes the reader better for the exercise.

In my brief comments here I will attempt to explain, react to and question the validity of the proposed use of auction theory to characterize bank lending. Each part of my discussion will be offered in a separate section, and in rather shortened form.

1   An overview of the approach taken

Let me begin by reviewing the approach taken. This paper is an application of auction theory (Milgrom and Weber, 1982) to the bank loan market. The paper analyses a representative lender in a market with n competitors. There is a representative borrower who seeks funds from the lender bank. There are two types of borrowers, good and bad, who are indistinguishable *ex ante*. Each lender, however, observes a signal about the loan quality, and a loan, if made, is supplied by the lender observing the best signal. Using signalling theory the author arrives at the representative bank's choice of the minimally acceptable project signal. If the signal, i.e. the estimated probability of repayment, is beyond some cut-off level, the loan is made. If it is below, it is rejected unilaterally. The paper goes on to solve for the symmetric Bayesian–Nash equilibrium of this game.

The paper next investigates the comparative statics of such a model, with a specific reference to the effect of competition on the individual bank's willingness to loan, its price or spread, and on total lending, which relates directly to total societal welfare. The results here form the substance of the paper and follow directly from the model's structure.

An increase in the number of competitors causes each bank to be more conservative, i.e. the required cut-off signal for offering a loan increases with the number of competitors. This is the standard 'winner's curse' result that emerges from all such models. If, however, bad loans are provided to borrowers who obtain no private gain from the ill-fated project, overall lending increases. This is because loans are made based upon the maximum order statistic, which increases with the number of competitors. This in turn may result in a decline in welfare. Increased aggressiveness in lending leads to welfare losses associated with the support of bad projects. If borrowers obtain some personal gain from such lending, the results lead unambiguously to a deterioration of social welfare as a direct result of new competition.

The purpose of this paper is to sound a note of caution about the upcoming market mergers associated with the integration of EC countries at the close of 1992. The Second Banking Directive, supported by commissioned studies (Price Waterhouse, 1988), suggests large benefits from banking market integration and enhanced competition. Riordan's view is that such enthusiasm may be ill founded. Competition may encourage aggressive bank lending, but it may not improve social welfare.

2   *Reactions to the model's structure*

From a technical point of view, the model is both well developed and neatly exposed. It transfers the technology of auction theory to the banking market and, along with several papers in this volume, brings disparate approaches to bear on the financial institution area.

With all such graftings, however, a key question is, does the model capture the right or critical features of the market in question? In short, is this a bank lending model? At some level, the answer is yes. It models the process of multiple lenders attempting to evaluate the repayment probability of various proposals offered to them daily. Bankers are aware of the presence of competitors, as well as their inability accurately to evaluate the nature of investment opportunities presented.

Yet, the model misses some vital characteristics of the bank lending market. First, the paper models the signal as idiosyncratic, but drawn from a single distribution for each borrower type. The signal is independent of the bank itself and its relationship to the borrower. The author recognizes this weakness in his later section when he writes of the need to develop endogenous screening in such a framework. To my mind, this is essential. Second, the model is atemporal. Yet, the majority of lending from the banking sector is repetitive and from credit facilities (Ham and Melnick, 1987). This suggests that an intertemporal model along the lines of Diamond (1989) may be more appropriate.

There is no doubt that many of the features of the current framework are consistent with open capital market lending. The issue is whether, with the absence of proprietary asset evaluation and intertemporal features, auction theory can be applied to bank lending specifically. To my mind, this is still an open question.

3   Implications of the theory

If the auction theory modelling structure is relevant to bank lending markets, then the data should be consistent with its predictions. What are these implications? One relates lending aggressiveness to the number of competitors. According to the theory, added competition makes lending more conservative, even as more total borrowing occurs. One could examine this issue in cross section, as we have in a matter similar to other questions of structure and performance (Gilbert, 1984). Such studies have tended to result in mixed results, at best, but the relationship here seems of considerable interest.

A second implication of the model is much more novel. According to the theory, an individual bank's loan standards are dependent upon the number of known competitors. Therefore, a borrower may well wish to pre-commit to not obtaining alternative bids as a way of obtaining a bank loan. I know of no such custom in the market, but perhaps the use of fees and lags in evaluation could be viewed as symptomatic of market pressure for the borrower to precommitment.

There may be more, but they are not apparent to this writer. The author and those who wish to apply this approach would do well, however, to pursue the empirical implications of the modelling structure. Data are readily available in this industry and support would add credence to the applicability of the theory.

4   Extensions suggested

Notwithstanding a request for proof, the author has presented an interesting beginning in the basic lending model presented. He suggests several areas that warrant extension and further work. Many of these are both intriguing and very worthwhile. To this writer, endogenous screening and incumbency advantage are the most likely to be valuable additions. In each case, the model would begin to take on more of the features of the bank loan market, and respond to the objections that I have raised above. While I recognize that each is a separate paper, their added insight would result in a richer understanding of this model's ultimate value in explaining the behaviour of the loan market. They would result also in more empirically testable hypotheses for validation of the fundamental approach.

In summary, then, the paper is well written, intriguing and proposes several avenues of further theoretical development. It has not yet made me a believer, but I am still very much listening to the story it weaves.

REFERENCES

Diamond, D.W. (1989) 'Reputation acquisition in debt markets', *Journal of Political Economy* **97**, 828–62.

Gilbert, R.A. (1984) 'Studies of bank market structure and competition: a review and evaluation', *Journal of Money, Credit and Banking* **16**, 617–44.

Ham, J.C. and A. Melnick (1987) 'Bank lending practices and the market for loan commitments: survey and analysis', *Review of Economics and Statistics* **69**, 704–8.

Milgrom, P.R. and R.J. Weber (1982) 'A theory of auctions and competitive bidding', *Econometrica* **50**, 679–88.

Price Waterhouse International Economic Consultants (1988) 'The cost of "New Europe"', in *Financial Services*, Commission of the European Communities, March.

Santomero, A.M. (1984) 'Modeling the banking firm', *Journal of Money, Credit and Banking* **16**, 576–602.

Index

absolute priority rule 222n.20
accounting practices
  bankruptcy 213–14
  United States of America 273
Admati, A. 95
adverse selection
  informational capacity 118, 120
  performance of banks 339
Aghion, P. 18, 46, 73, 205–6
agriculture
  characteristics 90
  stock markets 87
Allen, F. 95, 105
Ang, J. 207
applications, loan 125–6, 128–30
  costs 119, 121, 341
  fees 135
Arrow–Debreu theory 92
Asquith, P. 65
asset distribution 169
assets, resale value of 209–10
assured bail-out 216–17
Aumann, R. 93
automatic triggering of bankruptcy 209,
  211, 219
  Hungary 201–2, 210
Avery, R. B. 281

bad debts
  creditor passivity 216
  financial restructuring 231
Bagnoli, M. 342
bail-out, assured 216–17
Baird, D. 205
Bank Holding Company (BHC) Act 272
bankruptcy
  economic reform 9, 197–229
  financial restructuring 230, 231–2, 235–6
  renegotiation 65
Banks, J. 147

barriers to trade 165–6
Barro, Robert J. 164, 175, 176
Basle agreement 12
Bebchuk, L. 205
Begg, D. 241, 251, 253
Bencivenga, V. R. 187, 194
benefits, private 20–1, 42
Benston, G. J. 275
Berger, A. N. 281
Berglof, E. 69, 70
Bergstrom, T. 342
Berkovitch, E. 86, 87, 114
Berlin, M. 114, 115
Bernanke, B. 6, 120, 145, 148, 150
Bertrand competition 145n.3
Besanko, D. 281, 293, 294, 318
Bester, H. 120, 134
Bhattacharya, S. 87, 99, 108, 109, 110, 112,
  317
bids and bankruptcy 228
biotechnology industry 92
Blackmon, G. 283
Bliss, C. 231
Bofinger, P. 234, 253
Bolton, P. 18, 46, 70, 73
bond markets 7–8
bondholders, public 61–3, 66
Boot, A. W. A. 86, 87, 114, 265, 274, 275,
  280, 281, 283
borrowers
  banks as 15
  types of 296–8
  welfare of 312–14, 315–16, 326
bounded growth models 163, 164–5
Boyd, J. H. 163
Brady, S. 151
Braga de Macedo, J. 231
Brainard, L. 223
Brainard, W. 231
Broecker, T. 134, 330

Bryant, J. 318
Buiter, W. 251
Bulow, J. 61, 222
business cycle 190
business relationships, long-term 86–7

Calomiris, C. W. 34, 223
Calvo, G. 223, 241, 254
Cameron, R. 194
Campbell, T. S. 264
cancellation, debt 241, 261
capital
    accumulation 157, 160–4, 175
    investment 37
    regulation 266–7, 289–90
    requirements 28–9
    structure 19
capitalization of banks
    regulation 267
    see also recapitalization, of banks
Caprio, G., Jr 188
Carlin, W. 245
cartels 98
cash flow 225
cash limits 246–7
Central and Eastern Europe (CEE) 230–61
central bank lending 168–9
centralization of policy 230
Centre for Economic Policy Research
    (CEPR) 11
Chan, Y.-S. 264, 270, 282, 292, 317
Chandravarkar, A. 187
Chari, V. V. 318
charters, bank 292–3, 315
checking role 89, 92–101
Chemmanur, T. J. 265
Chile 237
Chua, J. 207
claims, creditors' 208–11
Clarke, R. 98
closure rules 280–1n.8
Cobb–Douglas production function 160–2
collusion, implicit 217–18
competition
    banks 3–4, 11: bankruptcy 220; Europe
        8–9, 276–7, 316–17; financial
        restructuring 241; performance
        328–48; refinancing 47, 48, 55–8, 64–5;
        regulation 15–16; relationship banking
        292–4, 299–301, 310–12, 315, 319–26;
        United States of America 8, 271–3
    Bertrand 145n.3
    financial system 270
    industries 92
    stock markets 84
completeness of markets 92

concessions 61, 65–6
Congressional Budget Office 282
Continental Illinois 15, 34n.18
contingent contracts 50–2
    banks 62, 63
    competition 64
    multiple initial lenders 60
    renegotiation 54–5
contracts, debt
    default law 197–8
    informational capacity 135–6
    maturity 47, 50–2, 68–9, 71–6
    see also renegotiation
contractual incompleteness 17–18
control see regulation
control rents 46–7, 49–53
    competition 56–7
    multiple initial lenders 59
convertibility, suspension of 15
Cooper, R. 134, 223
Coopers and Lybrand 210
Coricelli, F. 254
corporate control
    banks 233
    stock markets 98–100, 115
costs
    bankruptcy 207, 211
    financial restructuring 256–7
    loan applications 119, 121, 341
    monitoring 264, 265–6
cover-ups 30–1
Cramton, P. 98
credibility 243–4, 260–1
credit controls, selective 240, 245–6, 258
credit crunches
    informational capacity 118, 148–51
    real effects of banks 7
credit market model 118–30
credit ratings 49–50
current value accounting 273–4
Czech and Slovak Federal Republic
    (CSFR)
    creditor passivity 203, 214, 216
    financial restructuring 232, 238–9

Davies, S. M. 281
Davis, E. P. 7, 66
deadweight losses 237
debt conversion 241, 261
debt-holders
    incentive schemes 22–5
    optimal levels 43–4
    regulation of banks 28, 33
debt overhang 28
debt service capacity 73
    bankruptcy 225

debt socialization 241
debts
  bad: creditor passivity 216; financial
    restructuring 231
  financial restructuring 230–62
  inherited 215–16
  see also loans
decision-making process 90–2
  stock markets 88–9
defaults
  debt maturity 69–70
  laws 197–8: see also bankruptcy
delegated monitoring
  notion of a bank 14, 16
  rationale for banks 2
  and stock markets 6, 101–2
deposit insurance
  regulation of banks 5, 15, 27, 269–71:
    Europe 276–7; models 286–7; moral
    hazards 262–3; private 31–2; United
    States of America 272–6
  relationship banking 292–327
depositors
  efficient governance structure 36
  regulation of banks 17, 26–7, 28
deposits
  competition in banking 3
  efficient governance structure 26: ex ante
    regulation 28–9
deregulation of banking 315–16
design of bankruptcy laws 204–7, 211, 219,
  227
deviant lender's problem 332–3
Devinney, T. 329
Dewatripont, M. 13, 17, 34, 36–7, 42, 69,
  108, 111
Diamond, D. W. 2, 4, 14, 17, 33, 47, 49, 50,
  61, 66, 75, 76, 86, 87, 88, 89, 101–2,
  108, 109, 114, 134, 145, 267, 280, 318,
  347
Diamond, P. 87
direct regulation 274–5
discretionary regulation 274
dispersal of depositors 17
diversification of loans 344
division of labour 30–1
Dyba, K. 232
Dybvig, P. 2, 4, 14, 134, 267, 318

Eastern Europe 9–10
  stock markets 105
  see also Central and Eastern Europe
    (CEE); reforming socialist economies
    (RSEs)
economic development 156–96
economies of scale 10

effort levels 18, 37
Eichengreen, B. 244
Emmons, W. 282
enforcement of bankruptcy laws 204–5,
  211, 228
Englebrecht-Wiggans, R. 64
entrepreneurs
  economic development 158–9
  informational capacity 118, 121–2
enterprise sector reforms 186
entry into banking 292–3, 315
equity 205–6
equity financing 135
equity holders
  incentive schemes 22–6
  regulation of banks 28
Eurobond markets 7–8
Europe
  competition in banking 8–9
  performance of banks 328–9
  regulation of banking 276–7
  relationship banking 316–17
  see also Eastern Europe
Evans, J. 281
ex ante regulation 28–9
ex post regulation 29
exports 166
externalities 15–16

failures
  of banks: informational capacity 117–55;
    real effects of 6; spillovers 15, 16
  of credit market: implications 237–9;
    solutions 239–45
  of firms 8
Faulhaber, G. 95
Fazzari, S. 192
Federal Deposit Insurance Corporation
  (FDIC)
  Bank Insurance Fund 262, 271
  Improvement Act (FDICIA) 12, 26
Federal Trust Indenture Act 61
financial collapse see failures, of banks
financial indicators 166–82, 191–2, 194–5
financial structure 3
fiscal subsidies 246–7
Fitcher, G. 276
Flannery, M. J. 46
forcing contracts 136
Frankel, A. 83, 85
free-rider problems 206, 209, 234
Frenkel, J. 223, 241
Fulghieri, P. 265
funds, investment 82–5
Furlong, F. T. 267, 281
future of banks 7–8

Gal-Or, E. 98
Gale, D. 223, 280
gamble for resurrection 27–8
Gardner, E. 329
Geanokoplos, J. 93
Gelb, A. 194
General Inspectorate for Banking
    Supervision (GIBS) 214–15
Generally Accepted Auditing Principles
    (GAAP) 273–4
Gennotte, G. 344
Germany 84–6
Gertler, M. 145, 190
Gertner, R. 61, 65, 222
Giammarino, R. M. 281
Gilbert, R. A. 347
Gilson, S. C. 65
Glass–Steagall Act 271, 275
Glazer, J. 99, 112, 341
Goldsmith, R. W. 162, 190, 194
Gorton, G. 34
governance structure
    of banks 26–45
    of firms 17–26
governments
    bankruptcy 200
    financial restructuring 248–50
    intervention 195
    ownership of firms 89, 103–4
    United States of America 271–5
Green, E. 118, 145
Green, J. 108
Greenbaum, S. I. 86, 87, 114, 265, 270, 274,
    275, 282, 283, 292, 317
Greenwood, J. 187, 194
Griffith-Jones, S. 237
Grinblatt, M. 96
Grossman, S. J. 17, 37–8, 87, 94, 100, 108,
    110, 221
growth theory, new
    economic development 171
    real effects of banks 6
Guasch, J. L. 341
Gurley, J. G. 14, 190

Ham, J. C. 347
Hare, P. 237
Harris, M. 46, 221
Hart, O. 18, 37–8, 46, 66, 73, 80, 100, 110,
    205–6, 221
Haubrich, J. 145
Hellwig, M. 16, 33, 34, 83, 101, 109, 120,
    145, 223, 280
Hermalin, B. 340
holdout problem 100
Holmstrom, B. 35, 87, 88

Hubbard, G. 192
Hughes, G. 237
human capital 162–3
Hungary
    bankruptcy 199–204, 210, 214, 225–6:
        inherited debts 216
    financial restructuring 233, 238–9
Hwang, C. 96

Ibbotson, R. 95
imperfect competition 64
implementation of bankruptcy laws 204,
    207–21, 228
implicit collusion 217–18
incentive schemes
    ex post regulation 29
    managers 21–2
    outsiders 22–6
    perverse incentives problem 27–8
income elasticity 167
incumbency advantage 341
indirect regulation 274
Industrial Revolution 81, 104–5
inflation
    financial restructuring 244
    United States of America 272
information
    capacity 117–55
    debt maturity 46, 48–50, 68, 71–3:
        competition 64; monopolies 61, 64;
        returns 76; sensitivity 54–5
    gathering: by managers 91–2, 93–5;
        by stock markets 87–8, 98–100,
        110–13
    performance of banks 344
    structure 298–9
inherited debts 215–16
initial lenders
    multiple 58–60, 70
    single 57
initial public offering (IPO) 95–7
innovations
    economic development 158–9
    stock markets 102
insolvency 201
insurance *see* deposit insurance
integration, financial 8–9
inter-enterprise credit 234–6
interest rates
    Chile 237
    Poland 238
internal organization of banks 340–1
internalization of welfare 29–30
international community 251–2
intervention 19, 20, 23–5, 29
    cover-ups 30–1

investment
  bankruptcy 212–13
  economic development 160–5, 176, 182
  efficient governance structure 37–41
  relationship banking 296–8
investors
  efficient governance structure 38 41
  protection 5
involuntary credit 235

Jackson, T. 205, 221
Jagannathan, R. 318
Jappelli, T. 196
Jegadeesh, N. 96
Jensen, M. 46, 70, 76, 97, 221
John, A. 134, 223
John, K. 65, 262, 269
John, T. 262, 269
Johnston, B. J. 222
Journal of Economic Perspectives 330
Jovanovic, B. 187, 194
junior loans 59, 69
  banks 62–3

Kahane, Y. 266, 281
Kanatas, G. 281
Kane, E. 28, 217
Kareken, J. 267
Katz, M. 99
Kaufman, H. 15, 33
Keeley, M. C. 267, 270, 281, 317
Kihlstrom, R. 98
King, R. G. 158, 164, 166, 182, 187, 188
Klaus, Vaclav 203, 218
Knight, F. 158
Koehn, M. 266, 281
Kohlberg, E. 146
Kopcke, R. 33
Kornai, J. 221
Kraus, J. R. 281

Lang, L. 65
Lange, O. 103
large corporations 7
large debt-holders 33
Leamer, E. 176
Legros, P. 221
Leland, H. E. 108, 339
Levine, R. 158, 164, 166, 175, 176, 182,
  187, 188, 194
Lewis, T. R. 281
licences, banking 329
limited liability 287
liquidation
  bankruptcy 198, 204–7, 217: Hungary
    200, 201–2

debt maturity 46–7, 49–55, 68–9, 71–5:
  banks 61–3; competition 55–8, 64–5;
  multiple initial lenders 58–60
liquidity provision
  capital requirements 267
  rationale for banks 2–3
Litan, R. E. 275
loans
  competition 3–4
  efficient governance structure 26
  see also long-term loans; short-term
    loans
London Stock Exchange 81–2
long-term business relationships 86–7
long-term loans 46, 48, 68–9, 72–5
  banks 61, 63
  competition 55–6, 57, 65
  multiple initial lenders 59
Lown, C. 145, 148, 150
Lucas, R. E., Jr 157, 162

McConnell, J. 207
McFadden–Pepper Act 271
McGuire, T. 341
McKelvey, R. 93, 94
McKinnon, R. I. 194
McManus, D. A. 281
Maddison, A. 162
Mailath, G. J. 281
management function 19, 20
managers
  decision-making 90–2: stock markets 88–9
  efficient governance structure 37–40:
    incentive scheme 21–2; moral hazard
    18, 36–7
  financial restructuring 243
Mankiw, G. 120, 152, 164, 176
Manne, H. 99
margins, bank 240, 246, 258
Marino, A. M. 264
market structure 298–9, 313
Maskin, E. 108, 111
Matthews, S. 342
maturity of loans 46–80
Matutes, C. 3, 34, 134, 294, 330
Mayer, C. P. 7, 66, 82, 84, 86, 89, 96, 245
Mazumdar, S. 280
Meckling, W. 46, 70, 76
Melnick, A. 347
Meltzer, A. 145
mergers 100
Mertens, J.-F. 146
Merton, R. C. 262, 264, 269, 292
Mester, L. J. 114, 115, 281
Michaely, R. 96
Michie, R. 81, 82, 105

Milgrom, P. R. 64, 134, 265, 330, 331, 336,
    342, 345
Miller, M. 205
Mishkin, F. S. 272
Mitchell, J. 217, 220, 221, 222
Molyneux, P. 329
monetary incentives 20
money
    creation 236
    demand 166–7
monitoring
    by banks: delegated *see* delegated
        monitoring; regulation 263–5, 267–71,
        289–90
    of banks: cover-ups 30–1; objectives 5;
        by small depositors 27
monotone likelihood ratio property
        (MLRP)
    efficient governance structure 18–19,
        22
    performance of banks 331–2, 334–5
Montgomery, J. 83, 85
Mookherjee, D. 280
Moore, J. 46, 66, 73, 80, 205–6
moral hazard
    creditor passivity 212
    efficient governance structure 18, 36–7
    financial restructuring 243–4
    informational capacity 120
    performance of banks 339–40
    regulation of banks 263–5: capital
        regulation 266–7; deposit insurance
        262, 269–70, 286; narrow banking 275
multiple equilibria 134–5
multiple initial lenders 58–60, 70
multiple maturities 57

narrow banking
    future of banks 8
    regulation of banks 263, 275, 288–9
Neill, H. 83
*Nelson's Directory of Investment Research
    1992* 88
new growth theory
    economic development 171
    real effects of banks 6
New York Stock Exchange 81–3
non-performing claims 213–15, 220
notion of a bank 12–13, 14–17
Novshek, W. 98

Oh, S. 118, 145
overextension of credit 237–8
ownership
    of bonds 61
    of firms 212

Pagano, M. 196
Page, T. 93, 94
Palfrey, T. 98
passivity
    creditors 197–229, 234, 235: costs 237–9
    efficient governance structure: of banks
        29; of firms 23–5
payment system 14–15, 16
performance of banks
    competition 328–48
    regulation 27, 42, 43–4
Perotti, E. 234
perpetual growth models 163
perquisites 37–8
perturbed credit market model 130–2
perverse incentives problem 27–8
Peterson, B. 192
Pfleiderer, P. 95, 110
P'ng, I. 280
Poland
    creditor passivity 203, 214–15, 216
    financial restructuring 233, 238–9, 251:
        inter-enterprise credit 234; selective
        credit controls 235
Polemarchakis, H. 93
policies
    financial transformation 230–1, 252–3,
        260: inter-enterprise credit 236
    public 165–6
    regulation of banks 288–9
    relationship banking 314–17
political cover-ups 30–1
polyarchies 337–8
Portes, R. 231, 243, 244
portfolio choice 292–327
positive lending 127–30, 153
preferences 20–1
Prescott, E. C. 163
Price Waterhouse 346
prices
    economic development 186
    stocks 94–7
priority
    of creditors 205
    of loans 46–80
private benefits 20–1, 42
private deposit insurance 31–2
private lenders
    debt maturity 61–3
    economic development 168–9
private ownership 101
private ratings 31
private remedies, regulation of banking
        30–2
privatization process
    creditor passivity 212, 216

financial restructuring 230, 241, 244–5, 247–8
production process 90–2
productivity 159–62, 163–4, 175, 187
profits
   efficient governance structure 37–8
   informational capacity 122–3, 124–5, 133–4, 137–40
   portfolio choice 307–11
promissory notes 203
proxy fights 99
public bondholders 61–3, 66
public policies 165–6
Pyle, D. H. 108, 339

quiet times 25, 29

Rajan, R. 64–5, 114, 294, 295, 317
ratings
   credit 49–50
   private 31
rationale for banks 2–3
Raviv, A. 46
real effects of banks 6–7
realizations 50, 51–2, 62, 71–5
Rebelo, S. T. 188
recapitalization
   of banks: Central and Eastern Europe 9–10, 240–2, 247–8, 258; regulation 29, 31
   of state-owned enterprises 242–4
refinancing of loans 46–80
reforming socialist economies (RSEs) 197, 199–206, 210–29
regression 174–9
regulation
   of banks 12–17, 262–91: economic development 166; financial restructuring 246; importance 11; objectives 4–6; structure 26–45
   of firms 17–26
regulatory cover-ups 30–1
rehabilitation 200
relationship banking 2, 4, 292–327
renegotiation
   of contracts: banks 61–3, 65–6; debt maturity 53–4, 65; multiple initial lenders 58–60; seniority 69; stock markets 114–15
   efficient governance structure 19–20, 21
Renelt, D. 175, 176
rents
   control 46–7, 49–53: competition 56–7; multiple initial lenders 59
   regulation of banks 262–3, 265–6, 268–70

reorganization 205–6, 210, 219, 225–6
repression, financial 195
reputations
   of banks 2: regulation 262–3, 265–6, 268–71, 275, 288–91; rents 109
   of managers 34n.8
research and development (R&D) 97, 111–12
research joint ventures 99
resource allocation
   bankruptcy law 198, 205
   stock markets 81–116
restructuring
   by banks: future of banks 8, 10; of loans 61, 65
   of banks 42–3
   financial 230–61
resurrection, gamble for 27–8
reverse causality 182
risk
   aversion 45
   informational capacity 122
   regulation of banks 26, 270–1: deposit insurance 269, 286–7; moral hazard 264, 266–7
   relationship banking 320–1, 323
   shifting 117–18
   stock markets 87
Rey, P. 15
Ritter, B. 108, 112
Robbins, L. 103
Roberts, J. 134, 265
Roberts, K. 98
Rock, K. 95
Roe, M. 61, 205
Romer, D. 164, 176
Romer, P. 157, 162
Ronn, E. I. 269
Rosengren, E. 33
Rothschild, M. 108
Roubini, N. 187, 194, 195
runs
   capital requirements 267
   financial restructuring 234
   regulation of banking 15, 34n.5

Sah, R. J. 89, 112, 332, 336, 340–1
Saint-Paul, G. 187
Sala-i-Martin, X. 164, 176, 187, 194, 195
Santomero, A. M. 266, 281, 345
Sappington, D. 99, 112, 281
savings 170, 182
scale economies 10
Scharfstein, D. 61, 65, 70, 222
Schumpeter, J. A. 158
Scott, D. 188

screening
    endogenous 340
    informational capacity 119–22, 124–5,
        137–40, 151–4
    performance 328
    real effects 6–7
    relationship banking 299–300
securities
    distribution 21–2
    future of banks 7
selective credit controls 240, 245–6, 258
Senbet, L. 262, 269
senior loans 59, 69
    banks 62, 63
seniority of debt 46, 59, 69
shareholders 36
Sharpe, S. A. 66, 87, 108–9, 114, 292, 294,
    298, 317
Shaw, E. S. 14, 190, 194
Shaw, W. 96
Shleifer, A. 86
short-term loans 46, 48–9, 69–70, 71–6
    banks 61–3
    competition 55–7, 65
    multiple initial lenders 58–60
Shoven, J. 61, 222
Simons, H. C. 275
simultaneity 190–1
small depositors 17, 26–7, 28
Smith, B. D. 187, 194
Smith, C. W. 61, 105
Sobel, J. 147
social welfare 337–9
socialization, debt 241
soft budget constraints 198
Solow, R. M. 156–7, 162
solvency 211–13
Sonnenschein, H. 98
Soule, G. 105
spillovers
    of bank failures 15, 16
    of information 112
state-owned enterprises (SOEs) 242–4,
    248–50
State Property Agency (SPA) 225–6
Stiglitz, J. E. 15, 87, 88, 89, 94, 108, 112,
    120, 145, 151, 318, 336, 340–1
stock markets
    Eastern Europe 10
    resource allocation 81–116
subsidies
    financial restructuring 246–7
    regulatory 316
Summers, L. 86
survival probability of banks 306
Svejnar, J. 232

takeovers 100, 110
Tanzi, V. 250, 254
taxpayers 29–30
technological innovation 102
tenders 99–100
Thakor, A. V. 86, 87, 114, 265, 270, 274,
    280, 281, 282, 292, 293, 294, 317, 318
timing and efficient governance structure
    19–20
Tirole, J. 13, 17, 34, 35, 36–7, 42, 68, 69,
    87, 88
Townsend, R. M. 223, 280, 318
trade associations 98
trade barriers 165–6
transaction costs 14, 16
transferable utility 21
transformation function 14, 15, 16
transparency 246–7, 260
Treasury bills 242
turbulent times 24–5, 29

Udell, G. F. 86, 87, 114, 280
unbounded growth models 165
uncertainty and bankruptcy 211–12
under-investment 41
underpricing 95–6
unemployment 229
United Kingdom
    cash limits 247
    inter-enterprise credit 234–5
    stock markets 81–2
United States of America
    bank failures 118
    bankruptcy laws 205, 216–17
    regulation of banks 262, 271–6
    stock markets 81–4
United States Treasury 263, 271, 273
universal banking 276
Universal Divinity 147n.14

van Wijnbergen, S. 229, 244
variable costs 209
Verma, A. K. 269
Verrecchia, R. 87, 88
Vives, X. 3, 8, 34, 98, 134, 294, 329, 330
voluntary credit 235
von Thadden, E. L. 2, 69, 70, 108–9, 111,
    294

Wallace, N. 267
Warner, Jerrold B. 61
Weber, R. J. 64, 330, 336, 345
Webster, L. 238, 239
Weil, D. 164, 176
Weinstein, M. 96
Weiss, A. 120, 145, 151, 318, 341

Welch, I. 96
welfare
  borrowers 312–14, 315–16, 326
  social 337–9
White, L. J. 273
White, M. J. 205, 207, 222
Williams, J. 280
Wilson, P. 87, 114
Wilson, R. 342
winner's curse 330, 336, 346
Winton, A. 145, 294

Wong, K. P. 294
World Bank 203, 221, 231
write-offs, debt 244, 250–1, 258

Yanelle, M.-O. 34, 109, 137, 145
Yoon, S. H. 280
Yugoslavia 203

Zeckhauser, R. 283
zombie firms 28